The Letters of

SAMUEL JOHNSON

SAMUEL JOHNSON
by John Opie, 1783–1784 (Houghton Library, Harvard University)

The Letters of

SAMUEL JOHNSON

VOLUME III · 1777–1781

Edited by

BRUCE REDFORD

PRINCETON, NEW JERSEY

PRINCETON UNIVERSITY PRESS

MCM · LXXXXII

COPYRIGHT © 1992 BY PRINCETON UNIVERSITY PRESS
PUBLISHED BY PRINCETON UNIVERSITY PRESS, 41 WILLIAM STREET
PRINCETON, NEW JERSEY 08540

LIBRARY OF CONGRESS CATALOGING-IN-PUBLICATION DATA
(REVISED FOR VOLUMES 2 AND 3)

JOHNSON, SAMUEL, 1709–1784.
THE LETTERS OF SAMUEL JOHNSON.
INCLUDES BIBLIOGRAPHICAL REFERENCES AND INDEX.
CONTENTS: V. 1. 30 OCTOBER 1731 TO 15 DECEMBER 1772
—V. 2. 15 JANUARY 1773 TO 24 DECEMBER 1776—V. 3.
11 JANUARY 1777 TO 26 DECEMBER 1781.
ISBN 0–691–06929–8 (V. 3)
1. JOHNSON, SAMUEL—1709–1784—CORRESPONDENCE.
2. AUTHORS, ENGLISH—18TH CENTURY—CORRESPONDENCE.
3. LEXICOGRAPHERS—GREAT BRITAIN—CORRESPONDENCE.
I. REDFORD, BRUCE. II. TITLE.
PR3533.A4 1992   828'.609   90–8806

PRINCETON UNIVERSITY PRESS BOOKS
ARE PRINTED ON ACID-FREE PAPER, AND MEET THE
GUIDELINES FOR PERMANENCE AND DURABILITY OF
THE COMMITTEE ON PRODUCTION GUIDELINES
FOR BOOK LONGEVITY OF THE COUNCIL
ON LIBRARY RESOURCES

PRINTED IN THE UNITED STATES OF AMERICA
BY THE STINEHOUR PRESS, LUNENBURG, VERMONT

1 3 5 7 9 10 8 6 4 2

CONTENTS

ILLUSTRATIONS

EDITORIAL PROCEDURES

Policies of annotation and transcription have been modeled on the style sheet for the Yale Research Edition of the Private Papers of James Boswell. The most detailed version in print appears in the front matter to *The Correspondence of James Boswell with David Garrick, Edmund Burke, and Edmond Malone*, ed. P. S. Baker et al. (1986). The statement that follows adheres closely to this version.

THE TEXTS

Choice and Arrangement of Letters

The letters are presented in chronological order. Letters written for others, as well as public dissertations in the guise of letters, have been excluded. Undated letters that cannot be assigned with confidence to a specific year appear in Appendix I, where they are ordered alphabetically by correspondent. Appendix II gathers together the evidence for letters whose texts have not been recovered. Translations of Johnson's letters in Latin appear in Appendix III.

The copy-text has been the MSS of letters sent, whenever such MSS were available. In the absence of originals, we have used MS copies. When no MSS at all have been recovered, we have used printed texts as copy.

Transcription

In accordance with the policy of the Yale Research Series, "manuscript documents in this edition have been printed to correspond to the originals as closely as is feasible in the medium of type. A certain amount of compromise and apparent inconsistency seems unavoidable, but change has been kept within the limits of stated conventions."

The following editorial conventions are imposed silently:
Addresses. Elements appearing on separate lines in the MS are

run together and punctuated according to modern practice. On franked covers, handwriting is that of the franker unless otherwise specified.

Datelines. Places and dates are joined at the head of the letter regardless of their position in the MS. Punctuation has been normalized.

Salutations. Abbreviations are expanded. Commas and colons after salutations are retained; in the absence of punctuation, a colon is supplied.

Complimentary closes. Abbreviations are expanded. Punctuation has been normalized. Elements appearing on separate lines in the MS are run together. Complimentary closes paragraphed separately in the MS are printed as continuations of the last line of text.

Endorsements. Handwriting is that of the recipient unless otherwise specified.

Punctuation. At the ends of completed sentences periods may replace commas or dashes and are always supplied when omitted. A sentence following a period always begins with a capital letter.

Changes. Substantive additions and deletions in Johnson's hand are recorded in the notes.

Lacunae. Words and letters missing through a tear or obscured by a blot are supplied within angle brackets. Inadvertent omissions are supplied within square brackets. Nonauthorial deletions are not reported unless the reading is in doubt.

Abbreviations, contractions, and symbols. The following abbreviations, contractions, and symbols, and their variant forms, are expanded: abt (about), acct (account), agst (against), Bp (Bishop), cd (could), compts (compliments), Dr (Dear), Ld (Lord), Lop (Lordship), Ly (Lady), Lyship (Ladyship), recd (received), sd (should), Sr (Sir), wc (which), wd (would), yr (your), & (and), &c (etc.). All retained abbreviations and contractions are followed by a period. Periods following ordinals have been removed.

Superior letters. Superior letters are lowered.

Brackets. Parentheses replace square brackets in the text, brackets being reserved for editorial use.

Spelling. The original spelling has been retained, except for obvious inadvertencies, which are corrected in the text and recorded in the notes.

Capitalization and paragraphing. Original capitalization and paragraphing have been retained.

ANNOTATION

Headnotes. Postmarks, although partly illegible on some letters, are left unbracketed when not in doubt. Marks on the wrappers other than addresses, postmarks, endorsements, and stamped and written franks have been ignored.

Footnotes. When an abbreviated source is given, the full citation may be found in the list of cue titles and abbreviations on pp. xxvii–xxix. All other reference titles in the footnotes are sufficiently complete to enable ready identification; for each letter, these citations are presented in full the first time they occur and are shortened in all subsequent occurrences in the notes to that letter. Except where a work has been directly quoted, no source is given when the information is available in the *Dictionary of National Biography,* an encyclopedia, or other general reference work.

Reference to all letters is made by correspondent and date. *Post* and *Ante* references supplement but do not replace the index, which should be consulted whenever the identity of names or places is in doubt.

CHRONOLOGY

1709   Is born at Lichfield, 18 Sept.

1717–25   Attends Lichfield Grammar School.

1728   Enters Pembroke College, Oxford, in October.

1729   Leaves Oxford in December.

1731   Death of his father Michael.

1732   Usher at Market Bosworth School.

1733   Resides in Birmingham; translates Lobo's *Voyage to Abyssinia*.

1735   Marries Elizabeth Porter; opens school at Edial.

1737   Leaves for London in March; begins work for Edward Cave.

1738   *London*.

1744   *An Account of the Life of Richard Savage*; *Harleian Miscellany*.

1746   Signs contract for the *Dictionary*.

1749   *Irene* produced; *The Vanity of Human Wishes*.

1750   Begins *Rambler*.

1752   Death of Elizabeth Johnson; final *Rambler*.

1755   Oxford M.A.; publication of the *Dictionary*.

1758   Begins *Idler*.

1759   Death of his mother Sarah; publication of *Rasselas*.

1760   Final *Idler*.

1762   Is granted annual pension.

1763   Meets James Boswell.

1764   Founding of The Club.

1765   Meets Henry and Hester Thrale; Dublin LL.D.; *The Dramatic Works of William Shakespeare*.

1770   *The False Alarm*.

1771   *Thoughts on the late Transactions respecting Falkland's Islands*.

1773   Hebridean tour.

1774   *The Patriot*; tour of Wales.

1775   *A Journey to the Western Islands of Scotland*; *Taxation No Tyranny*; Oxford D.C.L.; trip to Paris.

1777   Trial of Dr. Dodd; begins work on *Lives of the Poets*.

1779   First installment of *Lives*.

1781   Death of Henry Thrale; second installment of *Lives*.

1783   Founding of Essex Head Club.

1784   Final break with Hester Thrale; dies 13 Dec.

Adam Cat.	R. B. ADAM, *The R. B. Adam Library Relating to Dr. Samuel Johnson and His Era*, 4 vols., 1929–30.
Alum. Cant. I	JOHN and J. A. VENN, *Alumni Cantabrigienses*, Part I (to 1751), 4 vols., 1922–27.
Alum. Cant. II	J. A. VENN, *Alumni Cantabrigienses*, Part II (1752–1900), 6 vols., 1940–54.
Alum. Oxon. I	JOSEPH FOSTER, *Alumni Oxonienses . . . 1500–1714*, 4 vols., 1891–92.
Alum. Oxon. II	JOSEPH FOSTER, *Alumni Oxonienses . . . 1715–1886*, 4 vols., 1887–88.
Baker	*The Correspondence of James Boswell with David Garrick, Edmund Burke, and Edmond Malone*, ed. P. S. Baker et al., 1986.
Bibliography	W. P. COURTNEY and DAVID NICHOL SMITH, *A Bibliography of Samuel Johnson*, 1915, 1925.
Bibliography Supplement	
	R. W. CHAPMAN and A. T. HAZEN, *Johnsonian Bibliography: A Supplement to Courtney*, 1939.
Bloom	E. A. BLOOM, *Samuel Johnson in Grub Street*, 1957.
Burke's Correspondence	
	The Correspondence of Edmund Burke, ed. T. W. Copeland et al., 1958–70.
Chapman	*The Letters of Samuel Johnson, with Mrs. Thrale's Genuine Letters to Him*, ed. R. W. Chapman, 3 vols., 1952.
Clifford, 1952	J. L. CLIFFORD, *Hester Lynch Piozzi*, 2d ed., 1952.
Clifford, 1955	J. L. CLIFFORD, *Young Samuel Johnson*, 1955.
Clifford, 1979	J. L. CLIFFORD, *Dictionary Johnson*, 1979.
Croker	JAMES BOSWELL, *The Life of Samuel Johnson, LL.D.*, ed. J. W. Croker, rev. John Wright, 10 vols., 1868.
SJ's *Dictionary*	SAMUEL JOHNSON, *Dictionary of the English Language*, 4th ed., 1773.
DNB	*Dictionary of National Biography.*

Earlier Years	F. A. POTTLE, *James Boswell: The Earlier Years, 1740–1769*, 1966.
Fifer	*The Correspondence of James Boswell with Certain Members of The Club*, ed. C. N. Fifer, 1976.
Fleeman	SAMUEL JOHNSON, *A Journey to the Western Islands of Scotland*, ed. J. D. Fleeman, 1985.
GM	*The Gentleman's Magazine*, 1731–1907.
Greene, 1975	DONALD GREENE, *Samuel Johnson's Library*, 1975.
Hawkins	SIR JOHN HAWKINS, *The Life of Samuel Johnson, LL.D.*, 2d ed., 1787.
Hazen	A. T. HAZEN, *Samuel Johnson's Prefaces and Dedications*, 1937.
Hebrides	*Boswell's Journal of a Tour to the Hebrides with Samuel Johnson, LL.D., 1773*, ed. from the original MS by F. A. Pottle and C. H. Bennett, 1961.
Hendy	J. G. HENDY, *The History of the Early Postmarks of the British Isles*, 1905.
Hill	*Letters of Samuel Johnson, LL.D.*, ed. G. B. Hill, 1892.
Hyde, 1972	MARY HYDE, *The Impossible Friendship: Boswell and Mrs. Thrale*, 1972.
Hyde, 1977	MARY HYDE, *The Thrales of Streatham Park*, 1977.
JB	James Boswell.
Johns. Glean.	A. L. READE, *Johnsonian Gleanings*, 11 vols., 1909–52.
Johns. Misc.	*Johnsonian Miscellanies*, ed. G. B. Hill, 2 vols., 1897.
JN	*Johnsonian Newsletter.*
Later Years	FRANK BRADY, *James Boswell: The Later Years, 1769–1795*, 1984.
Life	*Boswell's Life of Johnson, Together with Boswell's Journal of a Tour to the Hebrides and Johnson's Diary of a Journey into North Wales*, ed. G. B. Hill, rev. L. F. Powell, 6 vols., 1934–50; vols. V and VI, 2d ed., 1964.
Lit. Anec.	JOHN NICHOLS, *Literary Anecdotes of the Eighteenth Century*, 9 vols., 1812–15.
Lit. Car.	F. A. POTTLE, *The Literary Career of James Boswell, Esq.*, 1929.
Lives of the Poets	*Johnson's Lives of the English Poets*, ed. G. B. Hill, 1905.

Lond. Stage	*The London Stage*, Part III (1729–47), ed. A. H. Scouten, 1961; Part IV (1747–76), ed. G. W. Stone, Jr., 1962; Part V (1776–1800), ed. C. B. Hogan, 1968.
Namier and Brooke	
	SIR LEWIS NAMIER and JOHN BROOKE, *The House of Commons, 1754–1790*, 3 vols., 1964.
OED	*Oxford English Dictionary.*
Piozzi, *Letters*	HESTER LYNCH PIOZZI, *Letters to and from the Late Samuel Johnson, LL.D.*, 2 vols., 1788.
Piozzi	Annotated presentation copy, given to Sir James Fellowes, of H. L. Piozzi's *Letters to and from the Late Samuel Johnson, LL.D.*, 1788 (Birthplace Museum, Lichfield).
Plomer	H. R. PLOMER et al., *Dictionary of Printers and Booksellers, 1668–1725; 1726–1775*, 2 vols., 1922, 1932.
Poems	*The Poems of Samuel Johnson*, ed. David Nichol Smith and E. L. McAdam, rev. J. D. Fleeman, 1974.
Reades	A. L. READE, *The Reades of Blackwood Hill and Dr. Johnson's Ancestry*, 1906.
RES	*Review of English Studies.*
SJ	Samuel Johnson.
Sledd and Kolb	J. H. SLEDD and G. J. KOLB, *Dr. Johnson's Dictionary*, 1955.
Thraliana	*Thraliana: The Diary of Mrs. Hester Lynch Thrale*, ed. K. C. Balderston, 1942.
TLS	*Times Literary Supplement.*
Waingrow	*The Correspondence and Other Papers of James Boswell Relating to the Making of the "Life of Johnson,"* ed. Marshall Waingrow, 1969.
Walpole's Correspondence, Yale ed.	
	The Yale Edition of Horace Walpole's Correspondence, ed. W. S. Lewis et al., 1937–83.
Wheatley and Cunningham	
	H. B. WHEATLEY and PETER CUNNINGHAM, *London Past and Present*, 3 vols., 1891.
Works, Yale ed.	*The Yale Edition of the Works of Samuel Johnson*, J. H. Middendorf, gen. ed., 1958–.

The Letters of

SAMUEL JOHNSON

Hester Thrale

SATURDAY 11 JANUARY 1777

MS: Hyde Collection.

Jan. 11, 1777

Tempora mutantur.[1] I am to dine to day (Saturday) with Sir Joshua and Dr. Warton, on Sunday with Dr. Laurence, on Monday I am engaged to Miss Way,[2] on Tuesday to Mrs. Gardiner; on Wednesday I dine with Mr. Langton and the Bishop of Chester;[3] on Thursday with Mr. Paradise and Mr. Bryant.[4] Thus, dearest Lady, am I hindred from being with You and Miss Owen.[5] Mrs. Montague talks of You, and says she will come see you: but I hope, I shall come before her.

1. *Tempora mutantur, et nos mutamur in illis*: "Times change and we with them." Though it had attained proverbial status by the late sixteenth century, this saying has been attributed to Lothair I of Germany (T. B. Harbottle, *Dictionary of Quotations (Classical)*, 2d ed., 1958, p. 197; *Oxford Dictionary of English Proverbs*, rev. F. P. Wilson, 1970, p. 825).

2. Elizabeth Anne Cooke (1746–1825), eldest daughter of William Cooke (1711–97), D.D., Provost of King's College, Cambridge, married (1767) Benjamin Way (1740–1808), of Denham Place, Buckinghamshire, M.P. for Bridport (1765–68) (A.M.W. Stirling, *The Ways of Yesterday*, 1930, p. 310; Namier and Brooke III.614; *Lit. Anec.* IX.630; *Letters of Edward Gibbon*, ed. J. E. Norton, 1956, III.454). *Post* To Elizabeth Way, 4 May 1782.

3. *Ante* To Hester Thrale, 1 Apr. 1775.

4. Jacob Bryant (1715–1804), classical scholar, antiquarian and secretary to the fourth Duke of Marlborough. In 1774 Bryant had shown SJ the library at Blenheim "with great civility" (*Life* v.458).

5. Margaret Owen (1743–1816), Hester Thrale's distant cousin, "a woman of family and fortune" from Montgomeryshire, Wales, whom SJ persisted in finding "empty-headed" (*Life* III.48, 478; Hyde, 1977, p. 157). She was keeping Mrs. Thrale company during an especially difficult pregnancy.

Hester Thrale

MS: Hyde Collection.

Wednesday, Jan. 15, one in the morning, 1777

Omnium rerum vicissitudo.[1] The Night after last Thursday was so bad, that I took ipecacuanha the next day.[2] The next night was no better. On Saturday I dined with Sir Joshua. The night was such as I was forced to rise and pass some hours in a chair, with great labour of respiration. I found it now time to do something and went to Dr. Laurence, and told him I would do what he should order without reading the prescription. He sent for a Chirurgeon and took about twelve ounces of blood, and in the after noon I got sleep in a chair.

At night when I came to lie down, after trial of an hour or two I found sleep impracticable, and therefore did what the Doctor permitted in a case of distress, I rose and opening the orifice let out about ten ounces more. Frank[3] and I were but awkward, but with Mr. Levet's help we stopped the stream, and I lay down again, though to little purpose, the difficulty of breathing allowed no rest. I slept again in the day time in an erect posture. The Doctor has ordered me a second bleeding, which, I hope, will set my Breath at liberty. Last night I could lie but a little at a time.

Yet I do not make it a matter of much form. I was to day at Mrs. Gardiner's. When I have bled to morrow I will not give up Langton, nor Paradise.[4] But I beg that you will fetch me away on Fryday. I do not know but clearer air may do me

1. *Omnium rerum, heus, vicissitudost*: "It's a world of ups and downs" (Terence, *Eunuchus* II.276, trans. John Sargeaunt, Loeb ed.).

2. *ipecacoanha*: "a slender root, brought from the Spanish West Indies. . . . The mildest and safest emetic that has yet been discovered" (William Lewis, *Materia Medica*, 3d ed., 1784, pp. 354–55). Following Mark Akenside, SJ also considered it "a remedy for all constrictions of the breath" (*Post* To Hester Thrale, 23 Aug. 1777 and n. 2).

3. *Ante* To Thomas Birch, 8 Nov. 1755, n. 3.

4. *Ante* To Hester Thrale, 11 Jan. 1777.

good; but whether the air be clear or dark, let me come to You. I am, Madam, Your most humble servant,

SAM. JOHNSON

To sleep, or not to sleep.—

Hester Thrale

THURSDAY 16 JANUARY 1777[1]

PRINTED SOURCE: Piozzi, *Letters* I.209.

Madam,   Thursday

Master is very kind in being very angry; but he may spare his anger this time.[2] I have done exactly as Dr. Lawrence ordered, and am much better at the expence of about thirty-six ounces of blood.[3] Nothing in the world! For a good cause I have six-and-thirty more. I long though to come to Streatham, and you shall give me no solid flesh for a week; and I am to take physick. And hey boys, up go we.[4] I was in bed all last night, only a little sitting up. The box goes to *Calcutta*.[5] I am, Dearest, dearest Madam, Your, etc.

Let me come to you to-morrow.

1. Dated in relation to the preceding letter (15 Jan.) and Hester Thrale's reply (MS: Rylands Library 540.86), to which this letter responds.

2. In her reply to SJ's letter of 15 Jan., Hester Thrale had told him that her husband was "very angry already" at the news that SJ had been bleeding himself (MS: Rylands Library).

3. *Ante* To Hester Thrale, 15 Jan. 1777.

4. "And, hey! then up goe wee" is the refrain of Anarchus's song in Eclogue 11 of Francis Quarles's *The Shepheards Oracles* (*Complete Works*, ed. A. B. Grosart, 1881, III.235–36).

5. This unidentified "box" may have been intended for Warren Hastings (whose headquarters as Governor-General of India were in Calcutta) or Robert Chambers, since 1774 a judge of the Supreme Court in Bengal. *Ante* To Warren Hastings, 30 Mar. 1774.

Thomas Barnard [1]

FRIDAY 17 JANUARY 1777

MS: The Earl of Crawford and Balcarres.

Friday Jan. 17th

Mr. Johnson, not being to dine at the Club this day, as he intended,[2] waits on the Dean of Derry to take leave, and wish him a prosperous voyage.

Charade!
My first, shuts out Theives from your house or your Room,
My second, expresses a Syrian perfume;
My whole, is a Man in whose converse is shar'd,
The strength of a Bar, and sweetness of Nard.

1. Thomas Barnard (1726–1806), D.D., Dean of Derry (1769–80), Bishop of Killaloe (1780–94), Bishop of Limerick (1794–1806) (Fifer, pp. xxviii–xxxii). Barnard was elected to The Club in 1775. According to SJ, "no man ever paid more attention to another than he has done to me" (*Life* IV.115). For Goldsmith's poetical tribute, see "Retaliation," ll. 23–28.

2. In ill health, SJ was about to leave for several days in the "clearer air" of Streatham Park. *Ante* To Hester Thrale, 15 Jan. 1777; 16 Jan. 1777.

John Taylor

THURSDAY 23 JANUARY 1777

MS: Hyde Collection.
ADDRESS: To the Revd. Dr. Taylor in Ashbourne, Derbyshire.
POSTMARK: 23 IA.
ENDORSEMENTS: 1777, 23 Jany. 1777.

Dear Sir: Bolt court, Jan. 23, 1777

I am desired by Mrs. Williams to return thanks for the excellent Turkey and Hare, with the Turkey she made one feast and with the Hare she intends to make another.

You told me in your last nothing of your health, I hope it is as you wish. I was lately seized with a difficulty of breathing, which forced me out of bed, to pass part of the night in a chair.[1] Dr. Laurence has taken away, as is reckoned, about thirty six ounces of blood, and by purging and lower diet, I begin to breathe better than I have done for many months past.

I suppose you continue your purpose of residing in February.[2] Mrs. Thrale expects a little one in about three weeks.[3] I shall be glad to see you come up well and cheerful, and hope we may pass a good part of the time pleasantly together. I am, sir, your most affectionate,

SAM. JOHNSON

1. Cf. *Ante* To Hester Thrale, 15 Jan. 1777.
2. Since 1746, Taylor had been a prebendary of Westminster (Thomas Taylor, *Life of John Taylor*, 1910, p. 18).
3. Cecilia Margaretta (1777–1857), the Thrales' eleventh child and ninth daughter, was born 8 Feb. (Hyde, 1977, p. xii).

Bennet Langton
THURSDAY 13 FEBRUARY 1777

MS: Hyde Collection.

ADDRESS: To Benet Langton, Esq.

Sir: Thursday, Febr. 13, 1777

I suppose you do not doubt of my having written for Mr. Parr.[1]

If you dine with the Bishop of Chester to morrow, it will be kind to take up me.[2] If you come down Holbourn, and

1. Samuel Parr (1747–1825), LL.D. (1781), clergyman, schoolmaster, and classicist, began his teaching career at Harrow (1767–71), which he left to start his own school. "At the end of 1776 he applied successfully for the mastership of the Colchester grammar school. He obtained, through Bennet Langton, a recommendation from Dr. Johnson" (*DNB* xv.358). SJ, who "was much pleased with the conversation" of Parr, several times engaged him in friendly controversy (*Life* IV.15 and n. 5). "This great scholar, and warm admirer of Johnson" composed the epitaph for SJ's monument in St. Paul's (*Life* IV.423 n. 3).
2. *Ante* To Hester Thrale, 1 Apr. 1775; 11 Jan. 1777.

through Chancery Lane, you lose but little ground.[3] If I receive no answer, I shall expect you till three to morrow.

My Compliments etc. I am, sir, your most etc.

SAM. JOHNSON

3. SJ's house in Bolt Court was just off Fleet Street, a short distance from its junction with Chancery Lane.

James Boswell

TUESDAY 18 FEBRUARY 1777

PRINTED SOURCE: JB's *Life*, 1791, II.106.

Dear Sir,   Feb. 18, 1777

It is so long since I heard any thing from you, that I am not easy about it; write something to me next post.[1] When you sent your last letter every thing seemed to be mending, I hope nothing has lately grown worse.[2] I suppose young Alexander continues to thrive, and Veronica is now very pretty company. I do not suppose the lady is yet reconciled to me, yet let her know that I love her very well, and value her very much.

Dr. Blair is printing some sermons.[3] If they are all like the first, which I have read, they are *sermones aurei, ac auro magis aurei.*[4] It is excellently written both as to doctrine and language. Mr. Watson's book seems to be much esteemed.[5]

1. JB had mailed "a long letter" to SJ on 17 Feb. (*Boswell in Extremes*, ed. C. M. Weis and F. A. Pottle, 1970, p. 87; *Life* III.101–2).

2. The letter to which SJ refers was dated 16 Nov. 1776 (*Life* III.94), when JB's relations with his father were improving.

3. *Ante* To William Strahan, 24 Dec. 1776 and n. 1.

4. *sermones aurei, ac auro magis aurei*: "golden sermons—and even more golden than gold." *Auro auratior* and its variants, which had become tags or catchphrases by the mid-sixteenth century, derive from a Sapphic fragment, Χρύσω Χρυσοτέρα: "more golden than gold" (*Lyra Graeca* I.225, trans. J. M. Edmonds, Loeb ed.). The phrase may have come to SJ's attention through Dryden's *Original and Progress of Satire*: Dryden includes it in a paraphrase of Isaac Casaubon (*Critical Essays*, ed. George Watson, 1962, II.120).

5. *Ante* To William Strahan, 14 Oct. 1776 and n. 2.

* * * * * *

Poor Beauclerk still continues very ill.[6] Langton lives on as he is used to do. His children are very pretty,[7] and, I think, his lady loses her Scotch.[8] Paoli I never see.

I have been so distressed by difficulty of breathing, that I lost, as was computed, six-and-thirty ounces of blood in a few days.[9] I am better, but not well.

I wish you would be vigilant and get me Graham's "Telemachus" that was printed at Glasgow, a very little book,[10] and *Johnstoni Poemata*, another little book, printed at Middleburg.[11]

Mrs. Williams sends her compliments, and promises that when you come hither, she will accommodate you as well as ever she can in the old room. She wishes to know whether you sent her book to Sir Alexander Gordon.[12]

My dear Boswell, do not neglect to write to me, for your kindness is one of the pleasures of my life, which I should be very sorry to lose. I am, Sir, Your humble servant,

SAM. JOHNSON

6. *Ante* To JB, 21 Jan. 1775. Beauclerk, in chronic ill health, had spent part of the autumn and winter at Bath. By early July, however, Horace Walpole was able to report, "He looks so much less ill than he did, that one need never despair of any recovery after his and Lazarus's" (*Walpole's Correspondence*, Yale ed. XXXII.341, 365).

7. By Feb. 1777 Bennet Langton and his wife had produced four children: George (b. 1772), Mary (b. 1773), Diana (b. 1774), and Jane (b. 1776) (Fifer, p. lviii n. 29).   8. *Ante* To Bennet Langton, 24 Oct. 1770, n. 2.

9. *Ante* To Hester Thrale, 15 Jan. 1777; 16 Jan. 1777.

10. *Ante* To JB, 27 May 1775, n. 8.

11. *Poemata Omnia* (1642) by Arthur Johnston (1587–1641), Rector of King's College, Aberdeen, "who holds among the Latin poets of Scotland the next place to the elegant Buchanan" (*Works*, Yale ed. IX.15). SJ and JB had searched in vain for "Johnston's Poems" during their visit to Aberdeen in 1773 (*Life* v.95).

12. It is likely that the book in question is Anna Williams's *Miscellanies* (*Ante* To Elizabeth Montagu, 9 June 1759, n. 3).

George Steevens

TUESDAY 25 FEBRUARY 1777

PRINTED SOURCE: JB's *Life*, 1791, II.102.

Dear Sir,   February 25, 1777

You will be glad to hear that from Mrs. Goldsmith, whom we lamented as drowned, I have received a letter full of gratitude to us all, with promise to make the enquiries which we recommended to her.[1]

I would have had the honour of conveying this intelligence to Miss Caulfield,[2] but that her letter is not at hand, and I know not the direction. You will tell the good news. I am, Sir, Your most, etc.

SAM. JOHNSON

1. After Oliver Goldsmith's death in 1774, his friends began to gather together materials for a biography, the writing of which was entrusted to Thomas Percy. Sometime during the second half of 1776, however, the task was transferred to SJ (K. C. Balderston, *History and Sources of Percy's Memoir of Goldsmith*, 1926, pp. 18–21). SJ then began to solicit additional information from members of the Goldsmith family. According to K. C. Balderston, the "Mrs. Goldsmith" to whom he refers was "in all probability" the widow of Oliver's eldest brother Henry (d. 1768) (*Memoir*, p. 21).

2. Possibly a relation of James Caulfeild (1728–99), first Earl of Charlemont, Irish statesman and member of The Club (1773).

Elizabeth Aston

SATURDAY 8 MARCH 1777

MS: Maine Historical Society (Fogg Collection).
HEADING in an unidentified hand: To Mrs. Aston, Stow Hill.

Dear Madam: Boltcourt, Fleetstreet, March 8, 1777

As we pass on through the journey of life, we meet, and ought to expect many unpleasing occurrences, but many likewise encounter us unexpected. I have this morning heard from Lucy of your ilness. I heard indeed in the next sentence that you are to a great degree recovered. May your Recovery, Dearest

Madam, be compleat and lasting. The hope of paying you the annual visit is one of the few solaces, with which my imagination gratifies me, and my wish is that I may find you happy.

My health is much broken; my nights are very restless, and will not be made more comfortable, by remembering that one of the Friends whom I value most is suffering equally with my self.

Be pleased, dearest Lady, to let me know how you are, and if writing be troublesome, get dear Mrs. Gastrel to write for you.[1] I hope she is well and able to assist you, and wish that you may so well recover, as to repay her kindness, if she should want you. May you both live long happy together. I am, dear Madam, your most humble servant,

SAM. JOHNSON

1. *Post* To Elizabeth Aston, 15 Mar. 1777.

James Boswell

TUESDAY 11 MARCH 1777

PRINTED SOURCE: JB's *Life*, 1791, II.107–8.

Dear Sir,   March 11, 1777

I have been much pleased with your late letter, and am glad that my old enemy, Mrs. Boswell, begins to feel some remorse.[1] As to Miss Veronica's Scotch, I think it cannot be helped. An English maid you might easily have; but she would still imitate the greater number, as they would be likewise those whom she must most respect. Her dialect will not be gross. Her Mamma has not much Scotch, and you have yourself very little. I hope she knows my name, and does not call me *Johnston*.[2]

1. In his letter of 24 Feb., JB had told SJ that Mrs. Boswell would be sending him "some marmalade of oranges of her own making" (*Life* III.105).

2. "John*son* is the most common English formation of the Sirname from *John*; John*ston* the Scotch. My illustrious friend observed, that many North Britons pronounced his name in their own way" (JB's note).

The immediate cause of my writing is this:—One Shaw, who seems a modest and a decent man, has written an Erse Grammar,[3] which a very learned Highlander, Macbean,[4] has, at my request examined and approved.

The book is very little,[5] but Mr. Shaw has been persuaded by his friends to set it at half a guinea, though I had advised only a crown, and thought myself liberal. You, whom the authour considers as a great encourager of ingenious men, will receive a parcel of his proposals and receipts.[6] I have undertaken to give you notice of them, and to solicit your countenance. You must ask no poor man, because the price is really too high. Yet such a work deserves patronage.

It is proposed to augment our club from twenty to thirty, of which I am glad; for as we have several in it whom I do not much like to consort with,[7] I am for reducing it to a mere miscellaneous collection of conspicuous men, without any determinate character.[8] * * * * *. I am, dear Sir, Most affectionately yours,

SAM. JOHNSON

My respects to Madam, to Veronica, to Alexander, to Euphemia, to David.[9]

3. The Rev. William Shaw's *Analysis of the Galic Language* was published by subscription in 1778. Shaw (1749–1831), a Scots clergyman and Celtic philologist, had come to the notice of Lord Eglinton, who showed his MS to JB in Apr. 1776; JB then passed it on to SJ (*Life* III.107, 488; *Boswell: The Ominous Years*, ed. Charles Ryskamp and F. A. Pottle, 1963, p. 340).

4. *Ante* To Edward Cave, 1738, n. 2.

5. Shaw's *Analysis* is comparatively "little" in length (156 pages) but not in format (quarto).   6. Shaw's "Proposals" were written by SJ (*Life* III.107).

7. "On account of their differing from him as to religion and politicks" (JB's note).

8. During 1777 membership in The Club was expanded from twenty to twenty-six (*Life* III.488). The "several" to whom SJ took exception included Charles James Fox (elected 1774), Edward Gibbon (1774), and Adam Smith (1775).

9. David Boswell (1776–77), died 29 Mar., at age four months, of "a teething fever" (*Boswell in Extremes*, ed. C. M. Weis and F. A. Pottle, 1970, p. 103).

Elizabeth Aston

SATURDAY 15 MARCH 1777

MS: Pembroke College, Oxford.

Dearest Madam: March[1] 15, 1777

The letter with which I was favoured [by] the kindness of Mrs. Gastrel has contributed very little to quiet my solicitude. I am indeed more frighted than by Mrs. Porter's account.[2] Yet since you have had strength to conquer your disorder so as to obtain a partial recovery, I think it reasonable to believe that the favourable season which is now coming forward, may restore you to your former health. Do not, dear Madam, lose your courage, nor by despondence or inactivity give way to the disease. Use such exercise as you can bear, and excite cheerful thoughts in your own mind. Do not harrass your faculties with laborious attention, nothing is in my opinion of more mischievous tendency in a state of body like yours, than deep meditation, or perplexing solicitude. Gayety is a duty when health requires it. Entertain yourself as you can with small amusements or light conversation, and let nothing but your Devotion ever make you serious.

But while I exhort you, my dearest Lady, to merriment, I am very serious myself. The loss or danger of a friend is not to be considered with indifference; but I derive some consolation from the thought that You do not languish unattended, that You are not in the hands of strangers or servants, but have a Sister at hand to watch your wants and supply them.

If at this distance I can be of any use by consulting Physicians or for any other purpose I hope You will employ me. I have thought on a journey to Staffordshire, and hope in a few weeks to climb Stowhill, and to find there the pleasure which I have so often found.

Let me hear again from you. I am, Dear Madam, your most humble servant,

SAM. JOHNSON

1. MS: "March" superimposed upon "August" partially erased
2. *Ante* To Elizabeth Aston, 8 Mar. 1777.

13

Hester Thrale

MS: National Portrait Gallery, London.

Madam: March 19, 1777

Be pleased to procure the Bearer credit for a linen gown, and let her bring the bill to me.

Did you stay all night at Sir Joshua's? and keep Miss up again? Miss Owen had a sight. All the Burkes[1]—the Harris's[2]—Miss Reynolds—what has she to see more? And Mrs. Horneck and Miss.[3]—

You are all young and gay and easy. But I have miserable nights, and know not how to make them better. But I shift pretty well a-days, and so have at you all at Dr. Burney's to morrow.[4]

I never thought of meeting you at Sir Joshua's, nor knew that it was a great day. But things, as sages have observed happen unexpectedly, and you thought little of seeing me this fortnight except to morrow. But go where you will, and see if I do not catch You. When I am away, every body runs away with you, and carries You among the grisettes,[5] or[6] whither

---

1. Presumably "all the Burkes" refers to Edmund, his wife Jane, their son Richard (1758–94), and Edmund's putative cousin William (1729–98).

2. James Harris (1709–80), classical scholar and philologist, author of *Hermes, or a Philosophical Inquiry concerning Universal Grammar* (1751) and M.P. for Christchurch (1761–80). SJ judged Harris "a sound sullen scholar" but also "a prig, and a bad prig" (*Life* III.245). His wife Elizabeth (d. 1781) was the daughter of John Clarke of Sandford, Somerset; they were married in 1745 (Namier and Brooke II.588).

3. *Ante* To Hannah Horneck, 13 June 1770, n. 1.

4. Frances Burney met SJ for the first time when he, Hester and Queeney Thrale, Margaret Owen, and William Seward all called on the Burneys the morning of 20 Mar. (*Early Diary of Frances Burney*, ed. A. R. Ellis, 1907, II.152–58).

5. *grisette*: "a French girl or young woman of the working class ... a shop assistant or a seamstress" (*OED*). On the basis of a passage in Sir William Forbes's *Life of James Beattie* (1824, I.201), R. W. Chapman suggests that by "grisettes" SJ actually means "Blue-stockings" (Chapman II.167).

6. MS: "o" superimposed upon "a"

they will. I hope you will find the want of me twenty times before You see me. I am, Madam, your most humble servant,

SAM. JOHNSON

Hester Thrale

THURSDAY 27 MARCH 1777

PRINTED SOURCE: Sotheby's Catalogue, 30 Jan. 1918.

You have now been at court, your presentation was delayed too long.[1] What you intend to do at all it is wise to resolve on doing quickly. *Fugit irrevocabile tempus.*[2]

1. "Yesterday Mrs. Thrale was presented to their Majesties at St. James's by Lady Gage" (*London Chronicle*, 22–25 Mar. 1777, p. 282).

2. *Sed fugit interea, fugit inreparabile tempus*: "But time meanwhile is flying, flying beyond recall" (Virgil, *Georgics* III.284, trans. H. R. Fairclough, Loeb ed.).

John Perkins

FRIDAY 4 APRIL 1777

MS: Hyde Collection.

Apr. 4

Mr. Johnson sends compliments to Mr. Perkins, and though he believes this foolish newspaper to be false,[1] yet desires to know when Mr. Perkins heard of Mr. Thrale, and what he can tell of the ground of the report.[2]

1. "Yesterday morning died, suddenly, Henry Thrale, Esq: Member for the Borough" (*The Gazetteer and New Daily Advertiser*, 3 Apr. 1777, p. 3).

2. Writing in response to the same newspaper item, Hester Thrale reported that her husband was "alive and well" in Brighton, where they were having a brief holiday (5 Apr. 1777, MS: Rylands Library).

Henry Thrale

WEDNESDAY 9 APRIL 1777

MS: Kansai University Library, Osaka.
ADDRESS: ⟨   ⟩ Esq.[1]
HEADING in the hand of H. L. Piozzi: To Mr. Thrale.

Dear Sir: Apr. 9, 1777

This is a letter of pure congratulation. I congratulate you

1. That you are alive.[2]
2. That you have got my Mistress fixed again after her excentricities.[3]
3. That my Mistress has added to her conquests the Prince of Castiglione.[4]
4. That you will not be troubled with me till to morrow, when I shall come with Dr. Taylor.
5. That ⟨Taylor⟩[5] will go away in the evening. I am, sir, etc.

SAM. JOHNSON

1. MS: mutilated; rest of address missing

2. *Ante* To John Perkins, 4 Apr. 1777 and n. 1. "We are authorised to assure our Readers, that the Paragraph concerning the Death of Henry Thrale, Esq; has no Foundation in Truth" (*Public Advertiser*, 5 Apr. 1777, p. 3).

3. *eccentricity*: "deviation from a center; excursion from the proper orb" (SJ's *Dictionary*). On 8 Apr. the Thrales returned to Streatham after a period of two weeks, during which Mrs. Thrale had been "gay and easy" in London (*Ante* To Hester Thrale, 19 Mar. 1777).

4. Luigi Gonzaga (1745–1819), Prince of Castiglione and Solferino, traveler and *philosophe*, the author of *Il letterato buon cittadino* (1776) (*Thraliana* 1.403). On 1 Apr. Hester Thrale and SJ had dined at John Paradise's in a large company that included Castiglione (National Library of Wales, Brogyntyn MS: 38; information supplied by Dr. J. D. Fleeman).   5. MS: one or two words erased and del.

John Ryland

SATURDAY 12 APRIL 1777

MS: Hyde Collection.
ADDRESS: To Mr. Ryland.

Sir: Apr. 12, 1777

I have sent you the papers.[1] Of this parcel I have ejected no poetry. Of the letters there are some which I should be sorry to omit, some that it is not proper to insert, and very many which as we want room or want matter we may use or neglect. When we come to these we will have another selection. But to these I think our present plan of publication will never bring us. His poems with his play will I think make two volumes. The Adventurers will make at least one, and for the fourth, as I think you intend four which will make the subscription a Guinea, if you subscribe, we have so much more than we want that the difficulty will [be] to reject.

If Mrs. Hawkesworth sells the copy,[2] we are then to consider how many volumes she sells, and if they are fewer than we have matter to fill, we will be the more rigorous in our choice.

I am for letting none stand that are only relatively good as they were written in youth. The Buyer has no better bargain when he pays for mean performances, by being told that the authour wrote them young.

If the Lady can get an hundred pounds a volume, I should advise her to take it. She may ask more. I am not willing to take less.

If she prints them by subscription the volumes should be four, if, at her own expence, I still do not see considering the great quantity of our matter how they can be fewer. But in this I shall not be ob[s]tinate.

I have yet not mentioned Swift's Life,[3] nor the Novel[4] which together will go far towards a volume.

Who was his Amanuensis? that small hand strikes a reader with horrour. It is pale as well as small.

Many little things are, I believe, in the Magazines, which

1. *Ante* To John Ryland, 21 Sept. 1776; 14 Nov. 1776.

2. *copy*: "property in 'copy,' copyright" (*OED*).

3. Hawkesworth's edition of Swift's works (1755) was prefaced by his *Life of Swift*.

4. *Almoran and Hamet*, published in 1761, is an oriental tale much indebted to SJ's *Rasselas* (J. L. Abbott, *John Hawkesworth*, 1982, pp. 113–14).

should be marked and considered. I do not always know them but by conjecture.

The poetry I would have printed in order of time, which he seems to have intended by noting the dates, which dates I should like to preserve, they show the progress of his Mind, and of a very powerful Mind.[5] The same r⟨ule⟩ may be generally observed in the prose pieces.[6]

What we have to consider, and what I have considered are the Authours credit, and the Lady's advantage.

I should be glad to talk over the whole, when you can spend an hour or two with, sir, your most humble servant,

SAM. JOHNSON

5. For over ten years, beginning in June 1741, Hawkesworth contributed to the poetry section of the *GM*. He wrote in several genres, including the animal fable ("The Fop, Cock and Diamond"), the ode ("Life"), and the mock-epic ("The Death of Arachne") (Abbott, *Hawkesworth*, pp. 88–92).

6. "For over twenty-five years, from the mid-1740s to his death in 1773, Hawkesworth . . . contributed parliamentary 'debates,' translations, fiction, essays, and principally, dramatic and book reviews to the *Gentleman's Magazine*" (Abbott, *Hawkesworth*, p. 93).

Unidentified Correspondent
WEDNESDAY 16 APRIL 1777

MS: Beinecke Library.

Sir: Apr. 16, 1777

The Bearer is a poor Woman, who wants that assistance which I know not any man that can give her with so much skill, or will give her with so much generosity as yourself. I take the liberty therefore of recommending her to your kindness. I am, Sir, Your most humble Servant,

SAM. JOHNSON

James Boswell

SATURDAY 3 MAY 1777

PRINTED SOURCE: JB's *Life*, 1791, I.110–11.

Dear Sir,   May 3, 1777

The story of Mr. Thrale's death, as he had neither been sick nor in any other danger, made so little impression upon me, that I never thought about obviating its effects on any body else.[1] It is supposed to have been produced by the English custom of making April fools, that is, of sending one another on some foolish errand on the first of April.

Tell Mrs. Boswell that I shall taste her marmalade cautiously at first.[2] *Timeo Danaos et dona ferentes.*[3] Beware, says the Italian proverb, of a reconciled enemy. But when I find it does me no harm, I shall then receive it and be thankful for it, as a pledge of firm, and, I hope, of unalterable kindness. She is, after all, a dear, dear lady.

Please to return Dr. Blair thanks for his sermons.[4] The Scotch write English wonderfully well.

$$* \quad * \quad * \quad * \quad * \quad *$$

Your frequent visits to Auchinleck, and your short stay there are very laudable and very judicious. Your present concord with your father gives me great pleasure; it was all that you seemed to want.[5]

My health is very bad, and my nights are very unquiet. What can I do to mend them? I have for this summer nothing better

---

1. On 24 Apr. JB had written to SJ: "Our worthy friend Thrale's death having appeared in the newspapers, and been afterwards contradicted, I have been placed in a state of very uneasy uncertainty, from which I hoped to be relieved by you" (*Life* III.107–8). *Ante* To John Perkins, 4 Apr. 1777 and n. 1; *Ante* To Henry Thrale, 9 Apr. 1777, n. 2.   2. *Ante* To JB, 11 Mar. 1777 and n. 1.

3. *Timeo Danaos et dona ferentis*: "I fear the Greeks, even when bringing gifts" (Virgil, *Aeneid* II.49, trans. H. R. Fairclough, Loeb ed.).

4. *Ante* To William Strahan, 24 Dec. 1776 and n. 1; *Ante* To JB, 18 Feb. 1777.

5. JB had written to SJ: "I am going to Auchinleck to stay a fortnight with my father. It is better not to be there very long at one time. But frequent renewals of attention are agreeable to him" (*Life* III.108).

in prospect than a journey into Staffordshire and Derbyshire, perhaps with Oxford and Birmingham in my way.[6]

Make my compliments to Miss Veronica; I must leave it to *her* philosophy to comfort you for the loss of little David.[7] You must remember, that to keep three out of four is more than your share. Mrs. Thrale has but four out of eleven.[8]

I am engaged to write little Lives, and little Prefaces, to a little edition of the English Poets.[9] I think I have persuaded the booksellers to insert something of Thomson, and if you could give me some information about him, for the life which we have is very scanty, I should be glad.[10] I am, dear Sir, Your most affectionate humble servant,

SAM. JOHNSON

6. SJ left London for Oxford on 28 July, then traveled to Birmingham on 5 Aug. From 6 Aug. to 4 Nov. he stayed in Lichfield and Ashbourne, returning to London (via Birmingham) on 6 Nov. JB visited SJ at Ashbourne, 14–24 Sept. (*Life* III.135, 208).   7. *Ante* To JB, 11 Mar. 1777, n. 9.

8. The Thrales' four surviving children were Queeney, Susanna, Sophia, and Cecilia. Since 1765 they had lost seven in infancy or childhood: Frances, Henry, Anna Maria, Lucy, Penelope, Ralph, and Frances Anna (Hyde, 1977, p. xii).

9. On 29 Mar. SJ had contracted with thirty-six of "the most respectable book-sellers of London" (*Life* III.111) to produce prefaces, "biographical and critical," to a pocket (small octavo) edition of the English poets (*Life* III.488–89). The selection was limited to the period from *c*. 1660 to *c*. 1770; living poets were excluded. "The writing of these lives occupied Johnson for four years. The first four volumes, with twenty-two lives, came out in 1779; the remaining six, containing thirty lives, in 1781" (*Bibliography*, p. 132). For an authoritative account of the genesis of the *Lives*, see T. F. Bonnell, "John Bell's *Poets of Great Britain*: The 'Little Trifling Edition' Revisited," *Modern Philology* 85, 1987, pp. 128–52.

10. JB promptly located and interviewed James Thomson's sister, who showed him letters from her brother, one of which he copied and sent to SJ (*Life* III.116, 359–60).

John Taylor

SATURDAY 3 MAY 1777

MS: Pierpont Morgan Library.
ADDRESS: To the Reverend Dr. Taylor in Ashbourne, Derbyshire.
POSTMARK: 3 MA.
ENDORSEMENTS: 1777, 3 May 77.

Dear Sir: May 3, 1777

The Weather now begins to grow tempting, and brings my annual excursion into my mind. It is now an interesting question whether you intend to come hither again,[1] for if you do, I shall endeavour to accompany you back; if You let idleness prevail, and stay at home I have my own course to take.[2]

Mr. Lucas has just been with me. He has compelled me to read his tragedy, which is but a poor performance, and yet may perhaps put money into his pocket; it contains nothing immoral or indecent, and therefore, we may very reasonably wish it success.[3]

My nights continue to be very flatulent and restless, and my days are therefore sluggish and drowsy. After physick I have sometimes less uneasiness, as I had last night, but the effect is by no means constant; nor have I found any advantage from going to bed either with a full or an empty stomach.

Let me know what you resolve about your journey, as soon as you have taken your resolution. I am, sir, your affectionate, humble servant,

SAM. JOHNSON

1. *Ante* To Henry Thrale, 9 Apr. 1777.

2. Taylor must have replied that he did not intend to come to London again that spring. *Post* To John Taylor, 19 May 1777; *Ante* To JB, 3 May 1777, n. 6.

3. Henry Lucas (b. *c.* 1740), Irish lawyer and man of letters, requested that SJ revise his tragedy, *The Earl of Somerset* (*Life* III.532). In the preface to the published version of the play, Lucas thanks SJ for "the peculiar kindness of his perusal, emendations, and good opinion of this work" (1779, p. xxv). SJ, who told JB that he "did not strike out much," was displeased by this public expression of gratitude (*Boswell, Laird of Auchinleck*, ed. J. W. Reed and F. A. Pottle, 1977, p. 75 and n. 9; H. W. Liebert, "An Addition to the Bibliography of Samuel Johnson," *Papers of the Bibliographical Society of America* 41, 1947, pp. 231–38).

Mary Cholmondeley[1]

TUESDAY 6 MAY 1777

MS: Sir John Riddell, Bt.

Dear Madam,   May 6, 1777

No length of absence can make me so far forget the pleasure of your conversation, or the kindness of your friendship, as that I should not be still desirous of being numbered among those who partake both[2] of your comforts and your misfortunes. I will not omit therefore, as[3] this heavy blow has fallen upon you, to do what now only remains for human kindness, to entreat and counsel you to bear it with calmness and submission, and solace yourself with the amiable character which your Son has left behind him.[4] We all live on this condition that the ties of every endearment must at last be broken. The Mother must lose her Son, or the son his Mother.[5] This necessity, when such sorrowful separations happen, cannot indeed exclude[6] grief, but it may very properly restrain us from indulging it.[7] And I hope, dear Madam, this, or better considerations than I can suggest, will operate to your relief, and that You who have so often diffused pleasure, will in a short

1. Mary Cholmondeley (*c.* 1729–1811), wife (m. 1746) of the Rev. Hon. Robert Cholmondeley (1727–1804), second son of the third Earl of Cholmondeley and nephew of Horace Walpole. The Hon. Mrs. Cholmondeley was the younger sister of the celebrated actress Margaret Woffington (*c.* 1718–60). SJ, a member of her London coterie, had developed a gallant, relaxed, bantering friendship with this "very airy lady" (*Life* v.248). Mary Cholmondeley exemplified SJ's rule, "'tis not *Girls* but *Women* who inspire the violent and lasting passions"; according to Hester Thrale, "Mrs. Cholmondeley's Powr is still felt and acknowledged now at fifty Years old" (*Thraliana* 1.386).

2. MS: "both" altered from "bothe"

3. MS: "as" superimposed upon undeciphered erasure

4. Robert Francis Cholmondeley (1756–77), Mrs. Cholmondeley's younger son, died 29 Apr. (*Walpole's Correspondence*, Yale ed. vi.440 n. 2).

5. "But in the condition of mortal beings, one must lose another" (*Post* To James Elphinston, 27 July 1778).

6. MS: "indeed" del. before "exclude"

7. ". . . tears are neither to me nor to you of any further use, when once the tribute of nature has been paid" (*Ante* To James Elphinston, 25 Sept. 1750).

time be again able to receive it. I am, Madam, Your most humble servant,

SAM. JOHNSON

Charles O'Conor

MONDAY 19 MAY 1777

MS: Beinecke Library. The transcript (in the hand of J. C. Walker) used as copy for JB's *Life*.

Sir,   May 19, 1777

Having had the pleasure of conversing with Dr. Campbel about your Character and your literary Undertaking,[1] I am resolved to gratify myself by renewing a correspondence which began and ended a great while ago,[2] and ended, I am afraid, by my fault, a fault which, if you have not forgotten it, you must now forgive.

If I have ever disappointed you, give me leave to tell you that you have likewise disappointed me. I expected great discoveries in Irish Antiquity, and large publications in the Irish language. But the world still remains as it was, doubtful and ignorant.[3] What the Irish Language is in itself, and to what languages it has affinity are very interesting Questions, which every man wishes to see resolved that has any philological or historical curiosity. Dr. Leland begins his history too late;[4] the Ages which deserve an exact enquiry, are those times (for such

---

1. Thomas Campbell (1733–95), LL.D., Irish clergyman and antiquarian, met SJ through the Thrales in 1775 (*Dr. Campbell's Diary of a Visit to England*, ed. J. L. Clifford, 1947, pp. 1–5). Campbell spent the winter of 1776–77 in London, arranging for the publication of his *Philosophical Survey of the South of Ireland*, which appeared in Mar. 1778. "Since the manuscript was accepted for publication by W. Strahan and T. Cadell, it is possible that Johnson may have lent a friendly hand in the negotiations" (Clifford, *Diary*, pp. 10–11).

2. *Ante* To Charles O'Conor, 9 Apr. 1757.

3. Apparently the revised edition of O'Conor's *Dissertations on the History of Ireland* (1766) did not constitute the "large publication" SJ had in mind.

4. *Ante* To Thomas Leland, 17 Oct. 1765, n. 1. Though it contains a brief "Preliminary Discourse on the Antient State of that Kingdom," Leland's *History of Ireland* actually begins with the invasion of Henry II in 1171.

times there were), when Ireland was the School of the West, the quiet habitation of Sanctity and literature. If you could give a history, though imperfect, of the Irish Nation from its conversion to Christianity, to the invasion from England, you would amplify knowledge with new Views and new objects. Set about it therefore if you can, do what you can easily do, without anxious exactness. Lay the foundation, and leave the superstructure to posterity.[5] I am, Sir, your most humble Servant,

SAM. JOHNSON

5. In 1785 O'Conor informed J. C. Walker, "(tho' in an infirm state) I am following Dr. Johnsons Directions in drawing up a Memoir on the ancient State of this Island" (Waingrow, p. 124 n. 1). There is no record of the publication of such a memoir.

John Taylor

MONDAY 19 MAY 1777

MS: Berg Collection, New York Public Library.
ENDORSEMENT: 19 May 1777, about Dr. Dodd.

Dear Sir: May 19, 1777

I am required by Mrs. Thrale to solicit you to exert your interest, that she may have a ticket of admission to the entertainment at Devonshire house.[1] Do for her what You can.

I continue to have very troublesome and tedious nights, which I do not perceive any change of place to make better or worse. This is indeed at present my chief malady, but this is very heavy.

My thoughts were to have been in Staffordshire before now. But who does what he designs? My purpose is still to spend part of the Summer amongst you; and of that hope I have no particular reason to fear the disappointment.[2]

1. This fête, to be given by the Duke and Duchess of Devonshire at their mansion in Piccadilly, was "deferred to another Year" (Hester Thrale to SJ, 25 May 1777, MS: Rylands Library). *Post* To Hester Thrale, 19 May 1777 and nn. 3, 4.
2. *Ante* To JB, 3 May 1777, n. 6.

Poor Dod was sentenced last week.[3] It is a thing almost without example for a Clergyman of his rank to stand at the bar for a capital breach of morality. I am afraid he will suffer. The Clergy seem not to be his friends. The populace that was extremely clamorous against him, begins to pity him. The time that was gained by an objection which was never considered as having any force, was of great use, as it allowed the publick resentment to cool. To spare his life, and his life is all that ought to be spared, would be now rather popular than offensive. How little he thought six months ago of being what he now is. I am, Sir, etc.

SAM. JOHNSON

3. On 22 Feb. 1777 the Rev. William Dodd (1729–77), LL.D., popular preacher and King's Chaplain, had been convicted of forging the signature of his patron, Lord Chesterfield, to a bond for £4,200. Sentencing was delayed while part of the evidence against Dodd was reexamined and finally found admissible. On 16 May he was sentenced to be hanged. There was widespread hope that the King would grant a pardon; however, "the clergy opposed mercy as did some of the court, but especially Lord Mansfield who ... convinced George III that he must discountenance popular meddling with justice" (E. E. Willoughby, "The Unfortunate Dr. Dodd," in *Essays by Divers Hands*, ed. E. V. Rieu, *Transactions of the Royal Society of Literature*, 1958, XXIX.140). Accordingly, Dodd was executed on 27 June. SJ took an active role on Dodd's behalf. *Post* To Edmund Allen, 17 June 1777; 22 June 1777; *Post* To Charles Jenkinson, 20 June 1777; *Post* To William Dodd, 22 June 1777; *Post* To Lady Harrington, 25 June 1777.

Hester Thrale

MONDAY 19 MAY 1777

MS: Hyde Collection.

Madam: May 19, 1777

I have written to Dr. Taylor, you may be sure, but the business is pretty much out of the Doctors way.[1] His[2] acquaintance [is] with the Lord Cavendishes,[3] he barely knows the young Duke

1. *Ante* To John Taylor, 19 May 1777.   2. MS: "His" altered from "He"
3. SJ refers to the three uncles of the fifth Duke of Devonshire: Lord George Cavendish (?1727–94), Lord Frederick Cavendish (1729–1803), and Lord John

and Dutchess.[4] He will be proud to show that he can do it, but he will hardly try, if he suspects any danger of refusal.

You will become such a Gadder, that you will not care a peny for me. However, you are wise in wishing to know what life is made of: to try what are the pleasures, which are so eagerly sought, and so dearly purchased. We must know pleasure before we can rationally despise. And it is not desirable that when you are with matronal authority talking down juvenile hopes and maiden passions, your hearers should tell you, like Miss Pitches, "You never saw a Fête."[5]

That you may see this Show I have written because I am, Madam, your most humble servant, SAM. JOHNSON

Cavendish (1732–96). Taylor's acquaintance with them derived from his friendship with their father, the third Duke (*Ante* To John Taylor, 2 Jan. 1742, n. 2).

4. William Cavendish (1748–1811), fifth Duke of Devonshire (1764), married (1774) Lady Georgiana Spencer (1757–1806): "she . . . a lovely girl, natural, and full of grace; he, the first match in England" (*Walpole's Correspondence*, Yale ed. XXIII.562).

5. "Lady Pitches was haranguing about a Black Fox—Why (says her Daughter dryly) you never saw a Black Fox" (H. L. Piozzi's note in her copy of *Letters*, 1788, I.347: Trinity College, Cambridge). Presumably SJ refers to Sophia (d. 1779), the eldest daughter of Sir Abraham and Lady Pitches, neighbors of the Thrales (Hyde, 1977, p. 188 and n. 12; *Thraliana* I.200 n. 2, 393).

Hester Thrale

MONDAY 2 JUNE 1777

MS: Hyde Collection.

Dear Madam: Monday, June 2

I left my Watch and, I think, my Stockbuckle[1] in my Chamber. I spoke to Mr. Thrale and to Henderson,[2] but neither of them have minded me. Be so good as to send me my Chattels.

I wish You and Queeney a pleasant Wednesday.[3] I shall dine

1. *stockbuckle*: "a buckle used to secure the stock or cravat" (*OED*).

2. Henderson was Henry Thrale's valet (*Thraliana* I.455 and n. 7).

3. They had planned to go to the theater, but decided for lack of tickets to go to Ranelagh instead (Hester Thrale to SJ, 3 June 1777, MS: Rylands Library).

at the academy.[4] I was at Mrs. Vesey's last night[5] and so commended was my Prologue by fine Ladies—you can't think.[6]
Nor I tell.

And I got all that was got, for poor Mrs. Kelly had a miserable night. Only fifty pounds.[7] I am, Madam, Your slave,

SAM. JOHNSON

Do you make any new cloaths? How is Queeney to be
dressed?[8]

4. From 1771 until 1780, the Royal Academy had its headquarters in part of
Old Somerset House, the Strand (Wheatley and Cunningham III.177).

5. Elizabeth Vesey (*c*. 1715–91), close friend of Elizabeth Montagu and a prom-
inent Bluestocking hostess in her own right, the wife of Agmondesham Vesey,
Accountant-General of Ireland and member of The Club. In 1777 she lived on
Bolton Row, Piccadilly.

6. SJ had written a prologue for the benefit performance of Hugh Kelly's *A
Word to the Wise* at Covent Garden, 29 May 1777 (*Poems*, pp. 209–10).

7. See above, n. 6. The performance, which was intended to benefit Kelly's
widow and children, netted £56 15*s*. (*Lond. Stage*, Part v, 1.87).

8. Hester Thrale responded on 3 June: "How kind you are to be thinking of
my Clothes and Queeney's! mine are a plain White Silk ... trimmed with pale
Purple and Silver. ... My fair Daughter has no new clothes" (MS: Rylands Library).

Edmund Allen

TUESDAY 17 JUNE 1777

MS: Hyde Collection.

Sir: June 17, 1777

You know that my attention to Dr. Dodd has incited me to
enquire what is the real purpose of Government;[1] the dreadful answer I have put into your hands.[2]

1. SJ had been persuaded by Allen and the Countess of Harrington, both
friends of Dodd, to join in the attempt to secure him a royal pardon (*Life* III.141;
Post To Lady Harrington, 25 June 1777). SJ's writings on his behalf include a
sermon preached by Dodd in Newgate (*The Convict's Address to his Unhappy Brethren*), a *Speech to the Recorder Before Receiving Sentence of Death*, petitions to the King
and Queen, and letters to Lord Bathurst and Lord Mansfield (*Papers Written by Dr.
Johnson and Dr. Dodd*, ed. R. W. Chapman, 1926, pp. xv–xvi; Dodd MSS: Hyde
Collection; *Life* III.496).

2. On 16 June SJ wrote to Anthony Chamier, Under-Secretary of State, to de-

Nothing now remains but that he whose profession it has been to teach others to dye, learn now to dye himself.

It will be wise to deny admission from this time to all who do not come to assist his preparation; to addict himself wholly to prayer and meditation, and consider himself as no longer connected with the world. He has now nothing to do for the short time that remains, but to reconcile himself to God. To this end it will be proper to abstain totally from all strong liquors, and from all other sensual indulgencies, that his thoughts may be as clear and calm as his condition can allow.

If his remissions of anguish, and intervals of devotion leave him any time, he may perhaps spend it profitably in writing the history of his own depravation, and marking the gradual declination from innocence and quiet, to that state in which the law has found him. Of his advice to the Clergy or admonitions to Fathers of families there is no need; he will leave behind him those who can write them.[3] But the history of his own mind, if not written by himself, cannot be written, and the instruction that might be derived from it must be lost. This therefore he must leave, if he leaves any thing; but whether he can find leisure, or obtain tranquillity sufficient for this, I cannot judge. Let him however shut his doors against all hope, all trifles, and all sensuality. Let him endeavour to calm his thoughts by abstinence, and look out for a proper director in his penitence, and may God who would that all men should be saved, help him with his Holy Spirit, and have mercy on him for Jesus Christ's sake. I am, sir, your most humble servant,

SAM. JOHNSON

This may be communicated to Dr. Dodd.

---

termine whether the Privy Council might grant Dodd a pardon. On 17 June Chamier sent his "dreadful answer": "I do not hesitate to assure You that there is not the smallest Chance of even a Respite for Dr. Dodd. . . . I am thus explicit as I think it Cruelty to give this unhappy Man hopes that must be disappointed" (MS: Hyde Collection).

3. Dodd had meditated "a few words to the Clergy—on the Evil by which I was vanquish'd . . . a word to gay families, that live beyond their Incomes—fathers of families, living wholly without Religion" (Dodd to Allen, 15 June 1777, MS: Hyde Collection).

Charles Jenkinson

FRIDAY 20 JUNE 1777

PRINTED SOURCE: JB's *Life*, 1791, II.138–39.

Sir,

Since the conviction and condemnation of Dr. Dodd, I have had, by the intervention of a friend, some intercourse with him,[1] and I am sure I shall lose nothing in your opinion by tenderness and commiseration. Whatever be the crime, it is not easy to have any knowledge of the delinquent without a wish that his life may be spared, at least when no life has been taken away by him. I will, therefore, take the liberty of suggesting some reasons for which I wish this unhappy being to escape the utmost rigour of his sentence.

He is, so far as I can recollect, the first clergyman of our church who has suffered publick execution for immorality; and I know not whether it would not be more for the interest of religion to bury such an offender in the obscurity of perpetual exile, than to expose him in a cart, and on the gallows, to all who for any reason are enemies to the clergy.

The supreme power has, in all ages, paid some attention to the voice of the people; and that voice does not least deserve to be heard, when it calls out for mercy.[2] There is now a very general desire that Dodd's life should be spared. More is not wished; and, perhaps, this is not too much to be granted.

If you, Sir, have any opportunity of enforcing these reasons, you may, perhaps, think them worthy of consideration: but whatever you determine, I most respectfully intreat that you will be pleased to pardon for this intrusion, Sir, Your most obedient And most humble servant,

SAM. JOHNSON

1. SJ never visited Dodd in prison, but he corresponded with him through Edmund Allen, who was friendly with the Keeper of Newgate (*Life* III.145).

2. "Surely the voice of the publick, when it calls so loudly, and calls only for mercy, ought to be heard" (*Post* To JB, 28 June 1777). Petitions had poured in from a number of sources, including the Corporation of the City of London, 23,000 London householders, the two Universities, and even the jurors who had found Dodd guilty.

Edmund Allen

SUNDAY 22 JUNE 1777

MS: Hyde Collection.

ADDRESS: To Mr. Allen in Boltcourt, Fleetstreet.

Dear Sir: June 22, 1777

There was mention made of sending Dr. Dod's sermon to the great Officers of State.[1] I opposed it, but have now altered my Mind. Nothing can do harm, let every thing therefore be tried. Let Mr. Jenkinson have his letter wherever he be.[2] Let the Sermon be sent to every Body, and to the King if it can be done. He is, I believe more likely to read it, and to regard it than his Ministers. Let Lord Dartmouth have it,[3] and Lord North. I am, sir, your humble servant,

                                                    SAM. JOHNSON

   1. *Ante* To Edmund Allen, 17 June 1777, n. 1.

   2. *Ante* To Charles Jenkinson, 20 June 1777.

   3. William Legge (1731–1801), second Earl of Dartmouth, Lord Privy Seal (1775–82).

William Dodd

SUNDAY 22 JUNE 1777

MS: Hyde Collection. A copy in the hand of Edmund Allen.[1]

Sir,

I must seriously enjoin you not to let it be at all known that I have written this Letter, and to return the Copy to Mr. Allen in a Cover to me. I hope, I need not tell you that I wish it Success.—But do not indulge Hope.—Tell nobody.[2]

   1. This note was originally "subjoined" to the letter SJ wrote for Dodd to send to the King (*Life* III.145).

   2. MS: "Tell nobody" added in pencil in an unidentified hand

James Boswell
TUESDAY 24 JUNE 1777

PRINTED SOURCE: JB's *Life*, 1791, II.121–22.

Dear Sir,   June 24, 1777

This gentleman is a great favourite at Streatham, and there-fore you will easily believe that he has very valuable qualities.[1] Our narrative has kindled him with a desire of visiting the Highlands, after having already seen a great part of Europe. You must receive him as a friend, and when you have directed him to the curiosities of Edinburgh, give him instructions and recommendations for the rest of his journey.[2] I am, dear Sir, Your most humble servant,

SAM. JOHNSON

1. SJ repeats this information in his letter to JB of 28 June, where the "great favourite" is identified as William Seward.

2. On 15 July JB replied: "I received Mr. Seward as the friend of Mr. and Mrs. Thrale, and as a gentleman recommended by Dr. Johnson to my attention. I have introduced him to Lord Kames, Lord Monboddo, and Mr. Nairne. He is gone to the Highlands with Dr. Gregory; when he returns I shall do more for him" (*Life* III.126).

Lady Harrington[1]
WEDNESDAY 25 JUNE 1777

MS: Hyde Collection. A copy in the hand of Edmund Allen.
ADDRESS: To the Right Hon. Lady H.

Madam: June 25, 1777

That Humanity which disposed Your Ladyship to engage me in Favour of Dr. Dodd,[2] will incline You to forgive me when I

1. Lady Caroline Fitzroy (1722–84), daughter of the second Duke of Grafton and wife of the second Earl of Harrington. Lady Harrington was a flamboyant woman-about-town—notoriously unfaithful to her husband and an avid gambler. She had known Dodd since the early 1760s, when they both attended the masquerades at Carlisle House in Soho Square (Gerald Howson, *The Macaroni Parson*, 1973, pp. 59, 174).

2. According to JB, Lady Harrington "wrote a letter to Johnson, asking him to

take the Liberty of soliciting Your Influence in Support of my Endeavours, which, I am afraid, will otherwise be ineffectual. What could be done by the Powers which fall to my share, has been warmly and carefully performed.[3] The Time is now come when high Rank and high Spirit must begin their Operations. Dodd must die at last unless Your Ladyship shall be pleased to represent to his Majesty how properly the Life of a Delinquent may be granted to the Petition of that Society for the Sake of which he is to be punished;[4] that the greatest Princes have thought it the highest Part of their Praise, to be easily flexible to the Side of Mercy; and that whether the Case be consider'd as political or moral, the joint Petition of Three and Twenty Thousand Supplicants, ought not to be rejected, when even after all that they desire is granted, the Offender is still to suffer perpetual Exile, perpetual Infamy, and perpetual Poverty. I am, Madam, Your ladyship's Most obedient and most humble Servant,

SAM. JOHNSON

---

employ his pen in favour of Dodd. . . . Mr. Allen told me that he carried Lady Harrington's letter to Johnson, that Johnson read it walking up and down his chamber, and seemed much agitated, after which he said, 'I will do what I can'" (*Life* III.141). 3. *Ante* To Edmund Allen, 17 June 1777, n. 1.

4. No record of an appeal from Lady Harrington to the King has been recovered. Queen Charlotte herself was unsuccessful in persuading her husband to grant a pardon.

William Dodd

THURSDAY 26 JUNE 1777

PRINTED SOURCE: JB's *Life*, 1791, II.140.
ADDRESS: To the Reverend Dr. Dodd.

Dear Sir,   June 26, 1777

That which is appointed to all men is now coming upon you. Outward circumstances, the eyes and the thoughts of men, are below the notice of an immortal being about to stand the trial for eternity, before the Supreme Judge of heaven and earth. Be comforted: your crime, morally or religiously considered, has no very deep dye of turpitude. It corrupted no man's principles; it attacked no man's life. It involved only a temporary and reparable injury. Of this, and of all other sins, you are earnestly to repent; and may God, who knoweth our frailty and desireth not our death, accept your repentance, for the sake of his Son Jesus Christ our Lord.

In requital of those well-intended offices which you are pleased so emphatically to acknowledge, let me beg that you make in your devotions one petition for my eternal welfare. I am, dear Sir, Your affectionate servant,

SAM. JOHNSON

James Boswell

SATURDAY 28 JUNE 1777

PRINTED SOURCE: JB's *Life*, 1791, II.119–21.

Dear Sir,   June 28, 1777

I have just received your packet from Mr. Thrale's, but have not day-light enough to look much into it.[1] I am glad that I have credit enough with Lord Hailes to be trusted with more copy. I hope to take more care of it than of the last. I return Mrs. Boswell my affectionate thanks for her present, which I value as a token of reconciliation.[2]

Poor Dodd was put to death yesterday, in opposition to the recommendation of the jury[3]—the petition of the city of London—and a subsequent petition signed by three-and-twenty

1. JB had sent SJ "a large packet of Lord Hailes's 'Annals of Scotland'" (*Life* III.120). *Ante* To JB, 27 Aug. 1775.

2. Margaret Boswell had sent SJ a jar of homemade orange marmalade. *Ante* To JB, 11 Mar. 1777 and n. 1; 3 May 1777.

3. The jury found Dodd guilty with great reluctance, and in announcing its verdict also "recommended the prisoner to His Majesty's mercy" (Gerald Howson, *The Macaroni Parson*, 1973, p. 155).

thousand hands.[4] Surely the voice of the publick, when it calls so loudly, and calls only for mercy, ought to be heard.

The saying that was given me in the papers I never spoke;[5] but I wrote many of his petitions, and some of his letters.[6] He applied to me very often. He was, I am afraid, long flattered with hopes of life; but I had no part in the dreadful delusion; for as soon as the King had signed his sentence, I obtained from Mr. Chamier an account of the disposition of the court towards him, with a declaration that there was *no hope even of a respite.*[7] This letter immediately was laid before Dodd; but he believed those whom he wished to be right, as it is thought, till within three days of his end. He died with pious composure and resolution.[8] I have just seen the Ordinary that attended him.[9] His Address to his fellow-convicts offended the Methodists;[10] but he had a Moravian with him much of his time.[11]

4. *Ante* To Charles Jenkinson, 20 June 1777, n. 2.

5. In his letter of 9 June, JB told SJ that "the newspapers give us a saying of your's in favour of mercy to him" (*Life* III.119). L. F. Powell suggests that JB may have been referring to a paragraph that appeared in the *Public Advertiser*, 27 May 1777: "A Gentleman of Consequence asking the celebrated Dr. Johnson what he thought of the Propriety of pardoning a certain unhappy Clergyman, 'Think, Sir,' said he, 'I don't think; I am sure of that Propriety. Such a Life, so preserved, would be of more Utility to Mankind than a thousand Executions'" (*Life* III.491).

6. *Ante* To Edmund Allen, 17 June 1777, n. 1.

7. *Ante* To Edmund Allen, 17 June 1777, n. 2.

8. John Wesley visited Dodd two days before his execution and reported: "He was in exactly such a temper as I wished. He never at any time expressed the least murmuring or resentment at any one, but entirely and calmly gave himself up to the will of God" (*Journal of John Wesley*, ed. Nehemiah Curnock, 1938, VI.157).

9. The Rev. John Villette (d. 1799), Ordinary of Newgate (1774–99), whom JB praises for his "extraordinary diligence" and "earnest and humane exhortations" (*Life* IV.329; *Alum. Cant.* II.vi.290).

10. The sermon Dodd preached was written by SJ. *Ante* To Edmund Allen, 17 June 1777, n. 1.

11. The Rev. Benjamin La Trobe (1728–86), general director of the Moravian congregations in England and a friend of William Strahan, who first introduced La Trobe to SJ (M. J. Quinlan, "An Intermediary between Cowper and Johnson," *RES* 24, 1948, pp. 143–44; Waingrow, p. 468). According to James Hutton, the founder of the Moravian church in England, La Trobe "had great Merit indeed towards poor Dodd at my Request" (Waingrow, p. 468 and n. 12). Though much influenced by the Moravian Brethren during the early years of his ministry, John

His moral character is very bad: I hope all is not true that is charged upon him. Of his behaviour in prison an account will be published.[12]

I give you joy of your country-house, and your pretty garden;[13] and hope some time to see you in your felicity. I was much pleased with your two letters that had been kept so long in store;[14] and rejoice at Miss Rasay's advancement,[15] and wish Sir Allan success.[16]

I hope to meet you somewhere towards the north, but am loath to come quite to Carlisle.[17] Can we not meet at Manchester? But we will settle it in some other letters.

Mr. Seward, a great favourite at Streatham, has been, I think, enkindled by our travels, with a curiosity to see the Highlands. I have given him letters to you and Beattie.[18] He

---

Wesley began to oppose them in 1746, calling their pastors "Protestant Jesuits" (Martin Schmidt, *John Wesley*, 1962, I.270–71, II.67–68).

12. John Villette's *A Genuine Account of the Behaviour and Dying Words of William Dodd* (1777).

13. In his letter of 9 June, JB told SJ: "For the health of my wife and children I have taken the little country-house at which you visited my uncle, Dr. Boswell. . . . We have a garden of three quarters of an acre, well stocked with fruit-trees and flowers" (*Life* III.116). At the conclusion of their Hebridean tour, Nov. 1773, JB and SJ visited John Boswell at his house near the Meadows, outside of Edinburgh (*Hebrides*, p. 385; *Life* v.574).

14. JB sent two letters he had written but not posted, the first dated 30 Sept. 1764 ("at the tomb of Melancthon"), the second composed during his visit to Wilton, 19–22 Apr. 1775 (*Life* III.118).

15. "You will rejoice to hear that Miss Macleod, of Rasay, is married to Colonel Mure Campbell, an excellent man, with a pretty good estate of his own, and the prospect of having the Earl of Loudoun's fortune and honours" (JB to SJ, 9 June 1777, *Life* III.118).

16. "Sir Allan Maclean's suit against the Duke of Argyle, for recovering the ancient inheritance of his family, is now fairly before all our judges" (JB to SJ, 14 Feb. 1777, *Life* III.101). JB helped to argue Maclean's case before the Court of Session. At the beginning of July he won a partial victory—title to the lands of Brolass in Mull (*Boswell in Extremes*, ed. C. M. Weis and F. A. Pottle, 1970, p. 132 and n. 7).

17. "Dr. Johnson had himself talked of our seeing Carlisle together" (*Life* III.118 n. 3). In the event they met at Ashbourne and spent ten days together, 14–24 Sept.

18. *Ante* To JB, 24 June 1777.

desires that a lodging may be taken for him at Edinburgh, against his arrival. He is just setting out.

Langton has been exercising the militia.[19] Mrs. Williams is, I fear, declining.[20] Dr. Lawrence says he can do no more. She is gone to summer in the country, with as many conveniences about her as she can expect; but I have no great hope. We must all die: may we all be prepared!

I suppose Miss Boswell reads her book, and young Alexander takes to his learning. Let me hear about them; for every thing that belongs to you, belongs in a more remote degree, and not, I hope, very remote, to, dear Sir, Yours affectionately,

SAM. JOHNSON

19. Bennet Langton "served voluntarily for twenty-five years in the North Lincoln Militia, first as captain and then as major, and appears to have enjoyed his military duties and to have performed them commendably" (Fifer, p. lxxiii).

20. Anna Williams died on 6 Sept. 1783 "from mere inanition" (*Post* To Susanna Thrale, 9 Sept. 1783).

Bennet Langton

SUNDAY 29 JUNE 1777

MS: Hyde Collection.

HEADING in JB's hand: To Bennet Langton.

Dear Sir: June 29, 1777

I have lately been much disordered by a difficulty of breathing but am now better. I hope all your house is well.

You know we have been talking lately of St. Cross at Winchester.[1] I have an old acquaintance whose distress makes him very desirous of an hospital, and I am afraid, I have not strength enough to get him into the Chartreux.[2] He is a painter, who never rose higher than to get his immediate living;

1. *Ante* To Joseph Warton, 9 Oct. 1765, n. 3.

2. *Ante* To Richard Congreve, 25 June 1735, n. 14. In addition to the school, Charterhouse included a hospital for eighty old-age pensioners (Wheatley and Cunningham 1.364).

and from that at eighty three he is disabled by a slight stroke of the palsy, such as does not make him at all helpless on common occasions, though his hand is not steady enough for his art.[3]

My request is that you will try to obtain a promise of the next Vacancy from the Bishop of Chester.[4] It is not a great thing to ask, and I hope we shall obtain it.[5] Dr. Warton has promised to favour him with his notice, and I hope he may end his days in peace. I am, sir, your most humble servant,

SAM. JOHNSON

3. For a more detailed account of Isaac De Groot (*c.* 1694–1779), great-grandson of Hugo Grotius, *post* To William Vyse, 19 July 1777.
4. *Ante* To Hester Thrale, 1 Apr. 1775, n. 5; *Ante* To Bennet Langton, 13 Feb. 1777.   5. *Post* To William Vyse, 19 July 1777 and n. 6.

Bennet Langton
MONDAY 7 JULY 1777

MS: Hyde Collection.
ADDRESS: To Mr. Langton.

Dear Sir: July 7, 1777

I thank you for calling on me, and wish to meet. I am going out to morrow but shall be at home on Saturday. My respectful compliments to Lady Rothes. I hope my Miss Jenny is better.[1]

I am making a collection for a case of great distress, and hope You will favour me with a Guinea. I am, Sir, etc.

SAM. JOHNSON

1. Jane Langton (1776–1854), Langton's third daughter and SJ's godchild. *Post* To Jane Langton, 10 May 1784.

W. Sharp[1]

MONDAY 7 JULY 1777

PRINTED SOURCE: *GM* 1787, p. 99.

Sir,   London, 7th July, 1777

To the Collection of English Poets I have recommended the volume of Dr. Watts to be added.[2] His name has been long held by me in *veneration*; and I would not willingly be reduced to tell of him, only, that he was born and died.[3] Yet, of his life I know very little; and therefore must pass him in a manner very unworthy of his character, unless some of his friends will favour me with the necessary information. Many of them must be known to you;[4] and by your influence perhaps I may obtain some instruction. My plan does not exact much; but I wish to distinguish *Watts*; a man who never wrote but for a good purpose. Be pleased to do for me what you can. I am, Sir, your humble servant,   SAM. JOHNSON

1. The "W. Sharp" who furnished a copy of this letter to the *GM* may be William Sharp (*c.* 1730–1810), "a very eminent surgeon in the Old Jewry" and the brother of John Sharp (d. 1792), D.D., Archdeacon of Northumberland, who entertained SJ at Cambridge in 1765 (*Lit. Anec.* I.709, VIII.391; *Life* I.517).

2. Isaac Watts (1674–1748), D.D., the dissenting preacher and celebrated writer of hymns. SJ's "Life of Watts" begins, "The Poems of Dr. Watts were by my recommendation inserted in the late Collection" (*Lives of the Poets* III.302).

3. The short biographical section of SJ's "Life of Watts" depends on Thomas Gibbons's *Memoirs of Watts* (1780).

4. "At this time the writer had the honour of possessing Dr. Watts's correspondence with his great friends" (Sharp's note, *GM* 1787, p. 99).

William Vyse[1]

SATURDAY 19 JULY 1777

PRINTED SOURCE: JB's *Life*, 1791, II.123.
ADDRESS: To the Reverend Dr. Vyse, at Lambeth.

1. William Vyse (1742–1816), D.C.L., Rector of Lambeth and the son of Archdeacon William Vyse of Lichfield (*Ante* To Lucy Porter, 18 June 1768, n. 5).

Sir,   July 19, 1777

I doubt not but you will readily forgive me for taking the liberty of requesting your assistance in recommending an old friend to his Grace the Archbishop,[2] as Governour of the Charter-house.[3]

His name is De Groot; he was born at Gloucester; I have known him many years.[4] He has all the common claims to charity, being old, poor, and infirm, in a great degree. He has likewise another claim, to which no scholar can refuse attention; he is by several descents the nephew of Hugo Grotius;[5] of him, from whom perhaps every man of learning has learned something. Let it not be said that in any lettered country a nephew of Grotius asked a charity and was refused.[6] I am, reverend Sir, Your most humble servant,

SAM. JOHNSON

2. Frederick Cornwallis (1713–83), D.D., Archbishop of Canterbury (1768–83).

3. *Ante* To Bennet Langton, 29 June 1777, n. 2.

4. *Ante* To Bennet Langton, 29 June 1777.

5. Hugo Grotius (1583–1645), eminent Dutch statesman, jurist and scholar, author of *De satisfactione Christi* (1617) and *De jure belli ac pacis* (1625).

6. SJ's application to Archbishop Cornwallis was successful (*Life* III.125).

James Boswell

TUESDAY 22 JULY 1777

PRINTED SOURCE: JB's *Life*, 1791, II.125–26.

Dear Sir,   July 22, 1777

Your notion of the necessity of an yearly interview is very pleasing to both my vanity and tenderness. I shall, perhaps, come to Carlisle another year; but my money has not held out so well as it used to do.[1] I shall go to Ashbourne, and I purpose to make Dr. Taylor invite you. If you live awhile with me at his

1. JB had concluded his letter to SJ, 15 July: "I will meet you at Manchester, or where you please; but I wish you would complete your tour of the cathedrals, and

house, we shall have much time to ourselves, and our stay will be no expence to us or him.[2] I shall leave London the 28th; and after some stay at Oxford and Lichfield, shall probably come to Ashbourne about the end of your Session,[3] but of all this you shall have notice. Be satisfied we will meet somewhere.

What passed between me and poor Dr. Dodd you shall know more fully when we meet.[4]

Of lawsuits there is no end; poor Sir Allan must have another trial, for which, however, his antagonist cannot be much blamed, having two judges on his side.[5] I am more afraid of the debts than of the House of Lords. It is scarcely to be imagined to what debts will swell, that are daily encreasing by small additions, and how carelessly in a state of desperation debts are contracted. Poor Macquarry was far from thinking that when he sold his islands he should receive nothing.[6] For what were they sold? And what was their yearly value?[7] The admission of money into the Highlands will soon put an end to the feudal modes of life, by making those men landlords who were not chiefs. I do not know that the people will suffer by the change, but there was in the patriarchal authority something venerable and pleasing.[8] Every eye must look with pain

---

come to Carlisle, and I will accompany you a part of the way homewards" (*Life* III.127).

2. JB visited SJ at Ashbourne, 14–24 Sept.

3. The summer term of the Court of Session in Edinburgh ended 11 Aug.; SJ arrived at Ashbourne 30 Aug.

4. On 15 Sept. SJ let JB "carry with me to my room Dr. Dodd's letters to him, and several pieces which he had written for him" (*Boswell in Extremes*, ed. C. M. Weis and F. A. Pottle, 1970, p. 151).

5. *Ante* To JB, 28 June 1777, n. 16. Two of the fifteen judges of the Court of Session had voted in favor of the Duke of Argyll. According to JB, who sent SJ "a full state of the case," it was "certainly to be carried by appeal to the House of Lords" (JB to SJ, 14 Feb. 1777, *Life* III.102).

6. *Ante* To Hester Thrale, 23 Oct. 1773 and n. 7. Lauchlan Macquarrie's debts were so large that after the sale of his estate there was little or nothing left (*Life* v.556).

7. Macquarrie's land on Ulva brought in £156 5s. 1½d. per annum. It was sold for £5,540 (JB to SJ, 9 Sept. 1777, *Life* III.133).

8. SJ here condenses one of the themes of his *Journey to the Western Islands of Scotland*. See *Works*, Yale ed. IX.86, 112–13.

on a *Campbell* turning the *Macquarries* at will out of their *sedes avitae*,[9] their hereditary island.[10]

Sir Alexander Dick is the only Scotsman liberal enough not to be angry that I could not find trees, where trees were not. I was much delighted by his kind letter.[11]

I remember Rasay with too much pleasure not to partake of the happiness of any part of that amiable family.[12] Our ramble in the islands hangs upon my imagination, I can hardly help imagining that we shall go again. Pennant seems to have seen a great deal which we did not see:[13] When we travel again let us look better about us.

You have done right in taking your unkle's house.[14] Some change in the form of life, gives from time to time a new epocha of existence. In a new place there is something new to be done, and a different system of thoughts rises in the mind. I wish I could gather currants in your garden. Now fit up a little study, and have your books ready at hand; do not spare a little money, to make your habitation pleasing to yourself.

I have dined lately with poor dear ———.[15] I do not think he goes on well. His table is rather coarse, and he has his children too much about him. But he is a very good man.

Mrs. Williams is in the country to try if she can improve her

9. *quin etiam, sedes iubeat si vendere avitas*: "yea, if she bid me sell the home of my forefathers" (Tibullus, *Elegies* II.iv.53, trans. J. P. Postgate, Loeb ed.).

10. Macquarrie's two-thirds of Ulva had been purchased by a Mr. Campbell of Auchnaba (*Life* III.133).

11. Sir Alexander Dick (1703–85), Bt., M.D., of Prestonfield, Edinburgh, was a retired physician and close friend of JB; SJ met Dick at the start of the Hebridean tour. Sir Alexander had written to SJ, 17 Feb. 1777, thanking him for a copy of the *Journey to the Western Islands* and remarking on his complaint of treelessness: "Indeed our country of Scotland, in spite of the union of the crowns, is still in most places so devoid of clothing, or cover from hedges and plantations, that it was well you gave your readers a sound *Monitoire* with respect to that circumstance" (*Life* III.103). See *Works*, Yale ed. IX.9–10, 21, 60.

12. *Ante* To Hester Thrale, 14 Sept. 1773 and n. 7.

13. Thomas Pennant (1726–90), naturalist and traveler, author of *A Tour in Scotland and Voyage to the Hebrides* (1774). According to SJ, Pennant was "the best traveller I ever read; he observes more things than any one else does" (*Life* III.274).

14. *Ante* To JB, 28 June 1777 and n. 13.

15. SJ refers to Bennet Langton. *Ante* To JB, 18 Feb. 1777 and n. 7.

health; she is very ill.[16] Matters have come so about that she is in the country with very good accommodation; but, age and sickness, and pride, have made her so peevish that I was forced to bribe the maid to stay with her, by a secret stipulation of half a crown a week over her wages.

Our Club ended its session about six weeks ago. We now only meet to dine once a fortnight. Mr. Dunning, the great lawyer, is one of our members. The Thrales are well.

I long to know how the Negro's cause will be decided.[17] What is the opinion of Lord Auchinleck, or Lord Hailes, or Lord Monboddo?[18] I am, dear Sir, Your most affectionate, etc.

SAM. JOHNSON

16. *Ante* To JB, 28 June 1777 and n. 20.

17. Joseph Knight, an African slave, was purchased in Jamaica and brought to Scotland by his master. Knight then petitioned for liberty, contending that Scots law did not permit slavery. JB helped argue his case, which was decided by the Court of Session in Knight's favor, 15 Jan. 1778. At Ashbourne in September, SJ, who took a strong interest in the cause, dictated an argument to JB (*Life* III.202–3). *Post* To JB, 24 Jan. 1778.

18. Lord Auchinleck and Lord Hailes voted in favor of Knight, Lord Monboddo against him (*Life* III.213).

Margaret Boswell

TUESDAY 22 JULY 1777

PRINTED SOURCE: JB's *Life*, 1791, II.126–27.

Madam,   July 22, 1777

Though I am well enough pleased with the taste of sweet-meats, very little of the pleasure which I received at the arrival of your jar of marmalade arose from eating it.[1] I received it as a token of friendship, as a proof of reconciliation, things much sweeter than sweetmeats, and upon this consideration I return you, dear Madam, my sincerest thanks. By having your kind-ness I think I have a double security for the continuance of Mr. Boswell's, which it is not to be expected that any man can

1. *Ante* To JB, 11 Mar. 1777, n. 1; 3 May 1777.

long keep, when the influence of a lady so highly and so justly valued operates against him. Mr. Boswell will tell you, that I was always faithful to your interest, and always endeavoured to exalt you in his estimation. You must now do the same for me. We must all help one another, and you must now consider me, as, dear Madam, Your most obliged, And most humble servant,

SAM. JOHNSON

Richard Farmer
TUESDAY 22 JULY 1777

MS: Pierpont Morgan Library.

ADDRESS: To Dr. Farmer, Emanuel Coll., Cambridge.[1]

Sir: Boltcourt, Fleetstreet, July 22, 1777

The Booksellers of London have undertaken a kind of Body of English Poetry, excluding generally the dramas, and I have undertaken to put before each authors works a sketch of his life, and a character of his writings.[2] Of some, however I know very little, and am afraid I shall not easily supply my deficiencies. Be pleased to inform me whether among Mr. Bakers manuscripts, or any where else at Cambridge any materials are to be found.[3] If any such collection can be gleaned, I doubt not of your willingness to direct our search, and will tell[4] the Booksellers to employ a transcriber.[5] If you think my inspection necessary, I will come down, for who that has once experienced the civilities of Cambridge would not snatch the opportunity of another visit?[6] I am, Sir, Your most humble Servant,

SAM. JOHNSON

1. Address from text in *GM* 3 (N.S.), 1835, p. 47.
2. *Ante* To JB, 3 May 1777 and n. 9.
3. Thomas Baker (1656–1740), antiquarian and biographer, a fellow of St. John's College, Cambridge, who collected forty-two volumes of material for a projected *Athenae Cantabrigienses*. Volumes 24–42 were kept in the Cambridge University Library.   4. MS: "tell" superimposed upon "?ask" partially erased.
5. Cf. *Post* To Richard Farmer, 23 May 1780.
6. SJ had visited Cambridge in 1765 (*Ante* To Richard Farmer, 21 Mar. 1770, n. 1). There is no record of a second visit.

William Vyse
TUESDAY 22 JULY 1777

PRINTED SOURCE: JB's *Life*, ed. Edmond Malone, 1807, III.134.

July 22, 1777

If any notice should be taken of the recommendation which I took the liberty of sending you, it will be necessary to know that Mr. De Groot is to be found at No. 8, in Pye-street, Westminster.[1] This information, when I wrote, I could not give you; and being going soon to Lichfield, think it necessary to be left behind me.[2]

More I will not say. You will want no persuasion to succour the nephew of Grotius. I am, Sir, Your most humble servant,

SAM. JOHNSON

1. *Ante* To William Vyse, 19 July 1777.
2. *Ante* To JB, 3 May 1777 and n. 6; *Post* To Henry Thrale, 31 July 1777.

Thomas Lawrence
SATURDAY 26 JULY 1777

MS: Johnson House, London.
ADDRESS: To Dr. Laurence.

Dear Sir: Boltcourt, July 26, 1777

I send you a very handsome letter just received from Mr. Laurence.[1] There is great reason for hoping that you will live to derive pleasure from his character and conduct.

Be pleased to consider these two epitaphs which I purpose to have engraven.[2] I am going into Staffordshire.[3] I will send for them tonight. I am, Sir, your most humble servant,

SAM. JOHNSON

1. *Ante* To Thomas Lawrence, 30 Jan. 1775, n. 1.
2. It is likely that one of these epitaphs was for Oliver Goldsmith (*Life* III.82–83; *Post* To Joseph Nollekens, 27 Aug. 1777).
3. *Ante* To JB, 3 May 1777 and n. 6; *Post* To Henry Thrale, 31 July 1777.

Henry Thrale

THURSDAY 31 JULY 1777

MS: Historical Society of Pennsylvania.

HEADING in the hand of H. L. Piozzi: To Mr. Thrale.

Dear Sir: [Oxford] July 31, 1777

I came hither on Monday and find every thing much as I expected. I shall not stay long, but if you send any letters to me on Saturday, to University College, I shall receive them. Please to make my compliments to my Mistress and Queeny. I have picked up some little information for my Lives at the library.[1] I know not whether I shall go forward without some regret. I cannot break my promise to Boswel and the rest,[2] but I have a great mind to come back again. I am, sir, your most humble servant,

SAM. JOHNSON

1. Cf. *Post* To Hester Thrale, 4 Aug. 1777.

2. *Ante* To JB, 22 July 1777. "The rest" includes Lucy Porter, Elizabeth Aston, and John Taylor.

Hester Thrale

MONDAY 4 AUGUST 1777

MS: Hyde Collection.

Dear Madam: [Oxford] Aug. 4, 1777

I did not mean to express much discontent nor any ill humour in my letter.[1] When I went away I knew that I went partly because I had talked of going, and because I was a little restless. I have been searching the library for materials for my lives, and a little I have got.

Things have not gone quite well with poor Gwynne.[2] His

1. After reading SJ's letter of 31 July, Hester Thrale, concerned by his low spirits, had written an encouraging response (2 Aug. 1777, MS: Rylands Library).

2. John Gwynn (d. 1786), a Welsh architect and friend of SJ, who supported him in the controversy over elliptical vs. semi-circular arches for the Blackfriars Bridge (Clifford, 1979, p. 226) and contributed to his *Thoughts on the Coronation*

work was finished so ill that he has been condemned to pay three hundred pounds for damages, and the sentence is considered as very mild. He has however not lost his friends, and is still in the best houses, and at the best tables.

I shall enquire about the harvest when I come[3] into a region where any thing necessary to life is understood.[4] I do not believe that there is yet any great harm, if the weather should now mend. Reaping time will only be a little later than is usual.

Dr. Wetherel is abroad, I think at London; Mr. Coulson is here, and well. Every body that know[s] you enquires after you.

Boswel's project is disconcerted by a visit from a relation of Yorkshire, whom he mentions as the head of his clan.[5] Boszy, you know, makes a huge bustle about all his own motions, and all mine. I have inclosed a letter to pacify him and reconcile him to the uncertainties of human Life.[6]

I believe it was after I left your house that I received a pot of orange Marmalade from Mrs. Boswel. We have now, I hope, made it up.[7] I have not opened my pot.

I have determined to leave Oxford to morrow and on thursday hope to see Lichfield,[8] where I mean to rest till Dr. Taylor

---

(1761). Gwynn, "a fine lively rattling fellow" (*Life* II.439), designed and built bridges at Atcham, Shrewsbury, and Worcester. In his role as surveyor to the commissioners of the Oxford Paving Act, 1771–79, he built Magdalen Bridge, the Market, and the Workhouse. *Post* To Unidentified Correspondent, 30 Jan. 1778.

3. MS: "come" altered from "can"

4. "I wish you would tell me what folks at a Distance think of the harvest—the Weather here is abominable" (Hester Thrale to SJ, 2 Aug. 1777, MS: Rylands Library).

5. JB wrote SJ on 28 July, "puzzled about time of meeting . . . as Godfrey Bosville was coming." He wrote again on 29 July, "afraid" that SJ "would be angry at my uncertainty as to time of my meeting him" (*Boswell in Extremes*, ed. C. M. Weis and F. A. Pottle, 1970, p. 135). Godfrey Bosville (1717–84), of Gunthwaite and Thorpe, JB's "Yorkshire Chief" (*Life* III.439), visited Edinburgh the final week of August (Weis and Pottle, *Extremes*, pp. 140–41).

6. *Post* To JB, 4 Aug. 1777. SJ enclosed the letter so that it could be franked by Henry Thrale. JB received it in Edinburgh on 9 Aug. (Weis and Pottle, *Extremes*, p. 137).   7. *Ante* To Margaret Boswell, 22 July 1777.

8. SJ left Oxford as planned on 5 Aug., spent the night in Birmingham, and arrived in Lichfield on Wednesday the 6th (*Life* III.492).

fetches me to Ashbourne, and there I am likely enough to stay till you bid me come back to London.[9] I am, Madam, your most humble servant,

SAM. JOHNSON

9. SJ stayed in Ashbourne from 30 Aug. to *c.* 21 Oct.

James Boswell

MONDAY 4 AUGUST 1777

PRINTED SOURCE: JB's *Life*, 1791, II.127–28.

Dear Sir,   Oxford, Aug. 4, 1777

Do not disturb yourself about our interviews; I hope we shall have many; nor think it any thing hard or unusual, that your design of meeting me is interrupted.[1] We have both endured greater evils, and have greater evils to expect.

Mrs. Boswell's illness makes a more serious distress.[2] Does the blood rise from her lungs or from her stomach? From little vessels broken in the stomach there is no danger. Blood from the lungs is, I believe, always frothy, as mixed with wind. Your physicians know very well what is to be done. The loss of such a lady would, indeed, be very afflictive, and I hope she is in no danger. Take care to keep her mind as easy as is possible.

I have left Langton in London. He has been down with the militia,[3] and is again quiet at home, talking to his little people, as, I suppose, you do sometimes. Make my compliments to Miss Veronica. The rest are too young for ceremony.

I cannot but hope that you have taken your country-house at a very seasonable time, and that it may conduce to restore, or establish Mrs. Boswell's health, as well as provide room and

1. *Ante* To Hester Thrale, 4 Aug. 1777 and n. 5.

2. In his letter of 28 July, JB told SJ that Margaret Boswell "had been affected with complaints which threatened a consumption" (*Life* III.130). On 24 July she had begun to spit blood—an early sign of the tuberculosis that eventually killed her.   3. *Ante* To JB, 28 June 1777, n. 19.

47

exercise for the young ones.[4] That you and your lady may both be happy, and long enjoy your happiness, is the sincere and earnest wish of, dear Sir, Your most, etc.

SAM. JOHNSON

4. *Ante* To JB, 28 June 1777, n. 13.

Hester Thrale

THURSDAY 7 AUGUST 1777

MS: Hyde Collection.

ADDRESS: To Henry Thrale, Esq., in Southwark.

POSTMARKS: LITCHFIELD, 9 AV, FREE.

Dear Madam: Lichfield, Aug. 7, 1777

On Tuesday I left Oxford, and came to Birmingham. Mr. Hector is well, Mrs. Careless was not at home; Yesterday I came hither. Mrs. Porter is well. Mrs. Aston, to whom[1] I walked before I sat down, is very ill; but better. Whether she will recover I know not. If she dies I have a great loss.[2] Mr. Green is well, and Mrs. Adey, more I have not yet seen. At Birmingham I heard of the death of an old friend,[3] and at Lichfield of the death of another.[4] Anni praedantur euntes.[5] One was a little older, the other a little younger than myself.

But amidst these privations, the present must still be thought on, we must act as if we were to live. My Barber a man not unintelligent speaks magnificently of the Harvest,[6] and

1. MS: "whom" altered from "whose"

2. Though Elizabeth Aston had been "struck with a palsy" (*Post* To JB, 1 Sept. 1777), she lived until 1785.

3. Elizabeth Roebuck (1715–77), the daughter of Hannah Cambden, who kept the Castle Inn during SJ's stay in Birmingham, 1732–34 (*Life* III.492; *Johns. Glean.* v.268–69, XI.403).

4. *Ante* To Edmund Hector, 3 Nov. 1767, n. 3; *Life* III.492.

5. *singula de nobis anni praedantur euntes*: "the years, as they pass, plunder us of all joys" (Horace, *Epistles* II.ii.55, trans. H. R. Fairclough, Loeb ed.).

6. *Ante* To Hester Thrale, 4 Aug. 1777 and n. 4.

Frank whom I ordered to make his observations, noted fields[7] of very fine show as we passed along.

Lucy thinks nothing of my prologue for Kelly, and says she has always disowned it.[8] I have not let her know my transactions with Dr. Dod.[9] She says, she takes Miss's Correspondence very kindly. I am, Madam, your most humble servant,

SAM. JOHNSON

7. MS: "f" superimposed upon "th"
8. *Ante* To Hester Thrale, 2 June 1777 and n. 6.
9. *Ante* To John Taylor, 19 May 1777, n. 3.

Hester Thrale

SATURDAY 9 AUGUST 1777

MS: Birthplace Museum, Lichfield.

Dear Madam: Lichfield, August 9, 1777

No great matter has happened since I wrote, but this place grows more and more barren of entertainment. Two whom I hoped to have seen are dead.[1] I think that I am much more unwieldy and inert than when I was here last; my Nights are very tedious. But a light heart etc.

Lucy says "When I read Dod's Sermon to the prisoners I said, Dr. Johnson could not make a better."[2]

One of Lucy's Maids is dreadfully tormented by the taenia or long worm. She has taken many medicines without effect, and it is much wished that she could have the Knightsbridge powder.[3] I will pay for it, if You, dear Madam, will be so kind as to procure it, and send it with directions. Can it be franked?[4] If it cannot, the best way will be to unite it with

1. SJ refers to Catherine Turton and Harry Jackson (*Post* To Hester Thrale, 13 Aug. 1777). 2. *Ante* To Edmund Allen, 17 June 1777, n. 1.

3. A London apothecary, Mr. Evans of Knightsbridge, had devised for the treatment of worms a medicine that consisted of James's Fever Powders "with some Cinnabar added partly by the way of disguising, and partly by the way of altering them for the better" (*Thraliana* I.29).

4. Members of Parliament were not allowed to frank packages that exceeded two ounces in weight.

something of greater bulk. I have promised Lucy to give her Cook's last Voyage, for she loves prints;[5] but the last Voyage cannot be well understood without some knowledge of the former. If you will lend us Hawkesworth's Books, they shall be carefully returned.[6] If you will do this for us, the powders may be easily put up with the Books.

Please to make my compliments to Master, and to Queeney. I am, Madam, your most humble servant,

SAM. JOHNSON

5. Capt. James Cook's *Voyage towards the South Pole* (1777), a lavishly illustrated pair of quartos, describes his expedition of 1772–75.

6. Volumes 2 and 3 of John Hawkesworth's *Account of the Voyages undertaken . . . in the Southern Hemisphere* (3 vols., 1773) describe Cook's first Pacific voyage, 1768–71.

Hester Thrale

WEDNESDAY 13 AUGUST 1777

MS: Roger W. Barrett.

Dear Madam: Lichfield, Aug. 13, 1777

Such tattle as filled your last sweet Letter prevents one great inconvenience of absence, that of returning home a stranger and an enquirer. The variations of life consist of little things. Important innovations are soon heard, and easily understood. Men that meet to talk of Physicks or Metaphysicks, or law or history may be immediately acquainted. We look at each other in silence only for want of petty talk upon slight occurrences. Continue therefore to write all that you would say.

⟨*one word*⟩'s ⟨History⟩[1] I think, is in the Library in one volume in large octavo. It never was printed but once. You have Lord Westcote[2] and every body when I am away, and You go to Mr. Cator's,[3] and You are so happy.—

1. MS: two words del. and erased
2. *Ante* To Hester Thrale, 8 July 1771, n. 3.
3. In her letter of 2 Aug. Hester Thrale had told SJ, "We have dined at Cator's;

Miss Turton, and Harry Jackson are dead. Mrs. Aston is, I am afraid, in great danger.[4] Mr. Green, Mr. Garrick, and Mr. Newton[5] are all well. I have been very faint and breathless since I came hither, but fancy myself better this day. I hope Master's Walk will be finished when I come back and I shall perambulate it very often.

There seems to be in this country scarcely any fruit, there never indeed was much, but great things have been said of the harvest, and the only fear is of the weather. It rains here almost every day.

I dined yesterday with the corporation, and talked against a workhouse which they have in *contemplation*—there's the word now.[6] I do not know that they minded me, for they said nothing to me.[7]

I have had so little inclination to motion that I have always gone the shortest way to Stowhill, and hardly any where else, so that I can tell you nothing new of Green's Museum.[8] But I design to visit him, and all friends.

I hope for a letter to morrow, for you must not forget that I am, Madam, Your most humble servant,

SAM. JOHNSON

Why cannot Queeney write?

---

his house is splendid and his Countenance gay" (MS: Rylands Library). Cator lived at Beckenham Place in Kent, a short distance from Streatham Park (Hyde, 1977, p. 183).

4. *Ante* To Hester Thrale, 7 Aug. 1777, n. 2.

5. Andrew Newton (*c.* 1729–1806), a Lichfield wine merchant who had entertained SJ and the Thrales on their trip to Wales in 1774 (*Life* v.428; *Reades*, p. 200).

6. *contemplation*: "meditation; studious thought on any subject; continued attention" (SJ's *Dictionary*).

7. By 1781 a workhouse had been constructed on Sandford Street, in St. Mary's parish (John Snape, "A Plan of the City and Close of Lichfield," 1781). By 1819 there was also a workhouse in St. Chad's parish (*A Short Account . . . of Lichfield*, 1819, p. 101).

8. *Ante* To Lucy Porter, 12 July 1768, n. 2. SJ and the Thrales had visited Greene's collection of curiosities in 1774 (*Life* v.428).

Hester Thrale

MS: Hyde Collection.

Dear Madam: Lichfield, Aug. 23, 1777

At Lichfield?[1] yes, but not well. I have been trying a great ex-
periment with ipecacuanha which Akensyde had inclined me
to consider as a remedy for all constrictions of the breast.[2]
Lawrence indeed told me that he did not credit him, and no
credit can I find him to deserve. One night I thought my self
the better for it, but there is no certainty. On Wednesday
night I took ten grains, the night was restless. On thursday
morning I took ten grains the night again was restless. On friday night I took twenty grains, which Akensyde mentions as
the utmost that on these occasions he has *ventured* to give. The
night was perhaps rather worse. I shall therefore take truce
with ipecacuanha. Tell me, if you can what I shall do next.

Mr. Thrale's heart may be at rest. It is not fine Mrs. Anne
that has been caught by the taenia,[3] but Mrs. Anne tumbled
downstairs last night, and bruised her face. Both Maid and
Mistress are very grateful to You for the kindness with which
you procured the powders, and directed their use. They have
not yet been tried. It has been washing week, and I suppose
every body shrinks a little from such rough remedies, of which
at last the success is doubtful. However it will, I think, be tried
in all its formalities.

My Master may plant and dig till his pond is an ocean, if he
can find water, and his parterre adorn.[4] I hear no doubts of a
most abundant harvest, and it is said that the produce of Barley is particularly great. We are not far from the great year of

1. MS: comma preceding question mark
2. *Ante* To Hester Thrale, 15 Jan. 1777, n. 2. In an article in the *Medical Transactions*, Mark Akenside (1721–70), physician and poet, recommended ipecacoanha
in cases of spasmodic asthma (1768, 1.93).
3. *Ante* To Hester Thrale, 9 Aug. 1777.
4. As part of his extensive improvements to the grounds at Streatham Park,
Henry Thrale had dredged a small lake west of the house (Clifford, 1952, p. 165).

a hundred Thousand barrels,[5] which if three shillings be gained upon each[6] barrel, will bring us fifteen thousand pounds a year. ⟨Calvert⟩ never pretended to more than thirty pounds a day which is not eleven thousand a year. But suppose we should get but two shillings a barrel, that is, ten thousand a year. I hope we still have the advantage. Would you for the other thousand have my Master such a man as ⟨Calvert⟩?[7]

I showed dear Queeny's letter to Mrs. Aston and Mrs. Porter, they both took her remembrance of them very kindly.

It was well done by Mr. Brooke to send for you. His house is one of my favourite places. His Water is very commodious, and the whole place has the true old appearance of a little country town. I hope Miss goes, for she takes notice.[8]

The Races are next week.[9] People seem to be weary of them, for many go out of town, I suppose, to escape the cost of entertaining company. Dr. Taylor will probably come, and probably take me away;[10] and I shall leave Mistress Aston.

5. "Production leapt from the 32,000 barrel level at which Henry Thrale had found it in 1758 to 75,000 in 1776 and to 87,000 in 1778 under his great drive to gain the personal leadership of the London trade" (Peter Mathias, *The Brewing Industry in England 1700–1830*, 1959, p. 266).

6. MS: "each each"

7. H. L. Piozzi, who heavily deleted the name of this rival brewer, identified him as Samuel Whitbread (1720–1796) in her annotated copy of *Letters* (1788) (Trinity College, Cambridge). However, "Whitbread" is too long for the available space, and under the second deletion it is possible to read "Cal⟨vert⟩." Felix Calvert (1734–1802), of Calvert's Hour-Glass Brewhouse, was second only to Whitbread in terms of numbers of barrels brewed per annum. Hester Thrale described her husband's chief competitors as "Men whose Acquaintance he was ashamed of, and whose Persons he shrunk from if he met 'em in a Publick Place" (Hyde, 1977, p. 206).

8. In 1768 SJ and the Thrales had stayed with Francis Brooke (b. 1696), an attorney who lived in Town Malling, Kent. Brooke, a friend of Henry Thrale's father, was godfather to Susanna Arabella. The Thrales, accompanied by Queeney, visited Brooke again during the third week of August. In her letter to SJ of 28 Aug., Queeney mentions a cascade and several ponds (MS: Rylands Library). Hester Thrale speaks of "square canals" (Piozzi, *Letters* I.377).

9. Races were held annually on Whittington Heath, approximately two miles outside of Lichfield (*A Short Account . . . of Lichfield*, 1819, p. 102). *Post* To Hester Thrale, 27 Aug. 1777.

10. *Post* To Hester Thrale, 27 Aug. 1777.

Do not you lose nor let Master lose the kindness that you have for me. Nobody will ever love you both better, than, Dear Madam, your most obedient servant,

SAM. JOHNSON

Joseph Nollekens
WEDNESDAY 27 AUGUST 1777

MS: Hyde Collection.
ADDRESS: To Mr. Nollikens in Mortimer Street, Oxford Road, London.
POSTMARKS: LITCHFIELD, 29 AV.

Sir: [Lichfield]

I have at last sent you what remains, to put to poor dear Goldsmiths monument, and hope to see it erected at the abbey.[1]

You promised me a cast of the head.[2] If it could be sent to Lichfield directed to Mrs. Lucy Porter before I leave the country I should be glad, though the matter is not of such Consequence, as that you should incommode yourself about it.

I hope Mrs. Nollikens and our Friends in Italy[3] are all well, and that we shall all have some time or other a joyful meeting. I am, Sir, your most humble servant,

SAM. JOHNSON

Natus Hibernia, Forneiae Lonfordiensis, in loco
cui nomen Pallas, Nov. XXIX, MDCCXXXI,
Eblanae literis institutus,
Obiit Londini, Apr. IV. MDCCLXXIV.[4]

1. *Ante* To Joseph Nollekens, 24 Dec. 1776, n. 2.
2. Early that year Nollekens had completed a portrait bust of SJ, which was intended for the Royal Academy exhibition in April. A cast was sent to Lucy Porter, who did not admire it (H. W. Liebert, "Johnson's Head," privately printed for The Johnsonians, 1960; *Post* To Lucy Porter, 19 Feb. 1778).
3. *Ante* To Hester Thrale, 14 May 1776, n. 9.
4. For the text of the epitaph as it appears on Goldsmith's monument in Westminster Abbey, see *Life* III.83.

Hester Thrale

MS: British Library (Charnwood Collection).
ADDRESS: To Henry Thrale, Esq., in Southwark.
POSTMARKS: LITCHFIELD, 29 AV, FREE.

Dear Madam: Lichfield, Aug. 27, 1777

Our Correspondence is not so vigorous as it used to be; but now you know the people at Lichfield, it is vain to describe them,[1] and as no revolutions have happened, there is nothing to be said about them. We have a new Dean whose name is Proby,[2] he has the manners of a Gentleman, and some spirit of discipline which brings the cathedral into better method. He has a Lady that talks about Mrs. Montague and Mrs. Carter.[3]

On next Saturday I go to Ashbourne, and thither must my Letters be sent, if you are pleased ever to write to me.

When I came hither, I could hardly walk, but I have got better breath, and more agility. I intend to perambulate Master's dominions every day at least once. But I have miserable, distresful, tedious nights. Do you think they will mend at Brighthelmston?[4]

When I come to Ashbourne I will send my dear Queeney an account how I find things, for I hope she takes an interest in Dr. Taylor's prosperity.

This is race week, but Mrs. Aston, Mrs. Porter, and myself have no part in the course, or at the ball. We all sit at home and perhaps pretend to wonder that others go, though I can-

1. The Thrales visited Lichfield with SJ during their trip to Wales in 1774 (*Life* v.428–29).

2. The Rev. Baptist Proby (1727–1807), D.D., Dean of Lichfield Cathedral (1777–1807) (*GM* 1807, p. 183).

3. Mary Proby, daughter of the Rev. John Russell (d. 1791), Prebend of Peterborough and Lincoln (*Alum. Cant.* II.v.205; *GM* 1807, p. 183).

4. The Thrales left for Brighton on 30 Sept. SJ joined them there on 14 Nov., but stayed for only three days (*Post* To Hester Thrale, 10 Nov. 1777 and n. 2; Clifford, 1952, p. 156).

not charge any of us with much of that folly. Mrs. Gastrel who wraps her head in a towel, is very angry at the present mode of dress and feathers.

But amidst all these little things there is one great thing. The Harvest is abundant, and the weather a la merveille. No season ever was finer. Barley, Malt, Beer, and Money. There is the series of Ideas. The deep Logicians call it a sorites.[5] I hope my Master will no[6] longer endure the reproach of not keeping me a Horse.

The Puppies played us a vile trick when they tore my letter, but I hope my loss will be repaired to morrow. You are in the way of business and intelligence, and have something to write. I am here in unactive obscurity, and have little other pleasure, than to perceive that the poor languishing Lady is glad to see me.[7] I hope, dearest Lady, you will be glad to see me too, and that it will be long before disease lays hold upon You. I am, Dear Madam, Your most humble servant, SAM. JOHNSON

5. *sorites*: "a series of propositions, in which the predicate of each is the subject of the next, the conclusion being formed of the first subject and the last predicate" (*OED*).   6. MS: "no" repeated as catchword
7. *Ante* To Hester Thrale, 7 Aug. 1777 and n. 2.

James Boswell
SATURDAY 30 AUGUST 1777

PRINTED SOURCE: JB's *Life*, 1791, II.128.

Dear Sir,   August 30, 1777

I am this day come to Ashbourne, and have only to tell you, that Dr. Taylor says you shall be welcome to him, and you know how welcome you will be to me. Make haste to let me know when you may be expected.[1]

Make my compliments to Mrs. Boswell, and tell her, I hope we shall be at variance no more. I am, dear Sir, Your most humble servant,
                                                            SAM. JOHNSON
1. *Ante* To JB, 28 June 1777, n. 17.

James Boswell

PRINTED SOURCE: JB's *Life*, 1791, II.128–29.

Dear Sir,   Ashbourne, Sept. 1, 1777

On Saturday I wrote a very short letter, immediately upon my arrival hither, to shew you that I am not less desirous of the interview than yourself.[1] Life admits not of delays; when pleasure can be had it is fit to catch it: Every hour takes away part of the things that please us, and perhaps part of our disposition to be pleased. When I came to Lichfield, I found my old friend Harry Jackson dead. It was a loss, and a loss not to be repaired, as he was one of the companions of my childhood. I hope we may long continue to gain friends, but the friends which merit or usefulness can procure us, are not able to supply the place of old acquaintance, with whom the days of youth may be retraced, and those images revived which gave the earliest delight. If you and I live to be much older, we shall take great delight in talking over the Hebridean Journey.

In the mean time it may not be amiss to contrive some other little adventure, but what it can be I know not; leave it, as Sidney says,

"To virtue, fortune, wine, and woman's breast;"[2]

for I believe Mrs. Boswell must have some part in the consultation.

One thing you will like. The Doctor, so far as I can judge, is likely to leave us enough to ourselves. He was out to-day before I came down, and, I fancy, will stay out till dinner. I have

---

1. *Ante* To JB, 30 Aug. 1777.

2. "By an odd mistake, in the first three editions we find a reading in this line, to which Dr. Johnson would by no means have subscribed, *wine* having been substituted for *time*. That errour probably was a mistake in the transcript of Johnson's original letter" (Edmond Malone's note, *Life* III.131). SJ quotes the concluding line from a sonnet in Sidney's *Old Arcadia*: "This done, thou hast no more, but leave the rest / To vertue, fortune, time and woman's brest" (*The Poems of Sir Philip Sidney*, ed. W. A. Ringler, 1962, p. 98).

brought the papers about poor Dodd, to show you, but you will soon have dispatched them.[3]

Before I came away I sent poor Mrs. Williams into the country, very ill of a pituitous defluxion,[4] which wastes her gradually away, and which her physician declares himself unable to stop. I supplied her as far as could be desired, with all conveniencies to make her excursion and abode pleasant and useful, but I am afraid she can only linger a short time in a morbid state of weakness and pain.

The Thrales, little and great, are all well, and purpose to go to Brighthelmston at Michaelmas. They will invite me to go with them, and perhaps I may go, but I hardly think I shall like to stay the whole time;[5] but of futurity we know but little.

Mrs. Porter is well; but Mrs. Aston, one of the ladies at Stowhill, has been struck with a palsy, from which she is not likely ever to recover. How soon may such a stroke fall upon us!

Write to me, and let us know when we may expect you. I am, dear Sir, Your most humble servant,

SAM. JOHNSON

3. *Ante* To JB, 22 July 1777, n. 4.

4. *pituitous*: "consisting of phlegm"; *defluxion*: "the flow of humours downwards" (SJ's *Dictionary*). 5. *Ante* To Hester Thrale, 27 Aug. 1777, n. 4.

Hester Maria Thrale

THURSDAY 4 SEPTEMBER 1777

MS: The Earl of Shelburne.

ADDRESS: To Miss Thrale.

Dear Miss: Ashbourne, Sept. 4, 1777

And so between You and your Mamma, the postman has brought me no letter. Such usage—but this it is to be away. However I will shift a little longer as I can.

Dr. Taylor has put a very elegant iron palisade before his house; he has emptied his pool of the mud, and laid it upon the ground behind it. He thinks he has now six feet of water.

I see but few deer, and hardly any fowls. The Doctor has[1] transferred his attention to other things, and is become one of the sons of Harmony. To his Harpsichord he has added a very magnificent organ, a very fine hautbois, and if I count right, three fiddles. I hear that he makes the organist teach him to play, and hope to see You and him at the same instrument, like Miss Burney[2] and Master Wesley.[3]

The walk in the garden is covered with new gravel which will be continued to the waterfal, which now roars tolerably well.

The Cattle prosper pretty well, a Cow has just been sold to Mr. Chapplin a great breeder in Lincolnshire for one hundred and twenty pounds,[4] and for the other Cow one hundred and thirty have been refused. The young Bull is said to be bigger than his Sire. The horses are all well, but some of the cows are diseased, one in the udder, and one in the foot.

The Doctor thinks he shall get his Lawsuit against Mrs. Rudd.[5]

Tell Mamma that I hear every where of full crops though we have at present in Derbyshire bad weather, and that I reckon[6] on us to grow next year so rich, that what is now iron shall then be silver.

Mr. Langley and his Lady are well, but the Doctor and they are no friends.[7] I know not whether I ever told that my Cousin[8] Mr. Flint's wife is dead.[9]

1. MS: "his"

2. Esther Burney (1749–1832), Charles Burney's eldest daughter and a noted harpsichordist (Roger Lonsdale, *Dr. Charles Burney*, 1965, p. 54).

3. SJ could be referring either to Charles Wesley the younger (1757–1834) or to his brother Samuel (1766–1837), both musical prodigies and talented harpsichordists.

4. Charles Chaplin (1730–95), of Tathwell, Lincolnshire (*GM* 1795, p. 257). Twenty-eight letters from Chaplin to Sir Joseph Banks confirm his interest in raising sheep and cattle (MSS: Beinecke Library). *Post* To Hester Thrale, 22 Oct. 1777.   5. *Ante* To John Taylor, 13 Apr. 1776.

6. MS: "reckon" superimposed upon undeciphered erasure

7. *Ante* To John Taylor, 31 Aug. 1772, n. 2.

8. MS: "Cousin" altered from "Cousins"

9. Mary Dunn Collier (1733–76), wife of John Taylor's clerk, Thomas Flint

Neither at Lichfield nor Ashbourne is there any fruit and I am afraid you have not much upon all your Walls.

I hear no good of poor Mrs. Williams. Mrs. Porter is better than she uses to be. Mrs. Aston does not mend.[10]

I cannot boast of mending myself, nor much expect that Brighthelmston will mend me, yet I hope to pass a little time with you there.[11] I am, Dearest Miss, Your most humble servant,

SAM. JOHNSON

(1724–87) (*Life* v.581–82). It has still not been indisputably established that she was related to SJ (*Johns. Glean.* IX.40, 75).

  10. *Ante* To Elizabeth Aston, 15 Mar. 1777.

  11. *Ante* To Hester Thrale, 27 Aug. 1777, n. 4.

Hester Thrale

SATURDAY 6 SEPTEMBER 1777

MS: Hyde Collection.

Dearest Lady: [Lichfield] Sept. 6, 1777

It is true that I have loitered, and what is worse, loitered with very little[1] pleasure. The time has run away, as most time runs, without account, without use, and without memorial. But to say this of a few weeks, though not pleasing, might be born, but what ought[2] to be the regret of him who in a few days will have so nearly the same to say of sixty eight years. But complaint is vain.

If you have nothing to say from the neighborhood of the metropolis, what can occur to me in little cities, and petty towns. In places which we have both seen, and of which no description is wanted. I have left part of the company with which you dined here, to come and write this letter.[3] In which

  1. MS: initial "l" superimposed upon "p"

  2. MS: "must" del. before "ought"

  3. During their visit to Ashbourne in 1774, SJ and the Thrales dined with Richard Dyott of Lichfield, his wife Catherine, and their four daughters (*Ante* To

I have nothing to tell, but that my nights are very tedious. I cannot persuade myself to forbear trying something.

As you have now little to do, I suppose you are pretty diligent at the Thraliana, and a very [curious]4 collection posterity will find it.5 Do not remit the practice of writing down occurrences as they arise of whatever kind, and be very punctual in annexing the dates. Chronology you know is the eye of history;6 and every Man's life is of importance to himself. Do not omit painful casualties or unpleasing passages, they make the variegation of existence; and there are many transactions of which I will not promise with Æneas, et hæc olim meminisse juvabit.7 Yet that remembrance which is not pleasant may be useful. There is however an intemperate attention to slight circumstances which is to be avoided, lest a great part of life be spent in writing the history of the rest.8 Every day perhaps has something to be noted, but in a settled and uniform course, few days can have much.

Why do I write all this, which I had no thought of when I begun? The Thraliana drove it all into my head. It deserves however an hours reflection, to consider how with the9 least

---

Hester Thrale, *c.* 3 July 1775, n. 3), as well as with Philip Gell of Hopton Hall, Derbyshire (*Life* v.430–31).   4. MS: "curious" inserted by H. L. Piozzi

5. In Sept. 1776 Henry Thrale had presented his wife with six blank quarto books, each stamped in gold with the title "Thraliana." In this "Repository" she entered, following SJ's advice, "all the Observations I might make or hear; all the Verses never likely to be published, and in fine ev'ry thing which struck me at the Time" (*Thraliana* I.1; Clifford, 1952, pp. 145–47).

6. This sentiment, which had come close to attaining proverbial status, has been attributed to Isaac Vossius (W. B. Carnochan, *Gibbon's Solitude*, 1987, p. 196 n. 13). SJ may have had in mind a passage from the account of "Denys Petau, Jesuit" in John Ozell's translation (1704) of Charles Perrault's *Characters Historical and Panegyrical*. In his sequence of studies, Petau is said to have "pass'd to *History*, and at the same time to *Geography*, and to *Chronology*, which are as the two Eyes of History, and which ought never to be separated from it" (I.43).

7. *forsan et haec olim meminisse iuvabit*: "perchance even this distress it will some day be a joy to recall" (Virgil, *Aeneid* I.203, trans. H. R. Fairclough, Loeb ed.).

8. SJ had offered similar counsel to JB: "He again advised me to keep a journal fully and minutely, but not to mention such trifles as, that meat was too much or too little done, or that the weather was fair or rainy" (*Life* II.358).

9. MS: "the the"

loss of time, the loss of what we wish to retain may be prevented.

Do not neglect to write to me, for when a post comes empty, I am really disappointed.

Boswel, I believe, will meet me here.[10] I am, Dearest Lady, Your most humble Servant,
SAM. JOHNSON

10. *Ante* To JB, 28 June 1777, n. 17; 30 Aug. 1777.

Hester Thrale

MONDAY 8 SEPTEMBER 1777

MS: Hyde Collection.

Dear Madam: Ashbourne, Sept. 8, 1777

Surely the same vexatious interruption of our correspondence happens now that happened once when I was at Oxford. I write often, yet You seem not to have my Letters. I charged Frank with trusting some other hand to the postoffice, this he denies, and indeed I have answers to other letters.

I came hither on Saturday Aug. 30. The books were not then come; but I suppose according to Davies's letter, they came that evening.[1] Of the receipt of the Powders I wrote word, and told that the girl delayed a little while to take them.[2] From this place I wrote to Miss last thursday, and to You last Saturday. Nothing has been mentioned by You of which I have not taken proper notice, except that I have said nothing of Sir John Lade.[3] Many instances there are of the vanity of human solicitude, and it is not strange to find another. We were all planning out for him some mode of life, and disease was hovering over him. If he dies his Mother will lose what has en-

1. *Ante* To Hester Thrale, 9 Aug. 1777 and nn. 5, 6. Presumably Thomas Davies the bookseller had arranged for the shipping of the volumes to Lichfield.

2. *Ante* To Hester Thrale, 9 Aug. 1777 and n. 3.

3. Sir John Lade (1759–1838), second Bt., of Warbleton, Sussex, the nephew of Henry Thrale. Sir John was ill with consumption (Hyde, 1977, p. 178).

gaged her care, and incited her Vanity. The Son and the estate go away together. But Life occupies us all too much to leave us room for any care of others beyond what duty enjoyns; and no day enjoins sorrow or anxiety that is at once troublesome and useless. I would readily help the poor Lady, but, if I cannot do her good by assisting her I shall not disturb myself by lamenting her. Yet I suppose, his death will be as hard a blow as is commonly felt.[4] Let me know, if you hear, how he goes on.[5] I go on but uneasily.

I am in hopes of seeing Mr. Boswel, and then he may perhaps tell me something to write, for this is but a barren place. Not a mouse stirring.[6] I am, Madam, your most humble servant,

SAM. JOHNSON

4. MS: "suf" del. before "felt"

5. Within two weeks, Sir John's condition had improved markedly (Hester Thrale to SJ, 20 Sept. 1777, MS: Rylands Library; *Post* To Hester Thrale, 29 Oct. 1777).   6. *Hamlet* I.i.10.

James Boswell
THURSDAY 11 SEPTEMBER 1777

PRINTED SOURCE: JB's *Life*, 1791, II.131–32.

Dear Sir,   Ashbourne, Sept. 11, 1777

I write to be left at Carlisle, as you direct me, but you cannot have it. Your letter, dated Sept. 6, was not at this place till this day, Thursday, Sept 11;[1] and I hope you will be here before this is at Carlisle.[2] However, what you have not going, you may have returning; and as I believe I shall not love you less after our interview, it will then be as true as it is now, that I set a very high value upon your friendship, and count your kindness as one of the chief felicities of my life. Do not fancy that

1. In JB's journal this letter is recorded under 5 Sept. It does not appear in the *Life*.

2. "It so happened. The letter was forwarded to my house at Edinburgh" (JB's note).

an intermission of writing is a decay of kindness. No man is always in a disposition to write; nor has any man at all times something to say.[3]

That distrust which intrudes so often on your mind is a mode of melancholy, which, if it be the business of a wise man to be happy, it is foolish to indulge; and if it be a duty to preserve our faculties entire for their proper use, it is criminal. Suspicion is very often an useless pain. From that, and all other pains, I wish you free and safe; for I am, dear Sir, Most affectionately yours,

SAM. JOHNSON

3. Cf. *Ante* To JB, 8 Dec. 1763.

Elizabeth Aston

SATURDAY 13 SEPTEMBER 1777

MS: Pembroke College, Oxford.
ADDRESS: To Mrs. Aston at Stowhill, Lichfield.
POSTMARK: ASHBORNE.

Dear Madam: Ashbourne, Sept. 13, 1777

As I left you so much disordered, a fortnight is a long time to be without any account of your health.[1] I am willing to flatter myself that You are better, though you gave me no reason to believe that you intended to use any means for your recovery. Nature often performs wonders, and will, I hope, do for You more than You seem inclined to do for Yourself.[2]

In this[3] weakness of body with which it has pleased God to visit you, he has given you great cause of thankfulness, by the total exemption of your Mind from all effects of your disorder. Your Memory is not less comprehensive or distinct, nor your reason less vigorous and acute, nor your imagination less active and spritely than in any former time of your life. This is a

1. SJ left Lichfield for Ashbourne on 30 Aug. (*Ante* To JB, 30 Aug. 1777).
2. *Ante* To Hester Thrale, 7 Aug. 1777 and n. 1.
3. MS: "I" del. before "this"

great Blessing as it respects enjoyment of the present, and a Blessing yet far greater as it bestows power and opportunity to prepare for the future.

All sickness is a summons. But as You do not want exhortation, I will send you only my good wishes, and intreat you to believe the good wishes very sincere, of, Dear Madam, Your most humble servant,

SAM. JOHNSON

Hester Thrale

SATURDAY 13 SEPTEMBER 1777

PRINTED SOURCE: Piozzi, *Letters* 1.366–67.

Dear Madam,   Ashbourne, Sept. 13, 1777

Now I write again, having just received your letter dated the 10th.

You must not let foolish fancies take hold on your imagination. If Queeney grows tall, she is sufficiently bulky, and as much out of danger of a consumption as nature allows a young maiden to be. Of real evils the number is great, of possible evils there is no end. * * * * *[1] is really to be pitied. Her son in danger; the estate likely to pass not only from her, but to those on whom, I suppose, she would least wish it bestowed, and her system of life broken, are very heavy blows. But she will at last be rich, and will have much gratification in her power, both rational and sensual.

Boswell, I believe, is coming. He talks of being here today.[2] I shall be glad to see him. But he shrinks from the Baltick expedition, which I think is the best scheme in our power.[3]

1. "Lady Lade" (Piozzi 1.366). H. L. Piozzi makes the same identification in her own set of *Letters* (1788) (Trinity College, Cambridge).

2. JB arrived in Ashbourne "about eight o'clock" in the evening of 14 Sept. (*Boswell in Extremes*, ed. C. M. Weis and F. A. Pottle, 1970, p. 149).

3. In his letter of 9 Sept., JB had told SJ: "Let us, by all means, have another expedition. I shrink a little from our scheme of going up the Baltick" (*Life* III.134). This plan originated in a conversation during their Hebridean tour, 16 Sept. 1773: "Mr. Johnson said he would go to Sweden with me" (*Hebrides*, p. 175).

What we shall substitute, I know not. He wants to see Wales, but except the woods of Bachycraigh what is there in Wales? [4] What that can fill the hunger of ignorance, or quench the thirst of curiosity? We may perhaps form some scheme or other, but, in the phrase of Hockley in the Hole,[5] it is pity he has not a better bottom.[6]

Tell my young mistress that this day's letter is too short, and it brings me no news either foreign or domestick.

I am going to dine with Mr. Dyot, and Frank tells sternly, that it is past two o'clock. I am, dearest Madam, Your, etc.

4. Bach-y-Graig, Flintshire, the ancestral home of Hester Thrale's family, the Salusburys. Since Sept. 1775, SJ had been one of the trustees of the estate (Clifford, 1952, p. 129). According to H. L. Piozzi, the house was "bosom'd in Wood. Mr. Thrale cut 4000£ down—when he did *not* want it" (Piozzi 1.367).

5. Hockley in the Hole, Clerkenwell, London, "a place of public diversion—a kind of Bear Garden, celebrated for its bear and bull-baitings, trials of skill, and its breed of bull-dogs" (Wheatley and Cunningham 11.216).

6. *bottom*: "physical resources, 'staying power', power of endurance; said esp. of pugilists, wrestlers, race-horses, etc." (*OED*).

Hester Thrale

MONDAY 15 SEPTEMBER 1777

PRINTED SOURCE: Piozzi, *Letters* 1.368–69.

Dear Madam,   [Ashbourne] Sept. 15, 1777

Do you call this punctual correspondence? There was poor I writing, and writing, and writing, on the 8th, on the 11th, on the 13th; and on the 15th I looked for a letter, but I may look and look. Instead of writing to me you are writing the Thraliana.[1] But—he *must be humble who would please.*[2]

Last night came Boswell.[3] I am glad that he is come. He

1. *Ante* To Hester Thrale, 6 Sept. 1777 and n. 5.
2. *Ante* To Hester Thrale, 17 July 1775, n. 1.
3. *Ante* To Hester Thrale, 13 Sept. 1777, n. 2.

seems to be very brisk and lively, and laughs a little at
* * * * *.[4] I told him something of the scene at Richmond.[5]
You find, now you have seen the *progenies Langtoniana*, that I
did not praise them without reason; yet the second girl is my
favourite.[6]

You talk of pine-apples and venison.[7] Pine-apples it is sure
we have none; but venison, no forester that lived under the
green-wood-tree ever had more frequently upon his table. We
fry, and roast, and bake, and devour in every form.

We have at last fair weather in Derbyshire, and every where
the crops are spoken of as uncommonly exuberant. Let us now
get money and save it. All that is paid is saved, and all that is
laid out in land or malt. But I long to see twenty thousand
pounds in the bank,[8] and to see my master visiting this estate
and that, as purchases are advertised.[9] But perhaps all this
may be when Colin's forgotten and gone.[10] Do not let me be

4. In her own set of *Letters* (1788) and that presented to Sir James Fellowes,
H. L. Piozzi supplies "Langton." Hill, however, believes the correct reading to be
"Taylor" (Hill II.32 n. 6).

5. In her letter of 13 Aug., Hester Thrale had described to SJ a dinner at Sir
Joshua Reynolds's house on Richmond Hill. Bennet Langton, his wife, and their
"two pretty Babies" were present, and the Langton children proved "very troublesome" (MS: Rylands Library).

6. By Sept. 1777 the Langtons had four children, a boy and three girls. The
"second girl" was Diana (b. 1774) (Fifer, p. lviii).

7. In her letter of 6 Sept., Hester Thrale had told SJ, "We have Venison and
Pine Apple and not a Creature in London to come and eat them" (MS: Rylands
Library).

8. The profits from the brewery the previous year came to £14,000 (Clifford,
1952, p. 165).

9. On 20 Sept. Hester Thrale recorded in her *Family Book*: "Mr. Thrale's Affairs are now so very prosperous, that he thinks of nothing but to plan future
Expences: and rejects Counsel as Insult, and Restraint as Injury" (Hyde, 1977, p.
190). Her forebodings were justified: by the spring of 1778 Thrale had over-
brewed, speculated unwisely, and spent excessively on improvements at Streatham. The consequence was that his wife, although eight months pregnant, had to
travel to Brighton to beg a loan from Charles Scrase (Clifford, 1952, p. 166; Hyde,
1977, pp. 201–2).

10. "Then to her new Love let her go, / And deck her in Golden Array / . . .
While Colin, forgotten and gone, / No more shall be talk'd of, or seen" (Nicholas
Rowe, "Colin's Complaint," ll. 49–50, 53–54).

forgotten before I am gone, for you will never have such another, as, Dearest dear Madam, Your most humble servant.

Hester Thrale
THURSDAY 18 SEPTEMBER 1777

MS: Hyde Collection.

Dear Madam: Ashbourne, September the 18th 1777

Here is another Birthday. They come very fast. I am now sixty eight. To lament the past is vain, what remains is to look for hope in futurity. Queeny has now passed another year, I hope every year will bring her happiness.[1]

Boswel is with us in good humour, and play[s] his part with his usual vivacity. We are to go in the Doctors vehicle and dine at Derby to morrow.[2]

Do You know any thing of Bolt court? Invite Mr. Levet to dinner and make enquiry what family he has, and how they proceed. I had a letter lately from Mrs. Williams. Dr. Lewis visits her,[3] and has added ipecacuanha to her bark.[4] But I do not hear much of her amendment. Age is a very stuborn Disease. Yet Levet sleeps sound every Night. I am sorry for poor Sewards pain, but he[5] may live to be better.[6]

Mr. Myddelton's erection of an urn looks like an intention to bury me alive.[7] I would as willingly see my Friend, however

1. Queeney Thrale turned thirteen on 17 Sept.

2. *Post* To Hester Thrale, 20 Sept. 1777 and n. 4.

3. Possibly William Lewis (1714–81), M.D., author of *The New Dispensatory* (1753) (*Lit. Anec.* IX.764).   4. *Ante* To Hester Thrale, 15 Jan. 1777, n. 2.

5. MS: "he" altered from "the"

6. William Seward was suffering from severe pain in his teeth and face (Hester Thrale to SJ, 16 Sept. 1777, MS: Rylands Library). Cf. *Ante* To Hester Thrale, 11 July 1775.

7. John Myddelton (1724–92), of Gwaynynog, Denbighshire, was "erecting an Urn I think to your Memory" (Hester Thrale to SJ, 16 Sept. 1777, MS: Rylands Library). Myddelton had entertained SJ and the Thrales during their Welsh tour of 1774 (*Life* V.443, 587–88).

benevolent and hospitable quietly inurned. Let him think for the present of some more acceptable memorial.

Does nobody tell Lady Lade that a warmer climate and a clearer air is likely to help her Son, and that it may [be] convenient to run away from an English Winter, before he becomes too weak for travel.[8] It appears to me not improbable that change of air and the amusement and exercise of easy journeys might enable one so young to overcome his disease.

Dr. Taylor has another Buck. You must not talk to us of Venison.[9] Fruit indeed we have little, and that little not very good. But what there is, has been very liberally bestowed.

Mr. Langley and the Doctor still live on different sides of the Street.[10]

We have had for some time past such Harvest weather, as a Derbyshire Farmer dares scarcely hope. The Harvest has this year been every where a Month backward, but so far as I can hear, has recompensed the delay by uncommon plenty. Next Year will, I hope, complete Mr. Thrales wish of an hundred thousand barrels.[11] Ambition is then to have an end, and he must remember, that Non minor est Virtus quam quaerere, parta tueri.[12] When he has climbed so high, his[13] care must be to keep himself from falling. I am, Dear Madam, your most humble Servant,

SAM. JOHNSON

8. *Ante* To Hester Thrale, 8 Sept. 1777 and n. 3.

9. *Ante* To Hester Thrale, 15 Sept. 1777.

10. "Mr. Langley, a clergyman, the Head Master ... lives just on the opposite side of the street to Dr. Taylor's. But they are not on good terms" (*Boswell in Extremes*, ed. C. M. Weis and F. A. Pottle, 1970, p. 152). *Ante* To Hester Thrale, 12 July 1775.

11. *Ante* To Hester Thrale, 23 Aug. 1777 and n. 5; 15 Sept. 1777 and n. 9.

12. *Nec minor est virtus, quam quærere, parta tueri*: "Nor is there less prowess in guarding what is won than in seeking" (Ovid, *Ars Amatoria* II.13, trans. J. H. Mozley, Loeb ed.).

13. MS: "his" altered from "he"

Hester Thrale

MS: Hyde Collection.

Dear Madam: Ashbourne, Sept. 20, 1777

I do not remember what has happened that you write on mourning paper and use black wax.

Boswel liked Seward better as he knew him more,[1] and seems well pleased to be remembred by him and my Master.

Pretty dear Queeny I wish her many and many happy Birthdays.[2] I hope you will never lose her, though I should go to Lichfield, and though she should sit the thirteenth in many a company.[3]

You have nothing to say because you live at Streatham, and expect me to say much when I return from Lichfield and Ashbourne places to be considered as abounded in Novelty, and supplying every hour materials for history. It is as much as I can do to furnish every post with a letter, I keep nothing behind for oral communication.

I took Boswel yesterday to see Keddlestone and the Silkmils, and china work at Derby, he was pleased with all.[4] The Derby China is very pretty, but I think the gilding is all superficial,

1. JB had entertained William Seward during Seward's visit to Edinburgh in July. JB's verdict in his journal does not tally with his report to SJ: "Insipid and tiresome, *I* thought him" (*Boswell in Extremes*, ed. C. M. Weis and F. A. Pottle, 1970, p. 134).

2. *Ante* To Hester Thrale, 18 Sept. 1777 and n. 1.

3. "Something always happens when you go to Lichfield; and our sitting down thirteen to table yesterday made my fool's nerves flutter for Queeney" (Piozzi, *Letters* 1.375).

4. Traveling in John Taylor's "comfortable chaise and four," SJ and JB were driven to Derby via Kedleston Hall (1759–65), the magnificent country seat built by Lord Scarsdale and designed by Robert Adam (Weis and Pottle, *Extremes*, p. 160; Nikolaus Pevsner and Elizabeth Williamson, *Derbyshire*, 1978, pp. 255–58). In the town of Derby JB "admired the ingenuity and delicate art with which one man in particular fashioned clay into a cup, a saucer, or a teapot. . . . After dinner Mrs. Butter went with me to see the silk-mill. . . . I have no notion of mechanics. But the simplicity of this machine and its multiplied operations struck me with an agreeable surprise" (Weis and Pottle, *Extremes*, pp. 162–63). The mill was erected

and the finer pieces are so dear, that perhaps silver vessels of the same[5] capacity may be sometimes bought at the same price,[6] and I am not yet so infected with the contagion of Chinafancy, as to like any thing at that rate which can so easily be broken.

Master is very inconstant to Lady R——.[7] Did he not hold out against forty such repellents from Mrs. P——?[8] He grows nice I find let him try whether nicety will make him happy.[9]

Boswel has spent more money than he expected, and I must supply him with part of his expences home. I have not much with me, and beg Master to send me by the next post a note of ten pounds, which I will punctually return, not in opportunities of beneficence, though the noblest payment in the world, but in money or Bankpaper. Do not let him forget me.[10]

Do not suppose that I wrote this letter on purpose to borrow. *My Soul disdains it.* I did not think on it when I began to write. When I miss a post I consider myself as deviating from the true rule of action. Seeing things in this light, I consider every letter as something in the line of duty, upon this foot I make my arrangement, and under whatever circumstances of difficulty, endeavour to carry them into execution, for having in some degree pledged myself for the performance I think

---

in 1719 by Sir Thomas Lombe (1685–1739), who had acquired a patent for machines to wind, spin, and twist raw silk.

5. MS: "s" superimposed upon "c"

6. "The china was beautiful. But Dr. Johnson justly observed it was too dear; for that he could have vessels of silver of the same size as cheap as what were here made of porcelain" (Weis and Pottle, *Extremes*, p. 163).

7. H. L. Piozzi fills in the blank with "Rothes" (Piozzi 1.380). The identification is certain, given a passage in Hester Thrale's letter of 18 Sept.: "I asked Lady Rothes how She did that day. . . . Madam says She, in a pretty loud Voice, I have a *Poul*tice on now.—it has cured my Master of his Passion however" (MS: Rylands Library).

8. "Percy" (Piozzi 1.380). Thomas Percy's "Lady lived much with us at Brighthelmstone" (H. L. Piozzi to Richard Duppa, 26 Sept. 1816, MS: Hyde Collection).

9. *nicety*: "fastidious delicacy; squeamishness" (SJ's *Dictionary*).

10. *Post* To Hester Thrale, 25 Sept. 1777.

the reputation both of my head and my heart engaged, and reprobate every thought of desisting from the undertaking.[11]

Howel tells of a few words in Spanish, the true utterance of which will denominate the Speaker bueno Romanciador, the last sentence will un bueno politico.[12] He that can rattle those words well together may say all that political controversy generally produces. I am, Madam, Your most humble servant,

SAM. JOHNSON

Nay, but do enquire after Bolt court.[13]

11. SJ is parodying the stock rhetoric of contemporary politicians. See below, final paragraph and n. 12.

12. In his *Epistolae Ho-elianae* (Book II, No. 71), James Howell quotes "a Rhyme of certain hard throaty words which . . . are accounted the difficultest in all the whole *Castilian* Language; insomuch that he who is able to pronounce them is accounted *Buen Romancista*, a good speaker of *Spanish*" (*The Familiar Letters of James Howell*, ed. Joseph Jacobs, 1890, p. 498). According to SJ, "a good politician" will be able to pronounce the characteristic turns of phrase he parodies in the last sentence of the preceding paragraph.

13. *Post* To Hester Thrale, 29 Sept. 1777, n. 2.

Hester Thrale

MONDAY 22 SEPTEMBER 1777

MS: Hyde Collection.

Dear Madam: Ashbourne, Sept. 22, 1777

Now to sit down to tell me a long newspaper story about Lord Harcourt and his dog.[1]—I hoped when you had seen Levet, you would have learned something that concerned me.[2]

I hope Master has been so kind as to send me the ten

1. Hester Thrale had begun her letter of 20 Sept. with the story of the freakish accident that befell Simon Harcourt (1714–77), first Earl Harcourt, who drowned 16 Sept. while attempting to rescue his "dear little favourite dog" from a well (*Walpole's Correspondence*, Yale ed. XXVIII.327 and n. 3; *St. James's Chronicle*, 16–18 Sept. 1777, p. 4).

2. *Ante* To Hester Thrale, 18 Sept. 1777.

pounds else I shall be forced to borrow at Ashbourne or Lichfield.[3]

Boswel has been this morning with me to see Ilam Garden,[4] he talks of going away this week,[5] and I shall not think of staying here much longer though the wind whistles very prettily.[6] My Nights are still such as I do not like, but complaint will not mend them.

If Sir John holds life to one and twenty, he will probably live on, for his constitution if it does not grow weaker will become firmer.[7]

The harvest in Staffordshire has been such for plenty, and so well gathered as to be mentioned with admiration. Make your most of these golden years, and buy liberally what will now be liberally all[o]wed.[8] I hope to partake a little of the general abundance.—But I am now sixty eight. Make good use, my dear Lady of your days of health and spriteliness, sixty eight is coming fast upon you. Let it not find you wondering what is become of all the past.

If Aunt comes here she can do but little harm, for she will hardly go with you to Brighthelmston, and she cannot long trouble you at Stretham.[9]

3. *Ante* To Hester Thrale, 20 Sept. 1777.

4. The "beautiful romantic" garden at Islam, Dovedale, Staffordshire belonged to the Port family (*Boswell in Extremes*, ed. C. M. Weis and F. A. Pottle, 1970, p. 176). It comprised "a very fine amphitheatre, surrounded with hills covered with wood, and walks neatly formed along the side of a rocky steep ... with recesses under projections of rock, overshadowed with trees" (p. 178).

5. JB left Ashbourne for Edinburgh on 24 Sept. (Weis and Pottle, *Extremes*, p. 184).

6. In fact SJ remained at Ashbourne for almost another month (*Post* To Hester Thrale, 16 Oct. 1777; 22 Oct. 1777).

7. *Ante* To Hester Thrale, 8 Sept. 1777 and n. 3.

8. In her letter of 20 Sept., Hester Thrale had spoken of her husband's "golden Dreams," and announced that she had gone to London "to buy finery for Brighthelmston, that I may have my Share of the *Years of Plenty*" (MS: Rylands Library).

9. Since the beginning of August, Hester Thrale had been expecting a visit from Sidney Arabella Cotton (d. 1781), her garrulous and demanding aunt (Hester Thrale to SJ, 2 Aug. 1777, MS: Rylands Library). Mrs. Cotton eventually arrived at Streatham on 29 Sept. The Thrales left for Brighton without her on the

I hope soon to come to Lichfield, and from Lichfield to London.[10]

Taylor and Bosz. send their compliments with those of, Madam, Your most humble servant,

SAM. JOHNSON

30th (Hyde, 1977, pp. 190, 192; Hester Thrale to SJ, 26 Sept. 1777, MS: Rylands Library).

10. SJ did not return to London until 6 Nov. (*Post* To Hester Thrale, 6 Nov. 1777).

James Boswell

TUESDAY 23 SEPTEMBER 1777

MS: Beinecke Library.[1]

[Ashbourne]

Mr. Boswel's company is desired at the Blackmore's head.[2]

1. This note, in SJ's hand, is written on a page of JB's journal for 27 Sept.–3 Oct.

2. "After dinner the Doctor and I waited on Langton's mother and one of his sisters, who stopped at the Blackamoor's Head Inn" (JB's Ashbourne Journal, 23 Sept. 1777: *Boswell in Extremes*, ed. C. M. Weis and F. A. Pottle, 1970, p. 182).

Hester Thrale

THURSDAY 25 SEPTEMBER 1777

MS: Hyde Collection.

Dear Madam: Ashbourne, Sept. 25, 1777

Boswel is gone, and is I hope pleased that he has been here; though to look back on any thing with pleasure is not very common. He has been gay and good humoured in his usual way, but we have not agreed upon any other expedition.[1] He had spent more money than he intended, and I supplied him;

1. *Ante* To Hester Thrale, 13 Sept. 1777.

my deficiencies are[2] again made up by Mr. Thrales bill, for which I thank him.[3]

I will send directions to the Taylor to make me some cloaths according to Mr. Thrale's direction, though I cannot go with you to Brighthelmston, having loitered away the time I know not how, but, if you would have me I will endeavour to follow you, which upon the whole, perhaps may be as well.[4] I am here now on the 25th and am obliged by promise to take Lichfield in my way. So that the 30th will come upon me too soon.

The Levet that has been found in the register must be some other Levet; I dare say our Friend does not in his heart believe that it is he.[5]

I am glad that the Benedictines found you at last.[6] Father Wilkes, when he was amongst us, took Oxford in his way. I recommended him to Dr. Adams, on whom he impressed a high opinion of his Learning:[7] I am glad that my cell is reserved.[8] I may perhaps some time or other visit it, though I cannot easily tell why one should go to Paris twice. Our own beds are soft enough.[9] Yet my Master will tell you that one

2. MS: "a" superimposed upon "w"

3. *Ante* To Hester Thrale, 20 Sept. 1777.

4. SJ joined the Thrales at Brighton for three days in mid-November (Clifford, 1952, p. 156).

5. According to the printed text of her letter for 18 Sept., Hester Thrale had informed SJ, "My husband bids me tell you that he examined the register, and that Levet is only seventy-two years old" (Piozzi, *Letters* I.374). It is now accepted that Robert Levet was baptized at Kirk Ella, East Yorkshire, 30 Aug. 1705 (*Life* IV.137 n. 1). SJ and Hester Thrale both believed him to be older (*Thraliana* I.531).

6. "Father Prior too from the Paris Benedictines and another Monk came here to dinner" (Hester Thrale to SJ, 20 Sept. 1777, MS: Rylands Library). *Ante* To Robert Levet, 22 Oct. 1775, n. 5.

7. *Ante* To William Adams, 29 May 1776.

8. "A cell [in the English Benedictine monastery in Paris] is always kept ready for your use, he [the Prior] tells me; so when your cruel mistress turns you out, no harm will come of it" (Piozzi, *Letters* I.373–74).

9. "We talked of England and France—The beds are softer there than here, quoth my master. Softer, if you will, but not so clean, Sir, replied the Prior.—No, no, dirty enough to be sure, confessed Mr. Thrale, but exceeding soft" (Piozzi, *Letters* I.374).

wants to be doing some thing. I have some thing like a longing to see my Masters Performances, a pleasure which I shall hardly have till he returns from Brighthelmston.[10] I beg that before you go you will send the Bibliographia Britannica to my habitation.[11] I am, Dear Madam, your most humble servant,

SAM. JOHNSON

Let your next be sent to Lichfield.

10. "My Master has Prosperity in Sight, and in Possession . . . everybody tells me of some new Plan of Expence, he tells me nothing himself, but I hear it on all Sides, and shall I suppose see it anon" (Hester Thrale to SJ, 20 Sept. 1777, MS: Rylands Library).

11. "Bibliographia" is a slip for "Biographia." *Post* To Hester Thrale, 6 Nov. 1777. It is probable that SJ needed the *Biographia Britannica* (1747–66), a biographical dictionary edited by William Oldys and Joseph Towers, for his work on the *Lives of the Poets* (Lawrence Lipking, *The Ordering of the Arts in Eighteenth-Century England*, 1970, pp. 71, 78–81; Pat Rogers, "Johnson's *Lives of the Poets* and the Biographic Dictionaries," *RES* 31, 1980, pp. 149–71).

Hester Thrale

SATURDAY 27 SEPTEMBER 1777

MS: Hyde Collection.

Dear Madam: Ashbourne, Sept. 27, 1777

I think I have already told you that Bos. is gone.[1] The day before he went we[2] met the Duke and Dutchess of Argyle in the street, and went to speak to them while they changed Horses,[3] and in the afternoon Mrs. Langton and Juliet,

1. *Ante* To Hester Thrale, 22 Sept. 1777 and n. 5.

2. MS: "w" superimposed upon partially formed "h"

3. Toward the end of his Hebridean tour, SJ had been the guest at Inverary Castle of John Campbell, fifth Duke of Argyll (*Life* v.355–59). The Duke's wife, Elizabeth Gunning, former Duchess of Hamilton, had been attentive to SJ but deliberately neglectful of JB, who had opposed the claims of her son in the famous Douglas Cause (*Earlier Years*, pp. 311–17). When they met in Ashbourne, JB reported: "The Duchess was courteous to the Doctor. But, as at Inverary, would take hardly any notice of me" (*Boswell in Extremes*, ed. C. M. Weis and F. A. Pottle, 1970, p. 182).

stopped in their way to London, and sent for me, I went to them and sent for Boswel whom Mrs. Langton had never seen.[4]

And so, here is this post without a letter. I am old, I am old, says Sir John Falstaff.[5] "Take heed, my dear, youth flies apace." You will be wanting a letter sometime. I wish I were with you but I cannot come yet.—Glacies et frigora Rheni

> Me sine sola vides, ah! me te frigora laedant,
> Ah tibi ne glacies teneras secet aspera plantas. Ecl. x.[6]

I wish you well, Burney and all,[7] and shall be glad to know your adventures. Do not however think wholly to escape me, you will, I hope, see me at Brighthelmston.[8] Dare you answer me as Brutus answered his evil genius?[9] I know not when I shall write again now you [are] going to the world's end. Extra anni solisque vias,[10] where the post will be a long time in reaching you. I shall notwithstanding all distance continue to think on you, and to please my[11] self with the hope of being once again, Madam, your most humble servant,

SAM. JOHNSON

4. *Ante* To JB, 23 Sept. 1777.

5. "I am old, I am old" (*II Henry IV* II.iv.268).

6. *Alpinas a! dura, nives et frigora Rheni / me sine sola vides. a! te ne frigora laedant! / a! tibi ne teneras glacies secet aspera plantas!*: "thou art gazing, ah, heartless one! on Alpine snows and the frost-bound Rhine, apart from me, all alone. Ah, may the frosts not harm thee! Ah, may not the jagged ice cut thy tender feet!" (Virgil, *Eclogue* x.47–49, trans. H. R. Fairclough, Loeb ed.).

7. Charles Burney, who had been staying at Streatham Park, planned to accompany the Thrales to Brighton (Roger Lonsdale, *Dr. Charles Burney*, 1965, p. 240).

8. *Ante* To Hester Thrale, 25 Sept. 1777, n. 4.

9. "Why I will see thee at Philippi then" (*Julius Caesar* IV.iii.331).

10. *extra anni solisque vias*: "beyond the paths of the year and the sun" (Virgil, *Aeneid* VI.796, trans. H. R. Fairclough, Loeb ed.).

11. MS: "my" altered from "me"

Hester Thrale

MONDAY 29 SEPTEMBER 1777

MS: Hyde Collection.

Dear Madam: Ashbourn, Michaelmass day, 1777

And so because you hear that Mrs. Desmoulines has written, you hold it not necessary to write, as if she could write like you, or[1] I were equally content with hearing from her.[2]—Call you this backing your Friends?[3] She did write, and I remember nothing in her letter, but that she was discontented, that I wrote only Madam to her, and dear Madam to Mrs. Williams.[4] Without any great dearness in the comparison, Williams is I think, the dearer of the two. I am glad that she mends, but I am afraid she cannot get the start of the season, and Winter will come before she is prepared for it.

But at Streatham there are dears and dears, who before this letter reaches them will be at Brighthelmston.[5] Wherever they be, may they have no uneasiness but for want of me.

Now you are gone I wonder how long you design to stay, pray let me know when you write to Lichfield, for I have not lost hope of coming to you, yet that purpose may chance to fail.[6] But my comfort is, that you cannot charge me with forgetting you when I am away. You perhaps do not think how eagerly[7] I expect the post.

Mrs. Langton grows old, and has lost much of her undulation and mobility. Her voice likewise is spoiled. She can come upon the stage now only for her own benefit.[8] But Juliet is airy and cheerful, and has I hope done lamenting the inconstancy of Man. My Mistress is represented as unable to bear them company.[9] There was not time for many questions, and no op-

1. MS: "or" superimposed upon "a"

2. Hester Thrale had informed SJ on 26 Sept.: "I have this Moment been at Bolt Court myself to pick up News such as you like: Mrs. Des Moulines however wrote to you it seems two Days ago so now you know all without my help" (MS: Rylands Library).

3. "Call you that backing of your friends?" (*I Henry IV* II.iv.168).

4. Cf. *Ante* To Hester Thrale, 20 July 1771.

5. *Ante* To Hester Thrale, 22 Sept. 1777, n. 9.

6. *Ante* To Hester Thrale, 25 Sept. 1777, n. 4.   7. MS: "eargerly"

8. "He hated her perpetual Conversation about the Actors and Actresses, and said She waved her Head and hands in some awkward Manner" (Piozzi 1.389).

9. H. L. Piozzi identifies "My Mistress" as Elizabeth Langton, Bennet Langton's eldest sister (Piozzi 1.389).

portunity of winding and winding them, as Mr. Richardson has it, so as to get truth out without questions.[10] I do not indeed know that I am any great Winder. I suspect a Winder to be always a Man vacant, and commonly littleminded. I think my[11] dear little Mistress no great proficient at winding, though she could wind if she would, contemnit potius quam nescit.[12]

Dr. Taylor desires always to have his compliments sent.[13] He is, in his usual way very busy,—getting a Bull to his cows and a Dog to his bitches. His waterfall runs very well. Old Shakespeare is dead and he wants to buy another horse for his mares.[14] He is one of those who finds every hour something new to wish or to enjoy.[15]

Boswel while he was here saw Keddleston and the Silkmils,[16] and took Chatsworth in his way home.[17] He says, his Wife does not love me quite well yet, though we have made a formal peace.[18] He kept his journal very diligently, but then what was there to journalise. I should be glad to see what he says of ⟨the Dutchess⟩ of Argyle.[19] I think I told you that I took him to Ilam.[20]

Why should you suspect me of forgetting lilly lolly?[21] Now

10. "I have winded and winded about him, as he had done about me; but all to no purpose" (*Sir Charles Grandison*, 1753–54, 1.258, Letter 36).

11. MS: "m" superimposed upon "th"

12. *Aper omni eruditione imbutus contemnebat potius litteras quam nesciebat*: "Aper was a man of all-round learning, who as regards literature was not so much ignorant as disdainful" (Tacitus, *Dialogus de Oratoribus* 2, trans. Sir William Peterson, Loeb ed.).

13. MS: comma

14. *Ante* To Hester Thrale, 1 July 1775.

15. "Blest Madman, who coud every hour employ, / With something New to wish, or to enjoy!" (Dryden, "Absalom and Achitophel," ll. 553–54).

16. *Ante* To Hester Thrale, 20 Sept. 1777 and n. 4.

17. JB left Ashbourne on the morning of 24 Sept., and reached Chatsworth "in good time in the forenoon; was struck with the grandeur of the house and rich verdure of the park" (*Boswell in Extremes*, ed. C. M. Weis and F. A. Pottle, 1970, p. 184).

18. *Ante* To Margaret Boswell, 22 July 1777.

19. MS: heavily erased; conjectural reading based upon SJ's previous letter (*Ante* To Hester Thrale, 27 Sept. 1777)

20. *Ante* To Hester Thrale, 22 Sept. 1777 and n. 4.

21. "Give a thousand Compliments to Mr. Boswell, and tell Dr. Taylor I always send some to him, for if I *say* Lilly Lolly—I *mean* my Service to Doctor Taylor. I

you will see the Shellys,[22] and perhaps hear some thing about the Cottons,[23] and you will bathe, and walk, and dress, and dance and who knows how little you will think on, Madam, Your most humble servant, SAM. JOHNSON

hope you remember that nonsense or you will think me mad" (Hester Thrale to SJ, 18 Sept. 1777, MS: Rylands Library). The phrase derived from an anecdote concerning the "half-witted Son" of a Welsh squire, who said "Lilly Lolly" when he meant "How do you do Sir Robert Cotton" (Piozzi I.390).

22. Sir John Shelley (?1730–83), fifth Bt., of Mitchelgrove, Sussex, M.P. for New Shoreham (1774–80), Keeper of Records in the Tower of London, and an old friend of Henry Thrale (Namier and Brooke III.429). SJ had met Sir John, his wife Elizabeth (d. 1808), and their children in Brighton the previous year (Hyde, 1977, p. 169).

23. Sir John Shelley was related to Henry Shelley (1728–1805), the husband of Hester Thrale's first cousin, Philadelphia Cotton (d. 1819) (*Thraliana* I.298, II.1166).

Hester Thrale

MONDAY 6 OCTOBER 1777

MS: Hyde Collection.

Dear Madam: Ashbourne, Oct. 6, 1777

You are glad that I am absent, and I am glad that you are sick.[1] When you went away what did you do with your Aunt?[2] I am glad she liked my Susey, I was always a Susey, when nobody else was a Susy.[3] How have you managed at your new place?[4] Could you all get lodgings in one house, and meat at

1. Hester Thrale was pregnant with her twelfth child, whom they hoped would be a son (Hyde, 1977, pp. 189–90). The child proved to be a girl: Henrietta Sophia (1778–83).

2. *Ante* To Hester Thrale, 22 Sept. 1777 and n. 9.

3. "Susanna Arabella [Thrale], small and weak, received little admiration from anyone except Johnson. He was her staunch defender from the start" (Hyde, 1977, p. 37).

4. The Thrales had taken lodgings in Brighton until they could move into their own house (Clifford, 1952, p. 155).

one table? Let me hear the whole series[5] of misery, for as Dr. Young says, *I love horrour*.[6]

Methinks you are now a great way off, and, if I come, I have a great way to come to you. And then the Sea is so cold, and the rooms are so dull.[7] Yet I do love to hear[8] the sea roar and my Mistress talk. For when she talks ye Gods, how she will talk.[9] I wish I were with you, but we are now near half the length of England asunder. It is frightful to think how much time must pass between writing this letter and receiving an answer, if any answer were necessary. Taylor is now going to have a Ram, and then after aries and taurus we shall have gemini.[10] His oats are now in the wet, here is a deal of rain. Mr. Langdon bought at Nottingham fair fifteen tun of Cheese,[11] which at an ounce a piece will suffice after dinner for 480000 Men. This [is] all the news that the place affords. I purpose soon to be at Lichfield, but know not just when, having been defeated of my first design.[12] When I come to town I am to be very busy about my Lives.[13] Could not you do some of them for me?

I am glad Master huspelled you, and run you all on rucks,[14]

5. MS: "series" altered from "?story"

6. "But horrors now are not displeasing to me; / I like this rocking of the battlements" (Edward Young, *The Revenge*, 1721, I.i.3–4).

7. The principal meeting places in Brighton during the 1770s included the Assembly Room at the Ship Inn, built in 1767 by Robert Golden, and the Ballroom at the Castle Inn, built by John Crunden in 1766 (Ian Nairn and Nikolaus Pevsner, *Sussex*, 1965, pp. 426, 446, 452).   8. MS: "h" superimposed upon "t"

9. *Ante* To Hester Thrale, 19 Feb. 1773, n. 11.

10. SJ suggests whimsically that Taylor is progressing through the signs of the zodiac, beginning with Aries the Ram and Taurus the Bull.

11. *tun*: "the weight of two thousand pounds" (SJ's *Dictionary*).

12. *Post* To Hester Thrale, 22 Oct. 1777.

13. It is probable that SJ had begun writing what appears to be the first of his *Lives of the Poets*, the "Life of Cowley," after JB's departure on 24 Sept. (William McCarthy, "The Composition of Johnson's *Lives*: A Calendar," *Philological Quarterly* 60, 1981, p. 55). SJ finished "Cowley" on 11 Oct. (*Works*, Yale ed. 1.279).

14. *huspel*: "to treat with violence; to maltreat; to despoil; to harass" (*OED*). *ruck*: "a large number or quantity; a multitude, crowd, throng" (*OED*). SJ is lapsing into Midlands dialect; his meaning can be paraphrased as "I am glad Thrale is jostling you about in a confused group."

and drove you about, and made you stir. Never be cross about it. Quiet and calmness you have enough of, a little hurry stirs life, and brushing o'er adds motion to the pool. Dryden.[15] Now *Pool*, bring[s] my Masters excavations into my head.[16] I wonder how I shall like them, I should like not to see them, till we all see them together. We will have no waterfall to roar like the Doctors.[17] I sat by it yesterday and read, Erasmus's Militis Christiani Enchiridion.[18] Have you got that Book?

Make my compliments to dear Queeny. I suppose she will dance at the rooms, and your heart will go one knows not how. I am, Dearest and dearest Lady, Your most humble servant,

SAM. JOHNSON

15. "Nor Love is always of a vicious Kind, / But oft to virtuous Acts inflames the Mind. / Awakes the sleepy Vigour of the Soul, / And, brushing o'er, adds Motion to the Pool" (Dryden, "Cymon and Iphigenia," ll. 27–30).

16. *Ante* To Hester Thrale, 23 Aug. 1777, n. 4.

17. "One morning after breakfast, when the sun shone bright, we walked out together, and 'pored' for some time with placid indolence upon an artificial waterfall, which Dr. Taylor had made by building a strong dyke of stone across the river behind his garden" (*Life* III.190).

18. Erasmus's *Enchiridion Militis Christiani* (Antwerp, 1504) advocates a return to the New Testament and the Church Fathers for a more accurate and vigorous understanding of Christian dogma.

Hester Thrale

MONDAY 13 OCTOBER 1777

MS: Hyde Collection.

Dear Madam: [Ashbourne] Oct. 13, 1777

Yes I do love to hear from you.[1] Such pretty kind letters as you send—But it gives me great delight to find that my Master misses me. I begin to wish my self with you more than I should do if I were wanted less. It is a good thing to stay away till

1. "Lest you should not have had my last Letters, and as you kindly say you love to hear from me, I write again" (Hester Thrale to SJ, 4 Oct. 1777, MS: Rylands Library).

one's company is desired, but not so good to stay after it is desired.

You know, I have some work to do. I did not set to it very soon, and if I should go up to London with nothing done, what would be said, but that I was—who can tell what? I therefore stay till I can bring up something to stop their mouths,[2] and then—

Though I am still at Ashbourne I receive your dear Letters that come to Lichfield, and you continue that direction, for I think to get thither as soon as I can.

One of the Does died yesterday, and I am afraid, her fawn will be starved, I wish Miss Thrale had it to nurse, but the Doctor is now all for cattle, and minds very little either Does or Hens.

How did you and your Aunt part?[3] Did you turn her out of doors to begin your journey, or did she leave you by her usual shortness of visits. I love to know how you go on.

I cannot but think on your kindness and my Masters. Life has upon the whole fallen short, very short, of my early expectation, but the acquisition of such a friendship, at an age when new friendships are seldom acquired, is something better than the general course of things gives Man a right to expect. I think on it with great delight, I am not very apt to be delighted. I am, Madam, Your most obedient Servant,

SAM. JOHNSON

2. SJ had finished his "Cowley" and "Denham" by the time he returned to London (William McCarthy, "The Composition of Johnson's *Lives*: A Calendar," *Philological Quarterly* 60, 1981, p. 55). *Ante* To Hester Thrale, 6 Oct. 1777 and n. 12; *Post* To Hester Thrale, 3 Nov. 1777.

3. *Ante* To Hester Thrale, 22 Sept. 1777, n. 9.

Hester Thrale

MS: Houghton Library.

Dearest Lady: Ashbourne, Oct. 16

I am just going out and can write but little, how you should be long without a letter I know not, for I seldom miss a post. I purpose now to come to London as soon as I can, for I have a deal to look after, but hope I shall get through the whole business.[1]

I wish you had told me your adventure, or told me nothing. Be civil to Lord Lucan, he seems to be a good kind of Man.[2] Miss may change her mind, and will change it, when she finds herself get more credit by dancing than by Whist, and though she should continue to like as she likes now, the harm is none.[3]

Do not yet begin, dear Madam, to think about *the last*.[4] You may well dance these dozen years, if you keep your looks as you have yet kept them, and I am glad that Hetty has no design to dance you down.

The poor Pools.[5] I am sorry for the Girl,[6] she seems to be

1. *Ante* To Hester Thrale, 6 Oct. 1777 and n. 12; 13 Oct. 1777 and n. 2.

2. Charles Bingham (1735–99), first Baron Lucan (1776), later (1795) first Earl of Lucan, M.P. for Mayo County (1761–76), was elected to The Club in 1782. At Lord Lucan's house in Charles Street, Berkeley Square, SJ "often enjoyed all that an elegant table and the best company can contribute to Happiness" (*Life* IV.326).

3. Although she had been taking lessons for over two years, Queeney Thrale disliked dancing—so much so that she occasionally refused to dance at all (Hyde, 1977, pp. 113, 194).

4. SJ may be alluding to his final *Idler* essay: "There are few things not purely evil, of which we can say, without some emotion of uneasiness, 'this is the last.' . . . This secret horrour of the last is inseparable from a thinking being whose life is limited, and to whom death is dreadful" (*Works*, Yale ed. II.314–15).

5. Sir Ferdinando Poole (d. 1804), fourth Bt., of Lewes and Poole, Sussex, later (1789–90) Sheriff of Sussex. Lady Poole (d. 1786) was the daughter of Thomas White of Horsham, Sussex (*Complete Baronetage*, ed. G. E. Cokayne, 1904, IV.94).

6. "Of Miss Harriott Poole says he [SJ], how pleasing would this Girl's Softness and Innocency be if She had any thing else besides Softness and Innocency! but She is nothing, and can be nothing, and so one thanks her for nothing I think" (*Thraliana* I.169).

doomed before her time to weakness and solitude.[7] What is that Bedrider[8] the Supervisor? He will be up again. But life seems to be closing upon them.

I hope you still continue to be sick,[9] and my dear Master to be well.

I am no sender of compliments, but take them once for all, and deliver them to be kept as rarrities, by Miss Owen, Mrs. Nesbit, Miss Hetty, and Doctor Burney.

Still direct to Lichfield, for thither I am hastening, and from Lichfield to London, and from London, I hope to Brighthelmston, and from Brighthelmston—qua terra patet.[10] I am, Dearest of all dear Ladies, Your most humble servant,

SAM. JOHNSON

7. MS: "solidude"

8. SJ appears to have coined "bedrider" (not in SJ's *Dictionary* or *OED*) to describe someone who is, or causes another to be, bedridden.

9. *Ante* To Hester Thrale, 6 Oct. 1777 and n. 1.

10. *Ante* To Hester Thrale, 12 Aug. 1773, n. 24.

Hester Thrale

WEDNESDAY 22 OCTOBER 1777

MS: Hyde Collection.

Dear Madam: Lichfield, Oct. 22, 1777

I am come at last to Lichfield, and am really glad that I am got away from a place where there was indeed no evil, but very little good. You may I believe write once to Lichfield after you receive this, but after that, it will be best to direct to London.

Your throat is, I suppose, well by this time.[1] Poor Mrs. Burney it is impossible to think on without great compassion.[2]

1. In her letters of 4 and 18 Oct., Hester Thrale had complained of an "excessively" sore throat (MSS: Rylands Library).

2. On 17 Oct. Elizabeth Allen Burney (*c.* 1728–96), Charles Burney's second wife, arrived in Brighton from Paris, where she had gone to meet Elizabeth Allen (1761–?1826), her younger daughter by her first marriage. On 12 Oct. Elizabeth eloped with "an undesirable young man" named Samuel Meeke (Roger Lonsdale,

Against a blow so sudden and so unexpected I wonder that she supports herself. The consolations of Burney's girls must indeed be painful.[3] She had intended to enjoy the triumph of her daughter's superiority. They were prepared to wish them both ill, and their wishes are gratified. There is in this event a kind of system of calamity, a conflagration of the soul. Every avenue of pain is invaded at once. Pride is mortified, tenderness is wounded, hope is disappointed. Whither will the poor Lady run from herself.

My visit to Stow hill has been paid. I have seen there a collection of Misery. Mrs. Aston paralytick, Mrs. Walmsley lame,[4] Mrs. Hervey blind, and I think another Lady deaf. Ev'n such is life.

I hope dear Mrs. Aston is a little better; it is however very little. She was, I believe, glad to see me, and to have any body glad to see me is a great pleasure.

I will tell while I think on it, that I really saw with my own eyes Mr. Chaplin of Lincolnshire's letter for Taylors Cow,[5] accompanied with a draught on Hoare for one hundred and twenty six pounds to pay for her.[6] Frank says the young Bull is not quite so big as the old one. Taylor, I think, says he is bigger.

I have seen but one new place this journey, and that is Leek in the Morlands.[7] An old Church, but a poor Town.[8]

Dr. Charles Burney, 1965, p. 240; *Journals and Letters of Fanny Burney,* ed. Joyce Hemlow et al., 1972–84, I.lxxiv).

3. There was no love lost between Charles Burney's daughters by his first marriage (Esther, Frances, Susanna, Charlotte, and Sarah) and their stepmother (Joyce Hemlow, *History of Fanny Burney,* 1958, pp. 35–40).

4. Magdalen Walmsley (1709–86), fourth daughter of Sir Thomas Aston, third Bt., and the widow of SJ's friend Gilbert Walmsley (?1680–1751), whom she married in 1736 (*Johns. Glean.* v.251–52). Mrs. Walmsley, who lived in Bath, was paying a visit to her sisters in Lichfield (*Post* To Hester Thrale, 29 Oct. 1777; *Johns. Glean.* v.252).   5. *Ante* To Hester Maria Thrale, 4 Sept. 1777 and n. 4.

6. Hoare's Bank, Fleet Street, London, was established by Sir Richard Hoare (1648–1718) in 1693.

7. *moreland:* "a mountainous or hilly country: a tract of [North] Staffordshire is called the *Morlands,* from being hilly" (SJ's *Dictionary*).

8. The market town of Leek originated in the Norman manor of Lec (Sampson

The days grow short, and we have frosts, but I am, in all weathers, Madam, your most humble servant,

SAM. JOHNSON

Erdeswick, *A Survey of Staffordshire*, ed. Thomas Harwood, 1844, p. 494). The large, externally impressive parish church, dedicated to St. Edward the Confessor, was rebuilt after a fire in 1297 (Nikolaus Pevsner, *Staffordshire*, 1974, p. 168). On his way to Ashbourne, 14 Sept. 1777, JB attended afternoon prayers at St. Edward and spent several hours in the inn at Leek, which he found "a very pretty village, or rather . . . prettily situated" (*Boswell in Extremes*, ed. C. M. Weis and F. A. Pottle, 1970, p. 149).

Hester Thrale

SATURDAY 25 OCTOBER 1777

MS: Hyde Collection.

Dear Madam: Lichfield, Oct. 25, 1777

Cholmondely's Story shocks me, if it be true, which I can hardly think, for I am utterly unconscious of it, I am very sorry, and very much ashamed.[1]

I am here for about a week longer, and then I purpose to hasten to London. How long do you stay at Brighthelmston?[2] Now the Company is gone why should you be the lag. The season of Brewing will soon be here, if it [be] not already come. We have here cold weather, and loud winds.

Miss Porter is better than is usual, and Mrs. Aston is, I hope, not worse, but she is very bad, and being, I fancy, about sixty eight, is it likely that she will ever be better?

1. "When young Cholmondeley rode up to our Carriage as we drove through Derbyshire—Mr. Thrale—seeing him address Johnson in a Style civilly familiar, and knowing them to be acquainted;— tapped the Dr. who was reading, and said Sir, that is Mr. Cholmondeley,—well Sir replies Johnson raising His Eyes from the Book,—and *what if it is* Mr. Cholmondeley!" (*Thraliana* 1.189, Dec. 1777). George James Cholmondeley (1752–1830), later first Marquess of Cholmondeley, was the son of SJ's friend the Hon. Mrs. Robert Cholmondeley.

2. The Thrales remained at Brighton until 18 Nov. (Clifford, 1952, p. 156).

It is really now a long time that we have been writing and writing, and yet how small a part of our minds have we written? We shall meet, I hope, soon, and talk it out.

You are not yet sixty eight, but it will come, and perhaps you may then sometimes remembe[r] me.

In the mean time do not think to be young beyond the time, do not play Agnes,[3] and[4] do not grow old before your time nor suffer yourself to be too soon driven from the stage. You can yet give pleasure by your appearance, show yourself therefore, and be pleased by pleasing. It is not now too soon to be wise, nor is it yet too late to be gay.

Streatham is now I suppose the eighth wonder of the world,[5] I long to see it, but do not intend to go till, as I once said before, my Master and you and I, and nobody else shall be with us, perambulate it together.

Cicely, I warrant you, will do well enough.[6] I am glad you are so sick—and nobody to pity—Now for another pretty little Girl—But we know not what is best.[7] I am, Dearest Lady, your most humble servant,

SAM. JOHNSON

Pay my respects to Miss Owen.

3. SJ refers to Agnès, the young woman in Molière's *L'École des femmes* who is kept in a state of childish naivete by her prospective husband. *Post* To Hester Thrale, 16 Apr. 1781.

4. MS: "and" superimposed upon one word undeciphered

5. *Ante* To Hester Thrale, 17 July 1775; 23 Aug. 1777 and n. 4.

6. Hester Thrale had taken her youngest child, Cecilia (1777–1857), to Brighton in order "to dip her in the Sea, She looks pale and that will freshen her" (Hyde, 1977, p. 190). On 1 Dec. Hester Thrale recorded in her *Family Book*: "Caecilia *did* bathe at Brighton, but it did not agree with her . . . but She does very well upon the whole as to Person and Health" (Hyde, 1977, p. 196).

7. *Ante* To Hester Thrale, 6 Oct. 1777, n. 1.

Hester Thrale

MS: Hyde Collection.

Dear Madam: Lichfield, Oct. 27, 1777

You talk of writing and writing as if you had all the writing to yourself. If our Correspondence were printed I am sure Posterity, for Posterity is always the authours favourite, would say that I am a good writer too. Anch' io sonô Pittore.[1] To sit down so often with nothing to say, to say something so often, almost without consciousnesss of saying, and without any remembrance of having said, is a power of which I will not violate my modesty by boasting, but I do not believe that every body has it.

Some when they write to their friends are all affection, some are wise and sententious, some strain their powers for efforts of gayety, some write news, and some write secrets, but to make a letter without affection, without wisdom, without gayety, without news, and without a secret is, doub[t]less, the great epistolick art.

In a Man's Letters you know, Madam, his soul lies naked, his letters are only the mirrour of his breast, whatever passes within him is shown undisguised in its natural process. Nothing is inverted, nothing distorted, you see systems in their elements, you discover actions in their motives.[2]

Of this great truth sounded by the knowing to the ignorant, and so echoed by the ignorant to the knowing, what evidence have you now before you. Is not my soul laid open in these

1. *Anch'io sono pittore*: "I too am a painter" (an apocryphal remark attributed to Correggio as early as the late seventeenth century). "The remark is said to have been made by Correggio when looking at a work of Raphael's, variously identified with the *St. Cecilia* ... the *Sistine Madonna* ... and the Farnesina frescoes" (Cecil Gould, *The Paintings of Correggio*, 1976, p. 40). Correggio's saying may have reached SJ through Roger de Piles's *Abrégé de la Vie des Peintres* (1699) or through conversations with Sir Joshua Reynolds.

2. SJ's thoughts on "the great epistolick art" should be compared with his discussion of Pope's letters (*Lives of the Poets* III.206–8).

veracious pages? do not you see me reduced to my first principles? This is the pleasure of corresponding with a friend,
where doubt and distrust have no place, and every thing is
said as it is thought. The[3] original Idea is laid down in its simple purity, and all the supervenient conceptions, are spread
over it stratum super stratum, as they happen to be formed.
These are the letters by which souls are united, and by which
Minds naturally in unison move each other as they are moved
themselves. I know, dearest Lady, that in the perusal of this
such is the consanguinity of our intellects, you will be touched
as I am touched. I have indeed concealed nothing from you,
nor do I expect ever to repent of having thus opened my
heart. I am, Madam, Your most humble servant,

SAM. JOHNSON

3. MS: "The" superimposed upon "I"

Hester Thrale

WEDNESDAY 29 OCTOBER 1777

MS: Birthplace Museum, Lichfield.

Dear Madam: Lichfield, Oct.[1] 29, 1777

Though after my last letter I might justly claim an interval of
rest, yet I write again to tell you that for this turn you will hear
but once more from Lichfield. This day is Wednesday, on
Saturday I shall write again and on Monday I shall set out to
seek adventures, for you know, None but the Brave deserve
the Fair.[2]

On Monday we hope to see Birmingham, the seat of the
mechanick arts, and know not whether our next stage will be
Oxford, the mansion of the liberal arts, or London the residence of all the arts together. The Chymists call the world

1. MS: "O" superimposed upon "Se"
2. "None but the Brave deserves the Fair" (Dryden, "Alexander's Feast,"
chorus).

Academia Paracelsi,[3] my[4] ambition is to be his fellow student. To see the works of Nature, and hear the lectures of Truth. To London therefore—London may perhaps fill me, and I hope to fill my part of London.

In the meantime let me continue to keep the part which I have had so long in your kindness and my Master's, for if that should grow less I know not where to find that which may supply the diminution. But I hope what I have been so happy as to gain, I shall have the happiness of keeping.

I always omitted to tell you that Lucy's Maid took the worm powder with strict regularity, but with no great effect.[5] Lucy has had several letters from you, but cannot prevail on herself to write. But she is very grateful.

Mrs. Walmsley has been at Stowhill, and has invited me when I come to Bath, to be at her house. Poor Mrs. Aston either mends not at all, or not perceptibly; but she does [not] seem to grow worse.

Last year you gained 14000£. I long to know what are the prices of malt and hops, and what is the prospect for the year approaching.[6] I hope Master will soon put Viri's money into the funds,[7] and pay Lady Lade and her son, if that be not done already. I suppose Sir John is by this time recovered, and perhaps grown wiser, than to shake his constitution so violently a second time.[8]

Poor Mrs. Burney! One cannot think on her but with great compassion.[9] But it is impossible for her husbands da[u]ghters not to triumph, and the husband will feel, as Rochefoucault says, *something that does not displease him.*[10] You and I, who are

---

3. "He [Pope] studied in the academy of Paracelsus, and made the universe his favourite volume" (*Lives of the Poets* III.216).

4. MS: "m" superimposed upon "I"

5. *Ante* To Hester Thrale, 9 Aug. 1777 and n. 3.

6. *Ante* To Hester Thrale, 15 Sept. 1777 and n. 9.

7. Viry had loaned Thrale money for the brewery as long ago as 1773 (Clifford, 1952, p. 104 n. 3).   8. *Ante* To Hester Thrale, 8 Sept. 1777 and n. 3.

9. *Ante* To Hester Thrale, 22 Oct. 1777 and nn. 2, 3.

10. "Dans l'adversité de nos meilleurs amis, nous trouvons toujours quelque

neutral, whom her happiness could not have depressed, may be honestly sorry. I am, Dear Madam, your most humble servant,

SAM. JOHNSON

---

chose qui ne nous déplaît pas" (La Rochefoucauld, *Maximes*, ed. Jacques Truchet, 1967, p. 139).

Hester Thrale

MONDAY 3 NOVEMBER 1777

PRINTED SOURCE: Piozzi, *Letters* I.396–97.[1]

Dear Madam,   Lichfield, October[2] 3, 1777

This is the last time that I shall write, in this excursion, from this place. To-morrow I shall be, I hope, at Birmingham; from which place I shall do my best to find the nearest way home. I come home, I think, worse than I went; and do not like the state of my health. But, *vive hodie*,[3] make the most[4] of life. I hope to get better, and—sweep the cobwebs.[5] But I have sad nights. Mrs. Aston has sent me to Mr. Green to be cured.

Did you see Foote at Brighthelmstone?—Did you think he would so soon be gone?[6]—Life, says Falstaff, is a shuttle.[7] He was a fine fellow in his way; and the world is really im-

1. Printed text collated with excerpt in Maggs Catalogue 365, 1918, p. 416.
2. Deceived by SJ's "October" (Maggs), Piozzi misdated this letter. Cf. *Post* To Hester Thrale, 10 Nov. 1777.
3. *sera nimis vita est crastina: vive hodie*: "Too late is to-morrow's life; live thou to-day" (Martial, *Epigrams* I.xv.12, trans. W.C.A. Ker, Loeb ed.).
4. "best" (Maggs)
5. "Old woman, old woman, old woman, quoth I, / Where are you going to up so high? / To brush the cobwebs off the sky!" (*Oxford Dictionary of Nursery Rhymes*, ed. Iona and Peter Opie, 1951, p. 434). Other versions of the rhyme substitute "sweep" for "brush."
6. The comedian and playwright Samuel Foote (1720–77) died at Dover 21 Oct. In September he had been recuperating at Brighton from convulsions and repeated fits of fainting (Simon Trefman, *Sam. Foote, Comedian*, 1971, pp. 262–63).
7. "Life is a shuttle" (*Merry Wives of Windsor* v.i.23).

poverished by his sinking glories.[8] Murphy ought to write his life, at least to give the world a Footeana.[9] Now, will any of his contemporaries bewail him?[10] Will Genius change *his sex* to weep? I would really have his life written with diligence.[11]

It will be proper for me to work pretty diligently now for some time. I hope to get through, though so many weeks have passed. Little lives and little criticisms may serve.[12]

Having been in the country so long, with very little to detain me, I am rather glad to look homewards. I am, etc.

8. SJ's elegiac comment on David Garrick echoes his praise of Foote: Garrick's death "eclipsed the gaiety of nations and impoverished the publick stock of harmless pleasure" (*Lives of the Poets* II.21).

9. An anonymous *Memoirs of the Life and Writings of Samuel Foote* did appear before the end of the year, but no biography by Arthur Murphy has been recorded.

10. "Foote's death was regretted by the public; every newspaper and magazine in London carried an account of his life and praised the man in many ways. At least two close friends, [William] Jewel and [Arthur] Murphy, mourned him to their dying days" (Trefman, *Foote*, p. 263).

11. The first full-length biography appeared in 1805: William Cooke, *Memoirs of Samuel Foote Esq.*   12. *Ante* To JB, 3 May 1777 and n. 9.

Hester Thrale

THURSDAY 6 NOVEMBER 1777

MS: Hyde Collection.

Dear Lady: Boltcourt, Nov. 6, 1777

I am this evening come to Bolt court, after a ramble in which I have had very little pleasure and now have not you to talk to, nor My Master. I carried bad health out, and have brought it home. What else I bring is abundance of compliments to you from every body. Lucy I cannot persuade to write to you, but she is very much obliged.

Be pleased to write word to Streatham that they should find me the Biographia Britannica, as soon as is possible.[1]

1. *Ante* To Hester Thrale, 25 Sept. 1777 and n. 11.

I believe I owe Queeny a Letter, for which I hope she will forgive me. I am apt to omit things of more importance.

Let me hear from you now quick. Our letters will pass and repass like shuttlecocks. I am, Dearest Madam, your most humble servant,

SAM. JOHNSON

Hester Thrale

MONDAY 10 NOVEMBER 1777

MS: Hyde Collection.

Dear Madam: Oct.[1] 10, 1777

And so supposing that I might come to town and neglect to give you notice, or thinking some other strange thought, but certainly thinking wrong, you fall to writing about me to Tom. Davies, as if he could tell you any thing that I would not have you know. As soon as I came hither I let you know of my arrival, and the consequence is that I am summoned to Brighthelmston through storms and cold and dirt and all the hardships of wintry journeys.[2] You know my natural dread of all those evils, yet to show my Master an example of compliance, and to let you know how much I long to see you, and to boast how little I give way to disease, my purpose is to be with you on Friday.

I am sorry for poor Nezzy, and hope she will in time be better;[3] I hope the same for myself. The rejuvenescency[4] of Mr. Scrase gives us both[5] reason to hope, and therefore both

1. SJ misdated this letter by a month, as he did his letter to Hester Thrale of 3 Nov.

2. In her letter of 8 Nov., Hester Thrale had invited SJ to come down to Brighton on Friday the 14th and return with the Thrales to Streatham on Tuesday the 18th (MS: Rylands Library).

3. Susanna Nesbitt "has her Palpitation now once a fortnight, attended with great Pain and Spasms" (Hester Thrale to SJ, 8 Nov. 1777, MS: Rylands Library).

4. MS: undeciphered deletion before "rejuvenescency"

5. MS: "both" altered from "bothe"

of us rejoice in his recovery.[6] I wish him well besides as a friend to my Master.

I am just come home from not seeing my Lord Mayor's show, but I might have seen at least part of it.[7] But I saw Miss Wesley and her Brothers.[8] She sends her compliments. Mrs. Williams is come home, I think, a very little better.

Every body was an enemy to that Wig.[9] We will burn it, and get drunk, for what is joy without drink. Wagers are laid in the city about our success,[10] which is yet as the French call it, problematical.[11] Well, but seriously I think I shall be glad to [see] you in your own hair, but do not take too much time in combing, and twisting, and papering, and unpapering, and curling, and frizzing, and powdering, and getting out the powder, with all the other operations required in the cultivation of a head of hair. Yet let it be combed at least once in three months, on the quarter day;[12] I could wish it might be combed

6. Hester Thrale had told SJ that he might lose all his "Complaints at the Age of 72 like Mr. Scrase and begin the World anew" (8 Nov. 1777, MS: Rylands Library).

7. On Lord Mayor's Day (9 Nov. of every year, unless, as in 1777, the ninth fell on a Sunday) the mayor of London was inaugurated with lavish pageantry, processions, and feasting.

8. Sarah Wesley (1760–1828) was the daughter of the Rev. Charles Wesley (1707–88) (*Thraliana* 1.220). For her two brothers, *ante* To Hester Maria Thrale, 4 Sept. 1777 and n. 3.

9. For some time Hester Thrale, at her mother's urging, had been wearing a wig, but in Brighton Henry Thrale commanded her to "pull it off" and start dressing her own hair. "I did think to have burnt it for Joy of the great News from America but there comes no Confirmation of it they say" (Hester Thrale to SJ, 8 Nov. 1777, MS: Rylands Library).

10. Rumors were circulating about the defeat of the American forces at Brandywine, 11 Sept. 1777. General Howe's official report of the engagements at Brandywine and Germantown (4 Oct.) did not arrive in London until 1 Dec. "In the first [battle], Howe certainly had the advantage; and in the second . . . Washington . . . was repelled, and is retired into the Jerseys, the King having been restored to the sovereignty of Philadelphia" (*Walpole's Correspondence*, Yale ed. XXIV.338–39).

11. SJ's *Dictionary* records the derivation of "problematical" from the French *problématique*.

12. *quarter-day*: "one of the four days fixed by custom as marking off the quarters of the year, on which tenancy of houses usually begins and ends. . . . In Eng-

once at least in six weeks, if I were to indulge my wishes, but what are wishes without hopes, I should fancy the operation performed—one knows not when one has enough—perhaps—every morning. I am, Dearest Lady, Your most humble servant,

SAM. JOHNSON

land and Ireland the quarter-days are Lady Day (March 25), Midsummer Day (June 24), Michaelmas (Sept. 29), and Christmas (Dec. 25)" (*OED*).

Elizabeth Aston

THURSDAY 20 NOVEMBER 1777

MS: Pembroke College, Oxford.
ADDRESS: To Mrs. Aston, Stow Hill, Lichfield.
FRANK: Hfreethrale.
POSTMARKS: 20 NO, FREE.

Dear Madam: London, Nov. 20, 1777

Through Birmingham and Oxford I got without any difficulty or disaster to London, though not in so short a time as I expected, for I did not reach Oxford before the second day.[1] I came home very much incommoded by obstructed respiration, but by vigorous methods[2] am something better. I have since been at Brighthelmston,[3] and am now designing to settle.

Different things, Madam, are fit for different people. It is fit for me to settle, and for You to move. I wish I could hear of You at Bath,[4] but I am afraid that is hardly to be expected from your resolute inactivity. My next hope is that You will

1. SJ left Lichfield for London 4 Nov. (*Ante* To Hester Thrale, 3 Nov. 1777), and returned to Boltcourt 6 Nov. (*Ante* To Hester Thrale, 6 Nov. 1777).
2. SJ found "physick and opium" palliative (*Post* To Jane Gastrell, 23 Dec. 1777).
3. SJ joined the Thrales in Brighton on 14 Nov., and returned with them to Streatham on the 18th (*Ante* To Hester Thrale, 10 Nov. 1777 and n. 2).
4. *Ante* To Hester Thrale, 22 Oct. 1777 and n. 4.

endeavour to grow well where You are. I cannot help thinking that I saw a visible amendment between the time when I left You to go to Ashbourne, and the time when I came back.[5] I hope You will[6] go on mending and mending, to which exercise and cheerfulness will very much contribute. Take care therefore, dearest Madam, to be busy and cheerful.

I have great confidence in the care and conversation of dear Mrs. Gastrel. It is very much the interest of all that know her, that she should continue well, for she is one of [the] few people that has the proper regard for those that are sick. She was so kind to me, that I hope I never shall forget it, and if it be troublesome to You to write I shall hope that she will do me another act of kindness by answering this letter, for I beg that I may hear from You by some hand or another.[7] I am, Madam, Your most obedient servant,

SAM. JOHNSON

5. SJ refers to the interval between his departure for Ashbourne, 30 Aug., and his return to Lichfield, *c.* 21 Oct. His report to Hester Thrale was less sanguine: "I hope dear Mrs. Aston is a little better; it is however very little" (*Ante* To Hester Thrale, 22 Oct. 1777).   6. MS: "w" superimposed upon "g"

7. *Post* To Jane Gastrell, 23 Dec. 1777.

Lucy Porter

THURSDAY 20 NOVEMBER 1777

MS: Hyde Collection.

ADDRESS: To Mrs. Lucy Porter, Lichfield.

FRANK: Hfreethrale.

POSTMARKS: 20 NO, FREE.

Dear Love: London, Nov. 20, 1777

You ordered me to write you word when I came home. I have been for some days at Brighthelmston and came back on Tuesday night.[1]

1. *Ante* To Elizabeth Aston, 20 Nov. 1777, n. 3.

You know that when I left you I was not well, I have taken physick very diligently and am perceptibly better, so much better that I hope by care and perseverance to recover, and see you again from time to time.

Mr. Nollikens the Statuary has had my direction to send you a cast of my head.[2] I will pay the carriage when we meet. Let me know how you like it, and what the Ladies of your rout say to it.[3] I have heard different opinions.[4] I cannot think where you can put it.

I found every body here well. Miss has a mind to be womanly, and her womanhood does not sit well upon her.[5]

Please to make my compliments to all the Ladies and all the Gentlemen to whom I owe them, that is, to a great part of the town. I am, Dear Madam, your most humble servant,

SAM. JOHNSON

2. *Ante* To Joseph Nollekens, 29 Aug. 1777 and n. 2.

3. *rout*: "a fashionable gathering or assembly" (*OED*).

4. *Post* To Lucy Porter, 19 Feb. 1778.

5. SJ refers to Queeney Thrale, who had turned 13 on 17 Sept. (*Ante* To Hester Thrale, 18 Sept. 1777 and n. 1).

James Boswell

TUESDAY 25 NOVEMBER 1777

PRINTED SOURCE: JB's *Life*, 1791, II.177–78.

Dear Sir,   London, Nov. 25, 1777

You will wonder, or you have wondered, why no letter has come from me. What you wrote at your return, had in it such a strain of cowardly caution as gave me no pleasure.[1] I could

1. On 22 Sept., at Ashbourne, JB repeated to SJ an anecdote that Topham Beauclerk had told him the previous April. This story purported to give evidence of SJ's flagrant ingratitude toward his close friend Henry Hervey. SJ had assured JB that "the story was absolutely false" (*Life* III.195). In his letter of 29 Sept., JB regretted having divulged Beauclerk's identity, and asked SJ to tell no one of the incident (*Life* III.209–10).

not well do what you wished; I had no need to vex you with a refusal. I have seen Mr. —— ,[2] and as to him have set all right, without any inconvenience, so far as I know, to you. Mrs. Thrale had forgot the story. You may now be at ease.

And at ease I certainly wish you, for the kindness that you showed in coming so long a journey to see me. It was pity to keep you so long in pain, but, upon reviewing the matter, I do not see what I could have done better than as I did.

I hope you found at your return my dear enemy and all her little people quite well,[3] and had no reason to repent your journey. I think on it with great gratitude.

I was not well when you left me at the Doctor's,[4] and I grew worse; yet I staid on, and at Lichfield was very ill. Travelling, however, did not make me worse; and when I came to London I complied with a summons to go to Brighthelmston, where I saw Beauclerk, and staid three days.[5]

Our club has recommenced last Friday, but I was not there. Langton has another wench.[6] Mrs. Thrale is in hopes of a young brewer.[7] They got by their trade last year a very large sum, and their expences are proportionate.[8]

Mrs. Williams's health is very bad. And I have had for some time a very difficult and laborious respiration, but I am better by purges, abstinence, and other methods. I am yet however much behind-hand in my health and rest.

Dr. Blair's sermons are now universally commended, but let him think that I had the honour of first finding and first praising his excellencies.[9] I did not stay to add my voice to that of the publick.

My dear friend, let me thank you once more for your visit;

2. JB omits "Beauclerk": see above, n. 1.
3. *Ante* To Margaret Boswell, 22 July 1777.
4. *Ante* To Hester Thrale, 22 Sept. 1777 and n. 5; 25 Sept. 1777.
5. *Ante* To Hester Thrale, 10 Nov. 1777.
6. Elizabeth (1777–1804), Bennet Langton's fifth child and fourth daughter, was born 21 Oct. (Fifer, p. lviii n. 29).
7. *Ante* To Hester Thrale, 6 Oct. 1777, n. 1.
8. *Ante* To Hester Thrale, 15 Sept. 1777 and nn. 8, 9.
9. *Ante* To William Strahan, 24 Dec. 1776 and n. 1.

you did me great honour, and I hope met with nothing that displeased you. I staid long at Ashbourne, not much pleased, yet aukward at departing. I then went to Lichfield, where I found my friend at Stowhill very dangerously diseased.[10] Such is life. Let us try to pass it well, whatever it be, for there is surely something beyond it.

Well, now I hope all is well, write as soon as you can to, dear Sir, Your affectionate servant,

SAM. JOHNSON

10. *Ante* To Elizabeth Aston, 20 Nov. 1777.

Thomas Johnson
TUESDAY 16 DECEMBER 1777

MS: Clifton College, Bristol.
ADDRESS: To Mr. Thomas Johnson.

Dear Tom: Dec. 16, 1777

Our good friend Mr. Rann[1] very kindly requires that I should give you some token of reconciliation.[2] Neither you nor I have any time to spare for quarrels or grudges. I desire you to think no more of what you may have done wrong with respect to me, and to consider me as your affectionate Kinsman and friend,

SAM. JOHNSON

My service to your Wife.

1. The Rev. Joseph Rann (?1733–1811), Vicar of Holy Trinity, Coventry (1773–1811), and editor of *Dramatic Works of Shakespeare, with Notes* (1776–81) (*Reades*, p. 224; Benjamin Poole, *Coventry: Its History and Antiquities*, 1870, pp. 196, 205). Thomas Johnson was one of Rann's parishioners. *Post* To Hester Thrale, 29 May 1779.
2. *Ante* To John Hollyer, 6 Dec. 1774 and n. 3.

<h1>Jane Gastrell</h1>

TUESDAY 23 DECEMBER 1777

MS: Pembroke College, Oxford.

Dear Madam: Bolt court, Fleetstreet, Dec. 23, 1777

Your long silence portended no good, yet, I hope, the danger is not so near as our anxiety sometimes makes us fear.[1] Winter is indeed to all those that any distemper has enfeebled a very troublesome time but care and caution may pass safely through it, and from Spring and Summer some relief is always to be hoped.

When I came hither, I fell to taking care of myself, and by physick and opium had the constriction that obstructed my breath very suddenly removed. My nights still continue very laborious and tedious, but they do not grow worse.

I do not ask You, Dear Madam, to take care of Mrs. Aston, I know how little You want any such exhortation, but I earnestly entreat her to take care of herself.[2] Many lives are prolonged by a diligent attention to little things, and I am far from thinking it unlikely that she may grow better by degrees. However, it is her duty to try, and when we do our duty we have reason to hope. I am, Dear Madam, your most humble Servant,

                                      SAM. JOHNSON

1. *Ante* To Elizabeth Aston, 20 Nov. 1777.

2. SJ had chastised Elizabeth Aston for her "resolute inactivity," hoping that she would at least "endeavour to grow well where You are" (*Ante* To Elizabeth Aston, 20 Nov. 1777).

<h1>James Boswell</h1>

SATURDAY 27 DECEMBER 1777

PRINTED SOURCE: JB's *Life*, 1791, II.180–81.

Dear Sir,   December 27, 1777

This is the time of the year in which all express their good wishes to their friends, and I send mine to you and your family. May your lives be long, happy, and good. I have been much out of order, but, I hope, do not grow worse.

The crime of the schoolmaster whom you are engaged to prosecute is very great, and may be suspected to be too common.[1] In our law it would be a breach of the peace, and a misdemeanour; that is, a kind of indefinite crime, not capital, but punishable at the discretion of the Court. You cannot want matter: all that needs to be said will easily occur.

Mr. Shaw, the authour of the Gaelick Grammar,[2] desires me to make a request for him to Lord Eglintoune,[3] that he may be appointed Chaplain to one of the new-raised regiments.[4]

All our friends are as they were; little has happened to them of either good or bad. Mrs. Thrale ran a great black hair-dressing pin into her eye; but by great evacuation she kept it from inflaming,[5] and it is almost well. Miss Reynolds has been out of order, but is better. Mrs. Williams is in a very poor state of health.

If I should write on, I should, perhaps, write only complaints, and therefore I will content myself with telling you, that I love to think on you, and to hear from you; and that I am, dear Sir, Yours faithfully,

SAM. JOHNSON

1. On 29 Nov. JB had reported to SJ: "I am engaged in a criminal prosecution against a country schoolmaster, for indecent behaviour to his female scholars. There is no statute against such abominable conduct; but it is punishable at common law. I shall be obliged to you for your assistance in this extraordinary trial" (*Life* III.212). John Bell, schoolmaster at Stewarton, Ayrshire, was tried before the High Court of Justiciary, which dismissed the case. Bell was reindicted, however, found guilty, and banished from Scotland for life (*Boswell in Extremes*, ed. C. M. Weis and F. A. Pottle, 1970, pp. 196–97 and nn. 5, 9).

2. *Ante* To JB, 11 Mar. 1777 and n. 3.

3. Archibald Montgomerie (1726–96), eleventh Earl of Eglinton, "the most influential of Ayrshire peers and landowners" (*Later Years*, p. 92), Colonel of the 51st Regiment of Foot and a neighbor, patron, client, and distant relation of JB (*Life* III.503; *Later Years*, p. 93).

4. There is no record that such a request was transmitted or acted upon.

5. *evacuation*: "the practice of emptying the body by physick" (SJ's *Dictionary*).

James Boswell

PRINTED SOURCE: JB's *Life*, 1791, II.182.

Dear Sir,   January 24, 1778

To a letter so interesting as your last, it is proper to return some answer, however little I may be disposed to write.

Your alarm at your lady's illness was reasonable, and not disproportionate to the appearance of the disorder.[1] I hope your physical friend's conjecture is now verified, and all fear of a consumption at an end:[2] a little care and exercise will then restore her. London is a good air for ladies; and if you bring her hither, I will do for her what she did for me—I will retire from my apartments, for her accommodation.[3] Behave kindly to her, and keep her cheerful.

You always seem to call for tenderness. Know then, that in the first month of the present year I very highly esteem and very cordially love you. I hope to tell you this at the beginning of every year as long as we live; and why should we trouble ourselves to tell or hear it oftener?

Tell Veronica, Euphemia, and Alexander, that I wish them, as well as their parents, many happy years.

1. On 8 Jan. JB informed SJ that Margaret Boswell had "for some time been very ill, having been confined to the house these three months by a severe cold, attended with alarming symptoms" (*Life* III.215). These symptoms, which included the spitting of blood, signaled the consumption that eventually killed her.

2. This "physical friend" was probably the surgeon Alexander Wood (1725–1807), who had been attending Margaret Boswell and doing his best to encourage JB (*Boswell in Extremes*, ed. C. M. Weis and F. A. Pottle, 1970, pp. 196, 202–3).

3. Surgeon Wood had suggested that "travelling might do [Mrs. Boswell] good, at least prolong life" (Weis and Pottle, *Extremes*, p. 204). On 12 Jan. JB informed Lord Pembroke: "I intend to take her into England as exercise and amusement and change of air will be the best remedys for her. She never would go to London with me to leave her children merely to be entertained. But now that a long Journey is prescribed for her I plese myself with the hopes of shewing her the Metropolis" (MS: Beinecke Library). This prospective trip never took place, however. Consequently SJ did not have the opportunity to turn over his bedroom to Margaret Boswell, as she had done for him in Aug. 1773 (*Life* V.24).

You have ended the negro's cause much to my mind.[4] Lord Auchinleck and dear Lord Hailes were on the side of liberty. Lord Hailes's name reproaches me; but if he saw my languid neglect of my own affairs, he would rather pity than resent my neglect of his.[5] I hope to mend, *ut et mihi vivam et amicis.*[6] I am, dear Sir, Your's affectionately,

SAM. JOHNSON

My service to my fellow-traveller, Joseph.[7]

4. *Ante* To JB, 22 July 1777, nn. 17, 18.

5. *Ante* To JB, 28 June 1777 and n. 1.

6. *ut et mihi vivam et amicis*: "in order that I may live both for myself and for my friends." SJ seems to be recalling and amplifying a fragment of Horace, *et mihi vivam* (*Epistles* I.xviii.107).

7. Joseph Ritter, JB's Bohemian servant, had accompanied SJ and JB on their Hebridean tour.

Thomas Cadell

WEDNESDAY 28 JANUARY 1778

MS: Hyde Collection.

ADDRESS: To Mr. Cadel.

Sir: Jan. 28, 1778

If you should obtain what[1] Mr. Davies tells me you design to ask, the office of Bookseller and Printer to the royal Academy,[2] I take the liberty of requesting, and I request with great earnestness, that for any thing to be printed for the Academy, you will make use [of] Mr. Allen's press in Boltcourt.[3] Mr.

1. MS: "what" altered from "which"

2. On 10 Feb. 1778 Thomas Cadell succeeded Thomas Davies as Bookseller and Printer to the Royal Academy of Arts, and remained in office until Mar. 1794 (Minutes of the Royal Academy Council: information supplied by Mr. Nicholas Savage, Deputy Librarian, Royal Academy).

3. According to the Minutes of the Royal Academy, 10 Feb. 1778, Cadell promised that "if he is elected Bookseller and Printer . . . he will . . . employ Mr. Allen as Printer in the same Manner as he was employed by Mr. Davies, provided he does the business to the satisfaction of Mr. Cadell." Cadell's imprint in the

Allen has hitherto done the work without payment, and having so long laboured only to his loss, it is reasonable that he should at last have some profit, at least some recompense.

Mr. Alen's business is not extensive, and he will be glad of work which greater Printers do not want, nor value, and if you continue him in the employment you will confer a great favour upon, Sir, your most humble Servant,

SAM. JOHNSON

Academy's exhibition catalogues, however, makes no mention of Allen (information supplied by Mr. Nicholas Savage). Cf. *Ante* To Edward Lye, 17 Aug. 1765; *Ante* To Edmund Allen, 19 June 1775.

Unidentified Correspondent
FRIDAY 30 JANUARY 1778

PRINTED SOURCE: JB's *Life*, ed. G. B. Hill, 1887, v.454.

Sir,   Bolt Court, Fleet Street, Jan. 30, 1778

Poor Mr. Gwyn is in great distress under the weight of the late determination against him, and has still hopes that some mitigation may be obtained.[1] If it be true that whatever has by his negligence been amiss, may be redressed for a sum much less than has been awarded, the remaining part ought in equity to be returned, or, what is more desirable, abated. When the money is once paid, there is little hope of getting it again.

The load is, I believe, very hard upon him; he indulges some flattering opinions that by the influence of his academical friends it may be lightened, and will not be persuaded but that some testimony of my kindness may be beneficial. I hope he has been guilty of nothing worse than credulity, and he then certainly deserves commiseration. I never heard otherwise than that he was an honest man, and I hope that by your

1. *Ante* To Hester Thrale, 4 Aug. 1777 and n. 2. No record of the desired "mitigation" has been discovered.

countenance and that of other gentlemen who favour or pity him some relief may be obtained. I am, Sir, Your most humble servant,

SAM. JOHNSON

Saunders Welch

TUESDAY 3 FEBRUARY 1778

PRINTED SOURCE: JB's *Life*, 1791, II.269–70.
ADDRESS: To Saunders Welch, Esq., at the English Coffee-House, Rome.

Dear Sir,   Feb. 3, 1778

To have suffered one of my best and dearest friends to pass almost two years in foreign countries without a letter, has a very shameful appearance of inattention.[1] But the truth is, that there was no particular time in which I had any thing particular to say; and general expressions of good will, I hope, our long friendship is grown too solid to want.

Of publick affairs you have information from the newspapers wherever you go, for the English keep no secret; and of other things, Mrs. Nollekens informs you. My intelligence could therefore be of no use; and Miss Nancy's letters made it unnecessary to write to you for information: I was likewise for some time out of humour, to find that motion, and nearer approaches to the sun, did not restore your health so fast as I expected. Of your health, the accounts have lately been more pleasing; and I have the gratification of imaging to myself a length of years which I hope you have gained, and of which the enjoyment will be improved, by a vast accession of images and observations which your journeys and various residence have enabled you to make and accumulate. You have travelled with this felicity, almost peculiar to yourself, that your companion is not to part from you at your journey's end; but you are to live on together, to help each other's recollection, and to

1. *Ante* To Hester Thrale, 14 May 1776 and n. 9.

supply each other's omissions. The world has few greater pleasures than that which two friends enjoy, in tracing back, at some distant time, those transactions and events through which they have passed together. One of the old man's miseries is, that he cannot easily find a companion able to partake with him of the past. You and your fellow-traveller have this comfort in store, that your conversation will be not easily exhausted; one will always be glad to say what the other will always be willing to hear.

That you may enjoy this pleasure long, your health must have your constant attention. I suppose you purpose to return this year.[2] There is no need of haste: do not come hither before the height of summer, that you may fall gradually into the inconveniences of your native clime. July seems to be the proper month. August and September will prepare you for the winter. After having travelled so far to find health, you must take care not to lose it at home; and I hope a little care will effectually preserve it.

Miss Nancy has doubtless kept a constant and copious journal. She must not expect to be welcome when she returns without a great mass of information. Let her review her journal often, and set down what she finds herself to have omitted, that she may trust to memory as little as possible, for memory is soon confused by a quick succession of things; and she will grow every day less confident of the truth of her own narratives, unless she can recur to some written memorials. If she has satisfied herself with hints, instead of full representations, let her supply the deficiencies now while her memory is yet fresh, and while her father's memory may help her. If she observes this direction, she will not have travelled in vain; for she will bring home a book with which she may entertain herself to the end of life. If it were not now too late, I would advise her to note the impression which the first sight of any thing new and wonderful made upon her mind. Let her now

2. The precise date of Welch's return has not been determined. He and his daughter were definitely back in England by 1780 (J. T. Smith, *Nollekens and His Times*, ed. Wilfred Whitten, 1917, I.238).

set her thoughts down as she can recollect them; for faint as they already be, they will grow every day fainter.

Perhaps I do not flatter myself unreasonably when I imagine that you may wish to know something of me. I can gratify your benevolence with no account of health. The hand of time, or of disease, is very heavy upon me. I pass restless and uneasy nights, harassed with convulsions of my breast, and flatulencies at my stomach; and restless nights make heavy days. But nothing will be mended by complaints, and therefore I will make an end. When we meet, we will try to forget our cares and our maladies, and contribute, as we can, to the chearfulness of each other. If I had gone with you, I believe I should have been better; but I do not know that it was in my power. I am, dear Sir, Your most humble servant,

SAM. JOHNSON

Lucy Porter

THURSDAY 19 FEBRUARY 1778

MS: Hyde Collection.

Dear Madam: Febr. 19, 1778

I have several little things to mention which I have hitherto neglected.

You judged rightly in thinking that the Bust[1] would not please.[2] It is condemned by Mrs. Thrale, Mrs. Reynolds, and Mrs. Garrick, so that your disapprobation is not singular.

These things have never cost me any thing, so that I do not much know the price. My Bust was made for the exhibition, and shown for the honour of the artist, who is a man of reputation above any of the other Sculptors. To be modeled in clay

1. MS: "Bust" superimposed upon undeciphered erasure
2. *Ante* To Joseph Nollekens, 27 Aug. 1777 and n. 2; *Ante* To Lucy Porter, 20 Nov. 1777.

costs, I believe, twenty guineas, but the casts when the model is made, are of no great price, whether a guinea or two guineas I cannot tell.[3]

About Mrs. Thrale's table linen I was mistaken. She bought three tablecloths for twenty five pounds each, which coming to seventy five pound, caused the mistake.

When you complained for want of Oysters, I ordered you a barrel weekly for a month, you sent me word sooner that you had enough, but I did not countermand the rest. If you could not eat them you could give them away. When you want any thing send me word.

I am very poorly, and have very restless and oppressive nights, but always hope[4] for better. Pray for me. I am your most humble servant,

SAM. JOHNSON

3. Nollekens charged between two and three guineas for a cast (J. T. Smith, *Nollekens and His Times*, ed. Wilfred Whitten, 1917, II.13 n. 1).

4. MS: "hope" superimposed upon undeciphered erasure

John Nichols[1]

c. MARCH 1778[2]

MS: British Library.
ADDRESS: To Mr. Nichol.

In the Life of Waller Mr. Nichol will find a reference to the *Parliamentary Hist.* from which a long quotation is to be in-

1. John Nichols printed SJ's *Prefaces, Biographical and Critical, to the Works of the English Poets*, and assisted him by collecting and checking information (William McCarthy, "The Composition of Johnson's *Lives*: A Calendar," *Philological Quarterly* 60, 1981, p. 53). This letter begins the series of "little billets," which, according to Nichols, "tend to illustrate the history of that *Opus Magnum*" (GM 1785, p. 9).

2. F. W. Hilles, whose redating of SJ's "billets" I follow, assigns this letter conjecturally to Mar. 1778 ("Johnson's Correspondence with Nichols," *Philological Quarterly* 48, 1969, pp. 226, 228). As Hilles points out, SJ had received proofs of his "Life of Waller" by 17 Apr. (*Life* III.313).

serted,³ if Mr. Nichol cannot easily find the book, Mr. Johnson will send it from Streatham.

Clarendon is here returned.⁴

3. SJ quotes from Waller's speech (June 1641) on "the great question, whether Episcopacy ought to be abolished" (*Lives of the Poets* I.257–59).

4. In his biography SJ quotes and comments on Lord Clarendon's "character of Waller, both moral and intellectual" (*Lives of the Poets* I.277–79).

Elizabeth Montagu

THURSDAY 5 MARCH 1778

MS: Huntington Library.

ADDRESS: To Mrs. Montague.

Madam,   March 5, 1778

And so You are alarmed, naughty Lady; You might know that I was ill enough when Mr. Thrale brought You my excuse. Could You think that I missed the honour of being at ⟨your⟩¹ table for any slight reason? But You ⟨have⟩ too many to miss any one of us, and I am ⟨proud⟩ to be remembred at last.

I am much better. A little cough ⟨still⟩ remains which will not confine me. To houses, ⟨like yours⟩ of great delicacy I am not willing to bring it.

Now, dear Madam, we must talk of business. Poor Davies, the bankrupt Bookseller, is soliciting his Friends to collect a small sum for the repurchase of part of his household stuff.² Several of them give him five guineas. It would be an honour to him, to owe part of his relief to Mrs. Montague.³

Let me thank you, Madam, once more for your enquiry;

1. MS: torn along right-hand margin; missing words supplied in an unidentified hand

2. SJ "called upon all over whom he had any influence to assist Tom Davies; and prevailed on Mr. Sheridan, patentee of Drury-lane Theatre, to let him have a benefit" (*Lit. Anec.* VI.430). Receipts for this performance (of Congreve's *Way of the World,* 27 May 1778) came to £198 9s. 6d. (*Lond. Stage,* Part v, i.177).

3. *Post* To Elizabeth Montagu, 6 Mar. 1778.

You have perhaps among your numerous train, not ⟨one⟩ that values a kind word or a kind look more than, Madam, Your most humble Servant,

SAM. JOHNSON

Elizabeth Montagu

FRIDAY 6 MARCH 1778

PRINTED SOURCE: JB's *Life*, ed. Croker, 1831, IV.75.

Madam,   6th March 1778

I hope Davies, who does not want wit, does not want gratitude, and then he will be almost as thankful for the bill as I am for the letter that enclosed it.[1]

If I do not lose, what I hope always to keep, my reverence for transcendent merit, I shall continue to be with unalterable fidelity, Madam, Your most obliged, and most humble servant,

SAM. JOHNSON

1. *Ante* To Elizabeth Montagu, 5 Mar. 1778.

William Adams

TUESDAY 7 APRIL 1778

MS: Historical Society of Pennsylvania.

ENDORSEMENT: Dr. Johnson, 7 Apr. 1778 [*added in an unidentified hand*] to Dr. Adams, Master of Pembroke Coll.

Dear Sir: Boltcourt, Fleetstreet, Apr. 7, 1778

When I travelled in Scotland, I was one Night at the House of a Minister named Macaulay, who had been sent to visit the Island of St. Kilda, and under whose name the last account of it is published.[1] In our evening's conversation I gave an account of the University of Oxford, and excited first in the

1. *Ante* To JB, 27 May 1775 and n. 6.

Lady and then in the Minister a desire of having their Son educated amongst us. They were[2] content that he should be a Servitor, and I promised my endeavour in his favour.[3] This promise is now claimed, and I take the liberty of soliciting your assistance. If you have any vacancy I hope you will please to receive him, if you are[4] full, it will [be] a great favour if you will enquire after a vacancy in any other house.[5] I am, Sir, Your most obedient and most humble Servant,

SAM. JOHNSON

2. MS: "w" superimposed upon "d"

3. "Mr. Johnson had given an account of the education at Oxford in all its gradations. The advantages of being a servitor, to a youth of little fortune, struck Mrs. Macaulay much. . . . Mr. Johnson very handsomely and kindly said that if they would send their boy to him when he was ready for the University, he would get him made a servitor. . . . The father did not take it so warmly as I should have thought he would. . . . But Mrs. Macaulay was wisely and truly grateful" (*Hebrides*, p. 89).   4. MS: "are" repeated as catchword

5. Dr. Adams did obtain a servitorship for Aulay Macaulay, who chose a military career instead and became a lieutenant in the Marines in 1779 (*Life* v.122 n. 2, v.505).

Richard Clark

WEDNESDAY 22 APRIL 1778

MS: Houghton Library.
ADDRESS: To——Clark, Esq.
ENDORSEMENT: 22d April 1778, Dr. Johnson.

Dear Sir: Apr. 22, 1778

I think myself very much favoured by your invitation.[1] Mr. Langton will fix the day.

I have a request to make which, I hope, is not improper, nor such as will give you much trouble. There is in Christ's Hospi-

1. In his capacity as Sheriff of London, Clark had invited SJ to "a dinner given at the Old Bailey to the judges, counsel, and a few guests." At the dinner, 30 Apr., "Mr. Justice Blackstone conversed with Johnson on the subject of their absent friend, Sir Robert Chambers" (Croker VII.192–93 n. 3).

tal, a little boy one George Angel,[2] whose Grandfather I once knew, and who had hardly any friend left, but a Lady who happened to be his Godmother. This little boy desires himself and his Godmother desires for him, that he may be put into the Grammar School; which we hope, Sir, to effect by your influence,[3] and that You will be pleased to exert your influence in his favour, is very warmly desired by, Sir, your most obedient and most humble Servant,

SAM. JOHNSON

2. George Angell (b. 1766), the son of George Angell, "Citizen and Joyner," was an orphan, and, at the time of his admission to Christ's Hospital in 1773, "quite destitute of means to support him" (Guildhall Library MSS: 12,818/11, p. 16; 12,818A/43, No. 128).

3. Though Clark was not a governor of Christ's Hospital (Guildhall Library MS: 12,857B), he apparently acted successfully on SJ's application: George Angell continued as a student until Dec. 1782, when he was discharged to serve under "Thomas Lewes Esqr. Commander of His Majesty's Ship Romney" (Guildhall Library MS: 12,818/11, p. 16).

James Boswell
THURSDAY 23 APRIL 1778

MS: Beinecke Library. The transcript (in the hand of JB) used as copy for his *Life*.

Sir, Apr. 23, —78

The debate between Dr. Percy and me is one of those foolish controversies which begin upon a question of which neither party cares how it is decided, and which is nevertheless continued to acrimony, by the vanity with which every man resists confutation.[1] Dr. Percy's warmth proceeded from a cause

1. On 12 Apr. SJ and Thomas Percy had quarreled over the merits of Thomas Pennant's *Tour in Scotland*, SJ maintaining that Pennant "describes very well" and Percy criticizing Pennant *inter alia* for an inaccurate account of the Duke of Northumberland's estate (*Life* III.271–74). In his role as peacemaker, JB suggested to SJ a stratagem for mending the breach: "I will write a letter to you upon the subject of the unlucky contest of that day, and you will be kind enough to put in writing as an answer to that letter, what you have now said" (*Life* III.276). Both letters were duly read out loud in the presence of Lord Percy; "thus every unfavourable im-

which perhaps does him more honour than he could have derived from juster criticism. His abhorrence of Pennant proceeded from his opinion, that Pennant had wantonly and indecently censured his Patron, His anger made him resolve that for having been once wrong, he never should be right. Pennant has much in his notions that I do not like; but still I think him a very intelligent traveller. If Percy is[2] really offended, I am sorry, for he is a man whom I never knew to offend any one. He is a man very willing to learn, and very able to teach; A man out of whose company I never go without having learned something. It is sure that he vexes me sometimes, but I am afraid it is by making me feel my own ignorance. So much extension of mind, and so much minute accuracy of enquiry, if you survey your whole circle of acquaintance, you will find so scarce, if you find it at all, that you will value Percy by comparison. Lord Hailes is somewhat like him, But Lord Hailes does not perhaps go beyond him in research and I do not know, that he equals him in elegance. Percy's attention to Poetry, has given grace and splendour to his studies of Antiquity. A mere Antiquarian[3] is a rugged Being.

Upon the whole, you see that what I might say in sport or petulance to him, is very consistent with full conviction of his merit. I am, Dear Sir, Your most etc.

SAM. JOHNSON

---

pression was obviated that could possibly have been made on those by whom he [Thomas Percy] wished most to be regarded" (*Life* III.276).

2. MS: "is" repeated as catchword

3. MS: "Antiquarian" repeated as catchword

Mauritius Lowe[1]

TUESDAY 28 APRIL 1778

1. Mauritius Lowe (1746–93), an indigent painter and illegitimate son of the second Baron Southwell, for whom SJ did everything in his power, including soliciting patronage and charitable contributions (*Life* IV.201–2; *Post* To William Hunter, 2 June 1778). SJ was godfather to Lowe's son and to one of his daughters (*Life* IV.202–3 n. 1).

MS: Hyde Collection.

ADDRESS: To Mr.[2]

Sir: Apr. 28, 1778

I spoke at the exhibition to Sir Joshuah and Mr. Garrick,[3] and found both of them cold enough. Mr. Garrick however seemed to relent, and I think you have reason to expect some thing from him, but he must be tenderly handled. I have however just received what will please and surprise you. I have sent it just as it came, and give you joy.[4] I am, Sir, your humble Servant,

SAM. JOHNSON

Write to return thanks.[5]

2. MS: mutilated; name of addressee missing

3. The spring exhibition of the Royal Academy of Arts opened 24 Apr., as was the custom, following the annual dinner on St. George's Day, 23 Apr. (Sidney Hutchison, *The History of the Royal Academy, 1768–1986*, 1986, p. 39).

4. On their way to dine at Pasquale Paoli's, 28 Apr., JB and SJ "stopped first at the bottom of Hedge-lane, into which he went to leave a letter, 'with good news for a poor man in distress,' as he told me" (*Life* III.324). Lowe lived at No. 3 Hedge Lane.

5. Lowe wrote to Garrick on 15 May, acknowledging the gift of ten pounds (*Private Correspondence of David Garrick*, ed. James Boaden, 1831–32, II.306).

Hester Thrale

THURSDAY 30 APRIL 1778

MS: Hyde Collection.

Dear Madam: Apr. 30, 1778

Since I was fetched away from Streatham the journal stands thus[1]

Saturday, Sir J. R. Sunday, Mr. Hoole.
Monday, Lord Lucan. Tuesday, Gen. Paoli.

1. The calendar that follows runs from Saturday, 25 Apr., to Sunday, 3 May.

Wednesday Mr. Ramsay.[2] Thursday, Old Baily.[3]
Fryday, Club. Saturday Sir J. R.
Sunday Lady Lucan.[4]

Monday, pray let it be Streatham, and very early, do now let it be very early. For I may be carried away—just like Ganymede of Troy.

I hope my Master grows well, and my Mistress continues bad.[5] I am afraid the Ladies will be gone,[6] and[7] I shall say

She's gone, and never knew how much I lov'd her.

Do now let me know whether you will send for me—early— on Monday. But take some care, or your letter will not come till tuesday. I am, Dearest Lady, Your most humble Servant,

SAM. JOHNSON

2. Allan Ramsay (1713–84), prominent Scots portraitist and Principal Painter to the King, lived at No. 67 Harley Street, where he frequently entertained SJ and other members of The Club (*Life* III.391 n. 2). According to SJ, who appears to have met Ramsay through Sir Joshua Reynolds, "you will not find a man in whose conversation there is more instruction, more information, and more elegance, than in Ramsay's" (*Life* III.336).

3. *Ante* To Richard Clark, 22 Apr. 1778, n. 1.

4. Margaret Bingham (d. 1814), Baroness Lucan, daughter of James Smith of Canonsleigh, Devon, and wife (m. 1760) of Sir Charles Bingham, Bt., first Baron (and later first Earl of) Lucan. Lady Lucan, a prominent Bluestocking, was an amateur painter and poet (*Life* IV.540; *Walpole's Correspondence*, Yale ed. XXIX.104).

5. *Ante* To Hester Thrale, 6 Oct. 1777 and n. 1.

6. "The Ladies" may have included Sophia Streatfeild (1754–1835), the beautiful young Greek scholar whom Hester Thrale had met at Brighton the preceding fall and who rapidly became an intimate friend (Clifford, 1952, p. 168; Hyde, 1977, pp. 193, 202).

7. MS: "and and"

John Nichols

SATURDAY 2 MAY 1778

PRINTED SOURCE: *GM* 1785, p. 10.

May 2, 1779[1]

As Waller professed to have imitated Fairfax, do you think a

1. F. W. Hilles argues persuasively that, given the contents of this note, it must

few pages of Fairfax would enrich our edition? Few readers have seen it, and it may please them. But it is not necessary.[2]

belong to the spring of 1778. He suggests that "years later Nichols might have read Johnson's figure 8 as a 9 . . . or, of course, the compositor could have erred in setting up the date" ("Johnson's Correspondence with Nichols," *Philological Quarterly* 48, 1969, p. 232).

2. SJ's "Waller" concludes with an extract from Book VII of Edward Fairfax's translation of Tasso's *Gerusalemme Liberata* (*Lives of the Poets* 1.296–300).

William Hunter

TUESDAY 2 JUNE 1778

MS: Hyde Collection.

Sir: June 2, 1778

Though I am under great obligations to Mr. Hunter, your Brother,[1] for[2] the kind attention which he shows to my servant,[3] yet not having ever seen him I take the liberty of applying to him again[4] by your intervention.

Mr. Lowe, an artist who gained the prize in the academy,[5] has a disorder which Mr. Lockhart thinks very dangerous, and such as requires an operation which neither he nor the patient cares to venture without a consultation. It is therefore requested of Mr. Hunter that he will be pleased to appoint a time, as soon as is possible to meet Mr. Lockhart, and inspect the malady.

Mr. Ramsay's letter comes with mine, but Mr. Ramsay did

1. John Hunter (1728–93), M.D., celebrated surgeon and specialist in human and comparative anatomy. "As an investigator, original thinker, and stimulator of thought, Hunter stands at the head of British surgeons" (*DNB* x.291).

2. MS: "f" superimposed upon "y"

3. SJ refers to Francis Barber.

4. MS: "a" superimposed upon "b"

5. *Ante* To Mauritius Lowe, 28 Apr. 1778, n. 1. The prize, which Lowe received in 1769, was the first gold medal awarded by the Royal Academy for an historical painting. Its subject was *Time Discovering Truth*.

not well know what was desired, and I could not in company explain it. I am, Sir, Your most humble servant,

SAM. JOHNSON

When I came to turn my letter I found I had been writing on a broken sheet, but you can excuse greater things.

James Boswell
FRIDAY 3 JULY 1778

PRINTED SOURCE: JB's *Life*, 1791, II.274.

Dear Sir,   London, July 3, 1778

I have received two letters from you, of which the second complains of the neglect shown to the first.[1] You must not tye your friends to such punctual correspondence. You have all possible assurances of my affection and esteem; and there ought to be no need of reiterated professions. When it may happen that I can give you either counsel or comfort, I hope it will never happen to me that I should neglect you; but you must not think me criminal or cold if I say nothing, when I have nothing to say.

You are now happy enough. Mrs. Boswell is recovered; and I congratulate you upon the probability of her long life.[2] If general approbation will add any thing to your enjoyment, I can tell you that I have heard you mentioned as *a man whom every body likes*. I think life has little more to give.

—— has gone to his regiment.[3] He has laid down his coach, and talks of making more contractions of his expence: how he will succeed I know not. It is difficult to reform a household gradually; it may be better done by a system totally new. I am

1. JB had written to SJ on 25 May and again on 18 June (*Life* III.359).

2. *Ante* To JB, 24 Jan. 1778 and n. 1.

3. SJ refers to Bennet Langton. *Ante* To JB, 28 June 1777 and n. 19; *Post* To Bennet Langton, 29 Aug. 1778 and n. 1.

afraid he has always something to hide. When we pressed him to go to —— ,[4] he objected the necessity of attending his navigation;[5] yet he could talk of going to Aberdeen, a place not much nearer his navigation. I believe he cannot bear the thought of living at —— in a state of diminution; and of appearing among the gentlemen of the neighbourhood *shorn of his beams.*[6] This is natural, but it is cowardly. What I told him of the encreasing expence of a growing family seems to have struck him.[7] He certainly had gone on with very confused views, and we have, I think, shown him that he is wrong; though, with the common deficience of advisers, we have not shown him how to do right.

I wish you would a little correct or restrain your imagination, and imagine that happiness, such as life admits, may be had at other places as well as London.[8] Without asserting[9] Stoicism, it may be said, that it is our business to exempt ourselves as much as we can from the power of external things. There is but one solid basis of happiness; and that is, the reasonable hope of a happy futurity. This may be had every where.

I do not blame your preference of London to other places, for it is really to be preferred, if the choice is free; but few have the choice of their place, or their manner of life; and mere pleasure ought not to be the prime motive of action.

Mrs. Thrale, poor thing, has a daughter.[10] Mr. Thrale dislikes the times, like the rest of us. Mrs. Williams is sick; Mrs.

4. SJ presumably refers to the family seat at Langton, Lincolnshire. *Ante* To Bennet Langton, 6 May 1755, n. 2.

5. *Ante* To Bennet Langton, 20 Mar. 1771, n. 4.

6. SJ accomplishes a triple allusion by quoting a phrase from Milton (*Paradise Lost* 1.596) that appears in Dryden's translation of the *Aeneid* (IX.887); the Dryden in turn is quoted under *shorn* in SJ's *Dictionary.*

7. *Ante* To JB, 25 Nov. 1777 and n. 6.

8. JB had begun to consider transferring to the English Bar, a step he eventually took in 1786 (*Later Years*, pp. 312–14, 318).

9. Edmond Malone conjecturally emended "asserting" to "affecting" (*Life* III.363 n. a, 529).

10. *Ante* To Hester Thrale, 6 Oct. 1777, n. 1; *Ante* To JB, 25 Nov. 1777.

Desmoulins is poor. I have miserable nights. Nobody is well but Mr. Levett. I am, dear Sir, your most, etc.

SAM. JOHNSON

Richard Clark

FRIDAY 17 JULY 1778

MS: Guildhall Library.

ADDRESS: To Richard Clerk, Esq., Sheriff of London, Great Broad Street; Streatham, July 16.

POSTMARK: [Undeciphered].

ENDORSEMENT: Dr. Johnson, 17 July 1778.

Dear Sir: Streatham in Surrey, July 17, 1778

I know your kindness for literature, and therefore have not much difficulty in soliciting your help, even though You cannot give it but with considerable trouble.

In the Life of Dryden, of which I have written a great part it will be necessary to say something of Settle, who had once the honour of being his Antagonist.[1] Settle, as I have learned, was the City Poet, and the last who bore that[2] title.[3] If you have the power of making the necessary enquiries I would wish to know.

The history of the office—when or how it began—the succession of City Laureats—their salary—their employment—when Settle obtained it—how long he held it—[4]

Settle died in the Chartreux. I would wish to know the year

1. The controversy with Elkanah Settle (1648–1724), poet and dramatist, began with Dryden's attack in *Notes and Observations on the Empress of Morocco* (1674) (J. A. Winn, *John Dryden and His World*, 1987, pp. 255–61).

2. MS: "that" altered from "the"

3. In his "Dryden," SJ identifies Settle as "the city poet, whose annual office was to describe the glories of the Mayor's day. Of these bards he was the last" (*Lives of the Poets* 1.376).

4. Clark passed on SJ's letter to Thomas Whittell, who replied from the Guildhall, 26 Aug.: "Upon the strictest Search in the City Books I cannot find there was such an Officer as City Poet, under that Denomination. There is an Account and

of his reception, and of his death.[5] But unless You have some very ready means of obtaining this knowledge, I will not trouble you about it, for I think, I can find means of obtaining what is known at the Chartreux.

The account of the City Poet will be a great addition to my Work. I am, Sir, Your most humble servant,

SAM. JOHNSON

---

several Records of a City Cronologer; and as Ben. Johnson was admitted to that Office and after him Frans. Quarles ... it is likely they were poetical Chronologers" (Guildhall Library MS: 3790).

5. Settle was admitted to the Charterhouse *c.* 1718, and died there in 1724.

James Elphinston
MONDAY 27 JULY 1778

PRINTED SOURCE: William Shaw, *Memoirs of the Life and Writings of the Late Dr. Samuel Johnson*, 1785, pp. 168–70. Collated with the text in James Elphinston, *Forty Years' Correspondence*, 1791, II.246–48.

Sir,
                                          July 27, 1778

Having myself suffered what you are now suffering, I well know the weight of your distress, how much need you have of comfort, and how little comfort can be given.[1] A loss, such as yours, lacerates the mind, and breaks the whole system of purposes and hopes. It leaves a dismal vacuity in life, which[2] affords nothing on which the affections can fix, or to which endeavour may be directed.[3] All this I have known, and it is now, in the vicissitude of things, your turn to know it.

But in[4] the condition of mortal beings, one must lose another. What would be the wretchedness of life, if there was[5]

1. Clementina, Elphinston's wife (m. 1751), had just died. She was the daughter of James Gordon, brother of General Alexander Gordon of Auchintoul, Banffshire (*Scottish Notes and Queries* 5 [3d ser.], 1927, p. 29).
2. "dhat" (Elphinston)   3. Cf. *Post* To Thomas Lawrence, 20 Jan. 1780.
4. "dhis" (Elphinston)   5. "wer" (Elphinston)

not something always in view,[6] some Being, immutable and unfailing, to whose mercy man may have recourse. τὸν πρῶτον κινοῦντα ἀκίνητον.[7]

Here we must rest. The greatest Being is the most benevolent. We must not grieve for the dead as men without hope, because we know that they are in his hands.[8] We have, indeed, not leisure to grieve long, because we are hastening[9] to follow them. Your race and mine have been interrupted by many obstacles, but we must humbly hope for an[10] happy end. I am, Sir, Your most humble servant,

SAM. JOHNSON

6. "somthing to' be kept always in vew" (Elphinston)

7. τὸ πρῶτον κινοῦν ἀκίνητον αὐτό: "the 'prime mover' is itself unmoved" (Aristotle, *Metaphysics* IV.viii.8, trans. Hugh Tredennick, Loeb ed.).

8. "O Merciful God . . . who also hath taught us (by his holy Apostle Saint Paul) not to be sorry, as men without hope, for them that sleep in him: We meekly beseech thee, O Father, to raise us from the death of sin unto the life of righteousness" ("The Order for the Burial of the Dead," *Book of Common Prayer*).

9. "hasting" (Elphinston)   10. "a" (Elphinston)

John Nichols
MONDAY 27 JULY 1778

MS: British Library.
ADDRESS: To Mr. Nichol.

Sir: July 27, 1778

You have now all *Cowley.* I have been drawn to a great length, but *Cowley* or *Waller* never had any critical examination before. I am very far advanced in *Dryden,*[1] who will be long too. The next great life I purpose to be *Milton's.*

It will be kind if you will gather the Lives of *Denham, Butler,* and *Waller,* and bind them in half binding in a small volume, and let me have it to show to my Friends, as soon as may be.[2]

1. MS: underlining extends under "in" and part of "who"

2. "A volume containing the *Prefaces* to Cowley, Butler, Waller, and Denham, now in the Hyde Collection, has been described as an 'uncorrected proof' state, but it contains press-figures and some binder's directions in Butler. . . . No proofs

I sincerely hope the press shall stand no more. I am, Sir, Your most humble servant,

SAM. JOHNSON

---

ever have press-figures or directions, and it is clear that this book is an advance copy—probably the one asked for by Johnson in his letter of 27 July 1778" (J. D. Fleeman, "Some Proofs of Johnson's *Prefaces to the Poets*," *The Library* 17, 1962, p. 215 n. 2).

William Strahan

MONDAY 27 JULY 1778

MS: Beinecke Library. The transcript (in the hand of William Strahan) used as copy for JB's *Life*.

Sir:

It would be very foolish for us to continue Strangers any longer.[1] You can never by Persistency make wrong, right. If I resented too acrimoniously, I resented only to yourself. Nobody ever saw or heard what I wrote. You saw that my Anger was over, for in a Day or two, I came to your House. I have given you longer time,[2] and I hope you have made so good use of it, as to be no longer on evil Terms with, Sir, Your etc.

SAM. JOHNSON

1. The cause of the quarrel between SJ and Strahan has not been determined. JB considered the "particulars" of the affair "unnecessary to relate" (*Life* III.364), and Strahan's modern biographer has not uncovered the reasons for their estrangement (J. A. Cochrane, *Dr. Johnson's Printer*, 1964, p. 145).

2. "After this time, the same friendship as formerly continued between Dr. Johnson and Mr. Strahan" (*Life* III.364).

Joshua Reynolds

FRIDAY 14 AUGUST 1778

MS: Yale Center for British Art.

Aug. 14

Mr. Johnson hopes that Sir Joshua Reynolds will do this little book the honour of reading it, and that he will then return it.[1]

1. *Ante* To John Nichols, 27 July 1778 and n. 2.

John Nichols
c. MID-AUGUST 1778[1]

MS: British Library.
ADDRESS: To Mr. Nichols.

Sir:

You have now the life of Dryden and you see it is very long. It must however have an appendix.

1. The invocation to the Georgicks from Milbourne (this in the small print).[2]

2. Drydens remarks on Rymer, which are ready transcribed.[3]

3. Drydens letter from Lambeth, which is promised me.[4] I am, Sir, etc.

1. SJ's "Dryden" was in press by 23 Aug. (*Diary and Letters of Madame D'Arblay*, ed. Austin Dobson, 1904, I.86).

2. Toward the end of "Dryden," SJ inserts Luke Milbourne's version of the invocation to Virgil's *Georgics*, so that, "according to his [Milbourne's] own proposal, his verses may be compared with those which he censures" (*Lives of the Poets* I.470).

3. "Mr. Dryden, having received from [Thomas] Rymer his *Remarks on the Tragedies of the last Age*, wrote observations on the blank leaves, which, having been in the possession of Mr. Garrick, are by his favour communicated to the publick" (*Lives of the Poets* I.471).

4. William Vyse supplied SJ with a copy (from the original in the Lambeth Library) of a letter from Dryden to his sons in Rome, Sept. 1697 (*Lives of the Poets* I.479–81).

Bennet Langton
SATURDAY 29 AUGUST 1778

MS: Hyde Collection.
ADDRESS: To Captain Langton, at Warly Camp.[1]

1. During the summer of 1778, Langton (a captain in the North Lincolnshire militia) was stationed at the camp on Warley Common, Essex (*Life* III.360–61; Fifer, pp. 316–20, 386).

Dear Sir: Aug. 29, 1778

I received your letter, and thought you very kind in writing so soon, but one little hindrance or other making it difficult for me to fix a time for the visit which I am extremely desirous of making, I omitted to write. I have now another hindrance having lamed one of my knees so much, that I shall get no credit in the field. When it is well, I purpose to come, and will certainly send you word two or three days before. I am not indifferent about it, but shall grieve very much if I miss the sight, when by your friendship I can have it with so much convenience.[2]

I have lately heard from Boswel who seems to be in his *old lunes*.[3] He wants to come to town.[4] I hope your Lady and all the rest got well through their Journey. I am, Dear Sir, your most obliged and most humble servant,

SAM. JOHNSON

2. SJ visited Langton for five days in September (*Life* III.361 and n. 1; *Post* To JB, 21 Nov. 1778). *Post* To Bennet Langton, 31 Oct. 1778.

3. "Why, woman, your husband is in his old lines again" (*Merry Wives of Windsor* IV.ii.17–18). SJ subscribes to the traditional emendation of *lines* to *lunes*.

4. JB had written to SJ on 18 Aug. His next trip to London did not take place until Mar. 1779 (*Life* III.366, 373).

Thomas Lawrence
TUESDAY 13 OCTOBER 1778

MS: Hyde Collection.
ADDRESS: To Dr. Laurence.

Dear Sir: Oct. 13, 1778

I am much distressed in the night and have lately had such an account of Musk that I wish to try it,[1] unless you think it

1. Musk, prescribed for various nervous complaints, was thought to abate pain, raise the spirits, and promote sleep. "This medicine is now received in general practice, in different convulsive disorders; and its dose has been increased, with advantage, to a scruple, and half a dram, every four or six hours" (William Lewis, *Materia Medica*, 3d ed., 1784, p. 429).

improper.[2] If you consent to the use of it, my request is that you will send your servant, or my servant with a note, to Apothecaries Hall, to buy it.[3] I may then expect to have it good. It is, I find four pound an ounce, I would have a dram.[4] I am, Sir, Your most humble servant,   SAM. JOHNSON

2. *Post* To Hester Thrale, 15 Oct. 1778.

3. "Apothecaries Hall, Water Lane, Blackfriars, a brick and stone building, erected in 1670 as the Dispensary and Hall of the Incorporated Company of Apothecaries" (Wheatley and Cunningham 1.55).

4. *dram*: "in weight the eighth part of an ounce" (SJ's *Dictionary*).

Hester Thrale

THURSDAY 15 OCTOBER 1778

MS: Hyde Collection.

Dearest Madam: Octr. 15, 1778

You that are among all the Wits, delighting and delighted, have little need of Entertainment from me whom you left at home unregarded and unpitied, to shift in a world to which you have made me so much a stranger,[1] yet I know you will pretend to be angry if I do not write a letter which when you know the hand you will perhaps lay aside to be read when you are dressing to morrow, and which when you have read it, if that time ever comes you will throw away into the draw and say—Stuff!

As to Dr. Collier's Epitaph, Nollikens has had it so long, that I have forgotten how long. You never had it. So you may set the Stratfields at defiance.[2]

There is a print of Mrs. Montague, and I shall think my self

1. In order to divert Henry, who was suffering from depression, the Thrales had embarked on an excursion "to various watering-places in the south of England" (Clifford, 1952, p. 172). Their first stop was Tunbridge Wells.

2. Apparently Sophia Streatfeild and her mother had reproached Hester Thrale for failing to show them an epitaph (perhaps by SJ) for Arthur Collier (1707–77), the lawyer and classicist who had tutored both Hester and Sophia (Clifford, 1952, p. 168 and n. 2).

very ill rewarded for my love and admiration if she does not give me one, she will give it nobody in whom it will excite more respectful sentiments.[3] But I never could get any thing from her but by pushing a face, and so, if you please, you may tell her.

I hope you let Miss Stratfield know how safe you keep her book.[4] It was too fine for a Scholar's talons. I hope she gets books that she may handle with more freedom, and understand with less difficulty. Do not let her forget me.

When I called the other day at Burneys, I found only the young ones at home, at last came the Doctor and Madam from a dinner in the country, to tell how they had been robbed as the[y] returned. The Doctor saved his purse but gave them three guineas and some silver, of which they returned him three and sixpence unasked to pay the turnpike.

I have sat twice to Sir Joshua, and he seems to like his own performance.[5] He has projected another in which I am to be busy, but we can think on it at leisure.[6]

Mrs. Williams is come home better, and the habitation is all concord and Harmony; only Mr. Levet harbours discontent.

With Dr. Laurence's consent I have for the two last nights

3. It is likely that the print in question was J. R. Smith's engraving (1776) after the portrait by Sir Joshua Reynolds (1775–76) (Edward Hamilton, *The Engraved Works of Sir Joshua Reynolds*, 1884, p. 120). Mrs. Montagu graciously agreed to SJ's request (Hester Thrale to SJ, 17 Oct. 1778, MS: Rylands Library; *The Sale Catalogue of SJ's Library*, ed. J. D. Fleeman, 1975, p. 64).

4. "It was a Greek Demosthene, given her by Dr. Collier" (Piozzi II.21).

5. The portrait to which SJ refers has not been conclusively identified. According to H. L. Piozzi, "This was not the Portrait you saw in Streatham Park Library. ... *That* was painted in 1772" (Piozzi II.21). On the other hand, L. F. Powell, supported by H. W. Liebert, maintains that the Streatham portrait (now at the Tate Gallery) was indeed painted in 1778 (*Life* IV.450; H. W. Liebert, "Portraits of the Author: Lifetime Likenesses of Samuel Johnson," in *English Portraits of the Seventeenth and Eighteenth Centuries*, 1974, p. 56). If the earlier date is accepted, then the painting at issue here may be a version of the Streatham portrait painted in 1788–89 for Topham Beauclerk (K. K. Yung, *Samuel Johnson*, 1984, pp. 117–18). *Post* To Hester Thrale, 31 Oct. 1778.

6. What was thought to have been a fifth and final Reynolds portrait, dated 1782–84 (*Life* IV.452; Liebert, "Lifetime Likenesses," p. 57), has recently been attributed to an unknown artist (K. K. Yung, *Samuel Johnson*, 1984, pp. 135–36).

taken Musk, the first night was a worse night than common, the second a better, but not so much better as that I dare ascribe any virtue to the medicine. I took a scruple each time.[7]

Now Miss has seen the Camp, I think, she should write me some account of it.[8] A Camp, however familiarly we may speak of it, is one of the great scenes of human life. War and peace divide [the] business of the world. Camps are the habitations of those who conquer kingdoms or defend them.

But what are Wits, and Pictures, and Camps and Physick? There is still a nearer concern to most of us. Is my Master come to himself? Does he talk and walk and look about him, as if there were yet something in the world for which it is worth while to live? or does he yet sit and say nothing? He was mending before he went, and surely he has not relapsed. To grieve for evils is often wrong, but it is much more wrong to grieve without them. All sorrow that lasts longer than its cause is morbid, and should be shaken off as an attack of melancholy, as the forerunner of a greater evil than poverty or pain.

I never said with Dr. Dodd that *I love to prattle upon paper*, but I have prattled now till the paper will not hold much more, than my good wishes which I sincerely send you. I am, Madam, your most humble servant,   SAM. JOHNSON

7. *Ante* To Thomas Lawrence, 13 Oct. 1778 and n. 1.

8. The Thrales had recently visited Hester's cousin, Sir Robert Cotton (*c.* 1739–1809), fifth Bt., of Combermere, Cheshire. Sir Robert, a colonel in the Guards, was stationed at Coxheath Camp, Kent (Hyde, 1977, p. 210). *Post* To Hester Maria Thrale, 24 Oct. 1778.

Hester Maria Thrale

SATURDAY 24 OCTOBER 1778

MS: The Earl of Shelburne.

My dearest Love: London, Oct. 24, 1778

I was in hopes that your letter about the camp would have been longer, and that you would have considered yourself as surveying in a camp perhaps the most important scene of human existence, the real scene of heroic life.[1] If you are struck with the inconveniencies of the military in a camp where there is no danger, where all the materials of pleasure are supplied, and where there is little but Jollity and festivity, reflect what a camp must be surrounded by enemies in a wasted or a hostile country, where provisions can scarcely be had, and what can be had must be snatched in haste by men who when they put the bread into their mouths, are uncertain whether they shall swallow it.

Sir Robert Cotton, whose degradation seems to touch you, is not the greatest man that has inhabited a tent. He is not considered out of Cheshire, nor perhaps in it, as standing on even ground with Alexander and Darius; Cæsar and Pompey; Tamerlane and Bajazet; Charles, Peter, and Augustus. These and many more like these, have lived in a camp like Sir Robert Cotton.

In a camp You [see] what is the[2] lowest and most portable accommodation with which Life can be contented; what shelter it is that can be most expeditiously erected and removed. There is in a camp what human wit sharpened by the greatest exigencies has been able to contrive, and it gives Ladies the particular[3] pleasure of seeing evils which they are not to share. I am, Sweeting, your most humble servant,

SAM. JOHNSON

1. *Ante* To Hester Thrale, 15 Oct. 1778 and n. 8.
2. MS: "t" superimposed upon "l"
3. MS: "particular" superimposed upon undeciphered erasure

Hester Thrale

SATURDAY 24 OCTOBER 1778

MS: Beinecke Library.

ADDRESS: To Henry Thrale, Esq., at Tunbridge Wells [*Readdressed in an unidentified hand*] London.

POSTMARKS: TUNBRIDGE WELLS, 24 OC, 26 OC, FREE.

Dearest Lady: London, Oct. 24, 1778

I have written Miss such a long letter that I cannot tell how soon I shall be weary of writing another, having made no new discoveries since my last either in art or Nature which may not be kept till we see each other.[1] And sure that time is not far off. The Duchess is a good Duchess for courting you while she stays, and for not staying to court you, till my courtship loses all its value.[2] You are there as I would have you, except your humours. When my Master grows well, must You take your turn to be melancholy? You appear to me to be now floating on the Spring tide of Prosperity, on a tide not governed by the moon but as the moon governs your heads, on a tide therefore which is never likely to ebb but by your own faults? I think it very probably in your power to lay up eight thousand pounds a year for every year to come, encreasing all the time, what needs not be encreased, the splendor of all external appearance. And surely such a state is not to be put into yearly hazard, for the pleasure of *keeping the house full* or the ambition of *outbrewing Whitbread*.[3] Stop now and you are safe, stop a few years and you may go safely on hereafter if to go on shall seem worth the while.

I am sorry for Mrs Montague;[4] we never could make any thing of the Lawyer, when we had him among us.[5] Montague

1. *Ante* To Hester Maria Thrale, 24 Oct. 1778.

2. Lady Georgiana Spencer (1757–1806), "the most charming Duchess in his Majesty's dominions" (*Life* IV.109–10), the beautiful and glamorous wife (m. 1774) of William Cavendish, fifth Duke of Devonshire. Hester Thrale had told SJ that his letter of 15 Oct. arrived "while I was talking with the Duchess of Devonshire, who had desired to be introduced to me" (17 Oct. 1778, MS: Rylands Library).

3. *Ante* To Hester Thrale, 23 Aug. 1777, n. 7.

4. Frances Burney (1752–1840), second daughter of Charles Burney, had just become a protégée of SJ and Hester Thrale as a consequence of their admiration for her first novel, *Evelina* (published Jan. 1778) (Roger Lonsdale, *Dr. Charles Burney*, 1965, pp. 243–47). Hester Thrale had reported in her letter of 19 Oct. that "Mrs. Montagu cannot bear Evelina—let not that be published" (MS: Rylands Library).

5. SJ refers to Alexander Wedderburn, who shared Mrs. Montagu's negative opinion of *Evelina* (Piozzi II.25; Hester Thrale to SJ, 19 Oct. 1778, MS: Rylands Library).

has got some vanity in her head. Vanity always oversets a Lady's Judgement. I have not told unless it be Williams, and I do not know that I have told her. If Stratfield has a little kindness for me, I am glad. I call now and then on the Burneys, where You are at the top of mortality.—When will You come home?

Two days ago Dr. Laurence ordered a new medicine which I think to try to night, but my hopes are not high. I mean to try however, and not languish without resistance.

Young Desmoulins is taken in *an undersomething* of Drury Lane,[6] he knows not, I believe, his own ⟨denomi⟩nation.[7]

My two clerical friends Darby and Worthington have both died this month.[8] I have known Worthington long, and to die is dreadful. I believe he was a very good Man.[9] I am, Madam, your most etc.[10]

SAM. JOHNSON

6. John Desmoulins, the son of Elizabeth Desmoulins, was employed by Drury Lane Theatre at a salary of 25 shillings per week, "apparently as one of the house servants" (*A Biographical Dictionary of Actors, Actresses, Musicians, Dancers, Managers, and Other Stage Personnel in London, 1660–1800*, ed. P. H. Highfill et al., 1975, IV.344). *Post* To Hester Thrale, 21 Nov. 1778.

7. MS: torn along right-hand margin

8. The Rev. John Derby (*c.* 1720–78), Rector of Southfleet, Kent, and former chaplain to Dr. Zachary Pearce, Bishop of Rochester. Derby prepared for posthumous publication Pearce's *Commentary on the Four Evangelists* (1777), to which SJ contributed the dedication and an account of Pearce's life (Hazen, pp. 154–57).

9. *Ante* To Hester Thrale, 4 Feb. 1775, n. 2.   10. MS: "most etc. most etc."

Bennet Langton

SATURDAY 31 OCTOBER 1778

MS: Hyde Collection.

ADDRESS: To Captain Langton, at Warley Camp.

Dear Sir: Oct. 31, 1778

When I recollect how long ago I was received with so much kindness at Warley Common,[1] I am ashamed that I have not made some enquiries after my friends.

1. *Ante* To Bennet Langton, 29 Aug. 1778 and nn. 1, 2.

Pray how many sheepstealers did you convict, and how did you punish them?[2] When are you to be cantoned in better habitations? The air grows cold, and the ground damp. Longer stay in the camp cannot be without much danger to the health of the common Men, if even the Officers can escape.[3]

You see that Dr. Percy is now Dean of Carlisle, about five hundred a year with a power of presenting him self to some good Living.[4] He is provided for.

The session of the Club is to commence with that of the parliament. Mr. Banks desires to be admitted, he will be a very honourable accession.[5]

Did the King please you? The Coxheath Men, I think, have some reason to complain; Reynolds says your Camp is better than theirs.[6]

I hope you find yourself able to encounter this weather; take care of your own health, and as you can, of your Men. Be pleased to make[7] my compliments to all the Gentlemen whose notice I have had, and whose kindness I have experienced. I am, Dear sir, your most humble servant,

SAM. JOHNSON

2. In his account of SJ's visit to Warley Camp, Bennet Langton reported that he "sat, with a patient degree of Attention, to observe the proceedings of a Regimental Court Martial that happen'd to be called in the time of his stay with us" (Fifer, p. 316).

3. The encampment broke up 29 Nov. (Fifer, p. 94 n. 4).

4. On becoming Dean of Carlisle, Percy "retained his livings at Easton Maudit and Wilby, but because the income from the deanery depended upon rents and fines (renewal fees) that came due at different intervals, it fell short in some years of the more than £550 that he expected" (B. H. Davis, *Thomas Percy*, 1989, p. 240).

5. Joseph Banks was elected to The Club 11 Dec. 1778 (*Letters of Sir Joshua Reynolds*, ed. F. W. Hilles, 1929, p. 67).

6. The King visited Warley Camp on 20 Oct., and Coxheath Camp on 23 Nov. (*Annual Register* 21, 1778, pp. 237–38).

7. MS: "m" superimposed upon "h"

Hester Thrale

SATURDAY 31 OCTOBER 1778

MS: Bodleian Library.
ADDRESS: To Henry Thrale, Esq., at Brighthelmston, Sussex.
POSTMARK: 31 OC.

Dear Madam: Oct. 31, 1778

Your letter seemed very long a coming, and was very welcome at last, do not be so long again.[1]

Long live Sir John Shelly that lures my Master to hunt.[2] I hope he will soon shake off the black dog,[3] and come home as light as a feather. And long live Mrs. Greville,[4] that downs my Mistress. I hope she will come home as flexible as a rush. I see my wish is rather ambiguous, it is to my Mistress that I wish flexibility. As to the imitation imputed to Mrs. Greville, if she makes any thing like a copy, her powers of imitation are very great, for I do not remember that she ever saw me but once. If she copies me she will lose more credit by want of Judgement, than she will gain by quickness of apprehension.

Of Mrs. Byron I have no remembrance,[5] perhaps her voice is low.[6]

Miss Burney is just gone from me. I told her how you took

1. SJ is responding to Hester Thrale's letter of 28 Oct. Her previous letter is dated 19 Oct. (MSS: Rylands Library).

2. Hester Thrale had told SJ that Henry was "following Sir John Shelley's Pack of Dogs over the Sussex Downs" (28 Oct. 1778).

3. *Ante* To Hester Thrale, 15 Oct. 1778 and n. 1.

4. Frances Macartney (d. 1789), wife of Richard Fulke Greville, the godmother of Frances Burney and the author of "A Prayer for Indifference" (*Life* IV.535). Hester Thrale had reported to SJ: "Mrs. Greville has a commanding Manner and loud Voice. Why She downs every body I am sure; You never told me that She was so Lofty a Lady. . . . Mrs. Greville is said to have formed her Manner upon yours" (28 Oct. 1778).

5. Sophia Trevannion (d. 1790), wife of Vice Admiral John Byron (1723–86), was soon to become one of Hester Thrale's closest friends (*Thraliana* I.444).

6. According to Hester Thrale, Sophia Byron "tryed hard for your heart one Day at Stretham but found it impregnable either from Situation or Garrison" (28 Oct. 1778).

to them all, but I told her likewise how You took to Miss Streatfield.[7] All poysons have their antidotes.

Sir Joshua has finished my picture, and it seems to please every body, but I shall want to see how it pleases you.[8]

Of your conditions of happiness do not set your trust upon any but what Providence puts in your own power. Your duty you may pay,[9] twenty thousand pounds, ⟨at forty⟩[10] you may lay up. The rest you can only pray for. Of your Daughters three are out of the danger of childrens distempers, the other two have hardly yet tried whether they can live or no. You ought not yet to count them among your settled possessions.[11]

Is it true that Mrs. Davenant is enceinte? it will give her great influence.[12]

Today Mrs. Williams and Mrs. Desmoulins had a scold, and Williams was going away, but I bid her *not turn tail*, and she came back, and rather got the upper hand.

I wish you would come back again to us all; you will find nobody among your fine Ladies that will love you as You are loved by, Dearest Lady, your most humble servant,

SAM. JOHNSON

7. "Sophy Streatfield is so very lovely and singleminded a Creature that I am ready to say as you once kindly said to me of Doctor Bathurst, that you would not have trusted us with each other's Acquaintance. . . . These Burneys are a sweet Family, I love them all" (Hester Thrale to SJ, 28 Oct. 1778).

8. *Ante* To Hester Thrale, 15 Oct. 1778 and n. 5.

9. Hester Thrale had told SJ that she hoped soon to have repaid Charles Scrase for the money he had loaned them the previous spring (28 Oct. 1778).

10. MS: "twenty" through ⟨forty⟩ heavily del.

11. Queeney, Susanna, and Sophia were then fourteen, eight, and seven, respectively, Cecilia one and Henrietta four months. Henrietta died at the age of four (Hyde, 1977, p. xii).

12. "It was *not* true, yet is her Influence as I have heard—undimi[ni]sh'd. She is Lady Corbet now 1815" (Piozzi II.28).

Charles Burney

MS: Hyde Collection.
ADDRESS: To Dr. Burney.
ENDORSEMENTS: Dr. Johnson, From Dr. Johnson, Novr. 2d 1778, No. 5.

Dear Sir: Nov. 2, 1778

I have sent your letters, and hope they may be useful.[1] But
Mr. Warton can help you through all your difficulties, his acquaintance is large, and his influence powerful.

What could Madam Frances mean by leaving her little book
behind her? I hope Mrs. Burney grows well, and wish you a
happy Journey. I am, sir, your most affectionate,

                                                    SAM. JOHNSON

1. *Post* To Edward Edwards, 2 Nov. 1778; *Post* To Benjamin Wheeler, 2 Nov.
1778.

Edward Edwards[1]

MS: Jesus College, Oxford.
ADDRESS: To the Reverend Dr. Edwards of Jesus College, Oxford.

Sir: London, Nov.[2] 2, 1778

The Bearer, Doctor Burney, has had some account of a Welsh
Manuscript in the Bodleian library, from which he hopes to
gain some materials for his History of Musick, but being ignorant of the Language is at a loss where to find assistance.[3] I

1. Edward Edwards (*c.* 1726–83), D.D., classical scholar and Vice-Principal of
Jesus College, Oxford (1762–83) (*Life* III.529).
2. MS: "Nov." superimposed upon "Dec."
3. Burney was at work on the second volume of his *General History of Music*,
which appeared in 1782. It is probable that he wished to consult the "Welsh Manuscript" for the "Cambro British" section of chapter 4 ("Of the Origin of Modern
Languages . . . and general State of Music, till the invention of Printing, about the
year 1450"). The particular manuscript Burney had in mind, however, has not

make no doubt but You, Sir, can help him through his difficulties, and therefore take the liberty of recommending him to your favour, as I am sure that You will find him a Man worthy of every civility that can be shown, and every benefit that can be conferred.[4]

But we must not let Welsh drive us from our Greek. What comes of Xenophon?[5] If You do not like the trouble of publishing the book, do not let your emendations be lost, contrive that they may be printed somewhere. I am, Sir, Your most humble servant,

SAM. JOHNSON

---

been identified with certainty (Roger Lonsdale, *Dr. Charles Burney*, 1965, p. 247; Charles Burney, *General History of Music*, II. chap. 4).

4. Edwards responded favorably to SJ's request (*Post* To Hester Thrale, 14 Nov. 1778).

5. Edwards's edition of Xenophon's *Memorabilia* appeared posthumously in 1785 (*Life* III.367 n. 2).

Benjamin Wheeler

MONDAY 2 NOVEMBER 1778

MS: John Comyn. A copy in the hand of Charles Burney.

Dear Sir: London, Nov. 2d 1778

Dr. Burney, who brings this paper, is engaged in a History of Musick, and having been told by Dr. Markham[1] of some MSS. relating to his Subject which are in the library of your College, is desirous to examine them;[2] He is my Friend, and therefore I take the liberty of intreating your favour and assistance in his enquiry, and can assure you with great confidence, that if you knew him, he would not want any intervenient Solicitation

1. SJ may be referring either to Dr. William Markham or to Dr. Robert Markham (d. 1786), Rector of St. Mary, Whitechapel, and Chaplain to the King (*Life* VI.274).

2. At Christ Church "Burney particularly wished to examine the great musical collection assembled by Dr. Henry Aldrich (1647–1710)" (Roger Lonsdale, *Dr. Charles Burney*, 1965, p. 247).

to obtain the kindness of one who loves learning and virtue as you love them.[3]

I have been flattering myself all the Summer with the hope of paying my annual visit to my friends, but something has obstructed me. I still hope not to be long without seeing you.[4] I should be glad of a little literary talk, and glad to shew you by the frequency of my visits how eagerly I love it, when you talk it. I am, Dear Sir, Your most humble servant,

SAM. JOHNSON

3. As a result of SJ's letter, Burney was given unrestricted access to the Aldrich Collection, a catalogue of which he compiled and gave to Christ Church (Lonsdale, *Burney*, p. 247).

4. SJ did not visit Oxford again until Oct. 1781 (*Post* To Hester Thrale, 17 Oct. 1781).

William Strahan

SATURDAY 7 NOVEMBER 1778

PRINTED SOURCE: C. K. Shorter, *Unpublished Letters of Dr. Samuel Johnson*, 1915, p. 4.

Sir: November 7, 1778

I have a friend that wants a hundred pounds. Will you send by a safe hand. I will be glad if you will find me the bill for it. There is my old reckoning with Mr. Cadell.[1] Do look it out at last. If I can promise the hundred pounds for next week it will be sufficient. I am, Sir, your humble servant,

SAM. JOHNSON

1. It is unlikely that SJ refers to the money still owing to him for the *Journey to the Western Islands of Scotland*. The most probable source is income from SJ's four political tracts, all published by Cadell in multiple editions; profits from these came to £160 11s. 6d. (information supplied by Dr. J. D. Fleeman).

Charlotte Lennox

MONDAY 9 NOVEMBER 1778

MS: Houghton Library.

Nov. 9, 1778

Mrs. Desmoulings will show you Mr. Murphy's letter, and will tell you why it will be best for us to go to his Chambers. I shall be ready to wait on you. Do not be frighted, I believe there is no danger.[1] I am, Madam, Your most humble servant,

SAM. JOHNSON

1. SJ was advising Lennox and her husband in their dispute with the bookseller James Dodsley and his partners over the ownership of copyright to *Memoirs of the Duke of Sully*. "The popularity of her work had already encouraged the piratical publication of two inexpensive Scottish editions, and now she was apparently determined to stand firm against further encroachment" (Bloom, p. 230). Arthur Murphy had been drawn into the affair in his capacity as a barrister with experience in copyright law. Lennox and Dodsley reached a compromise, apparently through Murphy's mediation (Bloom, pp. 230–31; Duncan Isles, "The Lennox Collection," *Harvard Library Bulletin* 19, 1971, p. 178 n. 161).

Hester Thrale

MONDAY 9 NOVEMBER 1778

MS: Hyde Collection.

Dear Madam:

Nov. 9, 1778

The Lord Mayor has had a dismal day.[1] Will not this weather drive you home? Perhaps you know not any body that will be glad to see you. I hope our Well will yield water again, and something fuller you will find the pond; but then all the trees are naked, and the ground damp. But the year must go round.

While you are away, I take great delight in your letters, only when you talk so much of obligations to me you should consider how much you put me into the condition of *honest Joseph*.[2]

1. *Ante* To Hester Thrale, 10 Nov. 1777, n. 7.

2. SJ alludes to Richardson's *Clarissa*. In response to Lovelace's letter of 8 Apr.,

Young Desmoulins thinks he has got something, he knows not what at Drury Lane; his Mother talk[s] little of it.[3] Sure it is not a *humm*.[4] Mr. Levet who thinks his ancient rights invaded, stands at bay, *fierce as ten furies*.[5] Mrs. Williams growls and scolds, but Poll does not much flinch.[6] Every body is in want.[7] I shall be glad to see Streatham again, but I can find no reason for going to Brighthelmston, but that of seeing my Master and You three days sooner.[8] I am, Madam, Your most humble servant,

SAM. JOHNSON

in which he addresses Joseph Leman as "honest Joseph," Leman replies, 9 Apr.: "your Honner has such a fesseshious way with you, as that I hardly know whether you are in jest, or earnest, when your Honner calls me honnest so often" (*Clarissa*, 1748, III.22, 28).   3. *Ante* To Hester Thrale, 24 Oct. 1778 and n. 6.

4. *hum*: "a piece of humbug; an imposition, a hoax" (*OED*).

5. "Fierce as ten Furies, terrible as Hell" (*Paradise Lost* II.671).

6. *Ante* To John Hawkins, 15 Jan. 1773 and n. 1.

7. Cf. *Post* To Hester Thrale, 14 Nov. 1778.

8. SJ did not go to Brighton; the Thrales returned on 26 Nov. (Hyde, 1977, p. 213).

Hester Thrale

SATURDAY 14 NOVEMBER 1778

MS: E. Thorne.

Dearest Madam: Nov. 14, 1778

Then I really think I shall be very glad to see you all safe at home. I shall easily forgive my Master his long stay, if he leaves the dog behind him.[1] We will watch as well as we can that the dog shall never be let in again, for when he comes the first thing he does is to worry my Master. This time he gnawed him to the bone. Content, said Rider's almanack, makes a man richer than the Indies.[2] But surely he that has the Indies in his

1. "The dog" refers to Henry Thrale's depression. *Ante* To Hester Thrale, 15 Oct. 1778 and n. 1; 31 Oct. 1778.

2. "Contentment swells a Mite into a Talent, and makes a Man richer than the *Indies*" (*Rider's British Merlin*, 1728, "Observations on October").

possession may without very much philosophy make himself content. So much for my Master and his dog, a vile one it is, but I hope if he is not hanged, he is drowned, with another lusty shake he will pick my Masters heart out.

I have begun to take valerian; the two last nights I took half an ounce each night; a very loathsome quantity.[3] Dr. Laurence talked of a decoction, but I say, all or nothing.[4] The first night I thought myself better but the next it did me no good.

Young Desmoulins says he is settled at a weekly pay of 25 shillings, about forty pounds a year.[5] Mr. Macbean has no business.[6] We have tolerable concord at home, but no love. Williams hates every body. Levet hates Desmoulins and does not love Williams. Desmoulins hates them both. Poll loves none of them.

Dr. Burney had the luck to go to Oxford, the only week in the year when the library is shut up. He was however very kindly treated, as one Man is translating Arabick, and another Welsh for his service.[7] Murphy told me that you wrote to him about Evelina.[8] *Francis* wants to read it.

And on the 26. Burney is to bring me.[9] Pray why so. Is it not as fit that I should bring Burney?—My Master is in his old lunes, and so am I.[10] Well, I do not much care how it is, and yet—At it again—

Pray make my compliments to Mr. Scrase. He has many things which I wish to have, his knowledge of Business, and of

3. In his *Materia Medica* William Lewis describes valerian as "a medicine of great esteem in the present practice against . . . different kinds of nervous disorders, and is commonly looked upon as one of the principal antispasmodics. . . . The dose of the root in powder is from a scruple to a dram or two, which may be repeated, if the stomach will bear it, two or three times a day" (3d ed., 1784, p. 658). SJ was therefore doubling the suggested maximum dosage.

4. *decoction*: "a preparation made by boiling in water" (SJ's *Dictionary*).

5. *Ante* To Hester Thrale, 24 Oct. 1778 and n. 6.

6. *Post* To John Nichols, 23 Nov. 1778; 26 Nov. 1778 and n. 1.

7. *Ante* To Edward Edwards, 2 Nov. 1778; *Ante* To Benjamin Wheeler, 2 Nov. 1778.   8. *Ante* To Hester Thrale, 24 Oct. 1778, n. 4.

9. *Ante* To Hester Thrale, 9 Nov. 1778 and n. 8.

10. *Ante* To Bennet Langton, 29 Aug. 1778 and n. 3.

law. He has likewise a great chair. Such an one my Master talked of geting, but that vile black Dog.—

Mrs. Queeney might write to me, and do herself no harm, she will neglect me till I shall take to Susy, and then Queeney may break her heart, and who can be blamed? I am sure I stuck to Queeney as long as I could.

Dos not Master talk how full his canal will be when he comes home.[11] Now or never. I know not how the Soil was laid; if it slopes towards the canal, it may pour in a great deal of water, but I suspect it slopes the wrong way.

This is but the 14th day; there are twelve more to the twenty sixth. Did you ever hear of notching a stick? however we have it in Horace truditur dies die;[12] as twelve days have gone, twelve days will come.

Hector of Birmingham just looked in at me. He is come to his only niece, who is ill of a cancer, I believe, with very little hope, for it is knotted in two places.[13]

I think at least I grow no worse, perhaps valerian may make me better. Let me have your prayers. I am, Dearest Lady, Your most obedient Servant,

SAM. JOHNSON

11. *canal*: "a bason of water in a garden" (SJ's *Dictionary*). *Ante* To Hester Thrale, 23 Aug. 1777, n. 4.

12. *truditur dies die*: "day treads upon the heel of day" (Horace, *Odes* II.xviii.15, trans. C. E. Bennett, Loeb ed.).

13. SJ refers to Ann Carless Hopper (1742–82), the one surviving child of Edmund Hector's sister (*Reades*, p. 152).

James Boswell

SATURDAY 21 NOVEMBER 1778

PRINTED SOURCE: JB's *Life*, 1791, II.278.

Dear Sir: Nov. 21, 1778

It is indeed a long time since I wrote, and I think you have some reason to complain; however, you must not let small things disturb you, when you have such a fine addition to your happiness as a new boy,[1] and I hope your lady's health restored by bringing him.[2] It seems very probable that a little care will now restore her, if any remains of her complaints are left.

You seem, if I understand your letter, to be gaining ground at Auchinleck, an incident that would give me great delight.[3]

*   *   *   *   *   *

When any fit of anxiety, or gloominess, or perversion of mind, lays hold upon you, make it a rule not to publish it by complaints, but exert your whole care to hide it; by endeavouring to hide it, you will drive it away. Be always busy.

The Club is to meet with the parliament; we talk of electing Banks, the traveller; he will be a reputable member.[4]

Langton has been encamped with his company of militia on Warley-common; I spent five days amongst them, he signalized himself as a diligent officer, and has very high respect in the regiment.[5] He presided when I was there at a court-martial; he is now quartered in Hertfordshire; his lady and little ones are in Scotland. Paoli came to the camp and commended the soldiers.

Of myself I have no great matter to say, my health is not restored, my nights are restless and tedious. The best night that I have had these twenty years was at Fort-Augustus.[6]

1. James Boswell the younger (1778–1822), JB's second surviving son, was born 15 Sept. (*Boswell, Laird of Auchinleck*, ed. J. W. Reed and F. A. Pottle, 1977, p. 16).

2. Margaret Boswell's consumptive condition tended to improve during pregnancy (*Later Years*, p. 167).

3. JB's troubled relations with his father and stepmother had temporarily improved (Reed and Pottle, *Boswell, Laird of Auchinleck*, pp. 33, 37).

4. *Ante* To Bennet Langton, 31 Oct. 1778 and n. 5.

5. *Ante* To Bennet Langton, 29 Aug. 1778; 31 Oct. 1778.

6. On 30 Aug. 1773 SJ and JB stayed overnight with Governor Trapaud of Fort Augustus, in whose house they were "well entertained and well lodged" (*Ante* To Hester Thrale, 6 Sept. 1773). SJ "passed the night in . . . sweet uninterrupted sleep" (*Works*, Yale ed. 1.266).

I hope soon to send you a few lives to read.[7] I am, dear Sir, Your most affectionate,

SAM. JOHNSON

7. These "few lives" may have included "Dryden," proofs of which SJ had returned the previous month (Appendix II: To Thomas Cadell, 17 Oct. 1778).

Hester Thrale

SATURDAY 21 NOVEMBER 1778

MS: Hyde Collection.

ADDRESS: To Henry Thrale, Esq., at Brighthelmston, Sussex.

POSTMARK: 21 NO.

Dear Madam: Nov. 21, 1778

I will write to you once more before you come away but—nil mihi rescribas[1]—I hope soon to see you. Burney and I have settled it, and I will not take a postchaise[2] merely to show my independence.

Now the dog is drowned I shall see both you and my Master just as You are used to be, and with your being as you have been, your friends may very reasonably be satisfied.[3] Only, be better if you can.

Return my thanks, if you please, to Queeny for her letter. I do not yet design to leave her for Susy, but how near is the time when She will leave me, and leave me to Susy or any body else that will pick me up.

—Currit enim ferox
Ætas, et[4] illi quos tibi demserit
Apponet annos.—[5]

1. *nil mihi rescribas attinet: ipse veni!*: "writing back is pointless: come yourself!" (Ovid, *Heroides* I.2, trans. Grant Showerman, Loeb ed.).

2. MS: possibly "post-chaise"

3. *Ante* To Hester Thrale, 14 Nov. 1778 and n. 1. 4. MS: "it"

5. *currit enim ferox / aetas, et illi, quos tibi dempserit, / apponet annos*: "For Time courses madly on, and shall add to her the years it takes from thee" (Horace, *Odes* II.v.13–15, trans. C. E. Bennett, Loeb ed.).

Queeny, whom you watched while I held her, will soon think our care of her very superfluous.

Miss Biron, and, I suppose, Mrs. Biron, is gone.[6] You are by this time left alone to wander over the Steene, and listen to the waves.[7] This is but a dull life, come away and be busy and count your poultry, and look into your dairy, and at leisure hours learn what revolutions have happened at Streatham.

I believe I told you that Jack Desmoulins is rated upon the Book at Drury Lane five and twenty shillings a week.[8]

Baretti has told his musical scheme to Burney, and Burney *will neither grant the question nor deny.* He is of opinion, that, if it dos not fail, it will succeed, but, if it does not succeed he conceives it must fail.[9]

It is good to speak dubiously about futurity. It is likewise not amiss to hope.

Did I ever tell you that George Strahan was married?[10] It so fell out that George fell in love with a girl whose fortune was so small that he perhaps could not mention it to his Father; but it happened likewise by the lottery of love, that the Father liked her so well, as of himself to recommend her to George. Such coincidence is rare.

> Come, now, do come home as fast as you can,
> Come with a whoop, come with a call,

6. *Ante* To Hester Thrale, 31 Oct. 1778 and n. 5. Augusta (d. 1824), the third of Admiral and Mrs. Byron's four daughters, was a friend of Frances Burney. She later married Vice Admiral Christopher Parker (*Diary and Letters of Madame D'Arblay*, ed. Austin Dobson, 1904, I.333 and n. 1, 347–48; *Thraliana* II.739 n. 4).

7. SJ refers to the Steine (pronounced "Steen"), a square in Brighton that was a fashionable meeting place akin to the Pantiles at Tunbridge Wells.

8. *Ante* To Hester Thrale, 24 Oct. 1778 and n. 6.

9. Baretti had translated Horace's *Carmen seculare* into English and persuaded François Philidor, celebrated composer and chess player, to set the translation to music. SJ supplied an epilogue (*Poems*, p. 219). Three performances took place in the Free-Masons Hall, London (26 Feb., 5 and 12 Mar. 1779). Baretti later claimed that this "musical scheme . . . brought me a hundred and fifty pounds in three nights, and three times as much to Philidor" (*Life* III.373 n. 3).

10. On 25 June 1778 Strahan married Margaret Robertson (*c.* 1751– 1831), of Richmond (J. A. Cochrane, *Dr. Johnson's Printer*, 1964, p. 156).

Come with a good-will, or come not at all.[11]

I am, Madam, your most obedient,

SAM. JOHNSON

11. "Come with a whoop and come with a call, / Come with a good will or not at all" (*Oxford Dictionary of Nursery Rhymes*, ed. Iona and Peter Opie, 1951, p. 99).

John Nichols
MONDAY 23 NOVEMBER 1778[1]

MS: British Library.

Monday

Mr. Johnson will hope for Mr. Nichols' company to tea, about six this afternoon, to talk of the index, and settle the terms.[2]

1. Dated with reference to the following letter.
2. *Post* To John Nichols, 26 Nov. 1778 and n. 1.

John Nichols
THURSDAY 26 NOVEMBER 1778

MS: British Library.
ADDRESS: To Mr. Nichols.

Sir:

Nov. 26, 1778

I am very well contented that the Index is settled, for though the price is low, it is not penurious.

Mr. Macbean having been for some time out of business, is in some little perplexities from which twelve guineas will set him free. This, we hope, You will advance; and during the continuance of the work subject to your inspection he desires a weekly payment of sixteen shillings, the rest to remain till it is completed.[1] I am, Sir, You most humble servant,

SAM. JOHNSON

1. Alexander Macbean "was employed by the Booksellers in compiling the Poetical Index to Dr. Johnson's Edition of the English Poets" (*GM*, General Index 1787–1818, 1821, III.xx).

John Nichols
c. DECEMBER 1778

MS: British Library.

Sir:

By some accident I laid your note upon Duke, up so safely that I cannot find it.[1] Your informations have been of great use to me. I must beg it again,[2] with another list of our authours, for I have laid that with the other. I am, Sir, etc.

I have sent Stepney's Epitaph.[3] Let me have the revises as soon as can be.[4]

1. SJ was either composing or revising his biography of Richard Duke (1658–1711), poet and clergyman. It is probable that he refers here to one of the notes on Duke in Nichols's edition of *The Original Works of William King, LL.D* (1776) (Edward Hart, "Some New Sources of Johnson's *Lives*," *PMLA* 65, 1950, pp. 1089–90).   2. MS: period

3. Half of SJ's very brief "[George] Stepney" consists of the poet's elaborate Latin epitaph from Westminster Abbey (*Lives of the Poets* 1.310).

4. *Revises* are final proofs (J. D. Fleeman, "Some Proofs of Johnson's *Prefaces to the Poets*," *The Library* 17, 1962, p. 214).

Thomas Lawrence
SATURDAY 5 DECEMBER 1778

MS: Hyde Collection.

Dear Sir: Saturday, Dec. 5, 1778

I perceive that our business has not been properly done. I suppose the Will must be returned, that the exemplification may be verified. If you can send me the paper and necessary directions I will send them away to night. I am, Sir, Your most humble servant,

SAM. JOHNSON

Thomas Fitzmaurice[1]
MONDAY 7 DECEMBER 1778

1. The Hon. Thomas Fitzmaurice (1742–93), second son of the first Earl of Shelburne, M.P. for Calne (1762–74) and Chipping Wycombe (1774–80) (Namier

MS: Hyde Collection.

Sir: Dec. 7, 1778

Good wishes are the necessary consequence of friendship, and of my good wishes, I hope, you make no[2] doubt.[3] But now you have a son I know not well what more to wish you except more sons, and a few daughters; the sons to be all brave, and the daughters all beautiful, and both sons and daughters to be wise and good.

Now you have a son what can you want? You have a Mother to rejoice in her grandson,[4] and a Lady to partake in all your felicities.[5] With Lady Shelburn I once had the honour of conversing, and entreat[6] you, sir, to let her know that I have not forgotten it; to your Lady I am a stranger, but who can doubt the excellence of her who you have chosen, and who has chosen you?

If encrease of happiness cannot be expected it still remains to wish the continuance, and very long it will continue, if there be any power in the desires of, Sir, your most humble Servant,

SAM. JOHNSON

---

and Brooke II.430). It is probable that SJ had met Fitzmaurice through the Thrales.   2. MS: "no no"

3. Fitzmaurice's first and only child, John (1778–1820), styled Viscount Kirkwall, was born 9 Oct.

4. Mary Fitzmaurice (d. 1780), Dowager Countess of Shelburne.

5. Mary (1755–1831), *suo jure* Countess of Orkney (m. 1777).

6. MS: "treat" repeated as catchword

John Hussey[1]

TUESDAY 29 DECEMBER 1778

MS: National Library of Australia.

ADDRESS: To the Revd. Mr. Hussey.

ENDORSEMENT: from Dr. Johnson previous to my departure for Aleppo, John Hussey.

1. The Rev. John Hussey (1751–99), of Hertford College, Oxford, was about to take up a post as Chaplain to the English Factory at Aleppo. According to JB, SJ "had long been in habits of intimacy" with Hussey (*Life* III.369).

Dear Sir: Dec. 29, 1778

I have sent you the Grammar, and have left You two Books more by which I hope to be remembred. Write my name in them. We may perhaps see each other no more. You part with my good wishes, nor do I despair of seeing you return.[2] Let no opportunities of vice corrupt you, Let no bad examples seduce You. Let the blindness of Mahometans confirm you in Christianity. God bless you. I am, Dear Sir, your affectionate, humble servant,

SAM. JOHNSON

2. Hussey did return to England: in 1787 (writing from Newington, Kent) he supplied JB with information for the *Life* (Waingrow, pp. 230, 233–35). But whether he and SJ met again has not been determined.

Elizabeth Aston

SATURDAY 2 JANUARY 1779

MS: Pembroke College, Oxford.

Dear Madam: London, Boltcourt, Fleetstreet, Jan. 2, 1779

Now the new year is come of which I wish You and dear Mrs. Gastrel many and many returns, it is fit that I give You some account of the year past. In the beginning of it I had a difficulty of breathing, and other ilness from which however I by degrees recovered and from which I am now tolerably free. In the spring and summer I flattered myself that I should come to Lichfield, and forebore to write till I could tell of my intentions with some certainty, and, one thing or other making the Journey always improper, as I did not come, I omitted to write, till at last I grew afraid of hearing ill news. But the other day Mr. Prujean called,[1] and left word[2] that You, dear Madam, are grown better, I know not when I heard any thing

1. William Prujean (*fl.* 1755–90), the husband of Elizabeth Aston's sister Sophia (*Johns. Glean.* v.254–55).
2. MS: "left word" repeated for clarity below SJ's first, less legible "left word"

that pleased me so much. I shall now long more and more to see Lichfield, and partake the happiness of your recovery.[3]

Now You begin to mend You have great encouragement to take care of yourself, do not omit any thing that can conduce to your health, and when I come I shall hope to enjoy with You and dearest Mrs. Gastrel many pleasing hours.

Do not be angry at my long omission to write, but let me hear how you both do, for you will write to nobody to whom your welfare will give more pleasure, than to, Dearest Madam, Your most humble servant,
SAM. JOHNSON

3. SJ visited Lichfield and Ashbourne, 22 May–28 June (*Post* To Hester Thrale, 29 May 1779; 26 June 1779).

Lucy Porter
SATURDAY 2 JANUARY 1779

MS: Hyde Collection.

Dearest Love: Boltcourt, Fleetstreet, Jan. 2, 1779

Though I have so long omitted to write, I will omit it no longer. I hope the new Year finds you not worse than you have formerly been; and I wish that many years may pass over you without bringing either pain or discontent. For my part, I think my health, though not good, yet rather better than when I left you.

My purpose was to have paid you my annual visit in the Summer, but it happened otherwise, not by any journey another way, for I have never been many miles from London, but by such hindrances as it is hard to bring to any account.

Do not follow my bad example but write to me soon again, and let me know of you what you have to tell, I hope it is all good.

Please to make my compliments to Mrs. Cobb, Mrs. Adey, and Miss Adey, and all the Ladies and Gentlemen that frequent your Mansion.

If you want any books, or any thing else that I can send you, let me know. I am, Dear Madam, your most humble servant,

SAM. JOHNSON

Eva Maria Garrick

THURSDAY 21 JANUARY 1779

MS: Houghton Library.

Streatham, Jan. 21, 1779

Mr. Johnson sends his compliments to Mrs. Garrick, and desires to know how she does.[1]

1. David Garrick had died of uremia 20 Jan. (*Letters of David Garrick*, ed. D. M. Little and G. M. Kahrl, 1963, III.1263).

Eva Maria Garrick

TUESDAY 2 FEBRUARY 1779

MS: Hyde Collection.

Feb. 2, 1779

Dr. Johnson sends most respectful condolence to Mrs. Garrick, and wishes that any endeavour of his could enable her support a loss which the world cannot repair.[1]

1. *Ante* To Eva Maria Garrick, 21 Jan. 1779, n. 1. Mrs. Garrick included in the inscription on her husband's monument at Lichfield SJ's elegiac comment from his "Life of Edmund Smith": "His death eclipsed the gaiety of nations and impoverished the public stock of harmless pleasure" (*Letters of David Garrick*, ed. D. M. Little and G. M. Kahrl, 1963, III.1264; *Lives of the Poets* II.21).

Frances Reynolds

MS: Hyde Collection.

Dearest Madam: Febr. 15, 1779

I have never deserved to be treated as You treat me; when you employed me before, I undertook your affair, and succeeded, but then I succeeded by chusing a proper time, and a proper time I will try to chuse again.[1]

I have about a week's work to do, and then I shall come to live in town, and will first wait on You in Dover street. You are not to think that I neglect You, for your Nieces will tell you how rarely they have seen me.[2] I will wait on You as soon as I can, and yet You must resolve to talk things over without anger, and you must leave me to catch opportunities; and be assured, Dearest Dear, that[3] I should have very little enjoyment of the day in which I had rejected any opportunity of doing good to you. I am, dearest Madam, Your most humble servant,

SAM. JOHNSON

1. Even after she had ceased to manage his household, uneasy relations continued between Sir Joshua Reynolds and his sister, who often lamented "the unkindness and injustice of her Brother, of which she seems to think she can never say enough" (S. M. Radcliffe, *Sir Joshua's Nephew*, 1930, p. 132; cf. *Post* To Frances Reynolds, 28 May 1784). SJ several times intervened in their disputes, which appeared to center on Sir Joshua's alleged lack of respect and consideration (James Northcote, *Life of Sir Joshua Reynolds*, 1818, 1.203; *Johns. Misc.* 11.455–56).

2. SJ refers to the two daughters of Frances Reynolds's widowed sister Mary Palmer: Mary (*c.* 1750–1820), later (1800) Marchioness of Thomond, and Theophila (*c.* 1756–1848), later (1781) Mrs. Robert Gwatkin (*Walpole's Correspondence*, Yale ed. XLVII.1943). They lived with their uncle Sir Joshua in Leicester Square (Radcliffe, *Sir Joshua's Nephew*, p. 131).

3. MS: "that" repeated as catchword

John Nichols
MONDAY 1 MARCH 1779

MS: British Library.

Sir: March 1, 1779

I have sent Philips[1] with his epitaphs to be inserted.[2]

The fragment of a Preface is hardly worth the impression but that we may seem to do something. It may be added to the life of Phillips.[3]

The Latin Page is to be added to the life of Smith.[4]

I shall be at home to revise the two sheets of Milton.[5] I am, Sir, Your most humble servant,

                                              SAM. JOHNSON

1. MS: "Philip's"

2. SJ's biography of John Philips (1676–1709) includes epitaphs from Hereford Cathedral and Westminster Abbey (*Lives of the Poets* 1.314–16).

3. SJ's "Philips" concludes with an unfinished "prefatory Discourse ... with a character of his writings" by Edmund Smith (*Lives of the Poets* 1.320–27).

4. SJ appends to his "Smith" a "ludicrous Analysis" in Latin of Smith's *Pocockius* (*Lives of the Poets* 11.21–22).

5. According to John Nichols, "Milton was begun in January 1779, and finished in six weeks" (*GM* 1785, p. 9).

Elizabeth Aston
THURSDAY 4 MARCH 1779

MS: Bodleian Library.

Dear Madam: Boltcourt, Fleetstreet, March 4, 1779

Mrs. Gastrel and You are very often in my thoughts, though I do not write so often as might be expected from so much love and so much respect. I please myself with thinking that I shall see You again, and shall find You better. But futurity is uncertain, poor David had doubtless many futurities in his head, which death has intercepted, a death, I believe, totally unexpected; He did not in his last hour seem to think his life in danger.[1]

My old complaints hang heavy on me, and my nights are very uncomfortable and unquiet; and sleepless nights make heavy days. I think to go to my Physitian, and try what can be done. For why should not I grow better as well as You?

Now You are better, pray, dearest Madam, take care of yourself. I hope to come this Summer and watch You.[2] It will be a very pleasant Journey if I can find You and dear Mrs. Gastrel well.[3]

I sent you two barels of oysters. If You would wish for more, please to send your commands to, Madam, Your most humble servant,

SAM. JOHNSON

1. *Ante* To Eva Maria Garrick, 21 Jan. 1779, n. 1.
2. *Ante* To Elizabeth Aston, 2 Jan. 1779, n. 3.
3. *Post* To Hester Thrale, 10 June 1779.

Lucy Porter

THURSDAY 4 MARCH 1779

MS: A.D.H. Pennant.

My dear Love: Boltcourt, Fleetstreet, March 4, 1779

Since I heard from You, I sent you a little print, and two barrels of Oysters, and I shall have some little books to send You soon.[1]

I have seen Mr. Peirson, and am pleased to find that he has got a living.[2] I was hurried when he was with me, but had time to hear that my Friends were all well.

1. SJ undoubtedly refers to the first installment of his *Prefaces*, published 31 Mar. (J. D. Fleeman, "Some Proofs of Johnson's *Prefaces to the Poets*," *The Library* 17, 1962, p. 213 n. 8). Cf. *Post* To JB, 13 Mar. 1779.

2. The Rev. John Batteridge Pearson (1749–1808), Perpetual Curate of St. Michael's, Lichfield (1774–82), had recently been appointed Vicar of Croxall, Derbyshire. Pearson was to be Lucy Porter's "principal legatee, and inheritor from her of many valuable Johnsonian relics" (*Johns. Glean.* 1.13–14).

Poor Mrs. Adey was, I think, a good woman and therefore her death is the less to be lamented, but [it] is [3] not pleasant to think, how uncertain it is, that when Friends part, they will ever meet again.[4]

My old complaints of flatulence, and tight and short breath oppress me heavily; my nights are very restless. I think of consulting the Doctor to morrow.

This has been a mild Winter, for which I hope you have been the better. Take what care You can of yourself and do not forget to drink. I was some how or other hindred from coming into the country last summer, but I think of coming this year.[5] I am, Dear Love, Your most humble servant,

SAM. JOHNSON

3. MS: "is" altered from "it"

4. Felicia Adey had died in Apr. 1778. As A. L. Reade comments, "Lichfield news seems to have come through slowly to Dr. Johnson" (*Johns. Glean.* IV.145).

5. *Ante* To Lucy Porter, 2 Jan. 1779; *Ante* To Elizabeth Aston, 2 Jan. 1779, n. 3.

John Taylor

TUESDAY 9 MARCH 1779

MS: Hyde Collection.

ADDRESS: To the Revd. Dr. Taylor, Ashbourne, Derbyshire.

POSTMARK: 9 MR.

ENDORSEMENT: 1779, 9 March 79.

Dear Sir: London, March 9, 1779

When you went away you desired me to remind You of your health; if any Mementos of mine could do you good, You should not want them, though I should write the same advice by every post. I have not indeed any advice to give You but that you keep your mind from disturbance, by attending to such things as You can supervise without anxiety. Utter inattention is a state both wretched and dangerous, and too much is likewise pernicious. Attention should be some thing less than anxiety, as[1] exercise is some thing less than labour.

1. MS: "as" altered from "an"

About meat and drink I have no counsel to give; I wish you could take more of both without oppression. Whatever oppresses must be hurtful.

I am afraid that you have not gotten your casting weights. They will supply you with very commodious exercise, if you do not tire yourself with them, and throw them quite away. Keep yourself cheerful, yet not forgetting that every decay is sent us to remind us of another world, and of the shortness of life. I am glad your Sunday is changed to Monday.

I will in a post or two write to Mr. Langley, and tell him all that he ought to know. I am glad that we talked about it.

I have very unquiet and tedious nights. I am come home for a few weeks to be a little in the world. But I like walking so little, that I can scarcely persuade myself to go out doors. Take care of yourself, and consult Dr. Butter.[2] Heberden's talk was rather prudential than medical, You might however perceive from it how much he thought peace of mind necessary to your reestablishment. I am, Dear Sir, Your affectionate servant,

SAM. JOHNSON

2. Cf. *Ante* To John Taylor, 31 Aug. 1772 and n. 4.

Hester Thrale

WEDNESDAY 10 MARCH 1779

MS: Houghton Library.

March 10, 1779

And so, dear Madam, it is a Mumm to see who will speak first.[1] I will come to see You on Saturday only let me know whether I must come to the borough, or am to be taken up here.[2]

1. According to SJ, there is a competition at "playing mum" (viz. keeping silent). Cf. his use of "humm" (*Ante* To Hester Thrale, 9 Nov. 1778).

2. SJ asks whether he should meet the Thrales at their house in Southwark or whether they will pick him up at Bolt Court.

Baretti's golden dream is now but silver. He is of my mind, he says, that there is no money for diversions.[3] But we make another onset on Friday, and this is to be the last time this season.[4]

I got my lives, not yet quite printed, put neatly together, and sent them to the King,[5] what he says of them I know not. Mr. Barnard could not speak to him. If the King is a Whig, he will not like them; but is any King a Whig?

So far I had gone when—in came Mr. Thrale, who will have the honour of bringing it. I am, Madam, Your most humble Servant,

SAM. JOHNSON

3. The American War had caused a severe decline in trade and a sharp rise in taxation. In the House of Commons on 1 Mar., Lord North had proposed increasing the excise tax an additional five percent (*Public Advertiser*, 2 Mar. 1779, pp. 2–3).   4. *Ante* To Hester Thrale, 21 Nov. 1778 and n. 9.

5. *Ante* To Lucy Porter, 4 Mar. 1779, n. 1. In 1767 the King had "expressed a desire to have the literary biography of this country ably executed, and proposed to Dr. Johnson to undertake it. Johnson signified his readiness to comply with his Majesty's wishes" (*Life* II.40).

James Boswell

SATURDAY 13 MARCH 1779

PRINTED SOURCE: JB's *Life*, 1791, II.281.

Dear Sir,   March 13, 1779

Why should you take such delight to make a bustle, to write to Mr. Thrale that I am negligent,[1] and to Francis to do what is so very unnecessary.[2] Thrale, you may be sure, cared not

1. "On the 23rd of February I wrote to him again, complaining of his silence, as I had heard he was ill, and had written to Mr. Thrale, for information concerning him" (*Life* III.372).

2. JB had written to Francis Barber on 22 Jan. 1779, "reminding him to preserve for me the M.S. and Proof sheets of his Master's *Prefaces Biographical and Critical to the English Poets*" (JB's Register of Letters, MS: Beinecke Library). Barber reported to JB on 19 Feb. that he "found it impracticable to collect the proof sheets regularly as they are work'd off; notwithstand the few which fell in

about it; and I shall spare Francis the trouble, by ordering a set both of the Lives and Poets to dear Mrs. Boswell, in acknowledgment of her marmalade.[3] Persuade her to accept them, and accept them kindly. If I thought she would receive them scornfully, I would send them to Miss Boswell, who, I hope, has yet none of her mamma's ill-will to me.

I would send sets of Lives, four volumes, to some other friends, to Lord Hailes first. His second volume lies by my bedside; a book surely of great labour, and to every just thinker of great delight.[4] Write me word to whom I shall send besides;[5] would it please Lord Auchinleck? Mrs. Thrale waits in the coach. I am, dear Sir, etc.

SAM. JOHNSON

---

my way I have carefully laid by in order to transmit them to you: however my Master has since order'd me to enform you that you shall shortly have the Books insteed of the above sheets" (Waingrow, p. 15).

3. *Ante* To Margaret Boswell, 22 July 1777. "He sent a set elegantly bound and gilt, which was received as a very handsome present" (Boswell's note).

4. The second volume of Hailes's *Annals of Scotland*, covering the period "From the Accession of Robert I, Surnamed Bruce, to the Accession of the House of Stewart," had just been published (*Walpole's Correspondence*, Yale ed. xv.140 and n. 2).   5. "This letter crossed me on the road to London" (*Life* III.373).

Hester Thrale

THURSDAY 18 MARCH 1779

PRINTED SOURCE: Piozzi, *Letters* II.43–44.

Dear Madam,
March 18, 1779

There is some comfort in writing, when such praise is to be had. Plato is a multitude.[1]

On Monday I came late to Mrs. Vesey. Mrs. Montague was there; I called for the print, and got good words.[2] The evening was not brilliant, but I had thanks for my company. The night was troublesome. On Tuesday I fasted, and went to the Doc-

1. *Ante* To John Wesley, 6 Feb. 1776, n. 3.
2. *Ante* To Hester Thrale, 15 Oct. 1778 and n. 3.

tor: he ordered bleeding. On Wednesday I had the teapot, fasted, and was blooded. Wednesday night was better. To-day I have dined at Mr. Strahan's at Islington, with his new wife.[3] To-night there will be opium. To-morrow the teapot. Then heigh for Saturday. I wish the Doctor would bleed me again. Yet every body that I meet says that I look better than when I was last met. I am, dearest Lady, Your, etc.

3. *Ante* To Hester Thrale, 21 Nov. 1778 and n. 10.

Thomas Cadell

WEDNESDAY 31 MARCH 1779

MS: Hyde Collection.

May[1] 31

Mr. Johnson desi[r]es Mr. Cadel to send him
Duty of Man 8vo.[2]
Nelson on the Festivals 8vo.[3]
They must be handsomely bound being for a present.[4]

1. Though SJ clearly wrote "May," this letter must predate To Thomas Cadell, 13 Apr. 1779. I therefore conjecture that "May" is a slip for "March." Cf. *Post* To Lucy Porter, 8 Mar. 1781 and n. 1.

2. *The Whole Duty of Man* (1658), the popular devotional treatise attributed to Richard Allestree (1619–81).

3. *Companion for the Festivals and Fasts of the Church of England* (1704) by Robert Nelson (1656–1715).   4. *Post* To Thomas Cadell, 13 Apr. 1779.

Hester Thrale

FRIDAY 9 APRIL 1779

MS: Hyde Collection.
ADDRESS: To Mrs. Thrale.

Madam: Friday, Apr. 9, 1779

An unexpected invitation will keep me here to Monday, but do, dear, sweet, fine, fair, kind, etc. etc. etc. etc. etc. etc. send

for[1] me before sunrise on Monday. I have sent you the books.[2]
I am, Dearest Lady, Your most, and most etc.

SAM. JOHNSON

1. MS: "for" superimposed upon "me"
2. *Ante* To Lucy Porter, 4 Mar. 1779 and n. 1.

Thomas Cadell
TUESDAY 13 APRIL 1779

MS: Boston Public Library.
ADDRESS: To Mr. Cadel.

Sir:

Apr. 13, 1779

The Duty of Man is not the right.[1] Nelson is bound in Sheepskin, a thing I never saw before.[2] I was bred a Bookseller, and have not forgotten my trade.

Do not let us teize one another about books. That they are lent about I suppose is true, but it must be principally by those that have bought them, which would have been done much less, if you had united every writer's life to his works, for then the borrower[3] must have carried away near twenty volumes whereas he now takes but four. I will venture to say that of those which I have given very few are lent. But be that as it may. You must supply me with what I think it proper to distribute among my friends. Let us have no dispute about it. I think myself not well used.[4] I am, Sir, Your very humble Servant,

SAM. JOHNSON

1. *Ante* To Thomas Cadell, 31 Mar. 1779 and n. 2.
2. A lowly sheepskin binding for Robert Nelson's august *Companion* would not have been appropriate under any circumstances; moreover, SJ had explicitly asked that it be "handsomely bound" (*Ante* To Thomas Cadell, 31 Mar. 1779 and n. 3; Philip Gaskell, *A New Introduction to Bibliography*, 1972, p. 152).
3. MS: undeciphered deletion before "borrower"
4. The tone and the substance of this letter suggest that Cadell had refused to be generous with presentation copies of SJ's *Prefaces*, complaining that they had been "lent about" and that sales of the first installment (*Works* and *Prefaces*, sixty volumes in all) had thereby been impaired. SJ counters that, had his prefaces not

been clustered together in four separate volumes, such widespread borrowing would have been difficult. Moreover, most of the lenders had bought the books they were distributing. SJ's indignation at Cadell's parsimony derives from the fact that he had been paid comparatively little for the project. Cadell might have argued, however, that SJ's dilatory ways had forced the consortium of booksellers to group his prefaces together, instead of annexing them directly to the poetical texts (*Bibliography Supplement*, p. 156).

Lucy Porter
c. THURSDAY 22 APRIL 1779[1]

MS: Hyde Collection.
ADDRESS: To Mrs. Lucy Porter, Lichfield.
FRANK: Hfreethrale.
POSTMARKS: 22 AP, FREE, B·E.

Dearest Madam:

Now the days grow longer and the weather warmer, I hope that, notwithstanding your presages, your health will mend, and your strength increase. Continual disorder of body is but an uncomfortable State, but I am afraid that in the latter part of life much health is not often to be expected. My nights are very restless and tedious, and my days for want of Sleep often heavy. I do not find that I am worse or better by changing air, and therefore it is with no great expectation of amendment that I make every year a journey into the country. But it is pleasant to visit those, whose kindness has been often experienced.

I hope to see Lichfield about the middle of May in my way to Derbyshire, and perhaps in June at my return homewards. If you want any books, let me know that I may procure them for you. Make my compliments to Mrs. Cobb and all my friends. I am, Dear Madam, Your humble servant,

SAM. JOHNSON

1. The evidence of the cover (postmark, frank, and receiver's stamp), as well as the references to "books," SJ's and Porter's health, and a trip to Lichfield "about the middle of May"—all point to 1779 as the year in which this (undated) letter was written.

James Boswell

MONDAY 26 APRIL 1779

PRINTED SOURCE: JB's *Life*, 1791, II.292.

Harley-street[1]

Mr. Johnson laments the absence of Mr. Boswell, and will come to him.[2]

1. SJ was dining at Allan Ramsay's, No. 67 Harley Street (see below, n. 2).

2. JB had written to SJ earlier that same day: "I am in great pain with an inflamed foot, and obliged to keep my bed, so am prevented from having the pleasure to dine at Mr. Ramsay's to-day, which is very hard; and my spirits are sadly sunk. Will you be so friendly as to come and sit an hour with me in the evening" (*Life* III.391). SJ kept his promise, and paid a call with Sir Joshua Reynolds. "The very sound of Dr. Johnson's voice roused me from my dejection" (*Boswell, Laird of Auchinleck*, ed. J. W. Reed and F. A. Pottle, 1977, p. 101).

Edmund Burke

TUESDAY 27 APRIL 1779

MS: Sheffield City Libraries (Wentworth Woodhouse Muniments).
ENDORSEMENT: Eminent Men, Saml. Johnson, 27 May 1779.

Dear Sir:

Apr. 27, 1779

I flatter myself that you will not be offended that I solicite a Favour. The Vicar of Coventry whose case I have enclosed is my Friend, and his petition is in my opinion not only just but modest.[1] His business will be brought before a Committee to morrow, and I beg your attendance and patronage.[2] I am, Sir, your most obedient and most humble servant,

SAM. JOHNSON

1. The Rev. Joseph Rann had twice petitioned the House of Commons for legislation to permit him "to collect the tithes (or their equivalent)" due to him (*Burke's Correspondence* IV.64 n. 1).

2. "On 19 April the House had resolved 'That all have Voices, who come to the Committee' on Coventry tithes. This made it possible for Burke, if he wished, to assist Rann. An Act was passed . . . it substituted a rate of one shilling in the pound for the tithes previously due to the Vicar" (*Burke's Correspondence* IV.64 n. 2).

John Wesley

MONDAY 3 MAY 1779

PRINTED SOURCE: JB's *Life*, 1791, II.294.

Sir,   May 3, 1779

Mr. Boswell, a gentleman who has been long known to me, is desirous of being known to you, and has asked this recommendation, which I give him with great willingness, because I think it very much to be wished that worthy and religious men should be acquainted with each other.[1] I am, Sir, Your most humble servant,

SAM. JOHNSON

    1. "Mr. Wesley being in the course of his ministry at Edinburgh, I presented this letter to him, and was very politely received" (*Life* III.394).

Lucy Porter

TUESDAY 4 MAY 1779

MS: Hyde Collection.
ADDRESS: Mrs. Lucy Porter, Lichfield.
FRANK: ffree W. Strahan.
POSTMARKS: 5 MA, FREE.

Dear Madam: May 4, 1779

Mr. Green has informed me that you are much better. I hope I need not tell you that I am glad of it. I cannot boast of being much better, my old nocturnal complaint still persues me, and my respiration is difficult, though much easier than when I left you the summer before last.[1] Mr. and Mrs. Thrale are well, Miss has been a little indisposed, but she is got well again. They have since the loss of their boy had two daughters, but they seem likely to want a Son.[2]

    1. *Ante* To Hester Thrale, 6 Nov. 1777.
    2. Henry Thrale the younger died in 1776; Cecilia was born in 1777, Henrietta (the last child) in 1778.

I hope you had some books which I sent you.[3] I was sorry for poor Mrs. Adey's death,[4] and am afraid you will be sometimes solitary, but endeavour, whether alone, or in company, to keep yourself chearful. My friends likewise die very fast, but such is the state of Man. I am, Dear Love, your most humble servant,

SAM. JOHNSON

3. *Ante* To Lucy Porter, 4 Mar. 1779 and n. 1.
4. *Ante* To Lucy Porter, 4 Mar. 1779 and n. 4.

John Taylor

TUESDAY 4 MAY 1779

MS: Houghton Library.
ADDRESS: Revd. Dr. Taylor, Ashbourn, Derbyshire.
FRANK: ffree W. Strahan.
POSTMARKS: 5 MA, 6 MA, FREE.
ENDORSEMENTS: 1779, 4 May 79.

Dear Sir:

May 4, 1779

It is a long time since I wrote to you, but alas! what have two sick old Friends to say to one another?[1] commonly nothing but that they continue to be sick. This at least is my case. Your last letter gave me hopes that it is less yours. But though we may be by intervals better, we know that we are in the main growing worse. This decline may however be hastened or retarded, and I hope we shall both retard it, as far as the laws of Nature permit. You are so regular that I know not what to advise more than You already do. I believe a moderate use of the weights will be useful,[2] but nequid nimis,[3] fatigue is dangerous.

Mr. Green of Lichfield has been here, and is returned loaded with Sir Ashton Levers Superfluities.[4] He said nothing

1. *Ante* To John Taylor, 9 Mar. 1779.
2. *Ante* To John Taylor, 9 Mar. 1779.
3. *nequid nimis*: "nothing in excess" (proverbial).
4. Sir Ashton Lever (1729–88), Kt., had created a museum of curiosities, called

of the affair of Wood, nor was it mentioned:[5] I am, Dear Sir, your most humble servant,

SAM. JOHNSON

---

the "Holophusikon," in Leicester House, Leicester Square, London. His celebrated collections included fossils, shells, stuffed birds, geological specimens, and primitive weapons. 5. *Ante* To John Taylor, 23 Dec. 1775.

Elizabeth Aston

TUESDAY 4 MAY 1779

MS: Houghton Library.

Dear Madam,   May 4, 1779

When I sent You the little books, I was not sure that You were well enough to take the trouble of reading them,[1] but have lately heard from Mr. Greene that you are much recovered. I hope You will gain more and more strength, and live many and many years, and I shall come again to Stowhill, and live as I used to do, with You and dear Mrs. Gastrel.

I am not well, my Nights are very troublesome, and my breath is short, but I know not that It grows much worse. I wish to see You. Mrs. Hervey has just sent to me to dine with her, and I have promised to wait on her to morrow.

Mr. Green comes home loaded with curiosities, and will be able to give his friends new entertainment.[2] When I come, it will be great entertainment to me, if I can find You and Mrs. Gastrel well, and willing to receive me.[3] I am, Dearest Madam, Your most humble servant,

SAM. JOHNSON

1. *Ante* To Lucy Porter, 4 Mar. 1779 and n. 1.
2. *Ante* To John Taylor, 4 May 1779 and n. 4.
3. *Post* To Hester Thrale, 29 May 1779.

Hester Thrale

MS: Rylands Library.

Dear Madam: May 20, 1779

The vicissitudes of things and the Eddies of life are now carrying You southward,[1] and me northward.[2] When shall we meet
again?

I must beg of You to send Mr. Watson's papers to my house,
directed for him, and sealed up.[3] I know not whether he does
not think himself in danger of piracy.

Take care that Susy sees all that Sophy has seen, that she
may tell her travels, and give them a taste of the world,[4] and
take care, and write to me very often, till we meet again, and
keep Master in good thoughts of me. Vale.

1. MS: "southward" altered from "southwards"
2. SJ was about to leave for Lichfield, the Thrales for Brighton.
3. These papers may have been related to the "History of the Reign of Philip
III" upon which Robert Watson was working at the time of his death (1781).
4. Sophia Thrale had been to Brighton before, Susanna had not. Hester
Thrale replied: "Sophy shews Susan the Wonders of the Deep very ludicrously;
and they are both at this moment employed in writing to some of their Schoolfel-
lows to tell them how happily they live here" (26 May 1779, MS: Rylands Library).

Hester Thrale

MS: Hyde Collection.

Madam: Lichfield, May 29, 1779

I have now been here a week, and will try to give you my Journal, or such parts of it as are fit in my mind for communication.

On friday. We set out about twelve, and lay at Daventry.

On Saturday. We dined with Mr. Rann at Coventry. He intercepted us at the town's end. I saw Tom Johnson who had

hardly life to know that I was with him. I hear he is since dead. In the Evening I came to Lucy, and walked to Stow hill; Mrs. Aston was gone or[1] going to Bed. I did not see her.

Sunday. After diner I went to Stow hill, and was very kindly received. At night I saw my old Friend Brodhurst—you know him—the play fellow of my infancy, and gave him a Guinea.[2]

Monday. Dr. Taylor came, and we went with Mrs. Cobb to Greenhill Bower.[3] I had not seen it perhaps for fifty years. It is much degenerated. Every thing grows old. Taylor is to fetch me next Saturday.

Mr. Green came to see us, and I ordered some physick.

Tuesday. Physick, and a little company. I din'd I think, with Lucy both Monday and Tuesday.

Wednesday ⎫ I had a few visits, from Peter Garrick among
Thursday ⎬ the rest, and dined at Stow hill. My breath
⎭ very short.

Friday. I dined at Stowhill, I have taken Physick four days together.

Saturday. Mrs. Aston took me out in her chaise, and was very kind. I dined with Mrs. Cobb and came to Lucy with whom I found, as I had done the fi[r]st day, Lady Smith and Miss Vyse. I find that Dr. Vyse talks here of Miss Stratfield.

This is the course of my life. You do not think it much makes me forget Streatham. However it is good to wander a little, lest one should dream that all the world was Streatham, of which one may venture to say *None but itself can be its parallel.*[4] I am, Dear Madam, your most humble servant,

SAM. JOHNSON

1. MS: "or" superimposed upon "to"

2. Possibly Walter Broadhurst, watchmaker, who lived on Breadmarket Street (*Johns. Glean.* III.136). Hester Thrale may have met him during her visit to Lichfield in 1774.

3. On Whit Monday it was customary for the heads of the Lichfield wards to parade at Green Hill, accompanied by Morris dancers, and for the Corporation to provide free food and drink to all the inhabitants of the city (Thomas Harwood, *History and Antiquities of the Church and City of Lichfield*, 1806, p. 352).

4. "None but Itself can be its Parallel" (Lewis Theobald, *Double Falshood* III. i.18). Theobald's line is mocked by Pope in the *Dunciad*: "For works like these let deathless Journals tell, / 'None but Thy self can be thy parallel'" (1728, III.271–72).

Hester Thrale

THURSDAY 10 JUNE 1779

MS: Hyde Collection.
ADDRESS: To Henry Thrale, Esq., in Southwark.
POSTMARKS: ASHBORNE, 12 IV, FREE.

Dear Madam: Ashbourne, June 10, 1779

I am surprised to find that I can be away and write so seldom, but I have very little to say. Mr. Green was much delighted with his afternoon at your house, and returned home much enriched by Mr. Lever.[1]

Poor Lucy is so much enfeebled in her feet that she cannot walk to church, and what is far worse, has her hearing very much impaired. I wish Miss would write to her. She will be glad.

Mrs. Aston is better than when I left her two years ago; but she eats almost nothing. Every body else is as when you left us.

I have tried Phlebotomy[2] and Physick but with no great success, but, I think, I am not worse.

Here is Dr. Taylor, better in his health likewise than he was. He eats little, but drinks by measure a full quart of water every dinner, which he says has quite cured the swelling of his legs. I dined two days ago with the old set of friends, male and female. I am, Dear Madam, your most humble servant,

SAM. JOHNSON

1. *Ante* To John Taylor, 4 May 1779 and n. 4.
2. *phlebotomy*: "bloodletting; the act or practice of opening a vein for medical intentions" (SJ's *Dictionary*).

Hester Thrale

SATURDAY 12 JUNE 1779

MS: Hyde Collection.

Dear Madam: Ashbourne, June 12, 1779

Your account of Mr. Thrales ilness is very terrible, but when I remember that he seems to have it peculiar to his constitution, that whatever distemper he has, he always has his head affected, I am less frighted. The seizure was, I think, not apoplectical, but hysterical, and therefore not dangerous to life.[1] I would have you however consult such Physitians as you think, you can best trust. Bromfield seems to have done well, and by his practice appears not to suspect an apoplexy.[2] That is a solid and fundamental comfort. I remember Dr. Marsigli an Italian Physician whose seizure was more violent than Mr. Thrale's, for he fell down helpless, but his case was not considered as of much danger, and he went safe home, and is now a professor at Padua. His fit was considered as only hysterical.

I hope Sir Philip who franked your letter comforts you as well as Mr. Seward.[3] If I can comfort you, I will come to you, but I hope you are now no longer in want of any help to be happy. I am, Dearest Madam, your most humble servant,

SAM. JOHNSON

The Dr. sends his compliments, he is one of the people that are growing old.

1. On 8 June Henry Thrale had suffered a stroke "as he sate at Dinner with his Sister Nesbitt ... his Brain is apparently loaded if not for ever injured by the blow" (*Thraliana* I.389). According to J. L. Clifford, "Although Thrale rallied quickly from this stroke, he never quite recovered his full strength" (1952, p. 176).

2. "I called Dr. Burney; beg'd him to fly in the Post Chaise which was then waiting for him—and send me some Physician Sir R. Jebb or Pepys, or if no one else could be found, my old Accoucheur Doctor Bromfield of Gerard Street. 'Twas *he* that came; and convincing me it was an Apoplectic Seizure, acted accordingly" (Piozzi II.48).

3. Sir Philip Jennings Clerke (1722–88), of Duddleston Hall, Salop, and Lyndhurst, Hants., M.P. for Totnes (1768–88), a political associate and friend of Henry Thrale (Namier and Brooke II.680). On 1 Mar. 1779 Hester Thrale reported that Sir Philip "has been very assiduous about me of late, and seems to pant after our Society. ... Sir Phillip has nothing particular to recommend him but good plain sense and Manners highly polished" (*Thraliana* I.372).

Hester Thrale

MS: Hyde Collection.

Dear Madam: Ashbourne, June 14, 1779

How near we all are to extreme danger.[1] We are[2] merry or
sad, or busy or idle, and forget that Death is hovering over us.
You were a dear Lady for writing again. The case as you now
describe it is worse than I conceived it when I read your fi[r]st
letter. It is still however not apoplectick, but seems to have
something worse than hys[t]erical, a tendency to a palsy, which
I hope, however, is now over. I am glad that you have Heberden, and hope We are all safer. I am the more alarmed by this
violent seizure, as I can impute it to no wrong practices or
intemperance of any kind, and therefore know not how any
defence or preservatives can be obtained. Mr. Thrale has certainly less exercise than when he followed the foxes,[3] but he is
very far from unweildiness[4] or inactivity, and further still
from any vitious or dangerous excess. I fancy however he will
do well to ride more.

Do, dear Madam, let me know every post, how he goes on.
Such sudden violence is very dreadful, we know not by what it
is let loose upon us, nor by what its effects are limited.

If my coming can either assist or divert, or be useful to any
purpose, let me but know. I will soon be with you.

Mrs. Kennedy, Queeny's Baucis, ended last week a long life
of disease and poverty.[5] She had been married about fifty
years.

1. *Ante* To Hester Thrale, 12 June 1779 and n. 1.   2. MS: "are are"
3. *Ante* To Hester Thrale, 31 Oct. 1778 and n. 2.
4. MS: "ness" repeated as catchword
5. "Old Kennedy and his Wife were two of the greatest scholars in England. . . .
They were imagining at what Time the Sun shone first upon the Earth, instead of
minding how to live upon it themselves. Miss Thrale (whom we called Queeney)
said humourously that they resembled Baucis and Philemon in Ovid" (H. L.
Piozzi's note in *Letters*, 1788, II.50: Trinity College, Cambridge). The Rev. John
Kennedy (1698–1782), D.D., Rector of Bradley, Derbyshire, was the author of *A
Complete System of Astronomical Chronology* (1763), to which SJ had contributed the

Dr. Taylor is not much amiss, but always complaining. I am, Madam, your most humble servant,   SAM. JOHNSON

Direct the next to Lichfield.

dedication. Assisted by his wife Catherine (?1700–79), whom SJ considered "a Hebrew scholar of the very first Rate" (*Life* 1.547), Kennedy "studied for forty-two years to establish the date of the creation of the world" (Hazen, p. 74; *Johns. Glean.* xi.280).

Nathan Wetherell

MONDAY 14 JUNE 1779

MS: Huntington Library.

ADDRESS: To the Reverend Dr. Wetherel in Oxford.

POSTMARKS: ASHBORNE, 16 IV.

Sir: Ashbourne, June 14, 1779

Dr. Taylor one of the Prebenderies of Westminster has lately lost by sudden death a Curate who had served his Living of Bosworth in Leicestershire more than twenty years.[1] The allowance is fifty pounds a year. If Mr. Maurice of your College has not something better, he may perhaps think it worth his acceptance, and I beg that You will propose it to him.[2] It is a large parish, but there are two Curates.[3]

My first wish is to accommodate Mr. Maurice, but upon his

1. John Ledbrooke (*c.* 1733–79), B.A. (Emmanuel College, Cambridge, 1757), curate of Market Bosworth from *c.* 1758, had died at the beginning of June (*Alum. Cant.* II.iv.128; information supplied by Canon John Seymour, The Rectory, Market Bosworth).

2. The Rev. Thomas Maurice (1754–1824), poet, classical scholar, and orientalist, had graduated from University College, Oxford, in 1778. SJ, who met Maurice through Samuel Parr, contributed a preface to his translation of *Oedipus Rex* (Hazen, pp. 136–42). Soon after taking his B.A. Maurice was ordained and made curate (on the recommendation of Dr. Wetherell) to the Rev. John Shepherd, Rector of Woodford, Essex. Maurice apparently did not think the curacy of Bosworth "worth his acceptance": he continued at Woodford until 1785, when he became chaplain of Epping, Essex (*GM* 1824, pp. 468–69).

3. Taylor's other curate was James Richardson, who served from 1775 to 1788, when the living passed to Thomas Wright (information supplied by Canon John Seymour).

refusal, any Gentleman whom You shall be pleased to recommend will be received by Dr. Taylor.[4] As the want is immediate and pressing, it must be supplied with speed. A little delay might be perhaps endured in favour of Mr. Maurice, but if a stranger comes it will be expected that he should come quickly.

You will be pleased to direct your answer to Dr. Taylor in Ashbourne, Derbyshire, for perhaps I may not stay her[e] long enough to receive it. I am, Sir, Your most humble Servant,

SAM. JOHNSON

4. Ledbrooke was succeeded by Francis Simpson (*c.* 1757–1827), B.A. (University College, 1777) (*Alum. Oxon.* II.iv.1299; information supplied by Canon John Seymour).

Charles Burney

THURSDAY 17 JUNE 1779

MS: Marion Pottle.

Sir: [Ashbourne] June 17, 1779

I am extremely obliged to you for your attention, and intelligence. It was happy that You happened to be at Streatham, when this dreadful attack was made.[1] You will do what you can, and I hope soon to come and help you. I am, Dear Sir, Your obliged, humble Servant,

SAM. JOHNSON

1. *Ante* To Hester Thrale, 12 June 1779, n. 2.

Hester Thrale

THURSDAY 17 JUNE 1779

PRINTED SOURCE: Chapman II.293–94.

Dear Madam: Asbourne, June 17, 1779

It is certain that your first letter did not alarm me in proportion to the danger, for indeed it did not describe the danger as it was.[1] I am glad that you have Heberden, and hope his restoratives and his preservatives will both be effectual. In the preservatives dear Mr. Thrale must concur, yet what can he reform? or what can he add to his regularity and temperance? He can only sleep less. We will do however all we can. I go to Lichfield to morrow with intent to hasten to Streatham.

Both Mrs. Aston and Dr. Taylor have had strokes of the palsy. The Lady was sixty eight, and at that age has gained ground upon it.[2] The Dr. is you know not young and he is quite well, only suspicious of every sensation in the peccant arm. I hope My dear Master's case is yet slighter, and that as his age is less, his recovery will be more perfect. Let him keep his thoughts diverted, and his mind easy. I am, Dearest and dearest, Your most humble servant,   SAM. JOHNSON

1. *Ante* To Hester Thrale, 12 June 1779, n. 1.
2. *Ante* To Elizabeth Aston, 4 May 1779.

Hester Thrale

SATURDAY 19 JUNE 1779

MS: Hyde Collection.

Dear Madam: Lichfield, June 19, 1779

Whether it was that your description of dear Mr. Thrales disorder was indistinct, or that I am not ready at guessing calamity, I certainly did not know our danger, our danger for sure I have a part in it, till that danger was abated.[1]

I am glad that Dr. Heberden and that you perceive so plainly his recovery.[2] He certainly will not be without any warning that I can give him against pernicious practices. His

1. *Ante* To Hester Thrale, 12 June 1779; 14 June 1779.
2. Hester Thrale's letter of 17 June begins: "Heberden finds Mr. Thrale vastly better. ... His Spirits mend apace now, and his good humour returns with his looks, they were quite dreadful last Sunday, but the Convalescence since then has been prodigiously rapid" (MS: Rylands Library).

proportion of sleep if he slept in the night, was doubtless very uncommon, but I do not think,[3] that he slept himself into a palsy. But perhaps a lethargick is likewise a paralytical disposition. We will watch him as well as we can. I have known a Man who had a stroke like this dye forty[4] years afterward without another. I hope we have now nothing to fear, or no more than[5] is unalterably involved in the life of Man.

I begin now to let loose my mind after Queeny and Burney.[6] I hope they are[7] both well. It will not be long before I shall be among you, and it is a very great degree of pleasure to hope that I shall be welcome.[8] I am, Dear Madam, your most humble servant,

SAM. JOHNSON

3. MS: "think" superimposed upon undeciphered erasure
4. MS: "fo" superimposed upon "af"   5. MS: "than" altered from "that"
6. "They were learning Latin of him—but Dr. Burney would not let *his* Girl go on—he thought Grammar too Masculine a Study for Misses" (Piozzi II.53). On 20 July Frances Burney reported: "Dr. Johnson gives us a Latin lesson every morning. . . . What progress we may make in this most learned scheme I know not. . . . To devote so much time to acquire something I shall always dread to have known, is really unpleasant enough" (*Diary and Letters of Madame D'Arblay*, ed. Austin Dobson, 1904, I.252).   7. MS: "a" superimposed upon "h"
8. *Post* To Hester Thrale, 26 June 1779.

Henry Thrale

c. SUNDAY 20 JUNE 1779

MS: Hyde Collection.
ADDRESS: To Henry Thrale, Esq., in Southwark.
POSTMARKS: LITCHFIELD, FREE, [Undeciphered].

Dear Sir: [Lichfield] July 15,[1] 1779

Though I wrote yesterday to my Mistress, I cannot forbear writing immediately to you, my sincere congratulation upon

1. The Lichfield postmark establishes that this letter was incorrectly dated: on 15 July SJ was back in London. Chapman (II.293) assigns it to *c.* 18 June, the day SJ returned from Ashbourne to Lichfield (*Ante* To Hester Thrale, 17 June 1779). A more persuasive interpretation of the surviving evidence places this letter after

your recovery from so much disorder, and your escape from so much danger.[2] I should have had a very heavy part in the misfortune of losing you, for it is not likely that I should ever find such another friend, and proportionate at least to my Fear must be my pleasure.

As I know not that you brought this disease upon yourself by any irregularity I have no advice to give you. I can only wish, and I wish it sincerely, that you may live long and happily, and long count among those that love you best, Dear Sir, your most humble servant,

SAM. JOHNSON

To Hester Thrale, 19 June 1779, which responds to her good news from Streatham, dated 17 June (MS: Rylands Library). Although SJ preferred not to write on Sundays, he broke this rule in cases of urgency.

2. *Ante* To Hester Thrale, 12 June 1779 and n. 1.

Henry Thrale

WEDNESDAY 23 JUNE 1779

MS: William Strutz.

Dear Sir: Lichfield, June 23, 1779

To show You how well I think of your health I have sent you an hundred pounds to keep for me. It will come within the day of quarter day, and that day You must give me.[1] I came by it in a very uncommon manner, and would not confound it with the rest.[2]

1. In this instance, at least, SJ expected Henry Thrale to act as his personal banker. SJ's comment on the quarter-day (*Ante* To Hester Thrale, 10 Nov. 1777, n. 12) makes it clear that he looked for interest on his deposit. His meaning seems to be that, although the money will actually arrive one day late (on 25 instead of 24 June), Thrale must consider interest due for the entire quarter.

2. On 16 Mar. 1776 SJ was paid £100 by C. Rivington. According to J. D. Fleeman, the receipt for this payment marks "the most likely source, but it is still not clear what the money came from, or where it had been in the meantime" ("The Revenue of a Writer: Samuel Johnson's Literary Earnings," in *Studies in the Book Trade in Honour of Graham Pollard*, 1975, pp. 216, 227 n. 32). It is unlikely, moreover, that the sum in question here derives from literary earnings (information supplied by Dr. J. D. Fleeman).

My wicked Mistress talks as if she thought it possible for me to be indifferent or negligent about your health or hers. If I could have done any good, I had not delayed an hour to come to you, and I will come very soon to try if my advice can be of any use, or my Company of any entertainment.

What can be done, You must do for yourself. Do not let any uneasy thought settle in your mind. Chearfulness and exercise are your great remedies. Nothing is for the present worth your anxiety. Vivite læti is one of the great rules of health.[3] I believe it will be good to ride often but never to weariness, for weariness is itself a temporary resolution of the nerves, and is therefore to be avoided. Labour is exercise continued to fatigue, Exercise is labour used only while it produces pleasure.

Above all keep your mind quiet, do not think with earnestness even of your health, but think on such things as may please without too much agitation, among which, I hope, is, Dear Sir, your most obliged and most humble servant,

SAM. JOHNSON

3. *Dum fata sinunt* / *vivite laeti*: "While the fates permit, live happily" (Seneca, *Hercules Furens*, ll. 177–78, trans. F. J. Miller, Loeb ed.). SJ owned a copy of Seneca's tragedies at the time of his death (Greene, 1975, p. 102).

Hester Thrale

THURSDAY 24 JUNE 1779

MS: Hyde Collection.

Dear Madam: [Lichfield] June 24, 1779

Though I wrote yesterday to Mr. Thrale I think, I must write this day to you, and I hope this will be the last letter, for I am coming up as fast as I can, but to go down cost me seven guineas, and I am loth to come back at the same charge.

You really do not use me well in thinking that I am in less pain on this occasion than I ought to be. There is nobody left for me to care about but you and my Master, and I have now for many years known the value of his Friendship, and the importance of his life, too well not[1] to have him very near my heart. I did not at first understand his danger,[2] and when I knew it, I was told likewise that it was over—and over I hope it is for ever.[3] I have known a Man seized in the same manner, who, though very irregular and intemperate, was never seized again.[4] Do what you can however, to keep my Master cheerful and slightly busy till his health is confirmed, and if we can be sure of that let Mr. Perkins go to Ireland and come back, as opportunity offers, or necessity requires, and keep yourself airy[5] and be a *funny little thing.*[6] I am, Madam, your most humble servant,

SAM. JOHNSON

1. MS: "not" repeated as catchword
2. *Ante* To Hester Thrale, 12 June 1779.
3. *Ante* To Hester Thrale, 19 June 1779 and n. 2.   4. MS: semicolon
5. MS: "airy" superimposed upon "che" partially erased
6. "It was a Hack-Joke to call me a funny little thing" (Piozzi II.56).

Hester Thrale

SATURDAY 26 JUNE 1779

MS: British Library (Charnwood Collection).

Dearest Lady: Lichfield, June 26, 1779

Now I find that You are pacified,[1] I can more cheerfully tell You that I shall leave this place next Monday, to find from Birmingham the easiest way home, and when I come I will tell You what little I have to tell, which I hope my dear Masters health will allow You leisure to hear. But You will now have the whole tale to yourself, and a very interesting tale it is.

Taylor was well enough content to see me go. The Ladies at Stowhil are sorry to part and Lucy shows some tenderness.

1. "You have been exceedingly kind, and I have been exceedingly cross; and now my Master is got well, and my Wrath over, I ask your Pardon sincerely" (Hester Thrale to SJ, 24 June 1779, MS: Rylands Library).

But I hope to be welcome at Streatham, and hope nothing will make Streatham less pleasing to me. I am, Dearest and Dearest, Your most humble servant,

SAM. JOHNSON

Frances Reynolds

c. TUESDAY 29 JUNE 1779

MS: Hyde Collection. A copy in the hand of Frances Reynolds.

Dear Madam: London, June 27,[1] 1779

I have sent what I can for your German friend. At this time it is very difficult to get any money, and I cannot give much.[2] I am, Madam, Your most affectionate and most humble servant,

SAM. JOHNSON

1. This letter must have been misdated, for SJ did not leave Lichfield until 28 June (*Ante* To Hester Thrale, 26 June 1779). I have conjecturally assigned it to the first possible day on which he could have written from London.
2. *Ante* To Hester Thrale, 10 Mar. 1779 and n. 3.

Charles Dilly

TUESDAY 13 JULY 1779

PRINTED SOURCE: JB's *Life*, 1791, II.294.

Sir,

Since Mr. Boswell's departure I have never heard from him;[1] please to send word what you know of him, and whether you have sent my books to his lady.[2] I am, etc.

SAM. JOHNSON

1. "I did not write to Johnson, as usual, upon my return to my family; but tried how he would be affected by my silence" (*Life* III.394).
2. *Ante* To JB, 13 Mar. 1779 and n. 3. Dilly had despatched "Dr. Johnson's Present of a Set of Poets for your Lady" on 24 May (Charles Dilly to JB, 25 May 1779, MS: Beinecke Library).

James Boswell
TUESDAY 13 JULY 1779

PRINTED SOURCE: JB's *Life*, 1791, II.295.

Dear Sir,   July 13, 1779

What can possibly have happened, that keeps us two such strangers to each other? I expected to have heard from you when you came home; I expected afterwards. I went into the country and returned; and yet there is no letter from Mr. Boswell. No ill I hope has happened; and if ill should happen, why should it be concealed from him who loves you? Is it a fit of humour, that has disposed you to try who can hold out longest without writing?[1] If it be, you have the victory. But I am afraid of something bad; set me free from my suspicions.[2]

My thoughts are at present employed in guessing the reason of your silence: you must not expect that I should tell you any thing, if I had any thing to tell. Write, pray write to me, and let me know what is, or what has been the cause of this long interruption. I am, dear Sir, Your most affectionate servant,

SAM. JOHNSON

1. *Ante* To Charles Dilly, 13 July 1779, n. 1.

2. JB replied on 17 July, complaining of "a supine indolence of mind" but confessing as well that he had put SJ to a "test" (*Life* III.395–96).

Thomas Lawrence
THURSDAY 29 JULY 1779

PRINTED SOURCE: Maggs Catalogue No. 343, 1916, p. 290.

Something has happened that will detain me in the Country on Saturday.[1] We will therefore take some day next week for our business.

1. By "the country" SJ undoubtedly means Streatham Park.

John Taylor

TUESDAY 3 AUGUST 1779

MS: Berg Collection, New York Public Library.
ADDRESS: To the Revd. Dr. Taylor at Ashbourne, Derbyshire.
ENDORSEMENTS: 1779, 3 Augt. 79.

Dear Sir: August 3, 1779

Since my return hither I have applied myself very diligently to the care of my health.[1] My Nights grew better at your house, and have never since been bad; but my breath was very much obstructed; yet I have at last got it tolerably free. This has not been done without great efforts.[2] Of the last fifty days I have taken mercurial physick, I believe, forty, and have lived with much less animal food than has been my custom of[3] late.

From this account you may, I think, derive hope and comfort. I am older than You, my disorders had been of very long continuance, and if it should please God that this recovery is lasting,[4] You have reason to expect an abatement of all the pains that encumber your life.

Mr. Thrale has felt a very heavy blow.[5] He was for some time without reason, and I think without utterance. Heberden was in great doubt whether his powers of mind would ever return. He has however perfectly recovered all his faculties and all his vigour. He has a fontanel in his back.[6] I make little doubt but that, notwithstanding your dismal prognostication You may see one another again.

He purposes this autumn to spend some time in hunting on the downs of Sussex.[7] I hope You are diligent to take as much exercise as you can bear. I had rather you rode twice a day than tired yourself in the morning. I take the true definition of exercise to be labour without weariness.[8]

1. SJ returned to London *c.* 29 June (*Ante* To Hester Thrale, 26 June 1779).
2. MS: comma   3. MS: "o" superimposed upon "t"   4. MS: period
5. *Ante* To Hester Thrale, 12 June 1779 and n. 1.
6. *fontanel*: "an artificial ulcer or a natural issue for the discharge of humours from the body" (*OED*).   7. Cf. *Ante* To Hester Thrale, 31 Oct. 1778 and n. 2.
8. Cf. *Ante* To Henry Thrale, 23 June 1779.

When I left you, there hung over you a cloud of discontent which is I hope dispersed. Drive it away as fast as You can. Sadness only multiplies ⟨it⟩self.[9] Let us do our duty, and be cheerful. ⟨I am,⟩ Dear Sir, Your humble servant,

SAM. JOHNSON

9. MS: mutilated along right-hand margin

Lucy Porter

TUESDAY 24 AUGUST 1779

MS: Hyde Collection.

Dear Madam: London, Aug. 24, 1777[1]

I suppose you are all frighted at Lichfield and indeed the terror has been very general, but I am still of opinion that there is not yet any danger of invasion.[2] The French fleet were within sight of Plymouth, but no gun was, I believe fired on either side. I had a note from Mr. Chamier (the under secretary of State) yesterday, that tells me. *The combined fleet* (of French and Spaniards) *are not in sight of land. They are supposed to be driven out of the channel by the Easterly wind.*

The English fleet under Hardy is much inferiour to[3] that of the Enemy in number of vessels, but our ships are said to have greater guns, and to be better manned. The Battle, whenever

1. MS: misdated; correct year established by references to prospective Franco-Spanish invasion

2. On 4 June the French fleet, under the command of the Comte d'Orvilliers, had sailed from Brest to join the Spanish fleet and then launch a joint attack on the Isle of Wight and Portsmouth. The English fleet, consisting of forty-six sail of the line under Sir Charles Hardy, was unable to prevent an enemy rendezvous: together the invasion fleet consisted of sixty-six ships, in addition to twelve frigates. Assembled at Le Havre and St. Malo were forty thousand troops ready to cross the Channel, once a beachhead had been established. On 17 Aug. the enemy fleet appeared off Plymouth. After a series of confused maneuvers on both sides, the Franco-Spanish fleet, many of whose sailors were ill, sailed back to Brest, having failed to engage the English (Robert Beatson, *Naval and Military Memoirs*, 1804, VI.190–96; A. T. Patterson, *The Other Armada*, 1960, pp. 149–51, 160, 162, 194–212).   3. MS: "to" repeated as catchword

it happens, will be probably of greater consequence than any battle in our time. If the French get the better we shall perhaps be invaded, and must fight for ourselves upon our own ground, if Hardy prevails all danger of that kind is at an end. If we are invaded the King is said to have resolved that he will head his own army.

Do not pay any regard to the newspapers: you will only disturb yourself. When there is any thing worth telling you, I design to let you know it. At present, it is the general opinion that the first action of consequence will be a great naval battle, and till that is over, all other designs, whatever they are, will be suspended. I am, Dear Madam, your humble servant,

SAM. JOHNSON

James Boswell
THURSDAY 9 SEPTEMBER 1779

PRINTED SOURCE: JB's *Life*, 1791, II.296.

My Dear Sir,   Streatham, Sept. 9, 1779

Are you playing the same trick again, and trying who can keep silence longest?[1] Remember that all tricks are either knavish or childish; and that it is as foolish to make experiments upon the constancy of a friend, as upon the chastity of a wife.

What can be the cause of this second fit of silence, I cannot conjecture; but after one trick, I will not be cheated by another, nor will harrass my thoughts with conjectures about the motives of a man who, probably, acts only by caprice. I therefore suppose you are well, and that Mrs. Boswell is well too; and that the fine summer has restored Lord Auchinleck.[2] I am much better than you left me; I think I am better than when I was in Scotland.

1. *Ante* To JB, 13 July 1779 and n. 2. JB had last written on 22 July: "My letter was a pretty long one, and contained a variety of particulars; but he, it should seem, had not attended to it" (*Life* III.396).

2. JB's father had been suffering from his habitual complaint, stoppage of urine.

I forgot whether I informed you that poor Thrale has been in great danger.[3] Mrs. Thrale likewise has miscarried, and been much indisposed.[4] Every body else is well; Langton is in camp.[5] I intend to put Lord Hailes's description of Dryden into another edition,[6] and as I know his accuracy, wish he would consider the dates, which I could not always settle to my own mind.

Mr. Thrale goes to Brighthelmston, about Michaelmas, to be jolly and ride a hunting. I shall go to town, or perhaps to Oxford.[7] Exercise and gaiety, or rather carelessness, will, I hope, dissipate all remains of his malady; and I likewise hope by the change of place, to find some opportunities of growing yet better myself. I am, dear Sir, Your humble servant,

SAM. JOHNSON

3. *Ante* To Hester Thrale, 12 June 1779 and n. 1.

4. On 10 Aug. Hester Thrale "miscarried in the utmost Agony before they could get me into Bed, after fainting five Times" (*Thraliana* I.401). "The stillborn child was a boy, full term, and perfectly formed" (Hyde, 1977, p. 220).

5. *Ante* To Bennet Langton, 29 Aug. 1778 and n. 1.

6. Hailes's description, which had come to SJ via JB, was not included in the revised edition of the *Lives of the Poets*, 1783. JB later passed on to Edmond Malone "the few notices concerning Dryden, which Lord Hailes had collected" (*Life* III.397 n. 3).

7. On 17 Sept. SJ traveled to Epsom, Surrey, to stay in the country house of Anthony Chamier (*Works*, Yale ed. I.298–99). On 5 Oct. the Thrales left for Brighton via Tunbridge Wells (Clifford, 1952, p. 180).

John Taylor

THURSDAY 9 SEPTEMBER 1779

MS: Hyde Collection.

ADDRESS: To the Revd. Dr. Taylor, Ashbourne, Derbys.

FRANK: Hfreethrale.

POSTMARKS: 9 SE, FREE, B·E.

Dear Sir: Streatham, Sept. 9, 1779

It is now long since I wrote to You, and I have had no answer.[1]

1. *Ante* To John Taylor, 3 Aug. 1779.

Are you well? If you are let me know it. If you are afflicted with any disease, take care that you do not make it worse by discontent. I sometimes fancy that you feel a painful disappointment from the manner in which the Bishoprick of Glocester has been bestowed; which has defered your hopes to another removal.[2] The matter has not fallen out as You would wish, but You have no unkindness[3] or neglect to complain of in your friends, and have therefore no reason to think your importance lessened or your influence diminished; you have suffered no degradation; what you wished to obtain is not given to another, and you do not want preferment for the money that it would bring; you desire it only for the sake of more extensive influence, which you may be well enough content without, though I do not blame your eagerness to have it.

I have not relapsed, and hope yet to mend. I suspect that I have eaten too much fruit this summer, but that temptation is near an end. Mr. Thrale continues gradually mending.[4] The Lady has had a miscarriage worse she says than any child birth, but she likewise is well, or growing better very fast.[5]

Of publick affairs I can tell you nothing, that you have not in the newspapers. I have no conviction that any invasion was ever intended, or that the French have had any transports on the opposite coast.[6] Their fleet is certainly more numerous than ours, and therefore it will not be prudent to fight till we are stronger for the hazard of the battle is all our own. If we beat them we only save ourselves, if they beat us, it is hard to say where the mischief would end. I am, Sir, your most humble servant,

SAM. JOHNSON

2. William Warburton (1698–1779), Bishop of Gloucester (1759–79), had been replaced by the Hon. James Yorke (1730–1808), previously Bishop of St. David's. Although SJ's tactful phrasing leaves the matter in some doubt, it seems clear that the nomination of Yorke had blocked another one of Taylor's schemes for preferment—possibly to the cathedral deanery (*Post* To John Taylor, 19 Oct. 1779). His longing to be made a dean continued unabated and unsatisfied: *Post* To Hester Thrale, 14 Nov. 1781.　　　　　3. MS: "unkindnest"

4. *Ante* To Hester Thrale, 12 June 1779 and n. 1.

5. *Ante* To JB, 9 Sept. 1779, n. 4.

6. *Ante* To Lucy Porter, 24 Aug. 1779 and n. 2.

Hester Thrale

MS: Hyde Collection.

Dear Madam: Monday, Oct. 4, 1779

I had intended to send you such a card as I have inclosed, when I was alarmed by hearing, that my Servant had told in the house, for servants never tell their Masters, his[1] opinion that for the two last days Mr. Thrale was visibly worse. His eyes are keen, and his attention upon such occasions vigorous enough.

I therefore earnestly wish that before you set out, even though you should lose a day, you would go together to Heberden, and see what advice he will give you.[2] In this doubtful pendulous state of the distemper, advice may do much, and Physicians, be their power less or more, are the only refuge that we have in sickness. I wish you would do yet more, and propose to Heberden a consultation with some other of the Doctors, and if Laurence is at present fit for business, I wish he might be called, but call somebody. As you make yourselves of more importance, you will be more considered. Do not go away with any reason to tax yourselves with negligence. You are in a state in which nothing that can be done, ought to be omitted. We now do right or wrong for a great Stake. You may send the Children and Nurses forward to morrow, and go yourselves on Wednesday. Little things must not now be minded, and least of all must you mind a little money. What the world has, is[3] to be sold, and to be enjoyed by those that will pay its price. Do not give Heberden a single Guinea, and subscribe a hundred to keep out the French, we have an invasion more formidable, and an enemy

1. MS: "h" superimposed upon "f"
2. Before the Thrales' departure on 5 Oct., "Mr. Thrale had looked particularly ill for two or three Days, and his Head had wander'd in a Conversation he held with Lady Lade, but he was cupped by Dr. Heberden's advice and the Symptoms went off" (*Thraliana* I.409).   3. MS: "is" altered from "it"

less resistible by power and less avoidable by flight.[4] I have now done my duty. I am, Dearest Lady, your humble servant,

SAM. JOHNSON

4. *Ante* To Lucy Porter, 24 Aug. 1779 and n. 2.

Hester Thrale

TUESDAY 5 OCTOBER 1779

MS: Hyde Collection.

Dear Madam: Oct. 5, 1779

When Mr. Boswel waited on Mr. Thrale in Southwark, I directed him to watch all appearances with close attention, and bring me his observations. At his return he told me that without previous intelligence he should not have discovered that Mr. Thrale had been lately ill.

It appears to me that Mr. Thrales disorder whether grumous or serous,[1] must be cured by bleeding, and I would not have him begin a course of exercise without considerable evacuation.[2] To encrease the force of the blood, unless it be first diluted and attenuated may be dangerous. But the case is too im[por]tant for my theory.

The weakness in my ankles left them for a day but has now turned to a pain in my toe, much like that at Brighthelmston.[3] It is not bad nor much more than troublesome. I hope it will not be greater nor last long.[4] You all go with the good wishes of, Dear Madam, Your most humble servant,

SAM. JOHNSON

1. *grumous*: "thick; clotted"; *serous*: "thin; watery" (SJ's *Dictionary*).
2. *Ante* To Hester Thrale, 4 Oct. 1779 and n. 2.
3. SJ may be referring to his visit during the autumn of 1776: he had been suffering from gout the previous summer (*Ante* To JB, 6 July 1776).
4. *Post* To Hester Thrale, 8 Oct. 1779.

Hester Thrale

FRIDAY 8 OCTOBER 1779

MS: Hyde Collection.

Dear Madam: London, Oct.[1] 8, 1779

I begin to be frighted at your omission to write, do not torment me[2] any longer, but let me know where You are, how you got thither, how you live there and every thing else, that one friend loves to know of another.[3]

I will show you the way.

On Sunday the gout left my ankles, and I went very commodiously to Church. On Monday night I felt my foot uneasy. On Tuesday I was quite lame. That night I took an opiate, having first taken physick and fasted. Towards morning on Wednesday the pain remitted. Bozzy came to me, and much talk we had.[4] I fasted another day, and on[5] Wednesday night could walk tolerably.[6] On Thursday finding myself mending, I ventured on my dinner, which I think has a little interrupted my convalescence. To day I have again taken physick and eaten only some stewed apples. I hope to starve it away. It is now not worse than it was at Brighthelmston.[7]

This, Madam, is the history of one of my toes; the[8] history of my head would perhaps be much shorter. I thought it was the gout on Saturday. It has already lost me two dinners

1. MS: "Oct." superimposed upon "November" partially erased
2. MS: "me" altered from "my"
3. The Thrales and Frances Burney left Streatham on 5 Oct., visited Knole, spent two nights at Tunbridge Wells, then traveled on to Brighton (*Diary and Letters of Madame D'Arblay*, ed. Austin Dobson, 1904, 1.270–80; Clifford, 1952, p. 180).
4. JB's journal for this period has not been recovered. He was in London by 4 Oct., and remained there until the 18th. "During this visit to London I had several interviews with him, which it is unnecessary to distinguish particularly" (*Life* III.400, 411).   5. MS: "on" superimposed upon "at"
6. MS: "rably" repeated as catchword
7. *Ante* To Hester Thrale, 5 Oct. 1779 and n. 3.
8. MS: "the" altered from "this"

abroad, but then I have not been at much more charges for I have eaten little at home.

Surely I shall have a letter to morrow. I am, Madam, your most humble servant,

SAM. JOHNSON

Hester Thrale

MONDAY 11 OCTOBER 1779

MS: Huntington Library.

Dear Madam: London, Oct. 11, 1779

I thought [it] very long till I heard from you, having sent a second letter to Tunbridge, which I believe You cannot have received.[1] I do not see why You should trouble yourself with Physicians, while Mr. Thrale grows better. Company and bustle will I hope, compleat his cure. Let him gallop over the downs in the morning, call his friends about him to dinner, and frisk in the rooms at night,[2] and outrun time, and outface misfortune.

Notwithstanding all authorities against bleeding Mr. Thrale bled himself well ten days ago.[3]

You will lead a jolly life, and perhaps think little of me, but I have been invited twice to Mrs. Vesey's Conversation,[4] but have not gone. The Gout that was in my ankles, when Queeney criticised my gait, passed into my toe, but I have hunted it, and starved it, and it makes no figure. It has drawn some attention, for Lord and Lady Lucan sent to enquire after me. This is all the news that I have to tell you. Yesterday I dined with Mr. Strahan, and Boswel was there; We shall be

1. This letter has not been recovered.

2. *Ante* To Hester Thrale, 6 Oct. 1777, n. 7.

3. "Mr. Thrale *never* prescribed for himself in his Life—he was surrounded by Physicians, and did what they recommended except forbearing to eat to Excess" (Piozzi II.63). *Ante* To Hester Thrale, 4 Oct. 1779 and n. 2.

4. *conversation*: "an 'at home'; *conversazione*" (*OED*).

both to morrow at Mr. Ramsays. Now sure I have told you quite all, unless you yet want to be told that I am, Madam, Your most humble servant,

SAM. JOHNSON

Hester Thrale

SATURDAY 16 OCTOBER 1779

MS: Hyde Collection.

Dear Madam: Oct. 16, 1779

The advice given you by Dr. Pepys agrees very exactly with my notions.[1] I would not bleed but in exigencies. Riding and cheerfulness will, I hope, do all the business. All alive and merry, must be my Master's motto.[2]

How did you light on your specifick for the toothach? You have now been troubled with it long, I am glad you are at last relieved.

You say nothing of the *Younglings*,[3] I hope they are not spoiled with the pleasures of Brighthelmston, a dangerous place, we were told, for *children*. You will do well to keep them out of harm's way.

From the younglings let me pass to a Veteran, you tell me nothing of Mr. Scrase, I hope he is well and chearful and communicative. Dos Mr. Thrale go and talk with [him] and do you run in and out? You may both be the better for his conversation.

I am sorry for poor Thomas, who was a decent and civil Man. It is hard that he should be overwhelmed by a new-comer. But *Thou by some other shalt be laid as low.*[4] Bowen's day

1. Lucas Pepys (1742–1830), M.D., later (1784) Bt., a prominent London physician who attended both SJ and the Thrales.

2. Cf. *Ante* To Henry Thrale, 23 June 1779 and n. 3.

3. SJ refers to Frances Burney and Queeney Thrale (aged 27 and 15 respectively). He may be playing on the title of Burney's comedy *The Witlings*, which she had finished that spring (*Diary and Letters of Madame D'Arblay*, ed. Austin Dobson, 1904, I.213).

4. "Boast not my Fall (he cry'd) insulting Foe! / Thou by some other shalt be laid as low" (Pope, *The Rape of the Lock* v.97–98).

may come.[5] A finer shop may be erected, kept by yet a finer man, and crouded by greater numbers of fine Gentlemen and fine Ladies.

My Foot gives me very little trouble, but it is not yet well.[6] I have dined since you saw me not so often as once in two days. But I am told how well I look, and I really think I get more mobility. I dined on Tuesday with Ramsay, and on Thursday with Paoli, who talked of coming to see you, till I told him of your migration.

Mrs. Williams is not yet returned, but discord and discontent reign in my humble habitation as in the palaces of Monarchs. Mr. Levet and Mrs. Desmoulins have vowed eternal hate. Levet is the more insidious, and wants me to turn her out. Poor Williams writes word that she is no better, and has left off her physick. Mr. Levet has seen Dr. Lewis, who declares himself hopeless of doing her any good. Lawrence desponded some time ago.

I thought I had a little fever some time, but it seems to be starved away. Bozzy says, he never saw me so well.[7] I hope, you will say the same when you see me, methinks it be pleasant to see you all, there is no danger of my forgetting you. Only keep or grow all well, and then I hope our meeting will be happy. I am, Dear Madam, your most humble servant,

SAM. JOHNSON

5. "Mrs. Thrale entered all our names at Thomas's, the fashionable bookseller; but we find he has now a rival . . . who seems to carry away all the custom and all the company. This is a Mr. Bowen, who is just come from London, and who seems just the man to carry the world before him as a shopkeeper" (Dobson, *D'Arblay*, I.281). R. Thomas had opened a circulating library at Brighton in 1774 (Dobson, *D'Arblay*, I.281 n. 1).

6. *Ante* To Hester Thrale, 8 Oct. 1779; 11 Oct. 1779.

7. *Ante* To Hester Thrale, 8 Oct. 1779, n. 4.

Lucy Porter

MS: Hyde Collection.

Dear Madam: London, Octr. 19, 1779

You tell me I must write, and I would willingly please You, but we have so little in common that I have not much to write about. Publick affairs are very bad, and I do not see that they are mending,[1] yet I cannot advise you to sell your stock, for the same reasons as those which I mentioned in the last letter.[2] The interest of a Mortgage, if a Mortgage could be got, is seldom regular.

Poor Mr. Thrale has been struck with a palsy but he is so well recovered as to ride a hunting.[3] It has been a dreadful alarm. The family is gone to Brighthelmston.[4] Mrs. Thrale had violent pains about her face, but she is got well.[5]

The course of Physick which I began at Lichfield, I have scarcely discontinued, and it has done great things for me.[6] Every body tells me how well I look. The Gout however laid hold on my foot about ten days ago, but as I have no great opinion of the benefits which the Gout is said to bring, I gave it such a reception, that I got very nearly rid of it in two days.[7] I am however not quite as I wish but who is quite as he wishes.

Mrs. Desmoulins Doctor Swinfen's daughter, and her daughter are still with me, but the money which they cost me I should not spend perhaps better. She is agreeable enough but I do not think over well of her, and her Daughter by ill health or ill management is I am afraid what Ladies call a *dawdle*.

1. *Ante* To Hester Thrale, 10 Mar. 1779, n. 3.
2. SJ may be referring to an unrecovered letter: To Lucy Porter, 24 Aug. 1779, does not mention financial matters.
3. *Ante* To Hester Thrale, 12 June 1779 and n. 1.
4. *Ante* To Hester Thrale, 8 Oct. 1779, n. 3.
5. *Ante* To Hester Thrale, 16 Oct. 1779.
6. *Ante* To John Taylor, 3 Aug. 1779.
7. *Ante* To Hester Thrale, 8 Oct. 1779; 11 Oct. 1779; *Post* To John Taylor, 9 Dec. 1779.

Mrs. Williams is visiting her friends in the country. She and Desmoulins are fire and water, when they are together they quarrel, and when they are apart they abuse one another.[8]

Make my compliments to Mr. Pearson.[9]

There is yet talk of an invasion, but I am not yet convinced that there is any real danger.[10] I hope however you patrol the streets.

On the eighteenth of last month I was seventy years old. I have lived long, and how little have I done? Let us, my dear, love one another while we yet live, and let me be remembred in your prayers. I am, My dear, your most humble servant,

SAM. JOHNSON

I fancy before you have this letter, Mr. Boswel will have been among you at Lichfield. He set out on Sunday on his way to Chester.[11]

8. Cf. *Ante* To Hester Thrale, 9 Nov. 1778.

9. A manuscript note describes the descent of this letter from Lucy Porter to John Pearson to his wife Elizabeth, who gave it in 1813 "to Mrs. Curzon for Lady Bisshopp." 10. *Ante* To Lucy Porter, 24 Aug. 1779 and n. 2.

11. JB, on an autumn "jaunt" with Colonel James Stuart, arrived in Lichfield 18 Oct., and left on the 19th for Chester, where he stayed approximately two weeks before returning to Edinburgh via Carlisle (*Boswell, Laird of Auchinleck*, ed. J. W. Reed and F. A. Pottle, 1977, p. 139). *Post* To JB, 27 Oct. 1779.

Frances Reynolds

TUESDAY 19 OCTOBER 1779

MS: Loren Rothschild.

ADDRESS: To Mrs. Reynolds.

ENDORSEMENT: Dr. Johnson, Oct. 79.

Dearest Madam: Oct. 19, 1779

You are extremely kind in taking so much trouble. My foot is almost well,[1] and one of my first visits will certainly be to Dover Street.

1. *Ante* To Hester Thrale, 11 Oct. 1779.

You will do me a great favour if You will buy for me the prints of Mr. Burke, Mr. Dyer, and Dr. Goldsmith, as You know a good impression.[2]

If any of your own pictures be engraved buy them for me,[3] I am fitting a little room with prints.[4] I am, Dear Madam, Your most humble Servant,

SAM. JOHNSON

2. SJ refers to engravings after the portraits by Sir Joshua Reynolds of Edmund Burke, Samuel Dyer, and Oliver Goldsmith (Edward Hamilton, *The Engraved Works of Sir Joshua Reynolds*, 1884, pp. 12–13, 25, 31–32).

3. Charles Townley engraved at least two of Frances Reynolds's portraits— those of Elizabeth Montagu and John Hoole (Richard Wendorf and Charles Ryskamp, "A Blue-Stocking Friendship," *Princeton University Library Chronicle* 41, 1980, pp. 197–98).

4. The sale catalogue of SJ's library lists nine lots worth (654–662) of "prints framed and glazed" (ed. J. D. Fleeman, 1975, p. 64). Cf. *Ante* To Hester Thrale, 15 Oct. 1778 and n. 3.

John Taylor

TUESDAY 19 OCTOBER 1779

MS: Berg Collection, New York Public Library.
ADDRESS: To the Reverend Dr. Taylor in Ashbourne, Derbyshire.
POSTMARKS: 19 OC, [Undeciphered].
ENDORSEMENTS: 1779, 19 Octr. 79.

Dear Sir: London, Oct. 19, 1779

When I found that the Deanery had given you no uneasiness I was satisfied, and thought no more of writing.[1] You may indeed very well be without it, and [I] am glad to find that You think so yourself. You have enough, if you are satisfied.

Mr. Thrale, after whose case You will have a natural curiosity, is with his family at Brighthelmston.[2] He rides very vigorously, and runs much into company, and is very angry if it be thought that any thing ails him.[3] Mrs. Thrale thinks him for

1. *Ante* To John Taylor, 9 Sept. 1779 and n. 2.
2. *Ante* To Hester Thrale, 8 Oct. 1779, n. 3.
3. *Ante* To Hester Thrale, 12 June 1779 and n. 1.

the present in no danger. I had no mind to go with them, for I have had what Brighthelmston can give,[4] and I know not they much wanted me.

I have had a little catch of the gout, but as I have no great opinion of the benefits which it is supposed to convey, I made haste to be easy, and drove it away after two days.[5]

Publick affairs continue to go on without much mending,[6] and there are those still who either fright themselves or would fright others with an invasion;[7] but my opinion is that the French neither have nor had in any part of the summer a number of ships on the opposite coast equal to the transportation of twenty or of ten thousand Men. Such a fleet can not be hid in a creek, it must be easily visible and yet I believe no man has seen the man that has seen it. The Ships of war were within sight of Plymouth, and only within sight.

I wish, I knew how your health stands. My Friends congratulate me upon my looks,[8] and indeed I am very free from some of the most troublesome of my old complaints, but I have gained this relief by very steady use of mercury and purgatives, with some opium, and some abstinence.[9] I have eaten more fruit this summer than perhaps in any since I was twenty years old, but though it certainly did me no harm, I know not that I had any medicinal good from it.

Write to me soon. We are both old. How few of those whom we have known in our youth are left alive. May we yet live to some better purpose. I am, Sir, your most humble servant,

SAM. JOHNSON

4. MS: "give" repeated as catchword

5. *Ante* To Hester Thrale, 8 Oct. 1779; 11 Oct. 1779. It was widely believed that occurrences of the gout preserved one from potentially more serious maladies. Horace Walpole, a frequent and vocal sufferer, told William Cole, "the gout certainly carries off other complaints" (*Walpole's Correspondence*, Yale ed. 1.366). *Post* To John Taylor, 9 Dec. 1779.

6. *Ante* To Hester Thrale, 10 Mar. 1779, n. 3.

7. *Ante* To Lucy Porter, 24 Aug. 1779 and n. 2.

8. Cf. *Ante* To Hester Thrale, 16 Oct. 1779.

9. Cf. *Ante* To John Taylor, 3 Aug. 1779.

Frances Reynolds

THURSDAY 21 OCTOBER 1779

MS: Hyde Collection.
ADDRESS: To Mrs. Reynolds.
ENDORSEMENT: Dr. Johnson in believe 79.[1]

Dear Madam: Oct. 21

I want no company but yours, nor wish for any other. I will wait on you on Saturday, and am so well that I am very able to find my way without a carriage. I am, Dear Madam, Your most humble servant,

SAM. JOHNSON

1. MS: "80" del. before "79"

Hester Thrale

THURSDAY 21 OCTOBER 1779

MS: Hyde Collection.

Dear Madam: London, Oct. 21, 1779

Your treatment of little Perkins was undoubtedly right;[1] when there is so strong a reason against any thing as unconquerable terrour, there ought surely to be some mighty reason for it, before it is done. But for putting into the water a child already well it is not very [easy] to find any reason strong or weak. That the nurses fretted will supply me during life with an additional motive to keep every child, as far as is possible, out of a Nurse's power. A Nurse made of common mould will have a pride in overpowering a child's reluctance. There are few minds to which tyranny is not delightful; Power is nothing but

1. John Perkins's wife and eldest child were ill with scarlet fever. Hester Thrale had taken his second son Henry (1776–1855) with them to Brighton (Piozzi II.67; *Thraliana* I.407 and n. 6).

as it is felt, and the delight of superiority is proportionate to the resistance overcome.

I walked yesterday to Covent garden, and feel to day neither pain nor weakness. Send me, if you can, such an account of yourself and my Master.

Sir Philip sent me word that he should be in town, but he has not yet called.[2] Yesterday came Lady Lucan, and Miss Bingham,[3] and she said it was the first visit that she had paid.

Your new friend Mr. Bowen who has sold fifty sets, had but thirty to sell, and, I am afraid, has yet a set or two for a friend.[4] There is a great deal of fallacy in this world. I hope you do not teach the company wholly to forsake poor Thomas.[5]

The want of company is an inconvenience, but Mr. Cumberland is a Million, make the most of what you have. Send my Master out to hunt in the morning, and to walk the rooms in the evening, and bring him as active, as a stag on the mountain back to the Borough. When he is in motion he is mending.

The young ones are very good in mi[n]ding their book.[6] If I do not make something of them *'Twill reflect upon me, as I know not my trade*,[7] for their parts are sufficiently known, and every body will have a better opinion of their industry than of mine. However, I hope when they come back to accustom them to more lessons.

Your account of Mr. Scrase gives me[8] no delight. He was a friend upon all occasions, whether assistance was wanted from the purse or the understanding. When he[9] is gone our barrier against calamity is weakened, and we must act with more cau-

2. *Ante* To Hester Thrale, 12 June 1779, n. 3.

3. Lavinia Bingham (1762–1831), the eldest daughter of Lord and Lady Lucan, married (1781) Viscount Althorp, later (1783) second Earl Spencer.

4. Presumably SJ refers to the first installment of *The Works of the English Poets, with Prefaces, Biographical and Critical.* Four volumes of prefaces and fifty-six volumes of poets constituted a set, which sold for £7 10s. (*Bibliography Supplement,* p. 156).   5. *Ante* To Hester Thrale, 16 Oct. 1779 and n. 5.

6. *Ante* To Hester Thrale, 19 June 1779, n. 6.

7. "And what will Folks say, if they see You afraid? / It reflects upon Me; as I knew not my Trade" (Matthew Prior, "The Thief and the Cordelier," ll. 36–37).

8. MS: "m" altered from "n"   9. MS: "he" altered from "his"

tion, as we shall be in more danger. Consult him, while his advice is[10] yet to be had.[11]

What makes Cumberland hate Burney?[12] Delap is indeed a rival,[13] and can upon occasion *provoke a bugle*, but what has Burney done? Dos he not like her book?[14]

Dr. Burney has passed one Evening with me. He has made great discoveries in a library at Cambridge, and he finds so many precious materials, that his Book must be a Porters load.[15] He has sent me another sheet.[16] I am, Dearest of all dear Ladies, Your most humble servant,

SAM. JOHNSON

10. MS: "is" altered from "it"

11. Though Charles Scrase was not in good health, he survived until 1792.

12. Richard Cumberland had been behaving with ostentatious rudeness to Frances Burney at Brighton. "All the folks here impute the whole of this conduct to its having transpired that I am to bring out a play [*The Witlings*] this season; for Mr. Cumberland, though in all other respects an agreeable and a good man, is so notorious for hating and envying and spiting all authors in the dramatic line, that he is hardly decent in his behaviour towards them" (*Diary and Letters of Madame D'Arblay*, ed. Austin Dobson, 1904, 1.286). *Ante* To Hester Thrale, 16 Oct. 1779, n. 3.

13. Frances Burney referred caustically to Delap as "my brother-dramatist" (Dobson, *D'Arblay*, 1.222). In 1779 Delap "was writing a play called *Macaria* on the story of the widow and daughter of Hercules, probably that produced at Drury Lane in 1781 as *The Royal Suppliants*" (Dobson, *D'Arblay*, 1.219 n. 4).

14. SJ refers to Burney's first novel, *Evelina* (1778).

15. Charles Burney was amassing materials on medieval music for the second volume of his *General History*. He recorded in his poetic autobiography: "In September, to Cambridge I fly for a week / Fresh materials for Volume the Second to seek / In the manuscripts which have been ages interr'd / In Sepulchres whence they can ne'er be transferr'd" (Roger Lonsdale, *Dr. Charles Burney*, 1965, p. 251).

16. "Although it is not clear what useful criticism, other than stylistic, Johnson could offer, Burney obviously treasured the faintest signs of interest from his idol and continued showing him the proofs of his book, perhaps as some kind of return of confidence, since Burney saw the *Lives of the Poets* in both manuscript and proof at this period" (Lonsdale, *Burney*, p. 252).

Sir

The Booksellers of London have undertaken a kind of Body of English Poetry, excluding generally the dramas, and I have undertaken to put before each authours works a sketch of his life, and a character of his writings. Of some, however I know very little, and am afraid I shall not easily supply my deficiencies. Be pleased to inform me whether among Mr Bakers manuscripts, or any where else at Cambridge any materials are to be found. If any such collection can be gleaned, I doubt not of your willingness to direct our search, and will tell the booksellers to employ a transcriber. If you think my

TO RICHARD FARMER, 22 JULY 1777

(The Pierpont Morgan Library)

is, doubtless, the great epistolick art.

In a Man's Letters you know, Madam, his soul lies naked, his Letters are only the mirrors of his breast, whatever passes within him is shewn undisguised in its natural process, Nothing is inverted, nothing distorted, you see Systems in their elements, you discover actions in their motives.

Of this great truth sounded by the knowing to the ignorant, and so echoed by the ignorant to the knowing, what evidence have you now before you. Is not my Soul laid open in these voluntary pages? do not you see me reduced to my first principles? This is the pleasure of corresponding with a friend, where doubt and distrust have no place, and every thing is said as it is thought. The original Idea is laid down in its simple purity, and all the supervenient conceptions, are spread over it in Stratum super Stratum, as they happen to be formed. These are the Letters by which souls are united, and by which Minds naturally in unison move each other as they are mo-

TO HESTER THRALE, 27 OCTOBER 1777
(Hyde Collection)

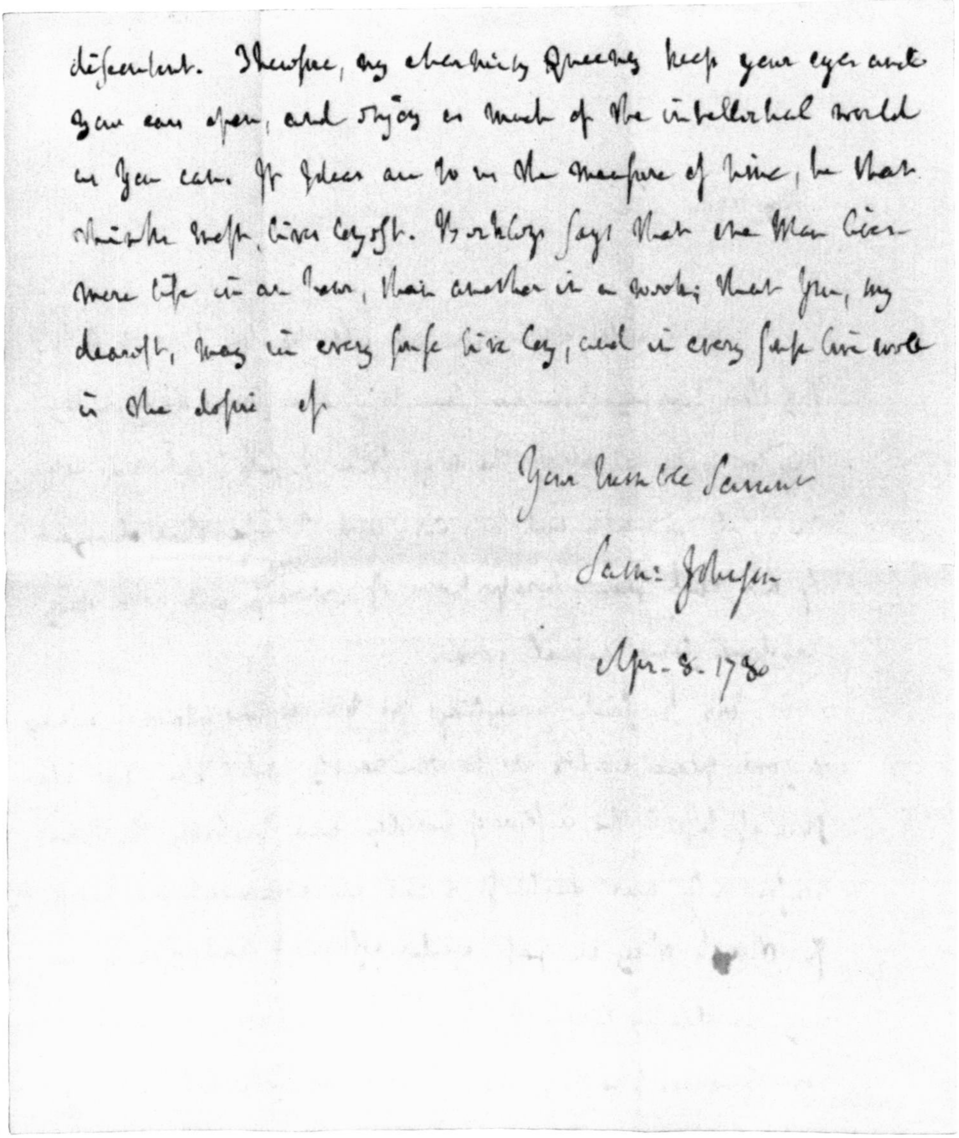
discontent. Therefore, my charming Queeney keep your eyes and
ears open, and enjoy as much of the intellectual world
as you can. If Ideas are to us the measure of time, he that
thinks most, lives longest. Berkeley says that one Man lives
more life in an hour, than another in a week; that you, my
dearest, may in every sense live long, and in every sense live well
is the desire of

Your humble Servant

Sam: Johnson

Apr. 8. 1780

TO HESTER MARIA THRALE, 8 APRIL 1780
(The Earl of Shelburne)

Mr Johnson knows that Sir Joshua Reynolds and the other Gentlemen will excuse his incompliance with the rule, when they are told that Mr Thrale died this morning.

Wolseley

(The date should have been 4 April 1781.)

TO SIR JOSHUA REYNOLDS, 4 APRIL 1781
annotated by James Boswell (The Beinecke Rare Book and Manuscript
Library, Yale University)

Elizabeth Aston

MS: Pembroke College, Oxford.

Dearest Madam: Bolt court, Fleetstreet, Oct. 25, 1779

Mrs. Gastrel is so kind as to write to me, and yet I always write to you, but I consider what is written to either as written to both.

Publick affairs do not seem to promise much amendment, and the nation is now full of distress.[1] What will be [the] event of things, none can tell, we may still hope for better times.

My health which I began to recover, when I was in the country, continues still in a good state, it costs me indeed some physick, and something of abstinence, but it pays the cost. I wish, dear Madam, I could hear a little of your improvements.[2]

Here is no news. The talk of the invasion seems to be over.[3] But a very turbulent session of Parliament is expected; though turbulence is not likely to do any good.[4] Those are happyest who are out of the noise and tumult. There will be no great violence of faction at Stowhill, and that it may [be] free from that and all other inconvenience and disturbance, is the sincere wish of all your Friends. I am, Dear Madam, your most humble servant,

SAM. JOHNSON

1. Cf. *Ante* To Lucy Porter, 19 Oct. 1779.
2. MS: "ments" repeated as catchword
3. *Ante* To Lucy Porter, 24 Aug. 1779 and n. 2.
4. In the autumn of 1779 there was considerable political unrest: the American War dragged on, the economic recession continued, and Ireland was clamoring for free trade. It was expected that Lord North's ministry might fall or at least be severely weakened. "The inglorious and unprosperous events of the summer, the general discontent and dissatisfaction that are arisen; but above all the crack that has happened in the administration itself ... such a concurrence of untoward circumstances naturally suggested a vision of much diminution of the majority" (*Walpole's Correspondence*, Yale ed. XXIV.533–34). When Parliament opened on 25 Nov., however, the Government beat back the challenge from the Opposition.

Hester Thrale

MONDAY 25 OCTOBER 1779

MS: Hyde Collection.

Dear Madam: London, Oct. 25, 1779

Let me repair an injury done by misinformation to Mr.
Bowen. He had at first indeed only thirty, that [1] is, two shares;
but he afterwards purchased two shares more. So all that he
says, I suppose, is true.[2]

On Saturday I walked to Dover Street, and back.[3] Yesterday
I dined with Sir Joshua. There was Mr. Elliot of Cornwal, who
enquired after my Master.[4] At night I was bespoken by Lady
Lucan, but she was taken ill, and the assembly was put off. I
am to dine with Renny to morrow.

I hope Mr. Thrale scours the country after the early horn,
and at night flutters about the rooms and once a day makes a
lusty dinner.[5] I eat meat but once in two days, at most but four
times a week, reckoning several weeks together, for it is neither necessary nor prudent to be nice in regimen. Renny told
me yesterday that I look better than when she knew me first.

It is now past the Postman's time and I have no letter, and
that is not well done, because I long for a letter, and you
should always let me know whether you and Mr. Thrale and
all the rest are, or are not well. Do not serve me so often, because your silence is always a disappointment.

Some old Gentlewomen at the next door are in very great
distress. Their little annuity comes from Jamaica, and is therefore uncertain,[6] and one of them has had a fall, and both are

1. MS: initial "t" superimposed upon "a"
2. *Ante* To Hester Thrale, 21 Oct. 1779 and n. 4.
3. *Ante* To Frances Reynolds, 21 Oct. 1779.
4. Edward Eliot (1727–1804), of Port Eliot, Cornwall, later (1784) first Baron
Eliot, M.P. for St. Germans (1748–68), Liskeard (1768–74), and Cornwall (1775–
1784); Receiver General of the Duchy of Cornwall (1749–1804) (Namier and
Brooke II.368). Eliot, "a patron of Reynolds and one of Reynolds's most valued
friends" (Fifer, p. xlvii), was elected to The Club in 1782.
5. *Ante* To Hester Thrale, 11 Oct. 1779.
6. It was widely expected that Jamaica would soon fall to the French (*Walpole's*

very helpless, and the poor have few to help them. Persuade my Master to let me give them some thing for him. It will be bestowed upon real Want.[7]

I hope all the Younglings go on well,[8] that the two eldest are very prudent, and the rest very merry. We are to be merry but a little while, Prudence soon comes to spoil our mirth. Old times have bequeathed us a precept directing us to *be merry and wise*,[9] but who has been able to observe it.

There is a very furious fellow writing with might and main against the life of Milton.[10] I am, Madam, your most humble servant,

SAM. JOHNSON

Correspondence, Yale ed. XXXIII.135). However, it remained under British control throughout the American War.

7. *Post* To Hester Thrale, 28 Oct. 1779; 2 Nov. 1779.

8. *Ante* To Hester Thrale, 16 Oct. 1779 and n. 3.

9. "It is good to be merry (witty) and wise" (*Oxford Dictionary of English Proverbs*, rev. F. P. Wilson, 1970, p. 527).

10. Attacks on SJ's "Milton" had begun in the *Westminster Magazine*, May 1779 (H. L. McGuffie, *SJ in the British Press*, 1976, p. 234). It was to prove the most controversial of his *Prefaces*: even the favorable reviewers tended to censure SJ for political prejudice. This particular "furious fellow" has not been identified.

James Boswell

WEDNESDAY 27 OCTOBER 1779

PRINTED SOURCE: JB's *Life*, 1791, II.307.

Dear Sir,   London, Oct. 27, 1779

Why should you importune me so earnestly to write?[1] Of what importance can it be to hear of distant friends, to a man who finds himself welcome wherever he goes, and makes new friends faster than he can want them?[2] If, to the delight of

1. JB had concluded his letter of 22 Oct., sent from Chester: "I beg it of you, my dear Sir, to favour me with a letter while I am here, and add to the happiness of a happy friend" (*Life* III.413).

2. After describing his warm reception from all SJ's friends in Lichfield, JB had remarked: "I cannot say that I ever passed two hours with more self-

such universal kindness of reception, any thing can be added by knowing that you retain my good-will, you may indulge yourself in the full enjoyment of that small addition.

I am glad that you made the round of Lichfield with so much success: the oftener you are seen, the more you will be liked. It was pleasing to me to read that Mrs. Aston was so well; and that Lucy Porter was so glad to see you.

In the place where you now are, there is much to be observed; and you will easily procure yourself skilful directors. But what will you do to keep away the *black dog* that worries you at home?[3] If you would, in compliance with your father's advice, enquire into the old tenures and old charters of Scotland, you would certainly open to yourself many striking scenes of the manners of the middle ages. The feudal system, in a country half-barbarous, is naturally productive of great anomalies in civil life. The knowledge of past times is naturally growing less in all cases not of publick record; and the past time of Scotland is so unlike the present, that it is already difficult for a Scotchman to image the oeconomy of his grandfather. Do not be tardy nor negligent; but gather up eagerly what can yet be found.[4]

We have, I think, once talked of another project, a History of the late insurrection in Scotland, with all its incidents.[5] Many falsehoods are passing into uncontradicted history. Voltaire, who loved a striking story, has told what we could not find to be true.[6]

You may make collections for either of these projects, or for both, as opportunities occur, and digest your materials at lei-

---

complacency than I did those two at Lichfield. Let me not entertain any suspicions that this is idle vanity. Will not you confirm me in my persuasion, that he who finds himself so regarded has just reason to be happy?" (*Life* III.412–13).

3. References to the "black dog" of depression occur most frequently in letters about Henry Thrale's melancholic moods.

4. *Ante* To JB, 31 Aug. 1772 and n. 5.

5. During JB's visit to Ashbourne, Sept. 1777, SJ had urged him to publish a "History of the Civil War in Great-Britain in 1745 and 1746" (*Life* III.162).

6. In chaps. XXIV–XXV of his *Siècle de Louis XV* (1763), Voltaire presents a romanticized account of the Young Pretender and the '45.

sure. The great direction which Burton has left to men disordered like you, is this, *Be not solitary; be not idle:*[7] which I would thus modify;—If you are idle, be not solitary; if you are solitary, be not idle.

There is a letter for you, from, Your humble servant,

SAM. JOHNSON

7. One of SJ's favorite maxims: *Ante* To Hester Thrale, 12 Nov. 1773, n. 3; 30 Mar. 1776.

Hester Thrale

THURSDAY 28 OCTOBER 1779

MS: Houghton Library.

Dear Madam: London, Oct. 28, 1779

Some days before our last separation, Mr. Thrale and I had one evening an earnest discourse about the business with Mr. Scrase.[1] It is indeed in a state of convalescence a melancholy affair, yet I am desirous that it may [be] despatched, while you may have the help of so much experience and understanding. I see no objection to entailing the Oxfordshire estate.[2] For my self, You may be sure I am very willing to be useful; but surely all use of such an office is at a very great distance.[3] Do not let those fears prevail which you know to be unreasonable, a will brings the end of life no nearer. But with this we will have done, and please ourselves with wishing my Master *multos et felices.*[4]

Charlotte Lennox accuses Cumberland of making a party against her play.[5] I always hissed away the charge, supposing

1. Henry Thrale was consulting Charles Scrase about his will (Clifford, 1952, p. 180 n. 4).

2. The estate of Crowmarsh, Oxfordshire, was ultimately bequeathed to Queeney Thrale (Clifford, 1952, pp. 45, 200 n. 2).

3. Thrale's will named SJ one of his four executors (Clifford, 1952, p. 200).

4. *multos et felices* [*annos*]: "many and happy years."

5. Charlotte Lennox's *The Sister*, produced at Covent Garden 18 Feb. 1769, had been withdrawn after the disastrous opening night (*Lond. Stage*, Part IV,

him a man of honour, but I shall now defend him with less confidence.[6] Nequid nimis.[7] Horace says, that nil admirari is the only thing that can make or keep a man happy.[8] It is with equal truth the only thing that can make or keep a man honest. The desire of fame not regulated, is as dangerous to virtue as that of money. I hope Charlotte scorns his little malice.

I have had a letter for ⟨*five or six letters*⟩,[9] which I have inclosed. Do not lose it, for it contains a testimony that there may be some pleasure in this World; and that I may have a little of the little that there is, pray write to me. I thought your last letter long in coming.

The two younglings; what hinders them from writing to me.[10] I hope they do not forget me.

Will Master give me any thing for my poor neighbours?[11] I have had from Sir Joshua and Mr. Strahan; they are very old Maids, very friendless, and very helpless.

Mrs. Williams talks of coming home this week from Kingston, and then there will be *merry doings.*[12]

I eat meat seldom, and take physick often, and fancy that I grow light and airy. A man that dos not begin to grow light and airy at seventy, is certainly losing time, if he intends ever to be light and airy.

I dined on Tuesday with Renny, and hope her little head begins to settle. She has however some scruples about the company of a Lady whom she has lately known. I pacified her as

---

iii.1386). "It must have been some satisfaction to her in this dismal failure to know that there was an active attempt to make the play unsuccessful and that such a sad outcome was not due entirely to a lack of merit in the play itself" (M. R. Small, *Charlotte Ramsay Lennox*, 1935, p. 173).

6. *Ante* To Hester Thrale, 21 Oct. 1779 and n. 12.

7. *Ante* To John Taylor, 4 May 1779, n. 3.

8. *Nil admirari prope res est una, Numici, / solaque quae possit facere et servare beatum*: "'Marvel at nothing'—that is perhaps the one and only thing, Numicius, that can make a man happy and keep him so" (Horace, *Epistles* I.vi.1–2, trans. H. R. Fairclough, Loeb ed.).   9. MS: one word heavily del.

10. *Ante* To Hester Thrale, 16 Oct. 1779 and n. 3.

11. *Ante* To Hester Thrale, 25 Oct. 1779; *Post* To Hester Thrale, 2 Nov. 1779.

12. *Ante* To Hester Thrale, 16 Oct. 1779.

well as I could. So no more at present but hoping you are all in good health as I am at this time of writing (excuse haste). I am, Dearest, dearest Lady, Your most obedient servant,

SAM. JOHNSON

Robert Chambers

SUNDAY 31 OCTOBER 1779

MS: Hyde Collection.

ENDORSEMENT: Doctor Sam. Johnson, 31 Octr. 1779, received about June 1780.

Dear Sir: Bolt court, Fleetstreet, Oct. 31, 1779

Your long letter and Lady Chambers's pretty journal gave me great delight, and I intend a long answer for which the bringer of this letter cannot stay, for he goes away to morrow. I believe it will please you to hear that my health has within this last half year been improved very perceptibly to myself, and very visibly to others. I am not without hope of seeing you again.[1]

I am very glad that you have thought it proper to show some countenance to Mr. Joseph Fowke, I always thought him a good Man, and I loved him as long as I knew him.[2] Do not let him be oppressed so far as you can protect him.

Mr. Levet, and Miss Williams are still with me; Levet is stout, but Williams is declining. I will not tell you more of my domestick affairs, because I reserve for[3] my long letter. The reason for which I now write, is that this young adventurer may have an opportunity of seeing you, and some kind of right to such notice as you can properly take of him, as the son of an ingenious man, and an amiable woman who were known to, Dear Sir, your faithful, humble servant,

SAM. JOHNSON

1. Chambers did not return from India until after SJ's death.
2. *Ante* To Francis Fowke, 11 July 1776, n. 2; *Post* To Joseph Fowke, 19 Apr. 1783.   3. MS: "from"

Hester Thrale

TUESDAY 2 NOVEMBER 1779

MS: Loren Rothschild.

Dear Madam: London, Nov. 2, 1779

This day I thought myself sure of a letter, but so I am constantly served. Mr. Cumberland, and Mrs. —— [1] and Mrs. Byron, and any body else puts me out of your head, and I know no more of You than if You were on the other side of the Caspian. I thought the two young things were to write too; but for them I do not much care.

On Saturday came home Mrs. Williams neither better nor worse than when she went, and I dined at Lord Lucan's, and found them well pleased with their Italian journey. He took his Lady, and Son,[2] and three Daughters.[3] They staid five months at Rome. They will have now something to talk of.

I gave my poor neighbour your half guinea and ventured upon making it two guineas at my Master's expence.[4] Pray, Madam, how do I owe You half a Guinea.

I dined on Sunday with Mr. Strahan, and have not been very well for some little time, last night I was afraid of the gout, but it is gone to day.

There was on Sunday night a fire at the north end of London Bridge, which has, they say, destroyed the water work.[5]

---

1. Possibly Mrs. Dickens, "a lady of Mrs. Thrale's acquaintance. . . . a sensible, hard-headed woman," who figures in Frances Burney's description of the visit to Brighton (*Diary and Letters of Madame D'Arblay*, ed. Austin Dobson, 1904, I.282).

2. Richard Bingham (1764–1839) succeeded his father as second Earl of Lucan in 1799.

3. Lord Lucan had four daughters: The Hon. Lavinia (*Ante* To Hester Thrale, 21 Oct. 1779, n. 3); the Hon. Louisa; the Hon. Margaret (1767–1839); and the Hon. Anne (1767–1840) (*Walpole's Correspondence*, Yale ed. XXIV.417 and n. 8).

4. *Ante* To Hester Thrale, 25 Oct. 1779.

5. "A Fire broke out last Night at a Hopfactor's close to London Bridge, which consumed Part of the same, and communicating to the Water-works, destroyed the lofty Pile there, which made a tremendous Blaze" (*Public Advertiser*, 1 Nov. 1779, p. 3).

Does Mr. Thrale continue *to hunt in fields for health unbought*,[6] if his taste of former pleasures returns, it is a strong proof of his recovery. When we meet we will be jolly blades.

I know not well how it has happenned, but I have never yet been at the Burneys. The Doctor has called twice on me, and I have seen some more sheets.—and away we go.[7] I am, Madam, your most humble servant,

SAM. JOHNSON

6. "Better to hunt in Fields, for Health unbought, / Than fee the Doctor for a nauseous Draught" (Dryden, "To my Honour'd Kinsman, John Driden, of Chesterton," ll. 92–93).

7. *Ante* To Hester Thrale, 21 Oct. 1779 and nn. 15, 16.

Hester Thrale

THURSDAY 4 NOVEMBER 1779

MS: Preston Manor, Brighton (Royal Pavilion, Art Gallery and Museum, Brighton).

Madam: London, Nov. 4, 1779

So I may write and write, and nobody care, but you can write often enough to Dr. Burney. Queeney sent me a pretty letter to which Burney added a silly short note, in such a silly white hand that I was glad it was no longer.[1]

I had heard before that Cumberland had lost not only ten thousand as you tell me, but twenty thousand as you with great consistency tell Dr. Burney, but knowing that no man can lose what he has not, I took it little to heart.[2] I did not think of borrowing, and indeed he that borrows money for adventures

1. SJ comments on Frances Burney's postscript to Queeney Thrale's letter, *c.* 2 Nov.: "'Dr. Johnson's other pupil a little longs to add a few lines to this letter,—but knows too well that all she has to say might be comprised in signing herself his obliged and most obedient servant, F.B.'" (*Diary and Letters of Madame D'Arblay*, ed. Austin Dobson, 1904, 1.300).

2. SJ refers to Richard Cumberland (*Post* To Hester Thrale, 8 Nov. 1779). Though Cumberland did indeed have a reputation for extravagance (*Walpole's Correspondence*, Yale ed. x.303), there seems to have been no foundation for this rumor.

deserves to lose it. No man should put into a lottery more than he can spare. Neither Delap however nor Burney have given occasion to his loss.[3]

Notice is taken that I have a cold and a cough but I have been so long used to disorders so much more afflictive that I have thought on them but little. If they grow worse something should be done.

I hear from every body that Mr. Thrale grows better. He is columen domus,[4] and if he stands firm, little evils may be overlooked. Drive him out in a morning, lead him out at night, keep him in what bustle you can.

Do not neglect Scrase,[5] You may perhaps do for him what you have done for Sir Philip.[6] The serious affair I do not wonder that you cannot mention, and yet I wish it were transacted while Scrase can direct and superintend it. No other man, if he shall have the same skill and kindness, which I know not where to find, will have the same influence.

Sir Philip never called upon me, though he promised me to do it.[7] Somebody else has laid hold upon him.

I live here in stark solitude, nobody has called upon me this livelong day, yet I comfort myself that I have no tortures in the night. I have not indeed much sleep, but I suppose I have enough, for I am not as sleepy in the daytime as formerly. I am, Dear Madam, Your most humble Servant,

SAM. JOHNSON

3. *Ante* To Hester Thrale, 21 Oct. 1779 and nn. 12, 13.

4. *columen domus*: "pillar of the house." Cf. *Ante* To Hester Thrale, 5 June 1776. SJ may have in mind a line from Terence, *bone custos, salve, columen vero familiae*: "faithful shepherd, pillar of my household" (*Phormio*, l. 287, trans. John Sargeaunt, Loeb ed.).

5. *Ante* To Hester Thrale, 21 Oct. 1779; 28 Oct. 1779.

6. SJ refers to Sir Philip Jennings Clerke. He may mean that, just as Hester Thrale had charmed Sir Philip into "extreme partiality and perfect Reverence," so she may influence Charles Scrase (*Thraliana* 1.388).

7. See above, n. 6.

Elizabeth Aston

FRIDAY 5 NOVEMBER 1779

MS: Pembroke College, Oxford.

Dearest Madam: London, Boltcourt, Fleetstreet, Nov. 5, 1779

Having had the pleasure of hearing from Mr. Boswel that he found you better than he expected, I will not forbear to tell You how much I was delighted with the news.[1] May your health encrease and encrease, till You are as well as You can wish yourself, or I can wish You.

My Friends tell me that my health improves too. It is certain that I use both physick and abstinence, and my endeavours have been blessed with more success than at my age I could reasonably hope. I please my self with the thoughts of visiting You next year in so robust a state that I shall not be afraid of the hill between Mrs. Gastrel's house and yours, nor think it necessary to rest my self between Stow hill and Lucy Porter's.[2]

Of publick affairs I can give You no very comfortable account. The Invasion has vanished for the present as I expected. I never believed that any invasion was intended.[3]

But whatever we have escaped we have done nothing, nor are likely to do better another year. We, however, who have no part of the nations welfare entrusted to our management, have nothing to do but to serve God, and leave the world submissively in his hands.

All trade is dead, and pleasure is scarce alive.[4] Nothing al-

1. In the letter (22 Oct. 1779) describing his day in Lichfield, JB had told SJ: "I hastened to Mrs. Aston's, whom I found much better than I feared I should" (*Life* III.412).

2. SJ did not visit Lichfield again until the autumn of 1781 (*Post* To Hester Thrale, 20 Oct. 1781).

3. *Ante* To Lucy Porter, 24 Aug. 1779 and n. 2. Cf. *Ante* To John Taylor, 19 Oct. 1779.

4. *Ante* To Hester Thrale, 10 Mar. 1779 and n. 3. The economic consequences of the War—drastically diminished trade and crippling taxation—outlasted the War itself. In 1784 Horace Walpole reported: "The majority of the nation persisted in approving and calling for the American War, and ought to swallow the

most is purchased but such things as the buyer cannot be with-out, so that a general sluggishness and general discontent are spread over the town. All the trades of luxury and elegance are nearly at a stand. What the parliament when it meets will do, and indeed what it ought to do is very difficult to say.[5]

Pray set Mrs. Gastrel, who is a dear good Lady, to write to me from time to time, for I have great delight in hearing from you, especially when I hear any good news of your health. I am, Dear Madam, your most humble servant,

SAM. JOHNSON

---

heavy consequences in silence. Instead of our colonies and trade we have a debt of two hundred and fourscore millions!" (*Walpole's Correspondence*, Yale ed. xxv.506).   5. *Ante* To Elizabeth Aston, 25 Oct. 1779 and n. 4.

Hester Thrale

SUNDAY 7 NOVEMBER 1779

MS: Hyde Collection.

London, Nov. 7, 1779

Poor Mrs. Byron, I am glad that she runs to you at last for Shelter, give her, dear Madam, what comfort you can.[1] Has any calamity fallen upon her? Her husband, so much as I hear, is well enough spoken of, nor is it supposed that he had power to do more than has been done. But Life must have its end, and commonly an end of gloomy discontent, and lingering distress.

While you are vigorous and spritely you must take into your

1. "Mrs. Byron too, another flightly Friend whom I love better than She deserves, is Distressed just now—her Husband is supposed to have forborne fighting in this last Affair, the Loss of the Grenada Islands.—and She is wild with Grief" (*Thraliana* 1.407). Vice Admiral Byron had returned to England on 10 Oct. after a long campaign against the French fleet in the West Indies. As the result of several strategic miscalculations, Byron had made it possible for the French to capture and retain Grenada. Though exonerated of any wrongdoing, Byron was not promoted or sent to sea again.

protection as many as you can of those who are tottering under their burden. When you want the same support, may you always find it.

I have for some time had a cough and a cold, but I did not mind it; continuance however makes it heavy, but it seems to be going away.

My Master, I hope, hunts, and walks, and courts the Belles, and shakes Brighthelmston. When he comes back frolick, and active, we will make a feast, and drink his health, and have a noble day.

Of the Lucans I have never heard since.[2] On Saturday after having fasted almost all the week, I dined with Renny. For Wednesday I am invited by the Veseys, and if I am well, purpose to go. I imagine there will be a large company. The invitation is to dine and spend the evening. Too much at a time. I shall be in danger of crying out with Mr. Head *catamaran* whatever that may mean, for it seemed to imply tediousness and disgust.[3] I do not much like to go, and I do not much like to stay away.

Have you any assemblies at this time of the year, and does Queeny dance? and does Burney dance too? I would have Burney dance with Cumberland, and so make all up.[4]

Discord keeps her residence in this habitation, but she has for some time been silent. We have much malice, but no mischief. Levet is rather a friend to Williams, because he hates

2. *Ante* To Hester Thrale, 2 Nov. 1779.

3. "This Mr. *Head*—whose real Name was *Plunkett*—a low Irish Parasite dependant on Mr. Thrale primarily, and I suppose secondarily on Mr. Murphy; was employed by them in various Schemes of Pleasure ... and on this Occasion was deputed to amuse them by personating some *Lord* whom His Patrons [proceeded] to introduce to the beautiful Miss Gunnings when they first came over with intent to make their Fortunes. He was received accordingly, and the Girls played off their best Airs, and cast kind Looks on his Introducers from Time to Time: Till the Fellow wearied as Johnson says, and disgusted with his ill-acted Character, burst out on a Sudden as they sate at Tea—and cried Catamoran! Young Gentlemen ... when will you have done with [this] Silly Joke now?" (Piozzi II.78–79). The *OED* defines *catamaran* as "a cross-grained or quarrelsome person, *esp.* a woman." 4. *Ante* To Hester Thrale, 21 Oct. 1779 and n. 12.

Desmoulins more, a thing that he should hate more than Desmoulins is not to be found.

I hear, but you never tell me any thing, that you have at last begun to bathe. I am sorry that your toothach kept you out of the water so long, because I know you love to be in it.

If such Letters as[5] this were to cost you any thing, I should hardly write them, but since they come to you for nothing,[6] I am willing enough to write though I have no thing to say, because a sorry letter serves to keep one from dropping totally out of your head, and I would not have you forget that there is in the world such a poor Being as, Madam, your most humble servant,

SAM. JOHNSON

5. MS: "as" altered from "are"
6. Henry Thrale, as M.P., received letters free of charge.

Hester Thrale

MONDAY 8 NOVEMBER 1779

MS: Hyde Collection.

Dear Madam: London, Nov. 8, 1779

You are a dear dear Lady. To write so often, and so sweetly makes some amends for your absence. Your last letter came about half an hour after my last letter was sent away,[1] but now I have another. You have much to tell me, and I have nothing to tell you, yet I am eager to write because I am eager for your answer.

I thought Cumberland had told You his loss.[2] If it be only report I do not much credit it. Something perhaps he may have ventured, but I do not believe he had ten thousand pounds, or the means of borrowing it. Of Beauclerc I suppose the fact is true that he is gone,[3] but for his loss, can any body

1. *Ante* To Hester Thrale, 7 Nov. 1779.
2. *Ante* To Hester Thrale, 4 Nov. 1779 and n. 2.
3. Topham Beauclerk and his wife had been in Brighton when the Thrales

tell who has been the winner? And if he has lost a sum disproportionate to his fortune, why should he run away when payment cannot be compelled?

Of Sir Thomas I can make no estimate, but if he is distressed
I am sorry, for he was in his prosperity civil and officious.[4]

It has happened to Scrase, as to many active and prosperous
men, that his mind has been wholly absorbed in business, or at
intervals dissolved in amusement, and habituated so long to
certain modes of employment or diversion, that in the decline
of life it can no more receive a new train of images than the
hand can acquire dexterity in a new mechanical operation. For
this reason a religious education is so necessary. Spiritual
Ideas may be recollected in old age, but can hardly be acquired.

You shall not hide Mrs. Byron from me,[5] for if she be a
feeler, I can bear a feeler as well as You, and hope that in
tenderness for what she feels from nature, I am able to forgive
or neglect what she feels by affectation. I pity her as one in a
state to which all must come, and I think well of her judgement in chusing You to be the depositary of her troubles, and
easer of her bosom. Fondle her and comfort[6] her.

Your letters have commonly one good paragraph concerning my Master, who appears to You and to every body to mend
upon the whole, though your vigilance perceives some accidental and temporary alterations, which however, I am willing
to hope are more rare and more slight than they were at first.
Let him hunt much, and think little, and avoid solitude. I hope
time has brought some company whom You can call now to
your table. Dos he take to Burney? Does he love her, as you
profess to love ⟨Mrs. Byron⟩[7] with a fifth part of the kindness

---

arrived the previous month (*Diary and Letters of Madame D'Arblay*, ed. Austin Dobson, 1904, I.282–83). They returned to London shortly before 13 Nov. (*Post To
JB*, 13 Nov. 1779).

4. Sir Thomas Mills (d. 1793), Kt., "a noisy fellow, who lived at a vast expense
without any visible means . . . supposed to be a natural son of Lord Mansfield, and
to be supported by him in that profusion" (*Walpole's Correspondence*, Yale ed.
XXIX.66 n. 5).   5. *Ante* To Hester Thrale, 7 Nov. 1779 and n. 1.

6. MS: "fort" repeated as catchword   7. MS: two words heavily del.

that she has for me. I am well rewarded[8] for what I have taught You of computation, by seeing our friendship divided into fractions; so we stand, do we? as 2 to 10 a pretty appearance upon paper, and still prettier in the heart. Well—go thy ways old Jack.[9]

Of the capture of Jamaica nothing is known, nor do I think it probable or possible.[10] How the French should in[11] a few days take from us an Island, which We could not in almost a century take from a few fugitive Negroes whom the Spaniards left behind them, is not easily imagined.[12] If You stay much longer in Sussex you may perhaps hear that London is taken.

We have a kind of epidemick cold amongst us, of which I have had my part, but not more than my part, and I think myself growing well. I have lived very sparingly, but shall have some dinner to day, and Baretti dines with me. I am, Dearest Madam, your most humble servant,

SAM. JOHNSON

8. MS: "f" del. before initial "r"

9. "Go thy ways, old Jack, die when thou wilt" (*1 Henry IV* II.iv.124–25).

10. *Ante* To Hester Thrale, 25 Oct. 1779, n. 6.

11. MS: "in" repeated as catchword

12. During the period of Spanish rule, 1509–1655, the aborigine population of Jamaica was exterminated and slaves were imported from Africa. The British took legal possession of the island in 1670, but for over a century thereafter had to combat a black insurgency based in the mountains.

Hester Maria Thrale

THURSDAY 11 NOVEMBER 1779

MS: The Earl of Shelburne.

ADDRESS: To Miss Thrale.

Dear Madam: London, Nov. 11, 1779

Your first letter was kind,[1] and your second kinder. It is fit that I should now take my turn to write though I have not much to tell You.

1. *Ante* To Hester Thrale, 4 Nov. 1779, n. 1.

Yesterday I dined at Mr. Vesey's with Lord Lucan and Mr. Pepys. After dinner came in Lady Lucan and her three daughters, who seem all pretty people. In the evening there was Lord Maccartney who has been taken by D'Estaigne in America, and stripped by him almost naked.[2] D'Estaigne took from him [his] Lady's picture because I suppose it was set with stones.[3] He is here now upon parole. He seems in some degree a literary Man.[4]

Lady Edgecomb was another of the company.[5] The talk was for a while about Burney's book, and the old objection to the Captain's grossness being mentioned, Lady Edgecombe said that she had known such a captain.[6]

Do not tell this to Burney for it will please her, and she takes no care to please me.

Of the rest I did not know all, Swinburne, the spanish traveller, I think, was there, but he did not speak or I did not hear him.[7]

Not a word was said all day upon publick affairs.[8] None care to present the condition in which we now are, to their own

2. George Macartney (1737–1806), Irish diplomat, first Baron and later (1792) first Earl Macartney, served as Governor of the Caribbean Islands from 1775 until his capture in July 1779 by the French forces under the command of Charles-Henri (1729–94), Comte d'Estaing.

3. In 1768 Macartney had married Lady Jane Stuart (1742–1828), the second daughter of the third Earl of Bute.

4. Macartney, author of *A Political Account of Ireland* (1773), was elected to The Club in 1786 (Fifer, p. xx).

5. Emma Edgcumbe (1729–1807), the daughter of John Gilbert, Archbishop of York, and wife of George, third Baron Edgcumbe and later (1789) first Earl of Mt. Edgcumbe.

6. One of the principal characters in Frances Burney's *Evelina* (1778) is Captain Mirvan, a rough-talking, boisterous naval officer.

7. Henry Swinburne (1743–1803), author of *Travels through Spain* (1779), a book lavishly illustrated with drawings of Roman and Moorish architecture. According to Horace Walpole, "These new *Travels* are simple, and do tell one a little more than late voyagers, by whose accounts one would think there was nothing in Spain but muleteers and fandangos" (*Walpole's Correspondence*, Yale ed. 11.149).

8. The impact of the economic recession is a constant theme in SJ's letters of 1779. *Ante* To Hester Thrale, 10 Mar. 1779; *Ante* To Lucy Porter, 19 Oct. 1779; *Ante* To Elizabeth Aston, 5 Nov. 1779.

minds, by expressing their hopes and fears or enquiring into those of others.

What can be come to my Mistress, that going into the sea disorders her. She was used to be quite amphibious, and could hardly be kept out of any water that she could get at. I am however not pleased with the change, and hope to see her original disposition prevail again.

Beauclerc ran no further than home, and is now, I hear, at his own house, perhaps Cumberland's distresses are in the same degree.[9] When stories of this kind are told you, receive them with indifference, and do not by telling them seem to be pleased, but attend to them[10] as traces of character, and hints for inquiry.

The last line of your letter was worth all the rest, if we can get and keep my Master well, we will try to shift for ourselves. I am, My dearest, your most humble servant,

SAM. JOHNSON

Your first letter had no date of time or place, the last had only time. Use to date fully. Mamma is negligent too.

9. *Ante* To Hester Thrale, 4 Nov. 1779 and nn. 2, 3; 8 Nov. 1779 and n. 3.
10. MS: "him"

James Boswell

SATURDAY 13 NOVEMBER 1779

PRINTED SOURCE: JB's *Life*, 1791, II.310.

Dear Sir, London, Nov. 13, 1779

Your last letter was not only kind but fond.[1] But I wish you to get rid of all intellectual excesses, and neither to exalt your pleasures, nor aggravate your vexations, beyond their real and natural state. Why should you not be as happy at Edinburgh

1. JB had written to SJ on 7 Nov., celebrating the delights of Chester and dreading the melancholy he expected to set in on his return to Edinburgh (*Life* III.415–16).

as at Chester. *In culpa est animus, qui se non effugit usquam.*[2] Please yourself with your wife and children, and studies, and practice.

I have sent a petition from Lucy Porter, with which I leave it to your discretion whether it is proper to comply.[3] Return me her letter, which I have sent, that you may know the whole case, and not be seduced to any thing that you may afterwards repent. Miss Doxy perhaps you know to be Mr. Garrick's niece.

If Dean Percy can be popular at Carlisle, he may be very happy.[4] He has in his disposal two livings, each equal, or almost equal in value to the deanery;[5] he may take one himself, and give the other to his son.[6]

How near is the Cathedral to Auchinleck, that you are so much delighted with it?[7] It is, I suppose, at least an hundred and fifty miles off.[8] However, if you are pleased, it is so far well.

Let me know what reception you have from your father, and the state of his health.[9] Please him as much as you can, and add no pain to his last years.

2. *in culpa est animus, qui se non effugit umquam*: "what is at fault is the mind, which never escapes from itself" (Horace, *Epistles* I.xiv.13, trans. H. R. Fairclough, Loeb ed.).

3. Lucy Porter requested that JB investigate the family connections of James Patton (1753–1812), of County Fife and Lichfield, who was paying court to David Garrick's niece, Merrial Docksey (b. 1761), daughter of Thomas Docksey of Snelston, Derbyshire. JB was able to give "a very favourable report of the family of Miss Doxy's lover" (*Life* III.418). Patton and Docksey were married in 1780 (*Life* III.536).

4. *Ante* To Bennet Langton, 31 Oct. 1778 and n. 4. JB had told SJ, "I am told at my inn, that he is very *populous* (popular)" (*Life* III.415–16).

5. SJ greatly exaggerated the value of Percy's Easton Maudit living (B. H. Davis, *Thomas Percy*, 1989, p. 19).

6. Percy's only son, Henry, died at the age of twenty in 1783 (*The Correspondence of Thomas Percy and Edmond Malone*, ed. Arthur Tillotson, 1944, p. 2 and n. 3).

7. Writing from Carlisle, JB had told SJ, "It is divinely cheering to me to think that there is a Cathedral so near Auchinleck" (*Life* III.416).

8. On 22 Nov. JB replied: "Carlisle is distant from Auchinleck scarcely a hundred miles. I know I can with ease reach it in a day from home" (MS: Beinecke Library).

9. In his response, JB reported that "I found my Father better both in body and mind than he has been for several years" (MS: Beinecke Library).

Of our friends here I can recollect nothing to tell you. I have neither seen nor heard of Langton. Beauclerk is just returned from Brighthelmston, I am told, much better.[10] Mr. Thrale and his family are still there; and his health is said to be visibly improved; he has not bathed, but hunted.[11]

At Bolt-court there is much malignity, but of late little open hostility. I have had a cold, but it is gone.

Make my compliments to Mrs. Boswell, etc. I am, Sir, Your humble servant,

SAM. JOHNSON

10. *Ante* To Hester Thrale, 8 Nov. 1779, n. 3. The alleged improvement in Beauclerk's health was short-lived: he died the following March (*Post* To JB, 8 Apr. 1780).   11. *Ante* To Hester Thrale, 25 Oct. 1779.

Hester Thrale

TUESDAY 16 NOVEMBER 1779

MS: Hyde Collection.

Dear Madam: London, Nov. 16, 1779

Pray how long does a letter hang between London and Brighthelmston. Your letter of the 12th I received on the 15th.

Poor Mrs. Byron is a feeler.[1] It is well that she has yet power to feel. Fiction durst not have driven upon a few months such a conflux of misery. Comfort her as You can.

I have look[ed] again into your grave letter. You mention trustees. I do not see who can be trustee for a casual and variable property, for a fortune yet to be acquired.[2] How can any man be trusted with what he cannot possess, cannot ascertain, and cannot regulate? The trade must be carried on by somebody who must be answerable for the debts contracted. This can be none but yourself, unless you deliver up the property

1. *Ante* To Hester Thrale, 7 Nov. 1779 and n. 1; 8 Nov. 1779.

2. In the event, Thrale appointed four trustees, who (along with John Perkins) were responsible for managing the brewery: SJ, John Cator, Jeremiah Crutchley, and Henry Smith (Clifford, 1952, p. 200).

to some other agent, and trust the chance both of his prudence and his honesty. Do not be frighted, Trade could not be managed by those who manage it, if it had much difficulty. Their great Books are soon understood, and their language

> If Speech it may be call'd, that speech is none
> Distinguishable in number mood or tense[3]

is understood with no very laborious application.

The help which you can have from any man as a trustee you may have from him as a friend, the trusteeship may give him power to perplex, but will neither encrease his benevolence to assist, nor his Wisdom to advise.

> Living on God, and on thyself rely.

Who should be trustee but You[4] for your own and your Children's prosperity? I hope this is an end of this unpleasing speculation, and lighter matters may take their turn.

What Mr. Scrase says about the Borough is true, but is nothing to the purpose. A house in the Square will not cost so much as building in Southwark, but buildings are more likely to go on in Southwark, if your dwelling is at St. James's.[5] Every body has some desire that deserts the great road of prosperity, to look for pleasure in a bye-path. I do not see with so much indignation Mr. Thrale's desire of being the first Brewer, as your despicable dread of living in the borough. Ambition in little things, is better than cowardice in little things, but both[6] these things however little to the publick eye are great in their consequences to yourselves. The world cares not how you brew, or where you live, but it is the business of the one to brew in a manner most advantageous to his Family, and of the

3. "If shape it might be called that shape had none / Distinguishable in member, joint, or limb" (*Paradise Lost* II.667–68).

4. MS: "you" altered from "your"

5. "In the midst of publick and private Distress, here is my mad Master going to build at the boro' House again:—new Store Cellars, Casks, and God knows what. I have however exerted my self and driv'n off his Workmen with a high Hand" (*Thraliana* I.391 n. 1).   6. MS: "both" altered from "bothe"

other to live where the general interest may best be superintended. It was by an accidental visit to the borough that you escaped great evil last Summer.[7] Of this folly let there [be] an end, at least, an intermission.[8]

I am glad that Queeny danced with Mr. Wade. She was the Sultaness of the evening, and I am glad that Mr. Thrale has found a riding companion whom he likes. Let him ride, say I, till he leaves dejection and disease behind him, and let them limp after him an hundred years without overtaking him. When he returns let me see him frolic and airy, and social, and busy, and as kind to me as in former times.[9]

You seem to be afraid that I should be starved before you come back. I have indeed practiced abstinence with some stubbornness, and with some success, but as Dryden talks of *writing with a hat*, I am sometimes very witty with a knife and fork.[10] I have managed my self very well, except that having no motive, I have no exercise.

At home we do not much quarrel, but perhaps the less we quarrel, the more we hate.[11] There is as much malignity amongst us as can well subsist, without any thought of daggers or poisons.

Mrs. Laurence is by the help of frequent operations still kept alive,[12] and such is the capricious destiny of mortals, that she will die more lamented by her husband, than I will promise to Usefulness, Wisdom, or Sanctity. There is always something operating distinct from [13] diligence or skill. Temple

---

7. SJ may refer to an incident that took place 10 Aug. 1779, when Hester Thrale detected "some Mismanagement among the Borough Clerks" and "set Things straight" (*Thraliana* 1.401).

8. SJ's "advice prevailed, and some time early in the new year the Thrales moved to Southwark" (Clifford, 1952, p. 181). In Jan. 1781, however, they rented a house on Grosvenor Square (p. 194).

9. MS: "times" repeated as catchword

10. "Thus they out-write each other with a hat" (Dryden, "Prologue to *The Conquest of Granada*," Part I, l. 12). 11. *Ante* To Hester Thrale, 7 Nov. 1779.

12. In 1744 Thomas Lawrence married Frances Chauncy of Derby, who died 2 Jan. 1780 (*GM* 1787, pp. 192–93). *Post* To Thomas Lawrence, 20 Jan. 1780.

13. MS: "from" altered from "for"

therefore in his composition of a hero, to the heroick virtues adds good fortune.[14] I am, Dearest Lady, your most humble servant,

SAM. JOHNSON

14. "Though it be easier to describe heroic virtue by the effects and examples than by causes or definitions, yet it may be said to arise from some great and native excellency of temper or genius transcending the common race of mankind in wisdom, goodness, and fortitude. These ingredients advantaged by birth, improved by education, and assisted by fortune, seem to make that noble composition" ("Of Heroic Virtue," in *Five Miscellaneous Essays by Sir William Temple*, ed. S. H. Monk, 1963, p. 98).

Hester Thrale

SATURDAY 20 NOVEMBER 1779

MS: National Portrait Gallery, London.

London, Nov. 20, 1779

Indeed, Dear Madam, I do not think that you have any reason to complain of Mr. Thrale or Mr. Scrase.[1] What I proposed is, I suppose unusual. However Mr. Thrale knows that I have suggested nothing to you that I had not first said to him. I hear he grows well so fast that we are not likely to try whose way is best, and I hope he will grow better, and better, and better, and then away with executors and executrixes. He may settle his family himself.

I am not vexed at you for not liking the Borough, but for not liking the Borough better than other[2] evils of greater magnitude. You must take physick, or be sick; you must live in the Borough, or live still worse.[3]

Pray tell my Queeny how I love her for her letters, and tell Burney that now she is a good girl, I can love her again.[4] Tell Mr. Scrase that I am sincerely glad to hear that he is better.

1. *Ante* To Hester Thrale, 16 Nov. 1779.
2. MS: undeciphered erasure before "other"
3. *Ante* To Hester Thrale, 16 Nov. 1779 and n. 8.
4. Frances Burney had written her first complete letter to SJ since leaving for Brighton. *Ante* To Hester Thrale, 4 Nov. 1779 and n. 1.

Tell my Master that I never was so glad to see him in my life, as I shall be now to see him well, and tell yourself that except my Master nobody has more kindness for you, than, Dear Madam, your most humble servant,

SAM. JOHNSON

Lucy Porter
THURSDAY 2 DECEMBER 1779

PRINTED SOURCE: *Johns. Misc.* II.450–51.

Dear Madam, Dec. 2, 1779

I have inclosed Mr. Boswels answer.[1]

I still continue better than when you saw me, but am not just at this time very well, but hope to mend again. Publick affairs remain as they were. Do not let the papers fright you.[2]

I have ordered you some oisters this week, which I hope you will get, though your oisters have sometimes miscarried. Write when you can. I am, My dear, Your humble servant,

SAM. JOHNSON

1. *Ante* To JB, 13 Nov. 1779 and n. 3.
2. *Ante* To Lucy Porter, 24 Aug. 1779 and n. 2.

John Taylor
THURSDAY 9 DECEMBER 1779

MS: Hyde Collection.
ENDORSEMENT: 9 Decr. 1779.

Dear Sir: Dec. 9, 1779

Your diet of Whey is, according to my opinion, the best that could have been invented. It will supply the defect of moisture which was probably the original cause of most of your complaints, and it will supply likewise something for nourishment. You may live ten years longer by the use of it. Therefore persist unless you find it disagreeable, and then after an interval try it again. For this reason, when you find it begin to displease you, leave it off, for if You drink it long against your appetite, your disgust will encrease to aversion, and you will not persuade yourself to begin it any more.

My Gout never came again.[1] You blame me, but I think very well of myself. Dr. Laurence does not seem much to like the trick, but he does not deny that it was very dexterously performed.[2] That the Gout is a remedy I never perceived, for when I had it most in my foot I had the spasms in my breast.[3] At best the Gout is only a dog that drives the wolf away, and eats the Sheep himself, for if the Gout has time for growth, it will certainly destroy, and destroy by[4] long and lingering torture. If it comes again I purpose to show it no better hospitality.

Mr. Thrale having by exercise and other means almost recovered from his first fit,[5] has been struck again with less violence indeed, but at a bad time of the year.[6] He is again recovering, but his convalescence is slow. He is not so bad however but that he does business, and goes daily from Strea[t]ham to Southwark. He must be nursed through the winter, and the Spring, I hope, will restore him.

Of publick affairs if I knew any good, I would tell you, but Good seems to be very distant. Nothing is to be seen but dejection and poverty.[7] I am, Dear Sir, Your affectionate, humble servant,

SAM. JOHNSON

1. In October SJ had suffered from gout in his feet (*Ante* To Hester Thrale, 8 Oct. 1779; 11 Oct. 1779).   2. *Ante* To Hester Thrale, 8 Oct. 1779.

3. *Ante* To John Taylor, 19 Oct. 1779 and n. 5.

4. MS: "but" del. before "by"

5. *Ante* To Hester Thrale, 12 June 1779 and n. 1.

6. On the way home from Brighton, 23 Nov., Henry Thrale had suffered a second stroke. Dr. Heberden "ordered Cupping which restored him so far that we are now just as we were before this last Attack" (*Thraliana* 1.410).

7. *Ante* To Elizabeth Aston, 5 Nov. 1779; *Ante* To Hester Maria Thrale, 11 Nov. 1779 and n. 8.

Hester Maria Thrale

SATURDAY 25 DECEMBER 1779

MS: The Earl of Shelburne.
ADDRESS: To Miss Thrale at Streatham.

Dec. 25, 1779

Pray, my dear Love, take the first opportunity of sending me my watch, which I left at the Bed. I hope, there is no need of telling You, that I wish You all, every good of the season, and of every season. I am, dear Sweet, Your most humble servant,

SAM. JOHNSON

Hester Maria Thrale

WEDNESDAY 29 DECEMBER 1779

MS: The Earl of Shelburne.
ADDRESS: To Miss Thrale.

Dear Love: Wednesday, Dec. 29, 1779

I wrote to You some days ago to send me my watch which I forgot;[1] and You have not sent it, which is not kind. Let[2] me have it as soon as ever You can. I am, dear Love, Your humble Servant,

SAM. JOHNSON

1. *Ante* To Hester Maria Thrale, 25 Dec. 1779.
2. MS: "Let" superimposed upon undeciphered erasure

Thomas Lawrence

THURSDAY 20 JANUARY 1780

MS: Hyde Collection.

Dear Sir: Jan. 20, 1780

At a time when all your friends ought to show their kindness, and with a character which ought to make all that know you, your friends, You may wonder that You have yet heard nothing of me.

I have been hindred by a vexatious and incessant cough, for which within these ten days, I have bled once, fasted four or five times, taken physick five times, and opiates, I think, six. This day it seems to remit.

The loss, dear Sir, which You have lately suffered, I felt many years ago, and know therefore how much has been taken from You, and how little help can be had from consolation.[1] He that outlives a Wife whom he has long loved, sees himself disjoined from the only Mind that had the same hopes and fears, and interest; from the only companion with whom he has shared much good or evil, and with whom he could set his mind at liberty to retrace the past, or anticipate the future. The continuity of being is lacerated. The settled course of sentiment and action is stopped, and life stands suspended and motionless till it is driven by external causes into a new channel. But the time of suspense is dreadful.

Our first recourse in[2] this distresful solitude, is perhaps for want of habitual piety, to a gloomy acquiescence in necessity. Of two mortal Being[s] one must lose the other. But surely there is a higher and a better comfort to be drawn from the consideration of that Providence which watches over all, and belief that the living and the dead are equally in the hands of God, who will reunite those whom he has separated, or who sees that it is best not to reunite them. I am, Dear Sir, your most affectionate and most humble servant,

SAM. JOHNSON

1. *Ante* To Hester Thrale, 16 Nov. 1779 and n. 12.   2. MS: "on"

John Nichols

EARLY 1780

MS: British Library.

Mr. Johnson purposes to make his next attempt upon Prior, at least to consider him very soon, and desires that some volumes published of his papers,[1] in two vol. 8vo may be procured.[2]

1. MS: "paperps" del. before "papers"
2. SJ asks for *Miscellaneous Works of his late Excellency Matthew Prior, Esq.* (1740).

John Nichols

c. FEBRUARY 1780

MS: British Library.

The turtle and sparrow can be but a fable. The Conversation I never read.[1]

1. Apparently Nichols had queried SJ's claim that Prior had written "only four" tales (*Lives of the Poets* II.201; *GM* 1785, p. 9). "The Turtle and the Sparrow" is described on the title page of 1723 as "A Poem" (*Literary Works of Matthew Prior*, ed. H. B. Wright and M. K. Spears, 1959, II.985). "The Conversation" is called "A Tale" (Wright and Spears, *Prior* 1.523).

John Nichols

c. FEBRUARY 1780[1]

PRINTED SOURCE: *GM* 1785, p. 10.

Please to get me the last edition of Hughes's Letters;[2] and try

1. For the dating of this note, see F. W. Hilles, "Johnson's Correspondence with Nichols," *Philological Quarterly* 48, 1969, pp. 232–33.
2. SJ calls for *Correspondence of John Hughes*, ed. John Duncombe, 2d ed., 1773. This edition includes five letters from Dyer to Duncombe, which constituted SJ's "sole source of biographical information" for his "Dyer" (Hilles, "Correspondence," p. 232; *Lives of the Poets* III.343 and n. 2).

to get Dennis upon Blackmore,[3] and upon Cato,[4] and any thing of the same writer against Pope.[5] Our materials are defective.

3. In his "Blackmore," SJ refers to John Dennis's *Remarks on Prince Arthur* (1696) as "a formal criticism, more tedious and disgusting than the work which he condemns" (*Lives of the Poets* II.238 and n. 4).

4. In his "Pope," SJ quotes extensively from Dennis's censorious *Remarks upon Cato* (1713) (*Lives of the Poets* II.134–44).

5. In the first section of his "Pope," SJ frequently quotes from and refers to Dennis's hostile remarks on the poet's appearance and his verse.

Unidentified Correspondent
FRIDAY 25 FEBRUARY 1780

PRINTED SOURCE: Sotheby's Catalogue, 3–8 Dec. 1900, Lot No. 1034, pp. 102–3.

The honor of being supposed to have some degree of your favour has exposed me to a request which I know not well how to reject. I am desired to solicit from you the resignation of Mr. Walpole's Tragedy,[1] which was stolen from Mr. Hardinge, and by you found upon a stall.[2] The appearance of negligence by which it was lost has made Mr. Walpole very angry, and you may restore peace to our friends by a very small concession, for the piece having satisfied your curiosity is to you

1. Horace Walpole completed his drama of incest, *The Mysterious Mother*, in 1768 (*Walpole's Correspondence*, Yale ed. x.259). Though never intended for publication or performance, the play did circulate in manuscript among a few select friends, "with strict injunctions that it should never be shown to Mr. *Garrick* or Dr. *Johnson*" (*Walpole's Correspondence*, Yale ed. XXXIII.578 n. 3). In 1781, however, it "wandered into the hands of some banditti booksellers," and Walpole was "forced to publish it" in order to fend off a spurious Irish printing (*Walpole's Correspondence*, Yale ed. II.270). There is no reference in Walpole's correspondence to the incident mentioned here.

2. George Hardinge (1743–1816), lawyer, man of letters, and later (1784–1802) M.P. for Old Sarum (Namier and Brooke II.581–82). Hardinge, Horace Walpole's correspondent and neighbor at Twickenham, called *The Mysterious Mother* "that striking play . . . which in a very original vein is full of dramatic genius and of picturesque effect" (*Walpole's Correspondence*, Yale ed. xxxv.648).

of very little value. If you will be (so) kind as to give me the credit of restoring it to the owner I will take care that your civility shall not be without the praise that belongs to it, and I cannot but think that what Mr. Hardinge asks of you, is what you would expect with reason in the like case.

John Nichols
c. MARCH 1780[1]

MS: Beinecke Library.

Mr. Johnson wishes that Mr. Nichol could favour him for an hour with the Drummer, and Steele's original preface.[2]

> 1. I follow F. W. Hilles in assigning this letter to *c*. Mar. 1780: SJ had finished his "Addison" by 6 Apr. (*Post* To Hester Thrale, 6 Apr. 1780; F. W. Hilles, "Johnson's Correspondence with Nichols," *Philological Quarterly* 48, 1969, p. 227).
>
> 2. SJ asks for Addison's play, *The Drummer* (1716), and for Richard Steele's preface, "published in 1716 and not easy to find. No doubt he was made curious to see it by what his chief source for this life, Andrew Kippis, had said of it in *Biographia Britannica*, 2nd ed., (1778) I.52, note O" (Hilles, "Correspondence," p. 229). According to SJ, that *The Drummer* "should have been ill received would raise wonder did we not daily see the capricious distribution of theatrical praise" (*Lives of the Poets* II.106).

John Nichols
c. APRIL 1780

MS: British Library.

Sir:

In reading Rowe in your Edition, which is very impudently called mine,[1] I observed a little piece unnaturally and odiously

> 1. To win a competitive advantage over John Bell's rival edition, the London booksellers had "deceived the buying public—and risked alienating Johnson—by lettering the spines of their volumes to read 'Johnson's Poets'" (T. F. Bonnell, "John Bell's *Poets of Great Britain*: The 'Little Trifling Edition' Revisited," *Modern Philology* 85, 1987, p. 152).

obscene. I was offended, but was still more offended when I could not find it in Rowe's genuine volumes.[2] To admit it had been wrong, to interpolate it is surely worse. If I had known of such a piece in the whole collection I should have been angry.— What can be done?[3]

2. SJ refers to Rowe's "Epigram on a Lady who shed her Water at seeing the Tragedy of *Cato*." The "Epigram" was included in the third edition of Rowe's *Poems on Several Occasions* (1714) and *The Poetical Works of Nicholas Rowe* (1720).

3. Nichols pointedly justified the inclusion of the offending poem (*GM* 1785, p. 10) and declined to remove it from the next edition (1790).

John Nichols

c. APRIL 1780

MS: British Library.

Dr. Warton tells me that Collins's first piece is in the G.M. for August, 1739. In August there is no such thing. *Amasius* was at that time the poetical name of Dr. *Swan* who translated Sydenham.[1] Where to find Collins I know not.[2]

1. John Swan, M.D., the editor and translator of Thomas Sydenham's *Works* (1742). Richard Wendorf and Charles Ryskamp argue that in the Jan. 1739 issue of the *GM* the pseudonym "Amasius" was used by both Collins (for "To Miss Aurelia C——R") and Swan (for "Left in Dr. Shaw's Translation of my Lord Bacon's Works") (*The Works of William Collins*, 1979, p. 100). In the August *GM* there is a poem ("To a Friend on his Marriage") that can plausibly be assigned to Swan but not to Collins (Wendorf and Ryskamp, *Collins*, p. 100).

2. I follow Wendorf and Ryskamp, who consider Collins's first published poem to be "To Miss Aurelia C——R, on her Weeping at her Sister's Wedding" (*GM* Jan. 1739, p. 41). For a detailed discussion, see *Collins*, pp. 99–101.

John Nichols

c. APRIL 1780

MS: British Library.

I think I must make some short addition to Thomsons sheet but will send it to day.

Hester Thrale

THURSDAY 6 APRIL 1780

MS: E. Thorne.

Dearest Lady: Apr. 6, 1780

You had written so often. I have had but two letters from
Bath,[1] and the second complains that the first which you call
so many, was neglected. And you pretend to be afraid of being
forgotten. I wonder what should put you out of my mind, you
say rightly that I shall not find such another, for there is not,
if I had the choice of all, such another to be found.

It is happy both for you and Mrs. Montague that the fates
bring you both to Bath at the same time. Do not let new
friends supplant the old, they who first distinguished you have
the best claim to your attention; those who flock about you
now take your excellence upon credit, and may hope to gain
upon the world by your countenance.

I have not quite neglected my Lives. Addison is a long one
but it is done. Prior is not short, and that is done too. I am
upon Rowe, who cannot fill much paper.[2] If I have done them
before you come again, I think to bolt upon you at Bath,[3] for
I shall not be now afraid of Mrs. Cotton.[4] Let Burney take
care that she does me no harm.

The diligence of Dr. Moisy I do not understand;[5] about
what is he diligent. If Mr. Thrale is well, or only not well be-

1. The Thrales and Frances Burney had arrived in Bath at the end of March,
and taken lodgings on the South Parade (*Thraliana* 1.436; Clifford, 1952, p. 182;
Diary and Letters of Madame D'Arblay, ed. Austin Dobson, 1904, 1.327). *Post* To Hester Maria Thrale, 8 Apr. 1780.   2. *Post* To Hester Thrale, 15 Apr. 1780.

3. SJ did not pay this intended visit: he fell behind schedule on the second
installment, and the Thrales had no spare apartment in their lodgings (Hester
Thrale to SJ, 20 Apr. 1780, MS: Rylands Library).

4. The day after their arrival in Bath, the Thrales and Frances Burney had
spent the afternoon with a group of relations that included Sidney Arabella Cotton, whom Burney described as "an ugly, proud old woman, but marvellous civil
to me" (Dobson, *D'Arblay*, 1.327).

5. Abel Moysey (1715–80), M.D., a prominent Bath physician (*Walpole's Correspondence*, Yale ed. XXIII.93 n. 5).

cause he has been ill, I do not see what the Physician can do. Dos he direct any regimen, or dos Mr. Thrale regulate himself? or is there no regularity among you? Nothing can keep him so safe as the method which has been so often mentioned, and which will be not only practicable but pleasant in the summer, and before summer is quite gone will be made supportable by custom.[6]

If health and reason can be preserved by changing three or four meals a week, or if such a change will but encrease the chances of preserving them, the purchase is surely not made at a very high price. Death is dreadful, and fatuity is more dreadful, and such Strokes bring both so near, that all their horrours ought to be felt. I hope that to our anxiety for him, Mr. Thrale will add some anxiety for himself.

Seward called on me one day, and read Spence.[7] I dined yesterday at Mr. Jodrel's in a great deal of company.[8] On sunday I dine with Dr. Laurence, and at night go to Mrs. Vesey. I have had a little cold, or two, or three, but I did not much mind them, for they were not very bad.

Make my compliments to my Master, and Queeney, and Burney, and Mrs. Cotton, and to all that care about me, and more than all—or else.

Now one courts you, and another caresses you, and one calls

6. In order to avoid another apoplectic stroke, Henry Thrale had been advised to regulate his diet. Apparently the suggested regimen included avoidance of meat every other day, a policy SJ had been following for some time (*Ante* To Hester Thrale, 25 Oct. 1779; *Post* To Hester Thrale, 18 Apr. 1780).

7. In May 1771 the executors of Joseph Spence (1699–1768) presented the Duke of Newcastle with a fair copy of Spence's "Observations, Anecdotes and Characters of Books and Men" (unpublished until 1820). "In January 1780 Sir Lucas Pepys ... was prevailed upon to ask the Duke of Newcastle to lend the manuscript for the use of Dr. Johnson, who had recently published the first four volumes of his *Prefaces* ... and now was preparing the life of Addison and of other poets for the concluding volumes" (*Spence's Anecdotes*, ed. J. M. Osborn, 1966, i.lxxxi, lxxxix). William Seward drew on Spence's collection for his *Anecdotes of Some Distinguished Persons* (1795–97) (Osborn, *Anecdotes* i.xc).

8. Richard Paul Jodrell (1745–1831), classicist and playwright, author of *The Persian Heroine* (1786), later (1783) a member of SJ's Essex Head Club (*Life* IV.254; *Lit. Anec.* IX.2–3).

you to cards, and another wants you to walk, and amidst all this pray try to think now and then a little of me, and write often. Mrs. Strahan is at Bath, but I believe, not well enough to be in the rooms.[9] I am, Dearest Madam, your most humble Servant,

SAM. JOHNSON

9. From 1755 until his wife's death in 1785, William Strahan's letters "are filled with references to her illnesses, in particular a form of gout and a 'bilious, cholicy disorder'" (J. A. Cochrane, *Dr. Johnson's Printer*, 1964, pp. 96, 206).

James Boswell
SATURDAY 8 APRIL 1780

PRINTED SOURCE: JB's *Life*, 1791, II.312.

Dear Sir,   April 8, 1780

Well, I had resolved to send you the Chesterfield letter; but I will write once again without it. Never impose tasks upon mortals. To require two things is the way to have them both undone.[1]

For the difficulties which you mention in your affairs I am sorry;[2] but difficulty is now very general: it is not therefore less grievous, for there is less hope of help. I pretend not to give you advice, not knowing the state of your affairs; and general counsels about prudence and frugality would do you little good. You are, however, in the right not to increase your own perplexity by a journey hither; and I hope that by staying at home you will please your father.

1. JB had repeatedly asked SJ to supply him with the text of the celebrated letter to Lord Chesterfield (*Ante* To Lord Chesterfield, 7 Feb. 1755), and to mark in his copies of Goldsmith's "Traveler" and "Deserted Village" those lines that SJ had contributed. SJ finally complied with the first request in 1781, with the second in 1783 (*Life* ii.478, IV.128).

2. JB had informed SJ that "the state of my affairs did not admit of my coming to London this year" (*Life* III.418). The winter of 1780 was a time of "acute financial pressure" as JB slid deeper into debt (*Later Years*, p. 195).

Poor dear Beauclerk[3]—*nec, ut soles, dabis joca.*[4] His wit and his folly, his acuteness and maliciousness, his merriment and reasoning, are now over. Such another will not often be found among mankind. He directed himself to be buried by the side of his mother, an instance of tenderness which I hardly expected.[5] He has left his children to the care of Lady Di,[6] and if she dies, of Mr. Langton, and of Mr. Leicester, his relation, and a man of good character.[7] His library has been offered to sale to the Russian ambassador.[8]

Dr. Percy, notwithstanding all the noise of the newspapers, has had no literary loss. Clothes and moveables were burnt to the value of about one hundred pounds; but his papers, and I think his books, were all preserved.[9]

Poor Mr. Thrale has been in extreme danger from an apoplectical disorder, and recovered, beyond the expectation of

3. Topham Beauclerk had died 11 Mar.

4. *animula vagula blandula,* / . . . *quae nunc abibis in loca,* / . . . *nec ut soles dabis iocos?*: "Dear fleeting sweeting, little soul, / What region now must be thy goal, / Unable, as of old, to jest?" ("Hadrian's Dying Farewell to his Soul," ll. 1, 3, 5, *Minor Latin Poets,* trans. J. W. Duff and A. M. Duff, Loeb ed.).

5. A letter from Bennet Langton to JB confirms and amplifies this information: "the first direction it [Beauclerk's will] contained was, that his Corps was to be carried down into Lancashire and deposited by the side of His Mother in the burying place of Her Family" (Fifer, p. 102). Beauclerk's mother, Lady Sidney Beauclerk (d. 1766), was the daughter of Thomas Norris of Speke, Lancashire (Fifer, pp. 102 n. 7, 108 n. 4).

6. Topham and Lady Diana Beauclerk had three children: Mary (1766–1851), Elizabeth (*c.* 1767–93), and Charles George (1774–1846).

7. George Leycester (*c.* 1733–1809), of Toft, Cheshire, Beauclerk's cousin (Fifer, p. 102 and n. 6).

8. Beauclerk's executors may have hoped that Empress Catherine II, a great collector and patron of the arts, would be interested in acquiring the library, which included over thirty thousand volumes (*Life* IV.105 n. 2). However, no purchaser could be found for the entire collection, and the library was sold at auction the following spring (*Life* III.420 n. 4).

9. Early on the morning of 18 Mar., a fire broke out in the servants' quarters at Northumberland House. According to the published reports, there were no fatalities, and damage was limited to the domestic offices (*Daily Advertiser,* 20 Mar. 1780, p. 1). "The alert firemen had literally snatched most of his [Percy's] prized books and papers from the flames" (B. H. Davis, *Thomas Percy,* 1989, p. 244).

his physicians; he is now at Bath, that his mind may be quiet, and Mrs. Thrale and Miss are with him.[10]

Having told you what has happened to your friends, let me say something to you of yourself. You are always complaining of melancholy, and I conclude from those complaints that you are fond of it. No man talks of that which he is desirous to conceal, and every man desires to conceal that of which he is ashamed. Do not pretend to deny it; *manifestum habemus furem*;[11] make it an invariable and obligatory law to yourself, never to mention your own mental diseases; if you are never to speak of them, you will think on them but little, and if you think little of them, they will molest you rarely. When you talk of them, it is plain that you want either praise or pity; for praise there is no room, and pity will do you no good; therefore, from this hour speak no more, think no more, about them.

Your transaction with Mrs. Stewart gave me great satisfaction; I am much obliged to you for your attention.[12] Do not lose sight of her; your countenance may be of great credit, and of consequence of great advantage to her. The memory of her brother is yet fresh in my mind; he was an ingenious and worthy man.

Please to make my compliments to your lady, and to the young ladies. I should like to see them, pretty loves. I am, dear Sir, Yours affectionately,

SAM. JOHNSON

10. *Ante* To Hester Thrale, 6 Apr. 1780, n. 1.

11. *manifestum habemus furem*: "we have the unmistakable thief" (legal maxim).

12. JB had reported "that after a good deal of enquiry I had discovered the sister of Mr. Francis Stewart, one of his amanuenses when writing his Dictionary;—that I had, as desired by him, paid her a guinea for an old pocket-book of her brother's which he had retained; and that the good woman, who was in very moderate circumstances, but contented and placid, wondered at his scrupulous and liberal honesty, and received the guinea as if sent her by Providence" (*Life* III.418). *Post* To JB, 27 Feb. 1784.

Lucy Porter

SATURDAY 8 APRIL 1780

MS: A.D.H. Pennant.

Dear Madam: London, April 8, 1780

I am indeed but a sluggish Correspondent, and know not when I shall much mend; however I will try.

I am glad that your oisters proved good, for I would have every thing good that belongs to You; and would have your health good that you may enjoy the rest. My health is better than it has been for some years past, and, if I see Lichfield again, I hope to walk about it.[1]

Your Brother's request I have not forgotten.[2] I have bought as many volumes as contain about an hundred and fifty Sermons which I will put in a Box, and get Mr. Mathias to send him. I shall add a Letter.

We have been lately much alarmed at Mr. Thrale's. He has had a stroke like that of an apoplexy, but he is at last got so well as to be at Bath, out of the way of trouble and business, and is likely to be in a short time quite well.[3]

I hope all the Lichfield Ladies are well, and that every thing is prosperous among them.

A few weeks ago I sent you a little stuff gown,[4] such as is all the fashion at this time. Yours is the same with Mrs. Thrale's and Miss bought it for us. These stuffs are very cheap, and are thought very pretty.

Pray give my compliments to Mr. Pierson, and to every body, if any such body there be, that cares about me.

I am now engaged about the rest of the lives, which I am afraid will take some time, though I purpose to use despatch, but something or other always hinders. I have a great number to do; but many of them will be short.[5]

1. SJ next visited Lichfield in Oct. 1781 (*Post* To Hester Thrale, 20 Oct. 1781).
2. *Ante* To Lucy Porter, 18 Apr. 1768, n. 6.
3. *Ante* To John Taylor, 9 Dec. 1779; *Ante* To Hester Thrale, 6 Apr. 1780, n. 1.
4. *stuff*: "textures of wool thinner and slighter than cloath" (SJ's *Dictionary*).
5. SJ had "at least these lives to do: *Rowe* (in progress), *Granville, Sheffield, Col-*

I have lately had colds, the first was pretty bad with a very troublesome and frequent cough, but by bleeding and physick it was sent away. I have a cold now, but not bad enough for bleeding.

For some time past, and indeed ever since I left Lichfield last year, I have abated much of my diet, and am, I think, the better for abstinence. I can breathe and move with less difficulty, and I am as well, as people of my age commonly are. I hope We shall [see] one another again sometime this year.[6] I am, Dear Love, Your humble Servant,   SAM. JOHNSON

---

lins, Pitt, Fenton, Congreve, Blackmore, A. Philips, Broome, Gray, Hammond, Lyttelton, West, Swift, Young, Pope, Akenside and *Shenstone*" (William McCarthy, "The Composition of Johnson's *Lives*: A Calendar," *Philological Quarterly* 60, 1981, p. 58).

6. See above, n. 1.

Hester *Maria* Thrale
SATURDAY 8 APRIL 1780

MS: The Earl of Shelburne.
ADDRESS: To Miss Thrale.

My dear Love: Apr. 8, 1780

It is well that you are all housed safe at last.[1] By this Journey you are sure to escape some danger. My Master will be out of the way both of political and commercial tumults and hurries, and I hope that change of air, and proper proportions of exercise and rest may produce some actual good.

As for such Younglings as you a new place is always a good place, unless it be eminently bad. The great pleasure of life is the influx of novelty, and probably for that reason only our earliest years are commonly our happiest, for though they are past under restraint, and often in a very unpleasing course of involuntary labour, yet while every hour produces something

1. *Ante* To Hester Thrale, 6 Apr. 1780, n. 1.

new, there is no deep impression of discontent. Therefore, my charming Queeney keep your eyes and your ears open, and enjoy as much of the intellectual world as You can. If Ideas are to us the measure of time, he that thinks most, lives longest. Berkley says that one Man lives more life in an hour, than another in a week;[2] that You, my dearest, may in every sense live long, and in every sense live well is the desire of, Your humble servant,

SAM. JOHNSON

2. "One man, by a brisker motion of his spirits and succession of his ideas, shall live more in one hour than another in two; and . . . the quantity of life is to be estimated, not merely from the duration, but also from the intenseness of living" (George Berkeley, *Siris*, paragraph 109, *The Works of George Berkeley*, ed. A. A. Luce and T. E. Jessop, 1953, v.68).

Hester Thrale

TUESDAY 11 APRIL 1780

MS: Princeton University Library.

Dear Madam: London, Apr. 11, 1780

On Sunday I dined with poor Laurence who is deafer than ever. When he was told that Dr. Moisy visited Mr. Thrale he enquired, for what? and said that there was nothing to be done, which Nature would not do for herself. On Sunday evening I was at Mrs. Veseys and there was enquiry about my Master, but I told them all good. There was Dr. Barnard of Eaton,[1] and we made a noise all the evening, and there was Pepys, and Wraxal till I drove him away. And I have no loss of my Mistress, who laughs, and frisks, and frolicks it all the long day, and never thinks of poor Colin.[2]

If Mr. Thrale will but continue to mend we shall, I hope, come together again, and do as good things as ever we did, but perhaps You will be made too proud to heed me, and yet,

1. Edward Barnard (1717–81), D.D., Provost of Eton (1764–81).
2. *Ante* To Hester Thrale, 15 Sept. 1777, n. 10.

as I have often told you, it will not be easy for you to find such another.

Queeney has been a good Girl, and wrote me a letter; if Burney said she would write, she told you a fib. She writes nothing to me. She can write home fast enough. I have a good mind to not let her know, that Dr. Bernard, to whom I had recommended her novel, speaks of it with great commendation, and that the copy which she lent me, has been read by Dr. Lawrence three times over.[3] And yet what a Gypsey it is. She no more minds me than if I were a Brangton.[4] Pray speak to Queeney to write again.

I have had a cold and[5] a cough, and taken opium, and think I am better. We have had very cold weather, bad riding weather for my Master, but he will surmount it all. Did Mrs. Browne make any reply to your comparison of business with solitude, or did You quite down her?[6] I am much pleased to think that Mrs. Cotton thinks me worth a frame, and a place upon her wall. Her kindness was hardly within my hope, but time does wonderful things. All my fear is, that if I should come again, my print would be taken down. I fear, I shall never hold it.

Who dines with you? Do you see Dr. Woodward or Dr. Harrington? Do you go to the House where they write for the myrtle?[7] You are at all places of high resort, and bring home

3. On 13 Apr. Frances Burney recorded in her diary: "Dr. Johnson has sent a bitter reproach to Mrs. Thrale of my not writing to him, for he has not yet received a scrawl I have sent him. He says Dr. Barnard, the provost of Eton, has been singing the praises of my book, and that old Dr. Lawrence has read it through three times within this last month!" (*Diary and Letters of Madame D'Arblay*, ed. Austin Dobson, 1904, I.339).

4. In her first novel, *Evelina* (1778), Burney satirically depicts a family of London tradespeople, the Branghtons, who prove a source of perpetual mortification to the heroine.

5. MS: "and and"

6. Mrs. Browne of Bath, a Methodist widow and friend of Hester Thrale, was "a pious, charitable, peaceful Christian, who at thirty years old, though elegant in her person, and high in health and fortune, resolved upon leading a single life, that she might the better and the easier dedicate her thoughts to God, and her money to such of his poor creatures who might want it" (Piozzi, *Letters* II.119).

7. "Poor Lady Miller's" (Piozzi II.100). Anna Riggs Miller (1741–81), wife of

hearts by dozens; while I am seeking for something to say about Men of whom I know nothing but their verses, and sometimes very little of them.[8] Now I have begun however, I do not despair of making an end. Mr. Nicols holds that Addison is the most *taking* of all that I have done. I doubt they will not be done before You come away.[9]

Now you think yourself the first Writer in the world for a letter about nothing. Can you write such a letter as this. So miscellaneous, with such noble disdain of regularity, like Shakespears works, such graceful negligence of transition like the ancient enthusiasts.[10] The pure voice of nature and of Friendship. Now of whom shall I proceed to speak? Of whom but Mrs. Montague, having mentioned Shakespeare and Nature does not the name of Montague force itself upon me.[11] Such were the transitions of the ancients, which now seem abrupt because the intermediate Idea is lost to modern understandings. I wish her name had connected itself with Friendship, but, ah Colin thy hopes are in vain, one thing however is left me, I have still to complain, but I hope I shall not complain much while You have any kindness for me. I am, Dearest and dearest Madam, Your most humble Servant,

SAM. JOHNSON

You do not date your Letters.

Sir John Miller (d. 1798), Bt., of Bath-Easton, was a Bluestocking hostess and the author of *Poetical Amusements at a Villa near Bath* (1775) and *Letters from Italy* (1776). "Mrs. Miller has been in Italy . . . and brought home a fine Vase which once belonged I think She says either to Cicero or Virgil I forget which; and when She makes a sort of Publick Breakfast in the Bath Season, a thing that happens two or three Times perhaps; She desires her Friends to bring with them a Copy of Verses to put in this Vase by way of Tribute: After the Dancing, Breakfast etc. is over— these Verses are read,—publickly to the Company, and Mrs. Miller presents a Wreath of Myrtle to the Lady or Gentleman who brought with him the best Lines" (*Thraliana* I.229–30).   8. *Ante* To Lucy Porter, 8 Apr. 1780 and n. 5.

9. The last of SJ's biographies ("Pope") was not finished until early in 1781 (F. W. Hilles, "The Making of *The Life of Pope*," in *New Light on Dr. Johnson*, ed. Hilles, 1959, p. 259).

10. SJ may have in mind chapter 33 of "Longinus'" *On the Sublime*. SJ twice refers to this treatise in his *Lives of the Poets*, once (I.412) in connection with Shakespeare.   11. *Ante* To Elizabeth Montagu, 9 June 1759, n. 1.

Hester Thrale

SATURDAY 15 APRIL 1780

MS: Hyde Collection.

Dearest Madam: April 15, 1780

I did not mistake Dr. Woodward's case, nor should have wanted any explanation. But broken is a very bad word in the city.[1]

There has just been with me Dr. Burney, who has given. What has he given? Nothing, I believe, gratis. He has given fifty seven lessons this week. Surely this is business.

I thought to have finished Rowe's life to day,[2] but I have five or six visitors who hindred me, and I have not been quite well. Next week I hope[3] to despatch four or five of them.

It is a great delight to hear so much good of all of you. Fanny tells me good news of you,[4] and you speak well of Fanny, and all of you say what one would wish of my Master. And my sweet Queeny, I hope is well. Does she drink the Waters? *One glass* would do her as much good as it does her father.

You and Mrs. Montague must keep Mrs. Cotton about you, and try to make a Wit of her. She will be a little unskilful in her first Essays, but you will see, how precept and example will bring her forwards.

Surely it is very fine to have your powers. The Wits court You, and Methodists love you,[5] and the whole world runs about You, and You write me word how well you can do without me, and so, go thy ways poor Jack.[6]

That Sovereign *glass of water* is the great medicine;[7] and

1. *Broken* in a mercantile context ("in the city") means "bankrupt" (see SJ's *Dictionary*, "break," def. 11).
2. *Ante* To Hester Thrale, 6 Apr. 1780; *Ante* To Lucy Porter, 8 Apr. 1780 and n. 5.   3. MS: "ho" altered from "ha"
4. *Ante* To Hester Thrale, 11 Apr. 1780, n. 3.
5. *Ante* To Hester Thrale, 11 Apr. 1780, n. 6.
6. *Ante* To Hester Thrale, 8 Nov. 1779 and n. 9.
7. Cf. *Post* To Hester Thrale, 25 Apr. 1780.

though his legs are rather too big, yet my Master takes a glass of water. This is bold practice. I believe, under the protection of a glass of water[8] drank at the pump, he may venture once a week upon a stew'd lamprey.[9]

I wish You all good, yet know not what to wish You which you have not. May all good continue and encrease. I am, Madam, Your most humble servant,

SAM. JOHNSON

You owe me silver Ʃ:

8. MS: "of water of water"

9. Henry Thrale, increasingly addicted to rich foods, was literally eating himself to death (Clifford, 1952, p. 184). Before his stroke, he had been accustomed to devour "stewed Lamprey at a valiant rate" (Hester Thrale to SJ, 3 June 1780, MS: Rylands Library). "Johnson thought little of the Power of Remedies, and less did he think on the power of stewed Lampreys to hinder all Remedies from being efficacious" (Piozzi, *Letters* II.103; annotated copy at Trinity College, Cambridge).

Hester Thrale

TUESDAY 18 APRIL 1780

MS: Current location unknown. Transcribed from photostat in the Hyde Collection.

Dear Madam: London, Apr. 18, 1780

Of the petticoat Government I had never heard. Of the Shakespeare I was once told by Miss Laurence, and that is all that I know of it. I have not seen nor heard of any body that has seen the wonders. You may be sure I should tell you any thing that would gratify your curiosity, and furnish you for your present expences of intellectual entertainment. But of this dramatick discovery I know nothing.

I cannot see but my Master may with stuborn regularity totally recover. But surely though the invasion has been repelled from life, the waste it has made will require some time and much attention to repair it. You must not grow weary of watching him, and he must not grow impatient of being watched.

Pray of what wonders do you tell me? You make verses, and they are read in publick, and I know nothing about them.[1] This very crime, I think, broke the link of amity between Richardson and Miss Mulso, after a tenderness and confidence of many years.[2] However you must do a great deal more before I leave you for Lucan or Montague, or any other charmer, if any other charmer would have me.

I am sorry that you have seen Mrs. Walmesley. She and her Husband exhibited two very different appearances of human Nature.—But busy, busy, still art thou.[3]—He prevailed on himself to treat her with great tenderness, and to show how little sense will serve for common life, she has passed through the world with less imprudence than any of her family.

Sir Philip's bill has been rejected by the Lords.[4] There was, I think, nothing to be objected to it, but the time at which it was propose[d], and the intention with which it was projected.[5]

1. Hester Thrale's poem "The Three Warnings" (originally published in Anna Williams's *Miscellanies*, 1766), had been recited by "a Man who gave publick Lectures upon Reading. . . . No Breach of Confidence there, except in suffering any body to tell on't except myself" (Hester Thrale to SJ, 20 Apr. 1780, MS: Rylands Library).

2. Hester Mulso Chapone (1727–1801), poet and essayist, had been one of Samuel Richardson's favorite correspondents in the early 1750s and an intimate member of his literary coterie. Richardson's biographers, T.C.D. Eaves and B. D. Kimpel, comment on SJ's theory: "It seems rather to have been the lady who neglected him. In 1756 he was hurt by her failure to answer a long letter. As late as 1758 he called Miss Mulso a favourite and wished she would write to him. . . . He seems also to have been neglected by Hester's future husband. . . . But they were not permanently alienated—Richardson left John Chapone a ring in his will" (*Samuel Richardson*, 1971, p. 348).

3. "But busy, busy still art thou, / To bind the loveless, joyless vow, / The heart from pleasure to delude, / And join the gentle to the rude" (James Thomson, "To Fortune," ll. 9–12).

4. In 1779 Sir Philip Jennings Clerk had introduced a bill to prevent corruption in the awarding of Government contracts. In Mar. 1780 it passed the House of Commons but was lost (14 Apr.) in the House of Lords. It was introduced again in 1782, when it passed both Houses (*Journals of the House of Commons, 1778–80*, XXXVII.187, 735–36; *Journals of the House of Lords, 1779–83*, XXXVI.504, 511).

5. The Contractors' Bill had become a legislative pawn in the struggle between Court and Ministry on the one hand and the Opposition on the other (*Walpole's Correspondence*, Yale ed. XXV.28).

It was fair in itself, but tended to weaken government, when it is too weak already.

Scrase is doubtless pleased with the payment of your debts.[6] My Master, if I understood him right, talked of putting the other eight thousand pounds into the Bank, till it could be commodiously received. I wish it were done. I love that money should lie in the Bank, and I love that debts should be discharged.

⟨*one or two words*⟩[7] has no business about you, but to be taught. Poor Byron's tenderness is very affecting. Comfort her all you can.[8] I sincerely wish her well. Declining life is a very awful scene.

Please to tell Mr. Thrale, that I think I grow rather less, and that I was last week almost dizzy with vacuity. I repeat my challenge to alternate diet,[9] and doubt not but both of us by adhering to it may live more at ease, and a much longer time. Though I am going to dine with Lady Craven,[10] I am, Madam, Your most humble servant,

SAM. JOHNSON

6. Charles Scrase had loaned the Thrales large sums to tide them over the financial crises of 1772 and 1778 (Clifford, 1952, pp. 93, 166).

7. MS: heavily del.

8. In addition to her own failing health and her husband's professional setback (*Ante* To Hester Thrale, 7 Nov. 1779, n. 1), Sophia Byron's distresses included the abrupt marriage of her son, Capt. George Anson Byron, to Charlotte Henrietta Dallas of Jamaica—"A pleasant circumstance for this proud family!" (*Diary and Letters of Madame D'Arblay*, ed. Austin Dobson, 1904, I.347 and n. 1).

9. *Ante* To Hester Thrale, 6 Apr. 1780 and n. 6.

10. Elizabeth Craven (1750–1828), daughter of the fourth Earl of Berkeley, wife of William (1738–91), sixth Baron Craven, later (1791) Margravine of Anspach, a popular dramatist and woman of fashion. "The beautiful, gay, and fascinating Lady Craven" (*Life* III.22), who was soon to separate from her husband, had already acquired a reputation for being "*infinitamente* indiscreet" (*Walpole's Correspondence*, Yale ed. XXV.611).

Charles Burney

WEDNESDAY 19 APRIL 1780[1]

MS: Boston Public Library.

ADDRESS: To Dr. Burney—or any Burney.

ENDORSEMENT in the hand of Frances Burney: From Dr. Johnson, A Note without date.

Wednesday

Mr. Johnson received an invitation from Mrs. Ord for to-morrow,[2] and having forgotten her street, desires to be informed where she lives. If Dr. Burney goes to morrow, Mr. Johnson will call on him, and beg the favour of going with him.

1. Dated by virtue of references to visiting Mrs. Ord. *Post* To Hester Thrale, 20 Apr. 1780; 25 Apr. 1780.

2. Anne Dillingham Ord (*c.* 1726–1808), wealthy widow of a Northumberland squire, prominent Bluestocking hostess, and a friend and admirer of Charles Burney, entertained frequently at her house on Queen Anne Street West (*GM* 1808, pp. 581–83; Roger Lonsdale, *Dr. Charles Burney*, 1965, pp. 181, 472).

John Taylor

THURSDAY 20 APRIL 1780

PRINTED SOURCE: Chapman II.345.

ADDRESS: To the Rev. Dr. Taylor in Ashbourne, Derbyshire.

Dear Sir: London, April 20, 1778[1]

The quantity of blood taken from you appears to me not sufficient. Thrale was almost lost by the scrupulosity of his Physicians, who never bled him copiously till they bled him in despair; he then bled till he fainted, and the stricture or obstruction immediately gave way, and from that instant he grew better.[2]

I can now give you no advice but to keep yourself totally quiet, and amused with some gentle exercise of the mind. If a

1. MS: misdated; see nn. 2, 3 below; cf. *Post* To Hester Thrale, 20 Apr. 1780

2. *Ante* To Hester Thrale, 12 June 1779 and nn. 1, 2.

suspected letter comes, throw it aside till your health is reestablished; keep easy and cheerful company about you, and never try to think but at those stated and solemn times when the thoughts are summoned to the cares of futurity, the only real cares of a rational Being.

As to my own health, I think it rather grows better, the convulsions which left me last year at Ashbourne have never returned, and I have, by the mercy of God, very comfortable nights.[3] Let me know very often how you are, till you are quite well. I am, Sir, Your affectionate, humble servant,

SAM. JOHNSON

3. On 18 June 1780 SJ recorded in his diary, "In the morning of this day last year I perceived the remission of those convulsions in my breast which had distressed me for more than twenty years" (*Works*, Yale ed. 1.300). Cf. *Post* To Hester Thrale, 21 June 1780.

Hester Thrale

THURSDAY 20 APRIL 1780

MS: Hyde Collection.

Dear Madam: London, Apr. 20, 1778[1]

Being to go dine with your favourite Hamilton, and to pass the evening with Mrs. Ord,[2] I write before your letter comes to me, if there comes any letter. I have not indeed much to say but inclose one from Lucy, and another from Taylor, keep them both for me.

I do not think they bled Taylor enough.[3] Mr. Thrale was saved by it, and I hope he will steadily remember that when evacuation is a cure, plenitude is a disease, and abstinence the true and only preventive.

1. MS: misdated; correct date established by virtue of references to Anne Ord, John Taylor, Henry Thrale, and Charles Burney
2. *Ante* To Charles Burney, 19 Apr. 1780 and n. 2.
3. *Ante* To John Taylor, 20 Apr. 1780.

I owe Miss Thrale and Miss Burney each a letter which I will pay them.

Dr. Burney gave fifty seven lessons last week, so you find, that we have recourse to musick in these days of publick distress.[4] Do not forget me. I am, Dearest Madam, Your most humble servant,

SAM. JOHNSON

You never date your letters.

4. *Ante* To Hester Maria Thrale, 11 Nov. 1779, n. 8.

Hester Thrale

TUESDAY 25 APRIL 1780

MS: A. Brooks.

London, Apr. 25, 1780

Dear Madam: Now there is a date; look at it.

Mr. Evans and Mr. Perkins called on me to day with your letter to the Electors, and another which they had drawn up, to serve in its place.[1] I thought all their objections just, and all their alterations proper. You had mentioned his sickness in terms which give his adversaries advantage by confirming the report which they already spread with great industry of his infirmity and inability. You speak in their opinion, and in mine, with too [little] confidence in your own interest. By fearing you teach others to fear. All this is now avoided, and it is to take its chances. Mr. Perkins is to imitate Mr. Thrale's hand.

How do You think I live? On thursday I dined with Hamilton, and went thence to Mrs. Ord. On Friday with much company at Reynolds's. On Saturday at Dr. Bell's. On Sunday at Dr. Burney's with your two sweets from Kensington, who are

1. This circular letter was meant to scotch rumors of Thrale's incapacity well in advance of the next general election (J. D. Fleeman, "Dr. Johnson and Henry Thrale, M.P.," in *Johnson, Boswell and Their Circle*, 1965, p. 184).

both well;[2] at night came Mrs. Ord, Mr. Harris, and Mr. Greville etc. On Monday with Reynolds, at night with Lady Lucan, to day with Mr. Langton; to morrow with the Bishop of St. Asaph;[3] on thursday with Mr. Bowles;[4] friday——Saturday at the Academy;[5] Sunday with Mr. Ramsay.

The Dean of Ossory's Lady once Miss Charlotte Cotterell, daughter of Admiral Cotterell, never complained to any body, but those whom she liked; and sister to Calamity who, I thought, had now lived with her.[6]

I told Lady Lucan how long it was since she sent to me, but she said I must consider how the world rolls about her. She seemed pleased that we met again.

The long intervals of starving I do not think best for Mr. Thrale nor perhaps for my self, but I know not how to attain any thing better, and every body tells me that I am very well, and I think there now remains not much cause for complaint, but O for a glass once in four and twenty hours of warm water! Can warm water be had only at Bath, as Steam was to be found only at Knightsbridge.[7] Nature distributes her gifts, they say, variously to show us that we have need of one another and in her bounty she bestowed warm water upon bath, and condemned the inhabitants of other places, if they would warm their water, to make a fire. I would have the young Ladies take half a glass every third day, and walk upon it.

2. Susanna and Sophia Thrale were attending school in Kensington (*Diary and Letters of Madame D'Arblay*, ed. Austin Dobson, 1904, I.91).

3. SJ refers to Jonathan Shipley.

4. William Bowles (1755–1826), of Heale House, Wiltshire, son of the Rev. William Bowles (1716–88), Canon of Salisbury, and later (1782) Sheriff of Wiltshire (*Life* IV.523). In 1784 Bowles was elected to SJ's Essex Head Club (*Post* To William Bowles, 23 Feb. 1784).   5. *Post* To Hester Thrale, 1 May 1780.

6. Though this entire paragraph has been heavily deleted, the text can be made out with comparative confidence. Apparently "Calamity" was the nickname of Charlotte Cotterell Lewis's sister Frances (*Post* To Hester Thrale, 5 June 1783).

7. "Sir, it is surprising how people will go to a distance for what they may have at home. Mrs. Langton came up to Knightsbridge with one of her daughters, and gave five guineas a week for a lodging and having a warm bath, that is, mere warm water. *That*, you know, could not be had in Lincolnshire. They said it was made either too hot or too cold there" (*Hebrides*, p. 255).

I not only scour the town from day to day, but many visitors come to me in the morning, so that my work makes no great haste, but I will try to quicken it.[8] I should certainly like to bustle a little among you, but I am unwilling to quit my post till I have made an end.

You did not tell me in your last letter how Mr. Thrale goes on. If he will be *ruled for aught appears he may live on these hundred years*.[9] Fix him when he comes in alternate diet.[10] I am, Dearest Lady, Your most humble servant.

SAM. JOHNSON

8. *Ante* To Lucy Porter, 8 Apr. 1780 and n. 5.

9. "Had he been rul'd, for ought appears, / He might have liv'd these Twenty Years" (Swift, "Verses on the Death of Dr. Swift," 1731, ll. 173–74).

10. *Ante* To Hester Thrale, 6 Apr. 1780 and n. 6.

John Nichols
c. MAY 1780 (1)

MS: British Library.
ADDRESS: To Mr. Nicol.

Sir: Friday

In examining this Book I find it necessary, to add to the life the preface to the *British Enchanters*[1] and You may add, if you will, the notes on *Unnatural flights*.[2] I am, Sir, etc.

1. The preface to Granville's drama, *The British Enchanters* (1710), duly appeared in the second installment (6 vols., 1781), but was dropped from the subsequent (four-volume) edition. See below, n. 2.

2. Commenting on the proofs of SJ's "Granville" and on this letter, J. D. Middendorf writes: "Johnson concluded his paragraph on Granville's *Essay upon Unnatural Flights in Poetry* with the statement, 'His poetical precepts are accompanied with agreeable and instructive notes, which ought not to have been omitted in this edition.' Nichols wrote, 'They shall be added, if Dr. J. pleases,' and Johnson replied, 'Let them be added'. . . . Prior to publication Johnson again suggested, in a letter to Nichols, that the notes be included, and they were, but the clause 'which ought not . . .' was not deleted until the four-volume edition of 1781, which at the same time also dropped the notes" (J. H. Middendorf, "Johnson as Editor: Some Proofs of the 'Prefaces,'" in *Eighteenth-Century Studies in Honor of D. F. Hyde*, ed. W. H. Bond, 1970, p. 93).

John Nichols

c. MAY 1780 (II)

MS: British Library.

ADDRESS: To Mr. Nicol.

There is a copy of verses by Fenton on the *first fit of the* gout, in Popes Miscellanies, and I think, in the last volume of Drydens. In Pope's I am sure.[1]

1. SJ believed that Elijah Fenton (1683–1730) was the author of "The First Fit of the Gout," which had first appeared, anonymously, in the *Oxford and Cambridge Miscellany Poems* (1708), edited by Fenton. Accordingly, SJ appended the poem to his "Fenton" (*Lives of the Poets* II.264 n. 8). In a thorough discussion of posthumous attributions, Earl Harlan argues that SJ found the poem in the 1720 edition of Bernard Lintot's *Miscellany,* "where a cursory examination of the index would seem to ascribe it to Fenton" (*Elijah Fenton*, 1937, p. 183). This *Miscellany,* first published in 1712, came to be known as "Pope's." Harlan concludes, however, that "The First Fit" does not belong in the Fenton canon (Harlan, *Fenton*, pp. 184–85).

John Nichols

MAY 1780

MS: British Library.

I should have given Fenton's birth to *Shelton* in Staffordshire, but that I am afraid there is no such place.[1]

The rest I have except his Secretaryship of which I know not what to make.[2]

1. SJ begins his account of Fenton's life, "He was born near Newcastle in Staffordshire of an ancient family" (*Lives of the Poets* II.257). Fenton's birthplace was indeed Shelton Old Hall, near Stoke-upon-Trent (Earl Harlan, *Elijah Fenton*, 1937, pp. 15–16).

2. "It is impossible to trace Fenton from year to year, or to discover what means he used for his support. He was a while secretary to Charles [fourth] earl of Orrery in Flanders, and tutor to his young son [the fifth Earl], who afterwards mentioned him with great esteem and tenderness" (*Lives of the Poets* II.258). According to Fenton's modern biographer, he served as secretary to the fourth Earl, 1711–20, and as tutor to his son and heir, John, 1714–20 (Harlan, *Fenton*, pp. 28, 41, 87).

When Lord Orrery was in an office Lewis was his Secretary. Lewis lived to my time, I knew him.[3]

The Gout verses were always given to Fenton, when I was young, and he was living.[4]

Lord Orrery told me that Fenton was his Tutor, but never that he was his father's secretary.[5]

Pray let me see the Oxford and Cambridge etc.,[6] if you are sure it was published by Fenton, I shall take notice of it.

3. SJ appears to be referring to Erasmus Lewis (1670–1754), a close friend of Jonathan Swift and Under-Secretary of State during the Oxford-Bolingbroke Ministry (Harold Williams, "Old Mr. Lewis," *RES* 21, 1945, pp. 56–57).

4. *Ante* To John Nichols, *c.* May 1780 (II), n. 1.   5. See above, n. 2.

6. *Ante* To John Nichols, *c.* May 1780 (II), n. 1.

Hester Thrale

MONDAY 1 MAY 1780

MS: A. Brooks.

Dearest Madam: London, May 1, 1780

Mr. Thrale never will live abstinently till he can persuade himself to abstain by rule. I lived on Potatoes on friday, and on spinach to day, but I have had I am afraid, too many dinners of late. I took physick too both days, and hope to fast to morrow. When he comes home, we will shame him, and Jebb shall scold him into regularity.[1] I am glad, however, that he is always one of the company, and that my dear Queeny is again another.[2] Encourage, as You can the musical girl.[3]

1. Sir Richard Jebb (1729–87), Bt., F.R.S., a distinguished London physician whose patients included the Thrale family and SJ.

2. "Poor Queeney's sore Eyes have just released her, she had a long Confinement and could neither read nor write" (Hester Thrale to SJ, 28 Apr. 1780, MS: Hyde Collection).

3. Jane Mary Guest (*c.* 1763–*c.* 1824), later (1789) Mrs. A. A. Miles, a precocious Bath pianist and pupil of J. C. Bach, was giving music lessons to Queeney Thrale (*A Biographical Dictionary of Actors, Actresses, Musicians, Dancers, Managers, and Other Stage Personnel in London, 1660–1800*, ed. P. H. Highfill et al., 1978, VI.442; Hester Thrale to SJ, 28 Apr. 1780, MS: Hyde Collection).

Nothing is more common than mutual dislike where mutual approbation is particularly expected.[4] There is often on both sides a vigilance not over benevolent, and as attention is strongly excited so that nothing drops unheeded, any difference in taste or opinion, and some difference where there is no restraint, will commonly appear, it immediately generates[5] dislike.

Never let criticisms operate upon your face or your mind; it is very rarely that an authour is hurt by his criticks. The blaze of reputation cannot be blown out, but it often dies in the socket, a very few names may be considered as perpetual lamps that shine unconsumed. From the authour of Fitzosborne's letters I cannot think myself in much danger.[6] I met him only once about thirty years ago, and in some small dispute reduced him to whistle; having not seen me since, that is the last impression. Poor Moore the fabulist was one of the company.[7]

Mrs. Montague's long stay, against her own inclination is very convenient. You would, by your own confession, want a companion, and she is par pluribus,[8] conversing with her You may *find variety in one.*[9]

At Mrs. Ord's I met one Mrs. Buller a travelled lady, of great spirit, and some consciousness of her own abilities.[10] We

4. On 28 Apr. Hester Thrale had reported: "Yesterday's Evening was passed at Mrs. Montagu's: there was Mr. Melmoth, I do not like him *though* nor he me; it was expected we should have pleased each other!'" (MS: Hyde Collection). See below, n. 6.   5. MS: "gene" repeated as catchword

6. William Melmoth (1710–99), poet, essayist, and translator, the author of *Letters of Sir Thomas Fitzosborne* (1742–49), a popular epistolarium. Hester Thrale had told SJ that Melmoth was "Whig enough to abhor" him for "Tor[y]ism" (28 Apr. 1780, MS: Hyde Collection).

7. Edward Moore (1712–57), playwright, editor, and author of *Fables for the Female Sex* (1744), had scratched a precarious living in Grub Street and died in poverty.   8. *par pluribus*: "equal to many."

9. "For here the false unconstant Lover, / After a thousand Beauties shown; / Does new surprising Charms discover, / And finds Variety in One" (Addison, *Spectator* No. 470).

10. Susanna Yarde Buller (1740–1810), wife of the eminent jurist Francis Buller (1746–1800), later (1790) first Bt. (*GM* 1810, p. 674). In 1783 Frances Burney described Mrs. Buller as "a famous Greek scholar, a celebrated traveller upon the Continent to see customs and manners; and a woman every way singular, for her

had a contest of gallantry an hour long so much to the diversion of the company, that at Ramsay's last night in a crouded room they would have pitted us again. There were[11] Smelt,[12] and the Bishop of St. Asaph, who comes to every place;[13] and Lord Monboddo, and Sir Joshua and Ladies out of tale.

The exhibition, how will You do either to see or not to see. The exhibition is eminently splendid. There is contour, and keeping and grace, and expression and all the varieties of artificial excellence. The apartments are really very noble.[14] The Pictures for the sake of a Skylight are at the top of the house, there we dined, and I sat over against the Archbishop of York.[15] See how I live when I am not under petticoat government. I am, Madam, your most humble servant,

SAM. JOHNSON

Mark that—you did not put the year to your last.

---

knowledge and enterprising way of life" (*Diary and Letters of Madame D'Arblay,* ed. Austin Dobson, 1904, II.187).   11. MS: "were" altered from "was"

12. Leonard Smelt (*c.* 1719–1800), of Langton, Yorkshire, had served as Deputy-governor to the Royal Princes, 1771–76.   13. Jonathan Shipley.

14. Begun in 1776, Somerset House was designed by Sir William Chambers to house various government offices, in addition to the Royal Academy, the Royal Society, and the Society of Antiquaries (John Harris, *Sir William Chambers,* 1970, p. 100). On the completion of the Strand block in Apr. 1780, the Royal Academy moved into the apartments allocated to it, west of the Vestibule. The official opening of the annual exhibition took place there on 1 May (*Public Advertiser,* 2 May 1780, p. 2).   15. William Markham.

Hester Thrale

SUNDAY 7 MAY 1780

PRINTED SOURCE: Piozzi, *Letters* II.112–13.

Madam,   Bolt-court, Fleet-street, May 7, 1780

Mr. P——[1] has just been with me, and has talked much talk, of

1. "Perkins" (Piozzi II.112).

which the result is, that he thinks your presence necessary for a few days.[2] I have not the same fulness of conviction; but your appearance would certainly operate in your favour, and you will judge better what measures of diligence and of expence are necessary. Money, Mr. P——[3] says, must be spent; and he is right in wishing that you be made able to judge how far it is spent properly. Perhaps, it is but perhaps, some desire that I have of seeing you, makes me think the better of his reasons. Can you leave Master? Can you appoint Mrs. ——[4] governess? If you can, the expence of coming is nothing, and the trouble not much; and therefore it were better gratify your agents.[5] Levy behaves well.

I dined on Wednesday with Mr. Fitzmaurice, who almost made me promise to pass part of the Summer at Llewenny.[6] To-morrow I dine with Mrs. Southwel;[7] and on Thursday with Lord Lucan. To-night I go to Miss Monkton's.[8] Thus I scramble, when you do not quite shut me up; but I am miserably

2. Given the widespread expectation of an impending general election, Henry Thrale was being urged by his supporters in the Borough to make an appearance, solicit votes, and put to rest the continuing rumors of his physical disability. In her letter to SJ of 4 May, Hester Thrale had ruled out such a campaign trip: "Mr. Thrale . . . is not safe from another Apoplexy . . . and his Appearance among his Constituents would *do him no good*" (MS: Rylands Library). She was now being pressed to appear in place of her husband (*Post* To Hester Thrale, 8 May 1780).

3. "Perkins" (Piozzi II.112).

4. "Byron" (Piozzi II.113). "Montague" is the likelier possibility.

5. Hester Thrale left Bath shortly after 9 May, and campaigned vigorously in Southwark until 19 May, when she returned to Bath (Clifford, 1952, pp. 184–85; *Post* To Hester Maria Thrale, 19 May 1780).

6. Thomas Fitzmaurice had purchased from Hester Thrale's cousin, Sir Robert Cotton, the family estate at Lleweney, Denbighshire, which SJ and the Thrales had visited on their Welsh trip of 1774 (*Life* v.435 and n. 2).

7. *Ante* To Hester Thrale, 12 May 1775 and n. 2.

8. Mary Monckton (1746–1840), daughter of the first Viscount Galway, later (1786) Countess of Cork and Orrery, a prominent Bluestocking hostess at her home on Berkeley Square—"one of those who stand foremost in collecting all extraordinary or curious people to her London conversaziones, which, like those of Mrs. Vesey, mix the rank and the literature, and exclude all beside" (*Diary and Letters of Madame D'Arblay*, ed. Austin Dobson, 1904, II.123). According to JB, the Hon. Miss Monckton's "vivacity enchanted the Sage, and they used to talk together with all imaginable ease" (*Life* IV.109).

under petticoat government, and yet am not very weary, nor much ashamed.

Pray tell my two dear girls that I will write to both of them next week; and let Burney know that I was *so* angry—I am, etc.

I know of Mrs. Desmouline's letter. It will be a great charity. Let me know when you are to come.

Hester Thrale

MONDAY 8 MAY 1780

MS: Sir Oliver Scott.

Dear Madam: Boltcourt, Fleetstreet, May 8, 1780

Would you desire better sympathy—At the very time when You were writing I was answering your letter.

Having seen nobody since I saw Mr. Perkins, I have little more to say, than when I wrote last.[1] My opinion is that You should come for a week, and show yourself, and talk in high terms, for it will certainly be propagated with great diligence that you despair and desist, and to those that declare the contrary, it will be answered why then do they not appear? To this no reply can be made that will keep your Friends in countenance. A little bustle, and a little ostentation will put a stop to clamours, and whispers, and suspicions of your friends, and calumnies of your opponents. Be brisk, and be splendid, and be publick. You will probably be received with much favour, and take from little people the opportunity which your absence gives them of magnifying their services, and exalting their importance. You may have more friends and fewer obligations.

It is always necessary to show some good opinion of those whose good opinion we solicit. Your friends solicit you to come, if you do not come, you make them less your friends by

1. *Ante* To Hester Thrale, 7 May 1780 and nn. 1, 2.

disregarding their advice. Nobody will persist long in helping those that will do nothing for themselves.

The voters of the borough are too proud and too little dependant to be solicited by deputies, they expect the gratification of seeing the Candidate bowing or courtesying before them. If You are proud, they can be sullen.

Such is the call for your presence; what is there to withold you. I see no pretence for hesitation. Mr. Thrale certainly shall not come, and yet somebody must appear whom the people think it worth the while to look at.

Do not think all this while that I want to see You. I dine on Thursday at Lord Lucan's, and on Saturday at Lady Craven's, and I dined yesterday with Mrs. Southwel.

As to my looks at the Academy,[2] I was not told of them, and as I remember, I was very well, and I am well enough now, and am, Dearest Madam, your most humble servant,

SAM. JOHNSON

2. *Ante* To Hester Thrale, 1 May 1780 and n. 14.

Hester Thrale

TUESDAY 9 MAY 1780

MS: Birthplace Museum, Lichfield.

Dear Madam: Boltcourt, Fleetstreet, London, May 9, 1780

This morning brought me the honour of a visit from Sir Philip Clerk, who has been to survey Streatham, and thinks it will be long before You can return thither, which he considers as a loss to him self of many pleasant days which your residence might have afforded.[1] We then talked about our Mistress, and ⟨Mrs. Montague⟩,[2] and I said You had most wit, and most literature.

Mr. Evans brought me your letter, to which I had already sent the answer, nor have I any thing to add but that the more I reflect, and the more I hear, the more I am convinced of the

1. Workmen were making extensive alterations at Streatham Park. *Post* To Hester Thrale, 27 July 1780.   2. MS: two or three words heavily del.

253

necessity of your presence.[3] Your adversaries will be for ever saying, that you despair of success, or disdain to obtain it by the usual Solicitation. Either of these suppositions generally received ruins your interest, and your appearance confutes both.

> Cette Anne si belle,
> Qu'on vante si fort,
> Pourquoi ne vient t'elle,
> Vraiment elle a tort.

While you stay away your friends have no answer to give.

Mr. Polhil, as I suppose you know, has refused to join with Hotham, and is thought to be in more danger than Mr. Thrale.[4]

Of J⟨*four or five letters*⟩'s[5] letter I would have You not take any notice, he is a man of no character.

My Lives creep on. I have done Addison, Prior, Rowe, Granville, Sheffield, Collins, Pit, and almost Fenton.[6] I design to take Congreve now into my hand.[7] I hope to have done before you can come home, and then whither shall I go?

What comes of my dear, sweet, charming, lovely, pretty, little, Queeney's learning?[8] This is a sad long interruption, and the wicked world will make us no allowance, but will call us ——

Lady Lucan says she hears Queeney is wonderfull[y] accomplished, and I did not speak bad of her.

Did I tell you that Scot and Jones both offer themselves to represent the University in the place of Sir Roger Newdigate. They are struggling hard for what, others think neither of them will obtain.[9]

3. *Ante* To Hester Thrale, 7 May 1780; 8 May 1780.

4. At the next general election, Sept. 1780, Sir Richard Hotham (?1722–99), a prosperous East India merchant, was returned head of the poll. Nathaniel Polhill (1723–82), a tobacco merchant who had represented Southwark since 1774, was reelected. Thrale was bottom of the poll (Namier and Brooke II.643, III.306, 529).

5. MS: name heavily del.   6. *Ante* To Lucy Porter, 8 Apr. 1780 and n. 5.

7. *Post* To Hester Thrale, 25 May 1780.

8. *Ante* To Hester Thrale, 19 June 1779, n. 6.

9. When Sir Roger Newdigate, who had represented Oxford since 1751, announced his intention not to stand again, the classicist William Scott and the orien-

I am not grown fat. I did thrive a little, but I checked the pernicious growth, and am now small as before.

Mrs. Strahan is at Bath, but, I am afraid, keeps her room, if she comes in your way, be civil to her, for she has a great kindness for me. I am, Dear Madam, your most humble servant,

SAM. JOHNSON

---

talist William Jones, both fellows of University College, declared themselves candidates for his seat. Both withdrew from the contest, however, and Sir William Dolben was returned unopposed (Namier and Brooke II.328, III.196, 198; Lord Teignmouth, *Memoirs . . . of Sir William Jones*, 1835, I.286–91).

Thomas Warton[1]

TUESDAY 9 MAY 1780

MS: Case Western Reserve.

Sir: Boltcourt, Fleetstreet, May 9, —80

I have your pardon to ask for an involuntary fault. In a parcel sent from Mr. Boswel[2] I found the inclosed letter,[3] which without looking on the direction I broke open, but finding that I did not understand it, soon saw it belonged to you. I am sorry for this appearance of a fault, but believe me, it is only the appearance. I did not read enough of the letter to know its purport. I am, Sir, Your most humble Servant,

SAM. JOHNSON

1. A note in the hand of J. W. Croker compares the style of this letter to SJ's "former letters to Mr. Warton." Croker prints the letter in his edition of JB's *Life* (1832, II.232).

2. JB's Register of Letters summarizes the contents of his report to SJ, 2 May 1780: "That I am at present quite well and to shew that my mind is not languid I send him my letter to Lord Braxfield of which I beg his opinion" (MS: Beinecke Library). JB refers to his pamphlet, *Letter to Lord Braxfield* (1780), which "consists of very outspoken advice to Braxfield as to the conduct to be expected of him" as Lord of Justiciary (*Lit. Car.*, pp. 101–4).

3. Warton had offered to send JB "two historical Ballads concerning Scotland," but JB replied that "he need not send the Ballads as they are to be in his third volume [of Warton's *History of English Poetry*]" (JB's Register of Letters, 2 May 1780, MS: Beinecke Library; Fifer, pp. 89–90, 100).

Hester Maria Thrale

FRIDAY 19 MAY 1780

MS: The Earl of Shelburne.

ADDRESS: To Miss Thrale.

Southwark, May 19, 1780,
about 5 in the morning

Dear Madam:

I am up first in the house; though my Mistress threatened last night how she would go away this morning without being seen or heard, yet I shall catch her.[1] She has been very busy, and has run about the Borough like a Tigress seizing upon every thing that she found in her way. I hope the Election is out of danger.[2]

So far things go on well, but is it not a long time since you and I sat in a corner together? and is it not likely to be still a longer time before we shall meet? Such is the lot of mortals that they can seldom gain one thing but by the loss of another. You are frisking and skipping about Bath, and every body talks of pretty Miss Thrale, and proud Miss Thrale, and Miss Thrale in this place, and Miss Thrale in that, but I am all for my own dear Miss Thrale in the Borough, unless I could be with her, and with her I could persuade my self that every place was the Borough. Since we must part, let us be more diligent when we meet again. Endeavour to preserve what You know, and I hope we shall have an opportunity of encreasing our knowledge. In the mean time throw your eyes about You; acquaintance with the world is knowledge, and knowledge very valuable and useful, and when we meet again, You shall tell me what You have seen and heard. I am, Dearest Sweeting, Your most humble servant,

SAM. JOHNSON

1. *Ante* To Hester Thrale, 7 May 1780, n. 5.
2. *Ante* To Hester Thrale, 9 May 1780, n. 4.

Richard Farmer

MS: Hyde Collection.

HEADING in JB's hand: To The Reverend Dr. Farmer.

Sir: May 23, 1780

I know your disposition to forward any literary attempt, and therefore venture upon the liberty of entreating you to procure from College or University registers, all the dates or other information which they can supply relating to Ambrose Philips, Broom, and Gray who were all of Cambridge, and of whose lives I am to give such accounts as I can gather.[1] Be pleased to forgive this trouble from, Sir, Your most humble Servant,

SAM. JOHNSON

Please to direct the papers to W. Strahan Esq. in Newstreet.

1. Apparently Farmer never sent the information requested (*Post* To John Nichols, 16 June 1780). As G. B. Hill notes, Farmer's "neglect to answer is apparent in the Lives of these men. The information which was not supplied by him was not obtained elsewhere" (Hill II.180 n. 3).

Hester Thrale

TUESDAY 23 MAY 1780

MS: Hyde Collection.

ADDRESS: To Henry Thrale, Esq., at Bath.

POSTMARKS: 23 MA, FREE.

Dear Madam: May 23, 1780

Your letter told me all the good news. Mr. Thrale well, Queeney good, ⟨Fanny⟩[1] pleasing and welcome, and yourself not so ill but that you know how to be made well, and now

1. MS: one word heavily del.

Montague is gone, you have the sole and undivided empire of Bath, and you talk to many whom you cannot make wiser, and enjoy the foolish face of praise.[2]

But Montague and you have had with all your adulations nothing finer said of you than was said last Saturday night of Burke and Me. We were at the Bishop of St. Asaph's,[3] a Bishop little better than *your* Bishop,[4] and towards twelve we fell into talk to which the Ladies listened just as they do to You, and said, as I heard, *there is no rising unless somebody will cry fire.*

I was last night at Miss Monkton's, and there were Lady Craven and Lady Cranburne,[5] and many Ladies and few Men. Next Saturday I am to be at Mr. Pepys's, and in the intermediate time am to provide for myself as I can.

You cannot think how doggedly I left your house on fryday morning, and yet Mrs. Abbess gave me some mushrooms,[6] but what are Mushrooms without my Mistress?

My Master has seen his handbill; will he stand to it?[7] I have not heard a word from the Borough since You went away.

Dr. Taylor is coming hastily to town that he may drive his lawsuit forward.[8] He seems to think himself very well. This Lawsuit will keep him in exercise, and exercise will keep him well. It is to be wished that the Law may double its delays. If Dr. Wilson dies, he will take St. Margaret's, and then he will

2. "And wonder with a foolish face of praise" (Pope, "Epistle to Dr. Arbuthnot," l. 212).　　　　　　　　　　　　　　　　　　　　3. Jonathan Shipley.

4. Hester Thrale's favorite bishop was John Hinchliffe (1731– 94), D.D., Bishop of Peterborough (1769–94), later (1792) a member of The Club (Fifer, p. 372 n. 7). "There is so much Dignity, so little *Pomposity*, so much Wit, so little Buffoonery, so much Christianity and so little Cant; that I have seldom seen a Character more truly to my Taste" (*Thraliana* 1.387).

5. Mary Amelia Cranbourne (1750–1835), wife of James Cecil (1748–1823), Viscount Cranbourne, who later that year succeeded his father as seventh Earl of Salisbury.

6. Presumably Mrs. Abbess was the housekeeper at the Thrales' house in Southwark, where SJ had been staying during Hester Thrale's bout of campaigning (*Ante* To Hester Maria Thrale, 19 May 1780).

7. *Ante* To Hester Thrale, 25 Apr. 1780 and n. 1.

8. *Ante* To John Taylor, 9 Feb. 1775, n. 1.

[have] the bustle of the Parish to amuse him.[9] I expect him every day.[10] I am, dear Lady, Your most humble servant,

SAM. JOHNSON

9. As senior prebendary of Westminster, Taylor had "his choice of the livings that are in the gift of the Chapter, of which St. Margaret's is one" (*Post* To Hester Thrale, 6 June 1780). When Thomas Wilson, rector since 1753, died in 1784, Taylor duly exercised his "personal Option" to succeed him (Charles Smyth, *Church and Parish . . . St Margaret's Westminster*, 1955, p. 197; Chapter Minute, 7 May 1784: information supplied by Mrs. E. Nixon, Muniment Room and Library, Westminster Abbey; *Post* To Hester Thrale, 13 May 1784).

10. *Post* To Hester Thrale, 25 May 1780.

Joseph Warton

TUESDAY 23 MAY 1780

PRINTED SOURCE: John Wooll, *Biographical Memoirs of the Late Revd. Joseph Warton, D.D.*, 1806, p. 390. Collated with text in JB's *Life*, ed. Croker, 1832, II.233.

Dear Sir,   May 23d, 1780

It is unnecessary to tell you how much I was obliged by your useful memorials. The shares of Fenton and Broom in the Odyssey I had before from Mr. Spence.[1] Dr. Warburton did not know them. I wish to be told, as the question is of great importance in the poetical world, whence you had your intelligence: if from Spence, it shows at least his consistency; if from any other, it confers corroboration. If any thing useful to me should occur, I depend upon your friendship.

Be pleased to make my compliments to the ladies of your house, and to the gentleman that honoured me with the Greek

1. Fenton contributed four books to Pope's translation of the *Odyssey* (1725), William Broome (1689–1745) eight books (as well as all the notes). "A natural curiosity, after the real conduct of so great an undertaking, incited me once to enquire of Dr. Warburton, who told me . . . that he was not able to ascertain the several shares. The intelligence which Dr. Warburton could not afford me, I obtained from Mr. Langton, to whom Mr. Spence had imparted it" (*Lives of the Poets* III.77–78). For Joseph Spence's *Anecdotes*, see *ante* To Hester Thrale, 6 Apr. 1780, n. 7.

Epigrams when I had, what I hope sometime to have again, the pleasure of spending a little time with you at Winchester.[2] I am, Dear Sir, Your most obliged and most humble servant,

SAM. JOHNSON

2. SJ had last visited Winchester early in 1778, when he accompanied Charles Burney and his son Richard to the school in order "to ensure that they were well received" (Roger Lonsdale, *Dr. Charles Burney*, 1965, p. 242). The "gentleman" in question may have been the Rev. George Huntingford (1748–1832), an assistant master at Winchester College who went on to become Bishop of Gloucester (1802) and Bishop of Hereford (1815). Huntingford was celebrated for his Greek and Latin verses.

John Nichols

WEDNESDAY 24 MAY 1780

MS: British Library.

May 24, 1780[1]

Mr. Johnson is obliged to Mr. Nicol for his communication and must have Hammond again.[2] Mr. Johnson would be glad of Blackmores Essays for a few days.[3]

1. MS: date in Nichols's hand
2. This "communication" was Nichols's memoir of Hammond, which had appeared in the *GM* the previous year (1779, p. 205) (Edward Hart, "Some New Sources of Johnson's *Lives*," *PMLA* 65, 1950, pp. 1090–93). The memoir "caused Johnson to rewrite his life of Hammond, as the existing proof sheets show" (F. W. Hilles, "Johnson's Correspondence with Nichols," *Philological Quarterly* 48, 1969, p. 229).
3. "Some years afterwards (1716 and 1717) he [Blackmore] published two volumes of essays in prose, which can be commended only as they are written for the highest and noblest purpose, the promotion of religion" (*Lives of the Poets* II.246).

Hester Thrale

MS: Hyde Collection.

No. 8 Boltcourt, Fleetstreet,
London, Thursday, May 25, 1780

Dear Madam: Look at this and learn.[1]

Here has been Dr. Laurence with me, and I showed him your letter, and you may easily believe we had some talk about my Master.[2] He said however little that was new, except this, which is of great importance, that if ever he feels any uncommon sensation in his head, such as, heaviness, pain, or noise, or giddiness, he should have immediate recourse to some evacuation, and thinks a cathartick most eligible. He told me a case of a Lady who said she felt a dizziness, and would bleed; to bleed however she neglected, and in a few days the dizziness became an apoplexy. He says, but do not tell it, that the use of Bath water, as far as it did any thing, did mischief. He presses abstinence very strongly, as that which must do all that can be done, and recommends the exercise of walking, as tending more to extenuation[3] than that of riding.

Dr. Taylor has let out another pound of blood,[4] and is come to town, brisk and vigorous, fierce and fell, to drive on his lawsuit.[5] Nothing in all life now can be more *profligater* than what he is, and if, in case, that so be, that they persist for to resist him he is resolved not to spare no money, nor no time. He is, I believe, thundering away. His solicitor has turned him

---

1. SJ is drawing attention to the precision of his record, as part of his campaign to induce Hester Thrale to date her letters (*Ante* To Hester Thrale, 20 Apr. 1780; 25 Apr. 1780; 1 May 1780).

2. In her letter of 23 May, Hester Thrale had reported that, according to Dr. Moisey of Bath, Henry Thrale might "be a well Man, if he continues that Care of his Diet with which he [Dr. Moisey] boasts to have inspired him" (MS: Rylands Library).

3. *extenuate*: "to lessen; to make small or slender in bulk" (SJ's *Dictionary*).

4. *Ante* To John Taylor, 20 Apr. 1780.

5. *Ante* To John Taylor, 9 Feb. 1775, n. 1; *Ante* To Hester Thrale, 23 May 1780.

off, and I think it not unlikely that he will tire his Lawyers. But now don't you talk.

My dear Queeny, what a good girl she is. Pray write to me about her, and let me know her progress in the world. Bath is a good place for the initiation of a young Lady. She can neither become negligent for want of observers, as in the country, nor by the imagination that she lies concealed in the croud, as in London. Lady Lucan told me between ourselves how much she had heard of Queeny's accomplishments; she must therefore now be careful since she begins to have the publick eye upon her.

A Lady has sent me a vial like Mrs. Nesbit's vial, of essence of roses. What am I come to?

Congreve, whom I despatched at the Borough, while I was attending the election,[6] is one of the best of the little lives; but then I had your conversation.

You seem to suspect that I think you too earnest about the success of your solicitation;[7] if I gave you any reason for that suspicion it was without intention. It would be with great discontent that I should see Mr. Thrale decline the representation of the borough, and with much greater should I see him ejected.[8] To sit in Parliament for Southwark is the highest honour that his Station permits him to attain, and his ambition to attain it is surely rational and laudable. I will not say that for an honest man to struggle for a vote in the legislature, at a time when honest votes are so much wanted, is absolutely a duty, but it is surely an act of virtue. The Expence, if it were more, I should wish him to despise. Money is made for such purposes as this, and the method to which the trade is now brought, will, I hope, secure him from any want of what he shall now spend.

Keep Mr. Thrale well, and make him keep himself well, and put all other care out of your dear head.

Sir Edward Littleton's business with me was to know the

6. *Ante* To Hester Maria Thrale, 19 May 1780.
7. *Ante* To Hester Thrale, 7 May 1780 and n. 2; 8 May 1780; 9 May 1780.
8. *Ante* To Hester Thrale, 9 May 1780, n. 4.

character of a Candidate for a School at Brewood in Staffordshire,[9] to which, I think, there are seventeen pretenders.[10]

Do not I tell you every thing? What would'st thou more of Man? It will, I fancy, be necessary for you to come up once again[11] a[t] least, to fix your friends, and terrify your enemies.[12] Take care to be informed as You can of the ebb or flow of your interest, and do not lose at Capua the victory of Cannæ.[13] I hope I need not tell You, dear Madam, that I am, Your most humble servant,

SAM. JOHNSON

9. Sir Edward Littleton (*c.* 1725–1812), fourth Bt., of Teddesley Park, Staffordshire, later (1784–1812) M.P. for Staffordshire, dined with SJ and the Thrales during their Welsh tour of 1774 (*Life* v.457). Sir Edward had studied with the master of Brewood Grammar School, Staffordshire, to whom SJ had applied in 1736 for the post of assistant master (*Lit. Anec.* III.332–34; *Life* IV.407 n. 4; Clifford, 1955, p. 161; Namier and Brooke III.46).

10. *pretender*: "one who lays claim to any thing" (SJ's *Dictionary*).

11. MS: "ag" superimposed upon "in"

12. Hester Thrale returned to Southwark once more before the dissolution of Parliament on 1 Sept. Her purpose was not to campaign, however, but rather to survey the damage done by the Gordon Riots (Clifford, 1952, p. 185).

13. After the great battle of Cannae, 216 B.C., the Carthaginians made the city of Capua, in southern Italy, the center of their struggle against Rome.

Henry Thrale

TUESDAY 30 MAY 1780

MS: Hyde Collection.

Dear Sir: London, May 30, 1780

You never desired me to write to You, and therefore cannot take it amiss that I have never written. I once began a letter in which I intended to exhort you to resolute abstinence, but I rejoice now that I never sent, nor troubled You with advice which You do not want. The advice that is wanted is commonly unwelcome, and that which is not wanted is evidently impertinent.

The accounts of your health and[1] of your caution with which I am favoured by my Mistress are just such as would be wished, and I congratulate You on your power over yourself, and on the success with which the exercise of that power has been hitherto rewarded. Do not remit your care, for in your condition it is certain, that security will produce danger.

You always used to tell me, that We could never eat too little, the time is now come to both of us in which your position is verified. I am really better than I have been for twenty years past, and if You persist in your present laudable practice, you may live to tell your great grandchildren the advantages of abstinence.

I have been so idle that I know not when I shall get either to You, or to any other place, for my resolution is to stay here till the work is finished, unless some call more pressing than I think likely to happen should summon me away. Taylor, who is gone away brisk and jolly,[2] asked me when I would come to him, but I could not tell him.[3] I hope however to see standing corn in some part of the earth this summer, but I shall hardly smell hay, or suck clover flowers. I am, Dear Sir, Your most obliged and most humble servant,

SAM. JOHNSON

1. MS: "of" del. before "and"   2. *Ante* To Hester Thrale, 25 May 1780.

3. Because he fell far behind schedule on his *Prefaces*, SJ only left London once in 1780, when he accompanied the Thrales to Brighton during the autumn (*Post* To JB, 17 Oct. 1780). His next visit to Ashbourne took place in 1781 (*Post* To Hester Thrale, 10 Nov. 1781).

John Taylor

TUESDAY 6 JUNE 1780

MS: Basil Barlow.

ADDRESS: To the Reverend Dr. Taylor in Ashbourne, Derbyshire.

ENDORSEMENTS: 1780, 6 June 80.

Dear Sir: London, June 6, 1780

Just as You went away you asked me whether I thought Mercury would do you any good. I never had considered it before, but the mention of it made an impression upon me, and I am of opinion, that as your disorders apparently arise from an obstructed circulation, Mercury may help You. I would have you try it cautiously, by adding two grains of calomel to your pill at night. Thus taken, it will remain in your body all night, and will be directed downwards in the morning. So small a quantity can have no sudden effect good or evil, but if in a Month You think yourself better continue it, if worse, leave it off, and rid yourself of it by a brisk purge. I hope it will do good. It will add very little to the bulk of your pill, and taste it has none, and as it is combined with a purgative it can never accumulate. Let me know whether You take it or not.

Be sure, whatever else You do, to keep your mind easy, and do not let little things disturb it. Bustle about your hay and your cattle, and keep yourself busy with such things as give you little solicitude. I am, Sir, Your affectionate etc.

SAM. JOHNSON

Hester Thrale

TUESDAY 6 JUNE 1780

MS: Hyde Collection.

London, No. 8 Boltcourt,
Fleetstreet, June 6, 1780

Dear Madam: Mind this, and tell Queeney.[1]

You mistake about Dr. Taylor's claim upon the Abby; the Prebends are equal, but the senior Prebendary has his choice of the livings that are in the gift of the Chapter, of which St. Margaret's is one—which if Wilson dies, he may take if he pleases.[2] He went home lusty and stout, having bustled ably about his Lawsuit, which at last, I think, he will not get.[3]

Mr. Thrale, you say, was pleased to find that I wish him

1. *Ante* To Hester Thrale, 25 May 1780, n. 1.
2. *Ante* To Hester Thrale, 23 May 1780, n. 9.
3. *Ante* To John Taylor, 9 Feb. 1775, n. 1; *Ante* To Hester Thrale, 23 May 1780.

well, which seems therefore to be a new discovery. I hoped he had known for many a year past that nobody can wish him better. It is strange to find that so many have heard of his fictitious relapse, and so few of his continual recovery.

And you think to run me down with the Bishop[4] and Mrs. Carter, and Sir James, and I know not whether you may not win a heat now the town grows empty.[5] Mrs. Vesey suspects still that I do not love them since that *skrimage*.[6] But I bustle pretty well, and show myself here and there, and do not like to be quite lost. However I have as many invitations to the Country as You, and I do not mind your breakfasts, nor your evenings.

Langton is gone to be an Engineer at Chatham,[7] and I suppose You know that Jones and Scot oppose each other for what neither will have.[8]

If Mr. Thrale at all remits his vigilance, let the Doctor loose upon him.[9] While he is watched he may be kept from mischief, but he never can be safe without a rule, and no rule will he find equal to that which has been so often mentioned of an alternate diet, in which at least in this season of vegetation, there is neither difficulty nor hardship.[10] I am, Dearest Madam, Your most humble servant,

SAM. JOHNSON

4. Presumably the Bishop of Peterborough (*Ante* To Hester Thrale, 23 May 1780 and n. 4).

5. In her letter from Bath of 3 June, Hester Thrale had reported, "Every body is going . . . all the folks: Sir James Caldwell has shone enough" (MS: Rylands Library).   6. *Ante* To Hester Thrale, 11 Apr. 1780.

7. Bennet Langton was on leave from the North Lincolnshire Militia, "probably to assist in repairing and augmenting the fortifications around the naval magazine and shipbuilding yards" at Chatham (Fifer, p. 111 n. 10).

8. *Ante* To Hester Thrale, 9 May 1780 and n. 9.

9. *Ante* To Hester Thrale, 6 Apr. 1780, n. 5.

10. *Ante* To Hester Thrale, 6 Apr. 1780 and n. 6; 18 Apr. 1780.

Hester Thrale

MS: Birthplace Museum, Lichfield.

Dear Madam:

London, June 9, 1780

To the question who was impressed with consternation it may with great truth be answered that every body was impressed, for nobody was sure of his safety.

On friday the good Protestants met in St. George's Fields at the summons of Lord George Gordon, and marching to Westminster insulted the Lords and Commons, who all bore it with great tameness.[1] At night the outrages began by the demolition of the Mass house by Lincolns Inn.[2]

An exact Journal of a weeks defiance of Government I cannot give you. On Monday Mr. Strahan who had been insulted spoke to Lord Mansfield who had I think been insulted too, of the licentiousness of the populace, and his Lordship treated it as a very slight irregularity.[3] On Tuesday night they pulled

---

1. The London riots began on 2 June 1780 when Lord George Gordon (1751–93), President of the Protestant Association, presented a petition to the House of Commons for repeal of the Toleration Act of 1778, which had removed certain disabilities from English Roman Catholics. He was accompanied on the march from St. George's Fields to Westminster by some 60,000 people (*Parliamentary History of England*, ed. William Cobbett, 1806–20, XXI.655). The mob blocked the approaches to the Houses of Parliament; attacked the coaches of Sir George Savile, Charles Turner, Lord Mansfield, and the Archbishop of York; and malreated, among others, the Bishops of Lincoln, Lichfield, and Rochester, and Lords Bathurst, Stormont, Boston, and Ashburnham (J. P. de Castro, *The Gordon Riots*, 1926, pp. 34–37; Cobbett, *Parliamentary History*, XXI.656–57).

2. "Amid the bawling and confusion detachments of the mob paraded off to satiate their vengeance on Catholic mass-houses, incited thereto by Gordon's recent reminder that chapel-burnings in Scotland had thwarted the intentions of the Government" (de Castro, *Riots*, pp. 41–42). Two "mass-houses" were burned that night: the Sardinian chapel of SS. Anselm and Cecilia in Duke Street, Lincoln's Inn Fields, and the private chapel of the Bavarian Envoy in Warwick Street, Golden Square (de Castro, *Riots*, pp. 42, 47).

3. See above, n. 1. "As King's Printer, Strahan perhaps was, and certainly imagined himself to be, an object of attack" (J. A. Cochrane, *Dr. Johnson's Printer*, 1964, p. 200).

down Fieldings house and burnt his goods in the Street.[4] They had gutted on Monday Sir George Saviles house, but the building was saved.[5] On Tuesday evening leaving Fieldings ruins they went to Newgate to demand their companions who had been seized demolishing the Chapel. The Keeper could not release them but by the Mayor's permission which he went to ask, at his return he found all the prisoners released, and Newgate in a blaze.[6] They then went to Bloomsbury and fastened upon Lord Mansfield's house, which they pulled down, and as for his goods they wholly burnt them. They have since gone to Cane Wood, but a guard was there before them.[7] They plundered some papists I think, and burnt a Mass house in Moorfields the same night.[8]

On Wednesday I walked with Dr. Scot to look at Newgate, and found it in ruins, with the fire yet glowing. As I went by, the protestants were plundering the Sessions house at the old Bailey.[9] There were not I believe a hundred, but they did their work at leisure, in full security, without Sentinels, without trepidation, as Men lawfully employed, in full day. Such is the Cowardice of a commercial place. On Wednesday they broke open the Fleet and the Kings bench and the Marshalsea, and Woodstreet counter and Clerkenwell Bridewell, and released all the prisoners.[10]

4. The magistrate Sir John Fielding (1721–80), half brother of the novelist, lived on Bow Street (Wheatley and Cunningham I.230).

5. Sir George Savile (1726–84), Bt., M.P. for Yorkshire (1759–83), had introduced the Roman Catholic Relief Bill in 1778 (Namier and Brooke III.405, 407). Sir George lived on Leicester Square (de Castro, *Riots*, p. 63).

6. The Keeper of Newgate Prison, Richard Akerman (c. 1722–92), did his best to keep the mob at bay. It broke through the gates, however, sacked the prison, released approximately three hundred prisoners, then set fire to the building, which burned to the ground (Wheatley and Cunningham II.591; Christopher Hibbert, *King Mob*, 1958, pp. 107–10).

7. Lord Mansfield's house on Bloomsbury Square was pillaged and burnt. However, a detachment of cavalry prevented his country seat, Kenwood, from being harmed (de Castro, *Riots*, pp. 112–13).

8. The Catholic chapel in Moorfields was destroyed on 4 June (*Life* III.538).

9. The Old Bailey Sessions House, also known as "Central Criminal Court," adjoined Newgate Prison (Wheatley and Cunningham II.590, 611).

10. The mob made a clean sweep of London's principal prisons: the Fleet, Far-

At night the[y] set fire to the fleet, and to the kingsbench, and I know not how many other places; you might see the glare of conflagration fill the sky from many parts.[11] The sight was dreadful.[12] Some people were threatned, Mr. Strahan moved what he could, and advised me to take care of my self. Such a time of terrour you have been happy in not seeing.

The King said in Council that the Magistrates had not done their duty, but that he would do his own, and a proclamation was published directing us to keep our servants within doors, as the peace was now to be preserved by force.[13] The Soldiers were sent out to different parts, and the town is now at quiet.

What has happened at your house you will know, the harm is only a few buts of beer, and I think, you may be sure that the danger is over.[14] There is a body of soldiers at St. Margaret's hill.[15]

Of Mr. Tyson I know nothing, nor can guess to what he can

---

ringdon Street; the King's Bench, Southwark; the Marshalsea, Southwark; Wood Street Compter, Cheapside; the New Prison, Clerkenwell; and the New Bridewell, Surrey.

11. MS: "places" del. before "parts"

12. On 8 June Horace Walpole reported to Lady Ossory: "I remember the Excise ... and the rebels at Derby ... and the French at Plimouth—or I should have a very bad memory—but I never till last night saw London and Southwark in flames!" (*Walpole's Correspondence*, Yale ed. XXXIII.190).

13. "All hell was loose in the City, and the civil powers seemed to have abdicated, paralysed by legal niceties concerning the Riot Act and the use of troops. So at least it appeared to the King, who complained of 'the great supineness of the civil magistrates'. . . . It was on the fifth day of rioting that an anxious and exasperated George took personal charge in the Privy Council, extracted an on-the-spot opinion from the Attorney-General, Wedderburn, on the propriety of calling in the military under common law *as citizens combating a felony*, and had them sent forthwith into action—necessarily bloody action—which succeeded promptly in quelling the riots" (Stanley Ayling, *George the Third*, 1972, p. 181).

14. "The mob had actually forced their way into the brewhouse, and in a few minutes would probably have burned it to the ground, had not Perkins, with rare presence of mind, plied the crowd with meat and drink, while Sir Philip Jennings Clerke hurried off to summon troops" (Clifford, 1952, p. 186).

15. St. Margaret's Hill included the open space in front of Streatham Town Hall (Wheatley and Cunningham II.469).

allude,[16] but I know that a young fellow of little[17] more than seventy, is naturally an unresisted conqueror of hearts.

Pray tell Mr. Thrale that I live here and have no fruit, and if he does not interpose, am not likely to have much, but I think, he might as well give me a little, as give all to the Gardiner.

Pray make my compliments to Queeny and Burney. I am, Madam, your most humble servant,

SAM. JOHNSON

16. Hester Thrale's letter reporting this incident has not been recovered. "Mr. Tyson" was Master of Ceremonies at Bath (*Diary and Letters of Madame D'Arblay*, ed. Austin Dobson, 1904, 1.394).   17. MS: "more" del. before "little"

Hester Thrale

SATURDAY 10 JUNE 1780

MS: McMaster University Library.

Dear Madam: June 10, 1780

You have ere now heard and read enough to convince you, that we have had something to suffer, and something to fear, and therefore I think it necessary to quiet the solicitude which You undoubtedly feel, by telling You that our calamities and terrors are now at an end.[1] The Soldiers are stationed so as to be every where within call; there is no longer any body of rioters, and the individuals are hunted to their holes, and led to prison;[2] the streets are safe and quiet; Lord George was last night sent to the tower;[3] Mr. John Wilkes was this day with a party of Soldiers in my neighborhood, to seize the publisher

1. *Ante* To Hester Thrale, 9 June 1780.

2. By 9 June the Army had finally restored order, but in the process over 450 rioters were either killed or wounded (J. P. de Castro, *The Gordon Riots*, 1926, chaps. 2–5).

3. Lord George Gordon, the principal fomenter of the riots, was arrested at his London house on 9 June and committed to the Tower on a charge of high treason (de Castro, *Riots*, p. 180).

of a seditious paper.[4] Every body walks, and eats, and sleeps in security. But the history of the last week would fill You with amazement, it is without any modern example.

Several chapels have been destroyed, and several inoffensive Papists have been plundered, but the high sport was to burn the Jayls.[5] This was a good rabble trick. The Debtors and the Criminals were all set at liberty,[6] but of the Criminals, as has always happened many are already retaken, and two Pirates have surrend[e]red themselves, and it is expected that they will be pardoned.[7]

Government now acts again with its proper force, and we are all again under the protection of the King and the Laws.[8] I thought that it would be agreeable to You and my Master to have my testimony to the publick security, and that you would sleep more quietly when I told You that You are safe. I am, Dearest Lady, Your most humble Servant,

SAM. JOHNSON

4. According to John Wilkes's diary, on the morning of 10 June he and his troops "dispersed a great mob in Fleetstreet at [the publisher] Wm. Moore's, No. 159, seiz'd several treasonable papers, and ... issued a warrant against Wm. Moore" (*Life* III.538).

5. *Ante* To Hester Thrale, 9 June 1780 and nn. 2, 6, 10.

6. *Ante* To Hester Thrale, 9 June 1780, nn. 6, 10.

7. In Mar. 1780 two crewmen on a privateer, John Williams and James Stoneham, had been tried and convicted for mutiny, but were granted a respite "in consequence of notice taken of the case in the house of commons. The captain, it seems, had been concerned in some illicit practices, and they had resisted going into port for fear of being pressed" (*GM* 1780, pp. 199, 248). After the Gordon Riots it was reported that Williams and Stoneham, "being set at large ... are said to have surrendered themselves to the judge, and offered to defend him, when he fled from the fury of the populace" (*GM* 1780, p. 374).

8. *Ante* To Hester Thrale, 9 June 1780 and n. 13.

Hester Thrale

MONDAY 12 JUNE 1780

MS: Beinecke Library.

Dear Madam: London, June 12, 1780

All is well, and all is likely to continue well. The Streets are all quiet, and the houses are all safe. This is a true answer to the first enquiry which obtrudes itself upon your tongue at the reception of a Letter from London. The publick has escaped a very heavy calamity. The Rioters attempted the bank, on wednesday night, but in no great number, and like other thieves, with no great resolution. Jack Wilkes headed the party that drove them away.[1] It is agreed that if they had seized the Bank on Tuesday, at the height of the panick, when no resistance had been prepared, they might have carried irrecoverably away whatever they had found. Jack, who was always zealous for order and decency, declares, that, if he be trusted with power, he will not leave a rioter alive. There is however now no longer any need of heroism or bloodshed, no blue riband is any longer worn.[2]

Lady Lade called on Friday at Mrs. Gardiners to see how she escaped, or[3] what she suffered, and told her that she had herself too much affliction within doors, to take much notice of the disturbances without.[4]

It was surely very happy that You and Mr. Thrale were away in the tumult; You could have done nothing better than has

1. John Wilkes, a rather improbable apostle of law and order, had helped to repel an attack on the Bank of England during the night of 7 June. The soldiers in his troupe "fired 6 or seven times on the rioters" and killed several of them (*Life* III.538).

2. Blue cockades and blue ribbons were the badges of Lord George Gordon's Protestant Association (*Ante* To Hester Thrale, 9 June 1780, n. 1). In the midst of the riots Horace Walpole did not leave his house before "decking myself with blue ribbands like a May-day garland" (*Walpole's Correspondence*, Yale ed. XXXIII.186).

3. MS: "or" altered from "in"

4. SJ alludes to the ill health and profligate behaviour of Lady Lade's son Sir John. *Post* To Hester Thrale, 8 Aug. 1780 and n. 8.

been done, and must have felt much terrour which your absence has spared you.[5]

We have accounts here of great violences committed by the Protestants at Bath, and of the demolition of the Masshouse.[6] We have seen so much here, that we are very credulous.

Pray tell Miss Burney that Mr. Hutton called on me yesterday,[7] and spoke of her with praise, not profuse, but very sincere, just as I do. And tell Queeny that if she does not write oftener, I will try to forget her. There are other pretty Girls that perhaps I could get, if I were not constant.

My Lives go on but slowly. I hope to add some to them this week. I wish they were well done.

Thus far I had written when I received your letter of battle and conflagration.[8] You certainly do right in retiring, for who can guess the caprice of the rabble? My Master and Queeny are dear people for not being frighted, and You and Burney are dear People for being frighted.[9] I wrote to you a letter of intelligence and consolation, which, if You staid for it, You had on Saturday, and I wrote another on Saturday which perhaps may follow You from Bath, with some atchievement of John Wilkes.[10]

5. See below, n. 8.

6. On 9 June a mob of several thousand people set fire to the Catholic chapel in Bath; they also destroyed six or seven houses belonging to Catholics (*The Daily Advertiser*, 13 June 1780, p. 1).

7. James Hutton (1715–95), a former bookseller and founder of the Moravian Church in England; "venerable, virtuous, pious, exemplary Hutton" (*Thraliana* II.926) had been "one of the most affectionate and affectionately regarded friends of the Burneys" since 1773 (Roger Lonsdale, *Dr. Charles Burney*, 1965, p. 125).

8. The original MS of this letter has not been recovered. In the published version (dated 10 June) Hester Thrale reports that she and Frances Burney had watched the burning of the Catholic chapel in Bath and the house of its priest (see above, n. 6). Because rumors had been spreading that Henry Thrale was a Catholic, the Thrales and Frances Burney decided to leave immediately for Brighton (Piozzi, *Letters* II.146–52; *Diary and Letters of Madame D'Arblay*, ed. Austin Dobson, 1904, I.424–26).

9. "Miss Burney is frighted, but she says better times will come. . . . Mr. Thrale seems thunderstricken, he don't mind any thing; and Queeney's curiosity is stronger than her fears" (Piozzi, *Letters* II.147).

10. *Ante* To Hester Thrale, 9 June 1780; 10 June 1780.

Do not be disturbed; all danger here is apparently over, but a little agitation still continues. We frighten one another with seventy thousand Scots to come hither with the dukes of Gordon and Argile, and eat us, and hang us, or drown us, but we are all at quiet.[11]

I am glad, though I hardly know why, that You are gone to Brighthelmston rather than to Bristol. You are somewhat nearer home, and I may perhaps come to see You.[12] Brighthelmston will soon begin to be peopled, and Mr. Thrale loves the place, and You will see Mr. Scrase, and though I am sorry that You should be so outrageously unrooted, I think that Bath has had You long enough.[13]

Of the commotions at Bath there has been talk here all day. An express must have been sent, for the report arrived many hours before the post, at least before the distribution of the letters. This report I mentioned in the first part of my letter, while I was yet uncertain of the fact.

When it is known that the Rioters are quelled in London, their Spirit will sink in every other place, and little more mischief will be done. I am, Dear Madam, Your most humble Servant,

SAM. JOHNSON

11. Alexander Gordon (1743–1827), fourth Duke of Gordon, was the brother of Lord George (*Ante* To Hester Thrale, 9 June 1780, n. 1), but the Duke of Argyll had no credible connection to the rioters.

12. When the Thrales returned to Brighton after the election in September, SJ accompanied them (*Post* To JB, 17 Oct. 1780).

13. *Ante* To Hester Thrale, 6 Apr. 1780, n. 1.

Hester Thrale

WEDNESDAY 14 JUNE 1780

PRINTED SOURCE: Piozzi, *Letters* II.158–59.

Dear Madam,   London, June 14, 1780

Every thing here is safe and quiet. This is the first thing to be told; and this I told in my last letter directed to Brighthelmstone.[1] There has indeed been an universal panick, from which the King was the first that recovered. Without the concurrence of his ministers, or the assistance of the civil magistrate, he put the soldiers into motion, and saved the town from calamities, such as a rabble's government must naturally produce.[2]

Now you are at ease about the publick, I may tell you that I am not well; I have had a cold and cough some time, but it is grown so bad, that yesterday I fasted and was blooded, and to day took physick and dined: but neither fasting nor bleeding, nor dinner, nor physick, have yet made me well.

No sooner was the danger over, than the people of the Borough found out how foolish it was to be afraid, and formed themselves into four bodies for the defence of the place; through which they now march morning and evening in a martial manner.

I am glad to find that Mr. Thrale continues to grow better; if he is well, I hope we shall be all well: but I am very weary of my cough, though I have had much worse. I am, etc.

1. *Ante* To Hester Thrale, 12 June 1780.
2. *Ante* To Hester Thrale, 9 June 1780, n. 13.

Hester Thrale

THURSDAY 15 JUNE 1780

MS: Colgate University Library.

Dear Madam,   London, June 15, 1780

Last night I told You that I was not well,[1] and though You have much else to think on, perhaps You may be willing enough to hear, that by the help of an opiate, I think myself better to day.

Whether I am or am not better, the town is quiet, and every

1. *Ante* To Hester Thrale, 14 June 1780.

body sleeps in quiet, except a few who please themselves with guarding us now the danger is over.[2] Perkins seems to have managed with great dexterity.[3] Every body, I believe, now sees that if the tumult had been opposed immediately, it had been immediately suppressed, and we are therefore now better provided against an insurrection, than if none had happened.

I hope You, and Master, and Queeny and Burney, are all well. I was contented last night to send an excuse to Vesey, and two days ago another to Mrs. Horneck; You may think I was bad, if you thought about it, and why should you not think about me who am so often thinking about You, and your appurtenances. But there is no gratitude in this world.

> But I could tell you, Doris, if I would
> And since you treat me so, methinks I should.

So sings the sublime and pathetick Mr. Walsh.[4] Well! and I will tell you too. Among the heroes of the Borough, who twice a-day perambulate, or perequitate Highstreet and the Clink,[5] rides that renowned and redoubted Knight, Sir Richard Hotham.[6] There is magnanimity which defies every danger that is past, and publick spirit that stands sentinel over property that he does not own. Tell me no more of the self devoted Decii, or of the leap of Curtius.[7] Let fame talk henceforward with all her tongues of Hotham the Hatmaker.

2. *Ante* To Hester Thrale, 14 June 1780.

3. *Ante* To Hester Thrale, 9 June 1780, n. 14.

4. "Yet I cou'd tell you, fair One, if I wou'd, / (And since you treat me thus, methinks I shou'd)" (William Walsh, "Galatea," Eclogue II, *Letters and Poems, Amorous and Gallant*, 1692, p. 114).

5. The Clink was a district in the northern section of Southwark, an area of about seventy acres that had once formed the Bishop of Winchester's liberty or manor (Wheatley and Cunningham 1.425–26). The famous prison took its name from this district.   6. *Ante* To Hester Thrale, 9 May 1780, n. 4.

7. Livy tells of a father and son, the Decii, who "devoted" themselves and the enemies of Rome to the gods of the underworld, then died fighting those same enemies. According to Roman legend, Marcus Curtius performed a similar act of self-sacrifice by leaping into a chasm in the Forum to save his country. SJ may have had in mind a sentence from Dryden's "Parallel Betwixt Painting and Poetry": "History is also fruitful of designs both for the painter and the tragic

I was last week at Renny's Conversatione, and Renny got her room pretty well filled, and there were Mrs. Ord, and Mrs. Horneck, and Mrs. Bunbury[8] and other illustrious names, and much would poor Renny have given to have had Mrs. Thrale too, and Queeny, and Burney, but human happiness is never perfect, there is always une vuide affreuse, as Maintenon complained, there is some craving void left aking in the breast.[9] Renny is going to Ramsgate, and thus the world drops away, and I am left in the sultry town, to see the sun in the Crab, and perhaps in the Lion, while You are paddling with the Nereids.[10] I am, Madam, Your most humble Servant,

SAM. JOHNSON

---

poet: Curtius throwing himself into a gulph, and the two Decii sacrificing themselves for the safety of their country, are subjects for tragedy and picture" (*Of Dramatic Poesy and Other Critical Essays*, ed. George Watson, 1962, II.188).

8. In 1771 Catherine Horneck had married the caricaturist Henry William Bunbury (1750–1811).

9. Voltaire quotes a letter from Madame de Maintenon to Madame de la Maisonfort: "Que ne puis-je vous donner mon expérience! que ne puis-je vous faire voir l'ennui qui dévore les grands et la peine qu'ils ont à remplir leurs journeés. . . . je suis venue à la faveur, et je vous proteste, ma chère fille, que tous les états laissent un vide affreux" (*Siècle de Louis XIV*, chap. XXVII). As Hester Thrale noted: "The vacuity of Life had at some early Period of his Life perhaps so struck upon the Mind of Mr. Johnson, that it became by repeated Impression his favourite hypothesis" (*Thraliana* I.179).

10. SJ waited out four signs of the zodiac in London, for he did not leave town until late October, when he accompanied the Thrales to Brighton (*Post* To JB, 17 Oct. 1780).

John Nichols

FRIDAY 16 JUNE 1780

MS: British Library.
ADDRESS: To Mr. Nicol.

Sir:

June 16, 1780

I have been out of order, but by bleeding and physick think I am better, and can go again to work.

Your note on Broome will do me much good.[1] Can you give me a few dates for A. Philips? I wrote to Cambridge about them, but have had no answer.[2] I am, Sir, Your humble servant,

SAM. JOHNSON

1. Nichols had sent SJ the biographical information on William Broome that was included in Nichols's *Select Collection of Poems* (1780, IV.283). SJ drew extensively on this memoir in his own "Broome" (Edward Hart, "Some New Sources of Johnson's *Lives*," *PMLA* 65, 1950, pp. 1093–95).

2. *Ante* To Richard Farmer, 23 May 1780 and n. 1.

Frances Reynolds

FRIDAY 16 JUNE 1780

MS: Hyde Collection.
ENDORSEMENT: Dr. Johnson, June 80.

Dear Madam: Bolt court, Fleetstreet, June 16, —80

I answer your letter as soon as I can, for I have just received it. I am very willing to wait on You at all times, and will sit for the picture, and, if it be necessary, will sit again, for wherever I sit, I shall be always with you.[1]

Mr. Langton has already read the volume, and had returned it, when you took it.[2]

Do not, my Love, burn your papers, I have mended little but some bad rhymes. I thought them very pretty, and was moved in reading them. The red ink is only lake and Gum,[3] and with a moist sponge will be washed off.

1. Frances Reynolds's portrait of SJ was over three years in the making (*Post* To Hester Thrale, 20 Aug. 1783). The painting at issue here may be the portrait attributed to her, which now hangs in the Albright-Knox Art Gallery, Buffalo, New York (Richard Wendorf and Charles Ryskamp, "A Blue-Stocking Friendship," *Princeton University Library Chronicle* 41, 1980, p. 186).

2. SJ may be referring to an advance copy of part of the second installment of the *Prefaces* (*Ante* To John Nichols, 27 July 1778 and n. 2; *Post* To Hester Thrale, 27 July 1780 and n. 1; 1 Aug. 1780).

3. *lake*: "a middle colour, betwixt ultramarine and vermilion. . . . It is made of cochineal" (SJ's *Dictionary*).

I have been out of order, but by bleeding and other means am now better. Let me know on which day I shall come to you. I am, dear Madam, your most humble Servant,

SAM. JOHNSON

To day I am engaged, and only to day.

Hester Thrale

WEDNESDAY 21 JUNE 1780

MS: Beinecke Library.

Dear Madam: Wednesday, June 21, 1780

Now You come to a settled place I have some inclination to write to You, for in writing after you there was no pleasure.[1] All is quiet; and that quietness is now more likely to continue than if it had never been disturbed.[2] Burney's care if it be not affected is ridiculous; but there is in the world much tenderness where there is no misfortune, and much courage where there is no danger.[3]

My cold is grown better, but is not quite well, nor bad enough now to be complained of. I wish I had been with you to see the Isle of Wight, but I shall perhaps go some time without You, and then we shall be even.

What you told me of Mr. Middleton frighted me,[4] but I am still of my old opinion, that a semivegetable diet will keep all well. I have dined on Monday and to day only on Peas.

1. The Thrales left Bath on 10 June and "drove in a leisurely fashion along country roads to Brighton, which they did not reach until the 18th" (Clifford, 1952, p. 185).

2. *Ante* To Hester Thrale, 14 June 1780.

3. "Frantic with fears for the Burney families in London, Fanny could take little joy in the leisurely progress of the route [from Bath to Brighton]. . . . Fanny was happy when Mrs. Thrale took her to London on June 23 and consented to leave her at home" (Joyce Hemlow, *The History of Fanny Burney*, 1958, p. 141).

4. This "Middelton" may be John Myddelton of Gwaynynog. *Ante* To Hester Thrale, 18 Sept. 1777, n. 7.

I suppose the town grows empty, for I have no invitations, and I begin to wish for something, I hardly know what, but I should like to move when every body is moving, and yet I purpose to stay till the work is done, which I take little care to do.[5] *Sic labitur ætas.*[6]

The world is full of troubles. Mrs. Lennox has just been with me to get a Chirurgeon to her Daughter,[7] the girl that Mrs. Cumins rejected, who has received a kick from a horse, that has broken five fore teeth on the upper side. The world is likewise full of escapes; had the blow been a little harder it had killed her.

It was a twelvemonth last Sunday since the convulsions in my Breast left me.[8] I hope I was thankful when I recollected it. By removing that disorder a great improvement was made in the enjoyment of life. I am now as well as men at my age can expect to be, and I yet think I shall be better.

I have had with me a brother of Boswel, a Spanish Merchant whom the war has driven from his residence at Valentia,[9] he is gone to see his friends, and will find Scotland but a sorry place after twelve years residence in a happier climate. He is a very agreeable man, and speaks no Scotch.

Keep Master to his diet, and tell him that his illwillers are very unwilling to think that he can ever sit more in parliament,

5. "Sometime in March [1781] I finished the lives of the Poets, which I wrote in my usual way, dilatorily and hastily, unwilling to work, and working with vigour, and haste" (*Works*, Yale ed. 1.303–4).

6. *utendum est aetate: cito pede labitur aetas*: "you must employ your time: time glides on with speedy foot" (Ovid, *Ars Amatoria* III.65, trans. J. H. Mozley, Loeb ed.).

7. Harriot Holles Lennox (1765–*c.* 1782/83), only daughter of Charlotte and Alexander Lennox. Her parents had debated whether to send Harriot to a boarding school in France; Duncan Isles suggests that "she stayed at home to share her mother's poverty until her early death" ("The Lennox Collection," *Harvard Library Bulletin* 19, 1971, p. 426 n. 212, p. 428 n. 218).

8. *Ante* To John Taylor, 20 Apr. 1780 and n. 3.

9. Thomas David Boswell (1748–1826), JB's youngest brother, had been living in Spain since 1767 (*Earlier Years*, pp. 14, 341, 456). After the declaration of war between England and Spain in 1779 he returned home and established himself as a business agent in London (*Later Years*, pp. 196–99).

but by caution and resolution he may see many parliaments.[10] Pay my respects to Queeny and Burney, living so apart we shall get no credit by our studies,[11] but I hope to see You all again sometime. Do not let separation make us forget one another. I am, Madam, Your most humble Servant,

SAM. JOHNSON

10. *Ante* To Hester Thrale, 8 May 1780; 9 May 1780.
11. *Ante* To Hester Thrale, 19 June 1779, n. 6.

Hester Thrale

TUESDAY 4 JULY 1780

MS: Hyde Collection.

Dear Madam: London, July 4, —80

You are too happy for any body but yourself to travel in such pretty company, and leave every thing safe behind you, and find every [one] well when you arrive,[1] and yet I question if you [are] quite contented, though every body envies You. Keep my Master tight in his geers,[2] for if he breaks loose the mischief will be very extensive.

Your account of Mr. Scrase[3] and of Miss Owen[4] is very melancholy, I wish them both their proper relief from their several maladies. But I am glad that Queeny continues well and hope she will not be too rigorous with the young ones, but allow them to be happy their own way, for what better way will they ever find?

1. On 20 June Hester Thrale left her husband and Queeney in Brighton, paid brief visits to Southwark and Streatham, then returned to Brighton with Susanna and Sophia (*Thraliana* I.437–38; Clifford, 1952, pp. 185–86).
2. *gear*: "the traces by which horses or oxen draw" (SJ's *Dictionary*).
3. On 29 June Hester Thrale reported to Frances Burney from Brighton, "This morning I carried a bunch of grapes to Mr. Scrase, who was too ill to swallow one, or to see even me" (*Diary and Letters of Madame D'Arblay*, ed. Austin Dobson, 1904, I.431).
4. According to Hester Thrale, Margaret Owen had been "fishing for Health in the Sea" (*Thraliana* I.438). *Post* To Hester Thrale, 10 July 1780.

C'est que L'Enfant toûjours est homme;
C'est que l'homme est toûjours Enfant.

I have not seen or done much since I had the misfortune of seeing You go away. I was one night at Burney's. There was Pepys, and there were Mrs. Ord, and Paradise, and Hoole, and Dr. Dunbar of Aberdeen,[5] and I know not how many more. And Pepys and I had all the talk.[6]

To day called on me the Dean of Hereford,[7] who says that the barley harvest is likely to be very abundant. There is something for our consolation. Don't forget that I am, Dear Madam, your most humble Servant,

SAM. JOHNSON

5. James Dunbar (d. 1798), LL.D., Professor of Philosophy at King's College, Aberdeen, and author of *Essays on the History of Mankind* (1780). SJ and JB had met him on their Hebridean tour (*Life* v.92, 495).

6. On 8 July Frances Burney informed Hester Thrale: "I have not seen Dr. Johnson since the day you left me, when he came hither . . . and then he was in high spirits and good humour, talked all the talk, affronted nobody, and delighted everybody. I never saw him more sweet, nor better attended to by his audience" (Dobson, *D'Arblay*, 1.435).

7. In 1780 the Dean of Hereford Cathedral was Nathan Wetherell.

Warren Hastings

FRIDAY 7 JULY 1780

MS: Hyde Collection.

ADDRESS: To the Honourable —— Hastings, Esq., Governour of Bengal.

ENDORSEMENT in an unidentified hand: Dr. Johnson, London, July 1780, Recomm. of Mr. Hickey—Painter.

Sir: London, July 7, 1780

Mr. Hickey who has the honour of conveying this to You, has been represented to me, by one of my kindest Friends,[1] not only as a skilful Painter of Portraits, but as a very virtuous and

1. This friend was Mary Cholmondeley (*Post* To John Hoole, 7 July 1780).

worthy Man.[2] By recommending such men to your favour and patronage I am in no fear of giving you offence, and I therefore take the liberty to which I have no right, of entreating You to favour him with such encouragement as may be proper. I am, Sir, Your most humble Servant,

SAM. JOHNSON

2. Thomas Hickey (1741–1824), Irish portrait painter, exhibited at the Royal Academy, 1772–92; his sitters included Dr. William Dodd and the Duke and Duchess of Cumberland. On the voyage to India in 1781, Hickey's ship was captured by the Franco-Spanish navy, but Hickey himself was permitted to return to England. In 1792 he accompanied Lord Macartney's embassy to China. After painting in China he traveled to India, where he spent the last twenty-five years of his life (*Allgemeines Lexikon der Bildenden Kuenstler*, 1924, XVII.47).

John Hoole
FRIDAY 7 JULY 1780

MS: Hyde Collection.

ADDRESS: To Mr. Hoole.

ENDORSEMENT: Dr. Johnson.

Sir:
                                                    July 7, 1780

Mrs. Cholmondely has ordered me to write a letter in favour of one Mr. Hickey who is going in this last Ship to India,[1] and I must desire You to fill up the direction, and send it to him, if it can yet be sent. I am, Sir, your most humble servant,

SAM. JOHNSON

1. *Ante* To Warren Hastings, 7 July 1780 and n. 2.

Hester Thrale
MONDAY 10 JULY 1780

MS: Texas Christian University Library.

Dear Madam: London, July 10, 1780

If Mr. Thrale eats but half his usual quantity, he can hardly eat too much. It were better however to have some rule, and some security. Last week I saw flesh but twice, and I think fish once, the rest was pease.

You are afraid, You say, lest I extenuate myself too fast, and are an enemy to Violence, but did you never hear nor read, dear Madam, that every Man has his *genius*,[1] and that the great rule by which all excellence is attained, and all success procure[d] is, to follow *genius*, and have You not observed in all our conversation that my *genius* is always in extremes, that I am very noisy, or very silent; very gloomy, or very merry; very sour or very kind? and would you have me cross my *genius* when[2] it leads me sometimes to voracity and sometimes to abstinence?[3] You know that the oracle said follow your *Genius*.[4] When we get together again but when alas will that be You can manage me, and spare me the solicitude of managing myself.[5]

Poor Miss Owen called on me on saturday, with that fond and tender application which is natural to misery when it looks to every body for that help which nobody can give.[6] I was

1. *genius*: "disposition of nature by which any one is qualified for some peculiar employment" (SJ's *Dictionary*).   2. MS: "w" superimposed upon "h"

3. As with his discussion of letter writing (*Ante* To Hester Thrale, 27 Oct. 1777), SJ here blends serious commentary with ironic exaggeration. The element of accurate self-analysis is complicated by mockery of the doctrine of the ruling passion, to which SJ strongly objected on the grounds of its deterministic implications. His most powerful attack on this doctrine occurs in his biography of Pope, which he was to begin writing later in 1780: "Those indeed who attain any excellence commonly spend life in one pursuit, for excellence is not often gained upon easier terms. But to the particular species of excellence, men are directed not by an ascendant planet or predominating humour, but by the first book which they read, some early conversation which they heard, or some accident which excited ardour and emulation" (*Lives of the Poets* III.174). Cf. *Rambler* No. 43.

4. SJ may be recalling, and combining, a tag from Persius and an anecdote from Plutarch. The tag (*Satires* v.151) is *indulge genio*: "give your Genius a chance!" (trans. G. G. Ramsay, Loeb ed.). The anecdote forms part of Plutarch's life of Cicero: "When he [Cicero] inquired, namely, of the god at Delphi how he could become most illustrious, the Pythian priestess enjoined upon him to make his own nature, and not the opinion of the multitude, his guide in life" (v.1, trans. Bernadotte Perrin, Loeb ed.).

5. Cf. *Ante* To Hester Thrale, Early June 1773.

6. *Ante* To Hester Thrale, 4 July 1780 and n. 4.

melted, and soothed and counselled her as well as I could, and am to visit her to morrow.

She gave a very honourable account of my dear Queeny, and says of my Master that she thinks his manner and temper more altered than his looks, but of this alteration she could give no particular account, and all that she could say ended in this, that he is now sleepy in the morning. I do not wonder at the Scantiness of her[7] narration, she is too busy within to turn her eyes abroad.

I am glad that Pepys is come, ⟨*three or four words*⟩,[8] but hope that resolute temperance will make him unnecessary. I doubt, he can do no good to poor Mr. Scrase.[9]

There is now at Brighthelmston a Girl of the name of Johnston, she is Granddaughter to Mr. Strahan;[10] I wish, You could properly take a little notice of her.

I stay at home to work, and yet do not work diligently, nor can tell when I shall have done, nor perhaps does any body but myself wish me to have done, for what can they hope I shall do better? Yet I wish the work was over, and I was at liberty.[11] And what would I do if I was at Liberty? Would I go to Mrs. Aston and Mrs. Porter, and see the old places, and sigh to find that my old friends are gone? Would I recal plans of life which I never brought into practice, and hopes of excellence which I once presumed,[12] and never have attained? Would I compare what I now am with what I once expected to have been? Is it reasonable to wish for suggestions of Shame, and opportunities of Sorrow?

If You please, Madam, we will have an end of this, and contrive some other wishes. I wish I had you in an Evening, and I wish I had you in a morning, and I wish I could hear a little

---

7. MS: "her" altered from "his"   8. MS: heavy deletion

9. *Ante* To Hester Thrale, 4 July 1780, n. 3.

10. Margaret Penelope Johnston (b. 1762) was the daughter of William Strahan's daughter Rachel (J. A. Cochrane, *Dr. Johnson's Printer*, 1964, pp. xiv, 109 n. 2). She later married Sir Alexander Monro, Bt. (*GM* 1809, p. 1057).

11. *Ante* To Hester Thrale, 21 June 1780 and n. 5.

12. MS: "presumed" superimposed upon "indulged" partially erased

talk, and see a little frolick. For all this I must stay, but life will not stay. I will end my letter and go to Blackmores life,[13] when I have told You that I am, Madam, Your most humble servant,

SAM. JOHNSON

13. SJ was correcting the proofs of his "Blackmore" (William McCarthy, "The Composition of Johnson's *Lives*: A Calendar," *Philological Quarterly* 60, 1981, p. 59; *Ante* To John Nichols, 24 May 1780).

Robert Lowth [1]
THURSDAY 13 JULY 1780

MS: Bodleian Library.

My Lord: Bolt court, Fleetstreet, July 13, 1780

If what I am about [to] lay before your Lordship has any thing of impropriety or intrusion, I entreat that it may be imputed to no other cause than my inability to contend with the importunity of a friend in distress.

Mr. Percival Stockdale, who has lately applied to your Lordship for orders, is of opinion that some testimony from me will promote his suit,[2] and I can declare that I believe his intention to be that which he professes of going immediately to Jamaica.[3] He cannot therefore without culpable duplicity show a title to a curacy, since he does not intend to serve a

1. Robert Lowth (1710–87), D.D., F.R.S., author of *Lectures on Hebrew Poetry* (1753), Bishop of Oxford (1766–77) and London (1777–87).

2. Percival Stockdale (1736–1811), poet, literary journalist, and deacon in the Church of England, the author of *Miscellanies in Prose and Verse* (1778), was SJ's neighbour in Bolt Court. Stockdale's copious later publications include *Lectures on the Truly Eminent English Poets* (1807) and *Memoirs* (1809), in which he demonstrates toward SJ an ambivalent attitude compounded of admiration, rivalry, and resentment (Lawrence Lipking, *The Ordering of the Arts in Eighteenth-Century England*, 1970, pp. 465–70). Though exasperated at times by Stockdale's eccentricities and ill-judged pleas for assistance, SJ continued to be his "kind protector" (*Life* II.113 and n. 2).

3. Stockdale had "procured a recommendation from Lord George Germaine to the Governer of Jamaica" (*Post* To Hester Thrale, 27 July 1780 and n. 9).

cure in this country. Is he not, my Lord in much the same state as a Clergyman ordained for the American Mission?

He has now a Curacy within his reach, but he wishes rather to try his fortune in Jamaica, and if he has the honour of being examined, he will be found, I believe, a better scholar than is often sent to the plantations. Though he is not rich, he is not distressed, nor likely, in any case, to bring disgrace upon the order by indigence.[4]

It is time for me now to apologise for my self. I hope your Lordship will not be offended, for I write with the submission and respect of one that honours your learning, and reverences your authority. I am, My Lord, Your Lordship's most obedient and most humble Servant,

SAM. JOHNSON

4. Bishop Lowth courteously but emphatically rejected this further plea for ordination: "Mr. Stockdale has passed by many opportunities of offering himself properly during ten or twelve years that he has been in Deacon's Orders. . . . If he finds inconveniences in his present situation, it is from his own neglect. . . . I find a notion seems to prevail, that the Bishop of London is a sort of Oecumenical Bishop, to whom all are to apply, who know not where to apply else for Orders. . . . It behoves me in regard to myself and Successors to take care not to encourage this practice" (MS: Bodleian Library). Later in 1780, Stockdale, who had been presented to the rectory of Hinxworth, Hertfordshire, did succeed in taking orders (*Bodleian Library Record* 1, 1940, p. 201).

Hester Maria Thrale

TUESDAY 18 JULY 1780

MS: The Earl of Shelburne.
ADDRESS: To Miss Thrale.

My dear Charmer: London, July 18, 1780

I take your correspondence very kindly, and blame my self for not answering you with more punctuality, as well because I would be exemplary as because I would be civil. But don't leave me off, but continue to do right, though I do wrong, and perhaps you may in time mend me.

Pray tell Mr. Thrale that last week I dined once upon peas, and three times upon gooseberry pie, and that none of the best; and that I hope to grow yet for a time less and less. Tell him that he must come back with all the health that he can get to face the world, which has some difficulty to believe that he is alive, and obstinately refuses to think that he is well.

Yesterday we were disappointed at Mrs. Horneck's of the Burneys, for Mrs. Burney was taken ill; how ill, I know not, for I need not tell you that at Burney Hall a little complaint makes a mighty bustle.[1]

Mrs. Williams continues at Kingston,[2] and says that her Friends are very kind to her. She is right to pick a little variety as she can.

From the Borough or from Streatham I have never heard since my Mistresses departure,[3] nor unless Mr. Evans has called seen any common friend except the Burneys.

You, dear Madam, I suppose wander philosophically by the Seaside, and survey the vast expanse of the world of waters, comparing as your predecessors in contemplation have done its ebb and flow, it[s] turbulence and tranquillity to the vicissitudes of human life. You, my Love, are now in the time of flood, your powers are hourly encreasing, do not lose the time. When you are alone read diligently, they who do not read can have nothing to think, and little to say; when you can get proper company talk freely and cheerfully, it is often by talking that [we] come to know the value of what we have read, to separate it[4] with distinctness, and fix it in the memory. Never delight your self with the dignity of silence or the superiority of inattention. To be silent or to be negligent are so easy, neither[5] can give any claim to praise, and there is no human

1. Elizabeth Burney's illness appears to have been "a little complaint": there is no record of a major crisis until the summer of 1782, when she nearly died (Joyce Hemlow, *The History of Fanny Burney*, 1958, pp. 153–54).

2. As a consequence of the Gordon riots in early June, "Mrs. Williams was frightened from London" (*Post* To Hester Thrale, 27 July 1780).

3. *Ante* To Hester Thrale, 4 July 1780 and n. 1.

4. MS: "it" altered from "in"   5. MS: "n" superimposed upon "th"

being so mean or useless, but his approbation and benevolence is to be desired.

I wonder when we shall meet again.[6] I know not when I shall get at liberty, and wish my work done, that I may do something which[7] I am not now doing, but then as now I intend to be, my sweetest, your most humble servant,

SAM. JOHNSON

6. The Thrales returned from Brighton immediately after the dissolution of Parliament on 1 Sept. (Clifford, 1952, p. 189).

7. MS: "w" superimposed upon "th"

Hester Thrale

THURSDAY 27 JULY 1780

MS: Hyde Collection.

London, July 27, 1780

And thus it is, Madam, that you serve me. After having kept me a whole week hoping and hoping, and wondering and wondering, what could have stopped your hand from writing, comes a letter to tell me that I suffer by my own fault. As if I might not correspond with my Queeney, and we might not tell one another our minds about politicks or morals, or any thing else. Queeney and I are both steady and may be trusted, we are none of the giddy gabblers, we think before we speak.

I am afraid that I shall hardly find my way this summer into the Country though the number of my lives now grows less. I will send you two little volumes in a few days.[1]

As the Workmen are still at Streatham, there is no likelihood of seeing You and my Master in any short time, but let my

1. As he had done in 1778, SJ appears to have distributed advance copies of his *Prefaces* to certain close friends. On 16 Aug. Frances Burney reported to Hester Thrale, "Dr. Johnson . . . has delighted me with another volume of his *Lives*,— that which contains Blackmore, Congreve, etc., which he tells me you have had" (*Diary and Letters of Madame D'Arblay*, ed. Austin Dobson, 1904, I.443). Cf. *Ante* To John Nichols, 27 July 1778 and n. 2.

Master be where he will so he be well.[2] I am not, I believe any fatter than when You saw me, and hope to keep corpulence away, for I am so lightsome, and so airy, and can so walk, you would talk of it if You were to see me. I do not always sleep well but I have no pain nor sickness in the night. Perhaps I only sleep ill because I am too long abed.

I dined yesterday at Sir Joshua's with Mrs. Cholmondely, and she told me, I was the best critick in the world, and I told her, that nobody in the world could judge like her of the merit of a Critick.

On sunday I went with Dr. Lawrence and his two Sisters in law to dine with Mr. Gawler at Putney. The Doctor cannot hear in a coach better than in a room, and it was but a dull day, only I saw two Crownbirds,[3] paltry creatures, and a red Curlew.

Every Body is gone out of town, only I am left behind and know not when I shall see either Naiad or Dryad; However it is as it has commonly been I have no complaint to make but of my self. I have been idle, and *of Idleness can come no goodness.*[4]

Mrs. Williams was frighted from London as You were frighted from Bath.[5] She is come back, as she thinks, better. Mrs. Desmoulins has a disorder resembling an asthma, which I am for curing with calomel[6] and Jalap,[7] but Mr. Levet treats it with antimonial wine.[8] Mr. Levet keeps on his legs stout, and walks, I suppose ten miles a day.

I stick pretty well to diet, and desire My Master may [be]

2. *Ante* To Hester Thrale, 9 May 1780 and n. 1.

3. SJ may be referring to the hoopoe, whose "Head is adorned with a most beautiful Crest, two inches high, consisting of a double row of feathers, reaching from the Bill to the nape of the Neck" (John Ray, *The Ornithology of Francis Willughby*, 1678, p. 145).

4. "Of Idleness comes no goodness" (*Oxford Dictionary of English Proverbs*, rev. F. P. Wilson, 1970, p. 396).

5. *Ante* To Hester Thrale, 12 June 1780 and n. 8.

6. *calomel*: "mercurous chloride" (*OED*).

7. *jalap*: "a purgative drug obtained from the tuberous roots of *Exogonium (Ipomoea) Purga* and some other convolvulaceous plants" (*OED*).

8. *antimonial wine*: "sherry containing tartar emetic" (*OED*).

told of it, for no man said oftener than he that *the less we eat the better.*

Poor Stockdale after having thrown away Lord Craven's patronage and three hundred a year, has had another disappointment. He procured a recommendation from Lord George Germaine to the Governer of Jamaica, but to make this useful something was to be done by the Bishop of London which has been refused.[9] Thus is the world filled with hope and fear and struggle and disappointment. Pray do you never add to the other vexations any diminution of your kindness for, Madam, Your humble Servant,

SAM. JOHNSON

9. In Apr. 1780 Percival Stockdale resigned his position as a tutor in Lord Craven's family and "thought of trying my fortune in my clerical capacity, in one of our WEST INDIA islands" (*Memoirs*, 1809, II.209). Lord George Germaine supplied him with a letter of recommendation to Sir John Dalling (c. 1731–98), Bt., Governor of Jamaica (1777–82). Stockdale was only a deacon, however, and when the Bishop of London repeatedly refused to ordain him (*Ante* To Robert Lowth, 13 July 1780 and n. 4), Stockdale found himself "totally without employment that was of any advantage" (*Memoirs* II.216).

Lord Westcote[1]
THURSDAY 27 JULY 1780

MS: Hyde Collection.

My Lord: Bolt Court, Fleet street, July 27, 1780[2]

The course of my undertaking will now require a short life of your Brother Lord Lyttelton. My desire is to avoid offence,[3] and to be totally out of danger. I take the liberty of proposing to your Lordship, that the historical account should be written under your direction by any friend whom you may be willing to employ, and I will only take upon my self to examine the

1. *Ante* To Hester Thrale, 8 July 1771, n. 3.
2. MS: location and date in the hand of J. W. Croker
3. *Post* To Lord Westcote, 28 July 1780 and n. 2.

poetry. Four pages like those of his works,[4] or even half so much, will be sufficient.

As the press is going on, it will be fit that I should know what you shall be pleased to determine.[5] I am, My Lord, Your Lordship's most humble Servant,

SAM. JOHNSON

4. *The Works of George, Lord Lyttelton*, ed. G. E. Ayscough (1774), had been published as a handsome folio, with approximately 350 words to a generously leaded page.

5. *Post* To Lord Westcote, 28 July 1780; *Post* To Hester Thrale, 1 Aug. 1780.

Lord Westcote

FRIDAY 28 JULY 1780

PRINTED SOURCE: JB's *Life*, ed. Croker, 1848, p. 650.

My Lord: Bolt Court, Fleet Street, July 28, 1780

I wish it had been convenient to have had that done which I proposed.[1] I shall certainly not wantonly nor willingly offend;[2] but when there are such near relations living, I had rather they would please themselves.[3] For the life of Lord Lyttelton I shall need no help—it was very public, and I have no need to be minute.[4] But I return your lordship thanks for your readiness to help me. I have another life in hand, that of Mr. West, about which I am quite at a loss;[5] any information

1. *Ante* To Lord Westcote, 27 July 1780.

2. "His expressing with a dignified freedom what he really thought of George, Lord Lyttelton, gave offence to some of the friends of that nobleman, and particularly produced a declaration of war against him from Mrs. Montagu ... between whom and his Lordship a commerce of reciprocal compliments had long been carried on" (*Life* IV.64).   3. *Post* To Hester Thrale, 1 Aug. 1780.

4. *Post* To John Nichols, 16 Aug. 1780.

5. Although Gilbert West (1703–56) was Lord Westcote's first cousin, he apparently had no helpful information to offer. SJ's "West" begins; "Gilbert West is one of the writers of whom I regret my inability to give a sufficient account; the intelligence which my enquiries have obtained is general and scanty" (*Lives of the Poets* III.328 and n. 3).

respecting him would be of great use to, my Lord, Your lordship's most humble servant,

SAM. JOHNSON

Charles Burney

MONDAY 31 JULY 1780

MS: Bodleian Library.

ADDRESS: To Dr. Burney at the Golden Cross in Oxford.

ENDORSEMENT: From Dr. Johnson, July 31st 1780, No. 7.

Dear Sir:

July 31, 1780

You did very kindly in letter know that You are at Oxford. You may do me a great favour if You can find in the libraries the Liber Londinensis, as I remember a small quarto printed perhaps in the first years of Henry the eighth; it is a miscellany containing among other things the Nutbrown Maid republished by Prior.

If you find it I beg you to transcribe literally the prophecy which is there and which lately Swift put in his works.[1] If there is any preface or note or any thing relating to it please to copy the whole, and tell nobody about it. Make my compliments to the Ladies. I am, Sir, Your most humble servant,

SAM. JOHNSON

1. Richard Arnold's *Chronicle, or Customs of London* (?1503) contains the ballad of "The Nut-brown Maid," which Matthew Prior imitated in "Henry and Emma" (1709) (*The Literary Works of Matthew Prior*, ed. H. B. Wright and M. K. Spears, 1959, II.909). Arnold's *Chronicle* does not include, however, any of the medieval and early Renaissance "prophecies" that Swift parodied in his *Famous Prediction of Merlin, the British Wizard* (1709). According to Herbert Davis, "It has caused some amusement that Dr. Johnson really believed that Swift was annotating a sixteenth century Prophecy of Merlin" (*Prose Works of Jonathan Swift*, ed. Davis, 1939, II.xxiv n. 2). SJ may have been intending to discuss Swift's satiric play with the prophetic genre in his biography, which he began writing at the end of the summer. However, he merely refers in passing to the *Famous Prediction* (*Lives of the Poets* III.14).

Hester Thrale

TUESDAY 1 AUGUST 1780

MS: Hyde Collection.

Madam: London, Aug. 1, 1780

I had your letter about Mr. Scrase and Miss Owen, but there was nothing to which I had any answer or to which any answer could be made.

This afternoon Dr. Lawrence drank tea, and as he always does, asked about Mr. Thrale; I told him how well he was when I heard, and, he does not eat too much said the Doctor, I said, not often, and the return was, that he who in that case should once eat too much, might eat no more. I keep my rule very well, and, I think, continue to grow better.

Tell my pretty dear Queeney that when we meet again, we will have, at least for some time two lessons in a day.[1] I love her, and think on her when I am alone, hope we shall be very happy together; and mind our books.

Now August and[2] autumn are begun, and the Virgin takes possession of the sky. Will the Virgin do any thing for a man of seventy? I have a great mind to end my work under the Virgin.[3]

I have sent two volumes to Mr. Perkins to be sent to you, and beg You to send them back as soon as You have all done with them.[4] I let the first volume get to the Reynolds's, and could never get it again.[5]

I sent to Lord Westcote about his Brother's life, but he says he knows not whom to employ, and is sure I shall do him no injury.[6] There is an ingenious scheme to save a day's work or part of a day, utterly defeated. Then what avails it to be wise?

---

1. *Ante* To Hester Thrale, 19 June 1779, n. 6.
2. MS: "a" superimposed upon "i"
3. *Ante* To Hester Thrale, 15 June 1780 and n. 10.
4. *Ante* To Hester Thrale, 27 July 1780 and n. 1.
5. *Ante* To Frances Reynolds, 16 June 1780 and n. 2.
6. *Ante* To Lord Westcote, 27 July 1780; 28 July 1780.

The plain and the artful Man must bothe do their own work.—But, I think, I have got a life of Dr. Young.[7]

Susy and Sophy have had a fine summer, it is a comfort to think that somebody is happy. And they make verses, and act plays.[8]

Mrs. Montague is, I think, in town, and has sent Mrs. Williams her annuity,[9] but I hear nothing from her, but I may be contented if I hear from You, for I am, dear Madam, Your most humble Servant,

SAM. JOHNSON

7. *Post* To John Nichols, Late 1780 and n. 2.

8. On 29 June Hester Thrale had reported to Frances Burney: "Susan and Sophy have taken to writing verses—'tis the fashion of the school they say, and Sophy's are the best performances of all the misses, except one monkey of eighteen years old" (*Diary and Letters of Madame D'Arblay*, ed. Austin Dobson, 1904, 1.432). 9. Cf. *Ante* To Elizabeth Montagu, 9 June 1759.

John Nichols

EARLY AUGUST 1780

MS: British Library.

ADDRESS: To Mr. Nicol.

Mr. Johnson desires Mr. Nicol to send him

Ruffhead's life of Pope[1]

Popes Works[2]

Swifts Works with Dr. Ha[w]kesworths life[3]

Lyttelton's Works[4]

and with those he hopes to have done.

The first to be got is Lyttelton.

1. The *Life of Alexander Pope* (1769) by Owen Ruffhead (1723–69). Although SJ had a very low opinion of Ruffhead's biography (*Life* II.166), he nonetheless drew upon it in his own "Pope" (*Lives of the Poets* III.100, 189, 190).

2. SJ used Warburton's nine-volume edition, published 1751 (F. W. Hilles, "The Making of *The Life of Pope*," in *New Light on Dr. Johnson*, ed. Hilles, 1959, p. 259 n. 3).

3. Hawkesworth's edition of Swift's works, prefaced by his *Life of Swift*, appeared in 1755. "An Account of Dr. Swift has been already collected, with great diligence and acuteness, by Dr. Hawkesworth, according to a scheme which I laid before him in the intimacy of our friendship" (*Lives of the Poets* III.1).

4. *Ante* To Lord Westcote, 27 July 1780, n. 4.

Hester Thrale

MS: Huntington Library.

Dear Madam: Aug. 8, 1780

What do you scold so for about Granville's Life, do you not see that the appendage neither gains nor saves any thing to me?[1] I shall have Young's life given me to spite You.[2]

Methinks it was pity to send the girls to school, they have indeed had a fine vacation, dear Loves, but if it had been longer it had been still finer.[3]

Did Master read my Books?[4] You say nothing of him in this letter, but I hope he is well, and growing every day nearer to perfect health. When do You think of coming home?

I have[5] not yet persuaded myself to work, and therefore know not when my work will be done. Yet I have a mind to see Lichfield.[6] Dr. Taylor seems to be well. He had written to me without a syllable of his lawsuit.[7]

You have heard in the papers how Sir John Lade is come to age, I have enclosed a short song of congratulation, which you must not show to any body.[8] It is odd that it should come into any bodies head. I hope you will read it with candour, it is, I believe, one of the authours first essays in that way of writing, and a beginner is always to be treated with tenderness.

My two Gentlewomen are both complaining. Mrs. Desmoulins had a mind of Dr. Turton,[9] I sent for him, and he has

1. *Ante* To John Nichols, *c.* May 1780 (I) and nn. 1, 2.
2. *Post* To John Nichols, Late 1780 and n. 2.
3. *Ante* To Hester Thrale, 1 Aug. 1780.
4. *Ante* To Hester Thrale, 27 July 1780 and n. 1; 1 Aug. 1780.
5. MS: "h" superimposed upon "c"
6. *Ante* To Lucy Porter, 8 Apr. 1780, n. 1.
7. *Ante* To John Taylor, 9 Feb. 1775; *Ante* To Hester Thrale, 23 May 1780.
8. SJ's "A Short Song of Congratulation," seven satirical quatrains in celebration of Sir John Lade's twenty-first birthday (1 Aug.), predicts that Sir John will squander his life and fortune in "vice and folly" (*Poems*, pp. 226–27).
9. John Turton (1735–1806), M.D., a prominent London physician who had attended Oliver Goldsmith in his last illness, was distantly related to SJ through Gregory Hickman's daughter Dorothy (*Life* III.500).

prescribed for Mrs. Williams, but I do not find that he promises himself much credit from either of them.[10]

I hope it will not be long before I shall have another little volume for You, and still there will be work undone. If it were not for those lives I think I could not forbear coming to look at You, now You have room for me. But I still think to stay till I have cleared my hands.

Queeney is not good. She seldom writes to me, and yet I love her, and I love you all, for I am, Madam, Your most humble servant,
SAM. JOHNSON

10. *Post* To Hester Thrale, 14 Aug. 1780.

Mary Prowse[1]

MONDAY 14 AUGUST 1780

MS: Hyde Collection.
ADDRESS: To Mrs. Prowse at Berkley, near Frome, Somersetshire.
POSTMARK: 14 AV.
ENDORSEMENT: Dr. Johnson, Augt. 1780.

Boltcourt (not Johnson's), Fleetstreet, London,
Madam: Aug. 14, 1780

For the loss which You have suffered I will not recall your grief by the formality of condolence. I believe, all to whom Mrs. Prowse was known, consider the world as deprived by her departure of a very bright and eminent example.[2]

The allowance which she was pleased to make towards the maintenance of the unhappy girl,[3] has been long discon-

1. Mary Prowse (1745–1800), the daughter of Thomas and Elizabeth Prowse of Compton Bishop, married (1783) the Rev. J. M. Rogers (?1749–1834), Rector of Berkeley, Somersetshire, and Wicken, Northamptonshire (*Johns. Glean.* XI.384–85, 404).

2. SJ laments the death of Elizabeth Prowse (1712–80), of Compton Bishop, Somersetshire, the widow of Thomas Prowse (1707–67), M.P. for Somerset (1740–67) (*Johns. Glean.* XI.384; Namier and Brooke III.336).

3. Elizabeth Herne (d. 1792), SJ's first cousin once removed, had been committed to Bethlehem Hospital in 1766. After being discharged as incurable, she was

tinued, how long, I really do not know, and am afraid of favouring myself by a conjectural account.[4]

Not knowing whether the payment was witheld by negligence or intention, I sometimes purposed to have written to the Lady, but never did it. Perhaps your accounts can set you right.[5]

It may be, Madam, in your power, to gratify my curiosity.[6] Your servants, I suppose, go frequently to Froome, and it will be thought by me a favour if You will be pleased, to bid them collect any little tradition that may yet remain, of one Johnson, who more than forty years ago was for a short time, a Bookbinder or Stationer in that town.[7] Such intelligence must be gotten by accident, and therefore cannot be immediately expected, but perhaps in time somebody may be found that knew him.

The great civility of your letter has encouraged me to this request.

The money which your excellent Mother's liberality makes payable to me, may be remitted by a note on a Banker, or on[8] the Bank, to, Madam, Your most humble Servant,

SAM. JOHNSON

---

placed in an insane asylum in Bethnal Green. In his will SJ left £100 for her care (*Johns. Glean.* VIII.179, XI.216).

4. In addition to the allowance she had been contributing, Elizabeth Prowse bequeathed SJ ten guineas a year "for the half maintenance of Miss Herne as long as she lives" (*Johns. Glean.* VIII.184). The connection between the Prowse family and Elizabeth Herne has not been established. A. L. Reade conjectures that she might have been "in the service of the Prowses, who in consequence felt some responsibility for her" (*Johns. Glean.* VIII.184).

5. Mary Prowse noted on the cover of the letter, "Not finding in my Mothers Books any account of the money having been paid for six years I sent him the whole arrears." *Post* To Mary Prowse, 9 Dec. 1780.

6. MS: "osity" repeated as catchword

7. It is likely that SJ here refers obliquely to his brother Nathaniel (1712–37), who appears to have worked in Frome shortly before his death (*Johns. Glean.* VI.60, X.125; Clifford, 1955, pp. 160–61; *Post* To Mary Prowse, 9 Dec. 1780).

8. MS: "on" superimposed upon "at"

Hester Thrale

PRINTED SOURCE: Chapman II.387–88.

Dear Madam:

Aug. 14, 1780

I hope my dear Queeney's suspicions are groundless. Whenever any alteration of manner happens, I believe, a small cathartick will set all right.[1]

I hope you have no design of stealing away to Italy before the election nor of leaving me behind you, though I am not only seventy, but seventy-one.[2] Could not you let me lose a year in round numbers. Sweetly, sweetly, sings Dr. Swift

> Some dire misfortune to portend,
> No enemy can match a friend.[3]

But what if I am seventy two, I remember Sulpitius says of Saint Martin (now that's above your reading), est animus victor annorum, et senectuti cedere nescius.[4] Match me that among your young folks. If you try to plague me I shall tell you that according to Galen life begins to decline from *thirty five*.[5]

But as We go off others come on: Queeney's last letter was very pretty, what a Hussey she is to write so seldom. She has no events, then let her write sentiment as you and I do, and sentiment you know is inexhaustible.

1. *Post* To Hester Thrale, 18 Aug. 1780 and n. 1.

2. According to Hester Thrale, her husband was "all on Fire for a Journey to Italy" (Clifford, 1952, p. 187). The Thrales and SJ had intended to travel to Italy in 1776—a trip that was canceled when Henry Thrale the younger died (Clifford, 1952, pp. 134, 138; *Ante* To Hester Thrale, 9 Apr. 1776 and n. 1).

3. "Some great Misfortune to portend, / No Enemy can match a Friend" ("Verses on the Death of Dr. Swift," 1731, ll. 119–20).

4. *et quamvis optata sit seni missio post laborem, est tamen animus victor annorum, et cedere nescius senectuti*: "and although an old man may desire release after his labor, nevertheless his spirit has conquered the years, and is unable to give way to old age" (Sulpitius Severus, *Epistola* III, in *Patrologiae Latinae*, ed. J. P. Migne, xx.182).

5. ἰστέον δὲ ὅτι ἡ ἀκμαστικὴ ἡλικία λε' ἔτεσι περιγράφεται, ἡ δὲ παρακμαστικὴ μθ': "further, one must know that the flourishing time of life is restricted to thirty-five years, and the declining time to forty-eight" (*Claudii Galeni Opera Omnia*, ed. D.C.G. Kuehn, 1829, XVII.ii.643).

If you want events here is Mr. Levet just come in at four-score from a walk to Hampstead, eight miles in August. This however is all that I have to tell you, except that I have three bunches of grapes on a vine in my garden, at least this is all that I will now tell of my garden.

Both my females are ill, both very ill, Mrs. Desmoulins thought that she wished for Dr. Turton, and I sent for him, and then took him to Mrs. Williams, and he prescribes for both, though without much hope of benefiting either.[6] Yet Physick has its powers, you see that I am better, and Mr. Shaw will maintain, that he and I saved my Master. But if he is to live always away from us, what did we get by saving him? If we cannot live together let us hear, when I have no letter from Brighthelmston, think how I fret, and write oftener; you write to this body and t'other body, and nobody loves you like, Your humble servant,

SAM. JOHNSON

6. *Ante* To Hester Thrale, 8 Aug. 1780 and n. 9.

John Nichols

WEDNESDAY 16 AUGUST 1780

MS: British Library.

Sir: Wednesday, Augt. 16, 1780[1]

I expected to have found a life of Lord Lyttelton prefixed to his Works.[2] Is there not one before the quarto Edition? I think there is—if not, I am, with[3] respect to him, quite aground.[4]

1. MS: "Augt. 16, 1780" in Nichols's hand
2. *Ante* To Lord Westcote, 27 July 1780.
3. MS: "with" altered from "without"
4. SJ's was the first biography of Lyttelton to appear in print (*Lives of the Poets* III.457; A. V. Rao, *A Minor Augustan*, 1934, p. 335). SJ wrote it unassisted by a previous memoir or by information from Lyttelton's family. *Ante* To Lord Westcote, 27 July 1780; 28 July 1780.

Hester Thrale

FRIDAY 18 AUGUST 1780

MS: Beinecke Library.

Dear Madam: Aug. 18, 1780

I lost no time, and have enclosed our Conversation.[1] You write
of late very seldom. I wish You would write upon *subjects*, any
thing to keep alive. You have your Beaux, and your flatterers,
and here am poor I forced to flatter myself, and any good of
myself I am not very easy to believe, so that I really live but a
sorry life. What shall I do with Lyttelton's Life?[2] I can make a
short life, and a short criticism, and conclude. Why did not
You like Collins, and Gay and Blackmore, as well as Akensyde?
I am, Madam, Your most humble servant,

SAM. JOHNSON

1. SJ encloses a memorandum (dated 18 Aug.) of his conversation with Dr.
Lawrence about Henry Thrale's health: "I have read the account and do not like
it—It looks like the forerunner of some disorder—To advise at this distance is
difficult—As he thinks himself well, he will do nothing.—Gentle purges will be of
great use, and if his pulse be quick and hard, I would advise to take a little blood,
by a little I mean ten ounces—He is a large Man" (MS: Hyde Collection).

2. *Ante* To John Nichols, 16 Aug. 1780 and n. 4.

James Beattie

MONDAY 21 AUGUST 1780

MS: National Library of Scotland.
ADDRESS: To Dr. Beattie [*added in an unidentified hand*] Peterhead.
ENDORSEMENT: from Dr. Sam. Johnson 1780, answered.

Sir: Boltcourt, Fleetstreet, Aug. 21, 1780

More years than I have any delight to reckon have past since
You and I saw one another, of this however there is no reason
for making any reprehensory complaint.[1] *Sic fata ferunt*.[2] But

1. According to Beattie, he "had been five years absent from London" (*Life*
III.434 n. 3).

2. *sive dolo seu iam Troiae sic fata ferebant*: "whether in treachery or that now the

methinks there might pass some small interchange of regard between us. If you say, that I ought to have written, I now write, and I write to tell you that I have much kindness for You and Mrs. Beattie, and that I wish your health better and your life long. Try change of air, and come a few degrees southwards; a softer climate may do you both good, Winter is coming on and London will be warmer, and gayer, and busier, and more fertile of amusement than Aberdeen.[3]

My health is better, but that will be little in the ballance when I tell you that Mrs. Montague has been very ill, and is, I doubt, now but weakly.[4] Mr. Thrale has been very dangerously disordered, but is much better, and I hope will totally recover. He has withdrawn himself from business the whole Summer. Sir Joshua and his Sister are well, and Mr. Davies has had great success as an authour generated by the corruption of a Bookseller.[5] More News I have not to tell you, and therefore You must be contented with hearing what I know not whether You much wish to hear, that, I am, Sir, Your most humble Servant,

SAM. JOHNSON

doom of Troy was thus setting" (Virgil, *Aeneid* II.34, trans. H. R. Fairclough, Loeb ed.).

3. Beattie and his son James visited London the following spring (Margaret Forbes, *Beattie and His Friends*, 1904, pp. 169–70).

4. "This illness had prevented her for some time from writing to Beattie, and when at last she was able to do so, she was so weak that she dared only say a few words to him on the subject of his anxieties about his children" (Forbes, *Beattie*, p. 167). Elizabeth Montagu may have been suffering from the "stomachic troubles" that tended to plague her (Reginald Blunt, *Mrs. Montagu*, 1923, II.102).

5. *Ante* To Elizabeth Montagu, 5 Mar. 1778 and n. 2. Davies' *Memoirs of the Life of David Garrick*, published in May, had gone rapidly into a second edition (*Walpole's Correspondence*, Yale ed. II.223 n. 10).

James Boswell

MONDAY 21 AUGUST 1780

PRINTED SOURCE: JB's *Life*, 1791, II.322.

Dear Sir,
                                    London, Aug. 21, 1780

I find you have taken one of your fits of taciturnity, and have resolved not to write till you are written to; it is but a peevish humour, but you shall have your way.[1]

I have sate at home in Bolt-court, all the summer, thinking to write the Lives, and a great part of the time only thinking.[2] Several of them, however, are done, and I still think to do the rest.[3]

Mr. Thrale and his family have, since his illness, passed their time first at Bath, and then at Brighthelmston; but I have been at neither place. I would have gone to Lichfield, if I could have had time, and I might have had time, if I had been active; but I have missed much, and done little.

In the late disturbances, Mr. Thrale's house and stock were in great danger; the mob was pacified at their first invasion, with about fifty pounds in drink and meat; and at their second, were driven away by the soldiers.[4] Mr. Strahan got a garrison into his house, and maintained them a fortnight; he was so frighted that he removed part of his goods.[5] Mrs. Williams took shelter in the country.

I know not whether I shall get a ramble this autumn; it is now about the time when we were travelling.[6] I have, however, better health than I had then, and hope you and I may yet shew ourselves on some part of Europe, Asia, or Africa. In the mean time let us play no trick, but keep each other's kindness by all means in our power.

1. JB wrote to SJ on 24 Aug. (*Boswell, Laird of Auchinleck*, ed. J. W. Reed and F. A. Pottle, 1977, p. 233).   2. *Ante* To Henry Thrale, 30 May 1780 and n. 3.
3. *Ante* To Hester Thrale, 11 Apr. 1780, n. 9.
4. *Ante* To Hester Thrale, 9 June 1780 and n. 14.
5. *Ante* To Hester Thrale, 9 June 1780 and n. 3.
6. SJ refers to their trip to the Hebrides, which began on 18 Aug. 1773 (*Ante* To Hester Thrale, 25 Aug. 1773).

The bearer of this is Dr. Dunbar, of Aberdeen, who has written and published a very ingenious book, and who I think has a kindness for me, and will when he knows you have a kindness for you.[7]

I suppose your little ladies are grown tall; and your son is become a learned young man. I love them all, and I love your naughty lady, whom I never shall persuade to love me. When the Lives are done, I shall send them to complete her collection, but must send them in paper, as for want of a pattern, I cannot bind them to fit the rest.[8] I am, Sir, Yours most affectionately,

SAM. JOHNSON

7. *Ante* To Hester Thrale, 4 July 1780, n. 5.

8. *Ante* To JB, 13 Mar. 1779 and n. 3. SJ had already sent sixty volumes; he was now planning to complete the set with Volumes v–x of the Prefaces and the two-volume index (Charles Dilly to JB, 25 May 1779, MS: Beinecke Library; *Bibliography Supplement*, p. 156). At the time of its dispersal, the Auchinleck library included a set of sixty-eight volumes (Volume LI missing) bound in calf, with "full gilt backs" (Sotheby's *Catalogue of the . . . Auchinleck Library*, 23–25 June 1893, Lot No. 322, p. 22).

Hester Thrale

THURSDAY 24 AUGUST 1780

MS: Hyde Collection.

Dear Madam: London, Aug. 24, 1780

I do not wonder that You can think and write but of one thing, yet concerning that thing You may be less uneasy, as You are now in the right way. You are at least doing, what I was always desirous to have you do, and which when despair put an end to the caution of men going in the dark, produced at least all the good that has been obtained. Gentle purges, and slight phlebotomies are not my favourites, they are popgun batteries,[1] which lose time and effect nothing. It was by bleeding

1. *popgun*: "a gun with which children play, that only makes a noise" (SJ's *Dictionary*). SJ illustrates this definition with a quotation from George Cheyne that includes the phrase "popgun artillery."

till he fainted that his life was saved. I would however now have him trust chiefly to vigorous and stimulating catharticks. To bleed is only proper when there is no time for slower remedies.

Does he sleep in the night; if he sleeps, there is not much danger, any thing[2] like wakefulness in a man either by nature or habit so uncommonly sleepy would put me in great fear. Do not now hinder him from sleeping whenever[3] heaviness comes upon him. Quiet Rest, light food, and strong purges will I think, set all right. Be you vigilant, but be not frighted.

Of Mr. Rushworth I very well remember all but the name.[4] "He had a nice discernment of loss and gain." This, I thought, a power not hard to be attained. What kept him out then must keep him out now, the want of a place for him. Mr. Perkins then observed that there was nothing upon which he could be employed. Matters will never be carried to extremities. Mr. Perkins cannot be discharged, and he will never suffer a superiour. That voluntary submission to a new mind, is not a heroick quality; but it has always been among us, and therefore I mind it less.

The expedition to foreign parts You will not much encourage, and you need not, I think, make any great effort to oppose it, for it is as likely to put us out of the way to mischief as to bring us into it. We can have no projects in Italy.[5] Exercise may relieve the body, and variety will amuse the mind. The expence will not be greater than at home in the regular course

2. MS: "thing" superimposed upon "time"

3. MS: "whenever" altered from "?wherever"

4. SJ's references in the following paragraph to "projects" and "instigators to schemes of waste" suggest that Rushworth was a speculator akin to Humphrey Jackson (*Ante* To Hester Thrale, 20 Mar. 1773 and n. 5). An entry in *Thraliana* (dated 13 Aug.) supports this interpretation: "My Master is got into most riotous Spirits somehow; he will go here and there, and has a hundred Projects in his Head, so gay, so wild" (*Thraliana* I.453). In her letter of 24 Aug. Hester Thrale informs SJ: "I have cleared the place of Mr. Rushworth too, and am once more tolerably easy, and at leisure to say I am sorry for the bad News, if it be true. We shall have ever so many Wretches breaking our Debt this Winter, and laying their Calamities to this Misfortune" (MS: Rylands Library).

5. *Ante* To Hester Thrale, 14 Aug. 1780 and n. 2.

of life. And he shall be safe from Brownes and Guilds, and all instigators to schemes of waste. Si te fata ferant, fer fata—[6]

The chief wish that I form is, that Mr. Thrale could be made to understand his real state, to know that he is tottering upon a point, to consider every change of his mental character as the symptom of a disease; to distrust any opinions or purposes that shoot up in his thoughts; to think that violent Mirth is the foam, and deep sadness the subsidence of a morbid fermentation; to watch himself, and counteract by[7] experienced remedies every new tendency, or uncommon sensation. This is a new and an ungrateful employment, but without this self examination he never can be safe. You must try to teach it and he to learn it gradually, and in this my sweet Queeny must help You; I am glad to hear of her vigilance and observation. She is my Pupil.

I suppose the Shelly Scheme is now past; I saw no great harm in it, though perhaps no good.[8] Do not suffer little things to embarrass you. Our great work is constant temperance and frequent, very frequent evacuation, and that they may not be intermitted, conviction of their necessity is to be prudently inculcated.

I am not at present so much distressed as You, because I think your present method likely to be efficacious. Dejection may indeed follow, and I should dread it from too copious bleeding for as purges are more under command, and more concurrent with the urgency of Nature, they seldom effect any irremediable change. However we must expect after such a

6. SJ quotes from George Buchanan's Latin translation (*Epigrammata* 1.62) of a poem from the Greek Anthology. Εἰ τὸ φέρον σε φέρει, φέρε καὶ φέρον· εἰ δ'ἀγανακτεῖς / καὶ σαυτὸν λυπεῖς, καὶ τὸ φέρον σε φέρει: "If the gale of Fortune bear thee, bear with it and be borne; but if thou rebellest and tormentest thyself, even so the gale bears thee" (*Anthologia Graeca* x.73, trans. W. R. Paton, Loeb ed.). See P. J. Ford, *George Buchanan*, 1982, pp. 37–38, 120 n. 14.

7. MS: "by" altered from "but"

8. "Mr. Thrale *would* go to Mitchel Grove the Seat of Sir John Shelley; I did not half like the Expedition, but Pepys bled him first 13 ounces, and gave some rough Medicines" (*Thraliana* 1.453). The Thrales left for Michelgrove on 28 Aug. and stayed until 2 Sept. (Hester Thrale to SJ, 27 Aug. 1780, MS: Rylands Library; *Thraliana* 1.453).

disease, that the mind will fluctuate long before it finds its center.

I will not tell you, nor Master, nor Queeney how I long to be among You, but I would be glad to know when we are to meet, and hope our meeting will be cheerful. I am, Dearest Lady, Your most humble servant,

SAM. JOHNSON

Hester Thrale

FRIDAY 25 AUGUST 1780

PRINTED SOURCE: Piozzi, *Letters* II.189–91.

Dear Madam,   London, August 25, 1780

Yesterday I could write but about one thing. I am sorry to find from my dear Queeney's letter to-day, that Mr. Thrale's sleep was too much shortened. He begins however now, she says, to recover it. Sound sleep will be the surest token of returning health. The swelling of his legs has nothing in it dangerous; it is the natural consequence of lax muscles, and when the laxity is known to be artificial, need not give any uneasiness. I told you so formerly. Every thing that I have told you about my dear master has been true. Let him take purgatives, and let him sleep. Bleeding seems to have been necessary now; but it was become necessary only by the omission of purges. Bleeding is only for exigences.

I wish you or Queeney would write to me every post while the danger lasts. I will come if I can do any good, or prevent any evil.

For any other purpose, I suppose, now poor Sam: may be spared; you are regaled with Greek and Latin, and you are *Thralia Castalio semper amata choro;*[1] and you have a daughter

1. "Michell, the Boy who won the Prize at Cambridge by his Verses in the Greek Language on the Death of Captain Cook, has sent them me with the following classical Compliment . . ." (*Thraliana* I.447). SJ quotes the second line of the eight-line poem: "Thrale, forever loved by the Castalian Choir." The poet was John Henry Michell (1759–1844), scholar of King's College, Cambridge, who in 1780

equal to yourself. I shall have enough to do with one and the other. Your admirer has more Greek than poetry; he was however worth the conquest, though you had conquered me. Whether you can hold him as fast, there may be *some dram of a scruple*,[2] for he thinks you have full tongue enough, as appears by some of his verses; he will leave you for somebody that will let him take his turn, and then I may come in again: for, I tell you, nobody loves you so well, and therefore never think of changing like the moon, and *being constant only in your inconstancy*.[3]

I have not dined out for some time but with Renny or Sir Joshua; and next week Sir Joshua goes to Devonshire,[4] and Renny to Richmond, and I am left by myself. I wish I could say *numquam minus*, *etc.* but I am not diligent.[5]

I am afraid that I shall not see Lichfield this year, yet it would please me to shew my friends how much better I am grown: but I am not grown, I am afraid, less idle; and of idleness I am now paying the fine by having no leisure.

Does the expedition to Sir John Shelly's go on?[6] The first week of September is now at no great distance; nor the eighteenth day, which concludes another of my wretched years. It is time to have done. I am, etc.

---

was awarded the Sir William Browne medal for the finest classical verses on a prescribed theme (*Alum. Cant.* II.iv.404).

2. SJ echoes the deluded Malvolio: "Why, everything adheres together, that no dram of a scruple, no scruple of a scruple, no obstacle . . . Nothing that can be can come between me and the full prospect of my hopes" (*Twelfth Night* III.iv.78–83).

3. "The *World*'s a *Scene* of *Changes*, and to be / *Constant*, in *Nature* were *Inconstancy*" (Abraham Cowley, "Inconstancy," ll. 19–20).

4. Sir Joshua left for Devonshire on 24 Aug. and stayed with various friends and patrons until his return to London on 22 Sept. (C. R. Leslie and T. Taylor, *Life and Times of Sir Joshua Reynolds*, 1865, II.305–6).

5. "P. Scipionem, M. fili, eum, qui primus Africanus appellatus est, dicere solitum scripsit Cato, qui fuit eius fere aequalis, numquam se minus otiosum esse, quam cum otiosus, nec minus solum, quam cum solus esset": "Cato, who was of about the same years, Marcus, my son, as that Publius Scipio who first bore the surname of Africanus, has given us the statement that Scipio used to say that he was never less idle than when he had nothing to do and never less lonely than when he was alone" (Cicero, *De Officiis* III.1, trans. Walter Miller, Loeb ed.).

6. *Ante* To Hester Thrale, 24 Aug. 1780 and n. 8.

Hester Maria Thrale

MONDAY 28 AUGUST 1780

MS: The Earl of Shelburne.

My dear Charmer: London, Aug. 28, 1780

I am very much obliged to you for your pretty letters. On
Saturday I opened my letter with terrour, but soon found that
all is mending. Every thing that I have ever proposed for Mr.
Thrale has been found right in the event. We must all com-
bine, as propriety shall permit, to impress him with the true
opinion of his danger, for without that he will naturally be
negligent of himself, and inattentive to his own sensations. Dr.
Laurence is of opinion that the tendency to an apoplexy might
always be perceived by one who knew how to distinguish it,
and if it was perceived at any distance it might be certainly
prevented. But if we cannot teach him to watch his own state
of body, we must all watch for him as we can.

It is well for me that a Lady so celebrated as Miss Thrale can
find time to write to me. I will recompense your condescension
with a maxim. Never treat old friends with neglect however
easily you may find new. There is a tenderness which seems
the meer growth of time, but which is in [fact] the[1] effect [of]
many combinations; those with whom we have shared enjoy-
ments, we remember with pleasure, those with whom we have
shared sorrow, we remember with tenderness. You must already have begun to observe that you love a book, or a box, or
an instrument that you have had a great part of your life, because it brings a great part of your life back to your view. You
can never say that your a very late acquaintance; you can only
like, or only admire. As others stand to you, must you stand to
others, and must therefore [know] that no new acquaintance
much love you, and therefore if you quit old friends for them,
you slight those who love you more in favour of those that love
you less. This I hope you will remember, and practice, though

1. MS: "effec" partially erased before "the"

far the greater part forget it, and therefore have no friend, as none they deserve.

I have been very grave, but you are a very thinking Lady. We shall now meet in a little time, I hope again, and love each other better and better.

Now am I turning to the second leaf just as if I was writing to your Mamma.

Dr. Burney and Fanny and Sophy[2] are gone to be happy with Mr. Crisp,[3] and Mrs. Burney and Susan[4] are left at home, and I am to go see them; indeed I have no other visit to make hardly, except that blind Mrs. Hervey has sent me a peremptory summons to dine with her on thursday, and I have promised to go lest she should think me intentionally uncivil; and you know, I am the civillest creature in nature.

Seward called on me two days ago, to get help for a poor woman.[5] This is all the news you can have from, Madam, your most humble servant,

SAM. JOHNSON

2. "Dr. Johnson always referred to Susan Burney's sister Charlotte as *Sophy,* from the analogy of *Susan and Sophy* Thrale" (Joyce Hemlow, "Dr. Johnson and the Young Burneys," in *New Light on Dr. Johnson,* ed. F. W. Hilles, 1959, p. 321). Charlotte Ann (1761–1838) was Charles Burney's ninth child by his first wife, Esther (Joyce Hemlow, *The History of Fanny Burney,* 1958, p. 11).

3. Samuel Crisp (1708–83), dramatist and critic, a close friend of the Burney family since *c.* 1764. Various Burneys often stayed with "Daddy" Crisp at Chessington Hall, near Kingston-upon-Thames, Surrey. On this occasion they spent about five weeks there (Hemlow, *Fanny Burney,* pp. 16–18, 142).

4. Susanna Elizabeth Burney (1755–1800), Charles Burney's sixth child by his first wife (Hemlow, *Fanny Burney,* p. 7).   5. SJ refers to William Seward.

Charles Lawrence[1]
WEDNESDAY 30 AUGUST 1780

MS: Beinecke Library.

1. Charles Lawrence (*c.* 1758–91), son of Thomas Lawrence and a fellow of St. John's College, Cambridge (1779–91), had been ordained deacon in June (*Alum. Cant.* II.iv.111; *Life* III.436 n. 2).

Dear Sir: Boltcourt, Aug. 30, 1780

Not many days ago Dr. Laurence shewed me a Letter in which You made kind mention of me. I hope therefore you will not be displeased that I endeavour to preserve your good will by some observations which your letter suggested to me.

You are afraid of falling into some improprieties in the daily service, by reading to an audience that requires no exactness. Your fear, I hope, secures you from danger, they who contract absurd habits, are such as have no fear. It is impossible to do the same thing very often without some peculiarity of manner, but that manner may be good or bad, and a little care will at least preserve it from being bad; to make it very good there must, I think, be something of natural or casual felicity which cannot be bought.

Your present method of making your sermons seems very[2] judicious. Few frequent Preachers can be supposed to have sermons more their own, than yours will be. Take care to register[3] some where or other the authours from whom your several discourses are borrowed, and do not imagine that you shall always remember even what perhaps You now think it impossible to forget.[4]

My advice however is that You attempt from time to time an original sermon, and in the labour of composition do not burden your mind with too much at once, do not exact from yourself at one effort of excogitation, propriety of thought and elegance of expression. Invent first and then embellish. The production of something where nothing was before, is an act of greater energy, than the expansion or decoration of the thing produced. Set down diligently your thoughts as they rise in the first words that occur, and when you have matter you will easily give it form.[5] Nor perhaps will this method be always

2. MS: "very" repeated as catchword

3. MS: undeciphered deletion before "register"

4. As Jean Hagstrum and James Gray observe: "For centuries, apparently, the habit of borrowing sermons from others was practised and encouraged. . . . In the eighteenth century the habit was widespread" (*Works*, Yale ed. XIV.xxvii–xxviii).

5. In conversation with JB and Robert Watson, 19 Aug. 1773, SJ had offered advice to "every young man beginning to compose": "I would say to a young

necessary, for by habit your thoughts and diction will flow together. The Composition of sermons is not very difficult; the divisions not only help the memory of the hearer but direct the judgment of the writer, they supply sources of invention, and keep every part in its proper place.[6]

What I like least in your letter is your account of the manners of the parish, from which I gather that it has been long neglected by the Parson. The Dean of Carlisle,[7] who was then a little rector in Northamptonshire, told me, that it might be discerned whether or no there was a Clergyman resident in a parish, by the civil or savage manners of the people. Such a congregation as yours stands in much need of reformation, and I would not have you think it impossible to reform them. A very savage parish was civilized, by a decayed gentlewoman who came among them to teach a petty school. My learned friend Dr. Wheeler of Oxford, when he was a young man had the care of a neighbouring parish for fifteen pounds a year which he was never paid, but he counted it a convenience that it compelled him to make a sermon weekly. One woman he could not bring to the Communion, and when he reproved or exhorted her, she only answered that she was no Scholar. He was advised to set some good Woman or Man of the parish a little wiser than herself to talk to her in language level to her mind. Such honest, I may call them holy artifices must be practiced by every Clergyman, for all means must be tried by which Souls may be saved. Talk to your people, however, as much as You can, and you will find that the more frequently you converse with them upon religious subjects, the more willingly

---

divine, 'Here is your text; let me see how soon you can make a sermon.' Then I'd say, 'Let me see how much better you can make it.' Thus I should see both his powers and his judgment" (*Hebrides*, pp. 44–45).

6. In his own sermons, SJ practiced what he preaches to Lawrence: "The sermon had, as a work of instruction, adapted the five divisions of the classical oration to its own purposes; it traditionally contained the *praecognitio textus* . . . the *partitio et propositio*, the *explicatio verborum*, the *amplificatio*, and the *applicatio*. Without pedantic regularity or detail, Johnson follows this ordering of material" (*Works*, Yale ed. XIV.xlii). 7. SJ refers to Thomas Percy.

they will attend, and the more submissively they will learn. A Clergyman's diligence always makes him venerable. I think, I have now only to say that in the momentous work that You have undertaken I pray God to bless You. I am, Sir, Your most humble servant,

SAM. JOHNSON

Lady Southwell[1]

SATURDAY 9 SEPTEMBER 1780

MS: Victoria and Albert Museum.
ADDRESS: To the Right Honourable Lady Sowthwel, Dublin.
POSTMARKS: [Undeciphered], SE 13.

Madam: Bolt court, Fleetstreet, London, Sept. 9, 1780

Among the numerous addresses of condolence which your great loss must have occasioned,[2] be pleased to receive this from one whose name perhaps You have never heard, and to whom your Ladyship is known only by the reputation of your virtue, and to whom your Lord was known only by his kindness and beneficence.

Your Ladyship is now again summoned to exert that piety of which You once gave in a state of pain and danger, so illustrious an example,[3] and your Lord's beneficence may be still continued by those who with his fortune inherit his virtues.

I hope to be forgiven the liberty which I shall take of informing your Ladyship, that Mr. Mauritius Lowe, a son of your late Lord's father, had by my recommendation to your Lord, a quarterly allowance of ten pounds, the last of which,

1. Margaret Hamilton (1722–1802), daughter of Arthur Hamilton of Castle Hamilton, County Cavan, who married, in 1741, Thomas George Southwell (1721–1780), third Baron and first Viscount Southwell.

2. Lord Southwell had died 29 Aug.

3. Lady Southwell had submitted to "an extremely painful surgical operation, which she endured with extraordinary firmness and composure, not allowing herself to be tied to her chair, nor uttering a single moan" (JB's *Life*, ed. Edmond Malone, 1804, III.476 n. 2).

313

due July 26, he has not received; he was in hourly hope of his remittance, or flattered himself that on October 26, he should have received the whole half-year's bounty, when he was struck with the dreadful news of his Benefactor's death.[4]

May I presume to hope that his want, his[5] relation, and his merit, which excited his Lordship's charity, will continue to have the same effect upon those whom he has left behind, and that though he has lost one friend he may not yet be destitute. Your Ladyship's charity cannot easily be exerted where it is wanted more; and to a mind like yours distress is a sufficient recommendation.

I hope to be allowed the honour of being, Madam, Your Ladyship's most humble Servant, SAM. JOHNSON

4. *Ante* To Mauritius Lowe, 28 Apr. 1778, n. 1; *Post* To Mauritius Lowe, 22 Oct. 1782. 5. MS: "he"

William Strahan

WEDNESDAY 13 SEPTEMBER 1780

PRINTED SOURCE: Hill II.203–4.
ADDRESS: To William Strahan, Esq.

Sir, Sept. 13, 1780

Having lost our Election at Southwark we are looking for a Borough less uncertain.[1] If you can find by enquiry any seat to be had, as seats are had without natural interest, you will by giving immediate notice do a great favour to Mr. Thrale. The messenger shall call to-morrow for your answer. There are, I suppose, men who transact these affairs, but we do not know them. Be so kind as to give us what information you can. I am, Sir, Your humble servant, SAM. JOHNSON

1. Henry Thrale had come in a distant third in the polls (*London Chronicle*, 9–12 Sept. 1780, p. 248). Despite his continuing ill health, "he refused to accept defeat, and swore he would try for another place. He actually wrote to Lord North of his hopes . . . but his condition being well known, nothing came of the request" (Clifford, 1952, p. 190).

Samuel Hardy [1]

SATURDAY 23 SEPTEMBER 1780

MS: Hyde Collection.

ADDRESS: To the Reverend Mr. Hardy at Enfield.

POSTMARKS: 23 SE, R·J.

Sir: Bolt court, Fleetstreet, Sept. 23, 1780

I should be very sorry to be thought capable of treating with neglect or disrespect such a Man as You, or such an attempt as yours.[2] I certainly wrote my opinion such as it was, long ago. I did not value it enough to keep a copy, and therefore must now tell it again, when the remembrance of your arguments is weakened by time.

You will be pleased, Sir, to recollect that I professed myself unskilful in Biblical criticism; my profession was very sincere, and I am far from desiring to obtrude my notions as decisive.

I admitted without difficulty your *prophesy by action*.[3] All types are prophesies of that kind.[4] But I know not whether the admission of such prophesies will support your interpretation as there seems to be no action done.

Whether your explication or that which is generally received be considered as true, the use and importance of the Sacra-

---

1. The Rev. Samuel Hardy (*c.* 1720–93), Rector of Little Blakenham, Suffolk, schoolmaster and theological writer, author of *On the Principal Prophecies of the Old and New Testament* (1771) and *The Scripture-Account of the Nature and Ends of the Holy Eucharist* (1784) (*Alum. Cant.* I.ii.304; *GM* 1793, p. 1156). "His writings in defence of Christianity are numerous, but confined to the doctrine of the Eucharist as a perpetual sacrifice, and to the explanation of the prophecies, and the epistle to the Hebrews" (*GM* 1793, p. 1156).

2. The letter to which SJ responds may well have been motivated by the impending publication of *Proposals for Printing by Subscription the Scripture-Account of the Nature and End of the Holy Eucharist* (1781).

3. "There are, in the Scriptures, such Things as *Prophecies by Action*. ... The intended Sacrifice of Isaac, and his Deliverance, foretold, *by Action*, that Christ should suffer, and that he should rise again *the third Day from the Dead*" (Hardy, *Scripture-Account*, pp. 15, 17).

4. SJ echoes Hardy on this point: "I consider *a Type* as *a Prophecy by Action*" (*Scripture-Account*, p. 302).

ment is the same,[5] and therefore I cannot think the question such as in the present disposition of the world can properly or usefully be moved. Why should you run the hazard of being wrong, when Religion gains nothing by your being right?

Your arguments from the Old Testament do not appear to me to have any force, or to be applied with any probability to your present purpose.[6] You will gain more upon the reader by omitting them, and trusting only to the passage in itself and to general reasoning. And if you publish your thoughts I think it best to give them the appearance rather of enquiry and conjecture, than of asertion and dogmatism.

Once more, Sir, I do not pretend to decide the question which was new to me, and of which I have not perhaps the previous knowledge necessary to the examination. Enquire of men more learned in the Scriptures. You have from Me the respect due to all diligent searchers after sacred Truth, and my wishes that you may be long able to continue your studies, to your own improvement, and instruction of others. I am, Sir, Your most humble Servant,

SAM. JOHNSON

5. According to Hardy, the miracle of the loaves and the fishes should be understood as a "*Prophecy by Action*"—a type of the Eucharist itself (*Scripture-Account*, p. 21).

6. In chapter VII of his *Scripture-Account*, Hardy collects examples from the Old Testament of what he considers "types of the Eucharist."

Hester Thrale

MONDAY 16 OCTOBER 1780

MS: William Andrews Clark Library.

Dear Madam: Oct. 16, 1780

Gell and Smith never came.[1] The Steyning affair was undertaken by one Mr. Jones, a Shoemaker, an old inhabitant of the

1. Possibly Philip Gell and Henry Smith (?1756–89), of New-House, St. Albans, a cousin of Henry Thrale (*Thraliana* 1.491 n. 2, II.1167).

King's Bench,[2] of whom Mr. Robson had that morning given me the character.

Pray let me know when it is that we *must* go. I will keep the day, but if it could be saturday I should be glad,[3] but the difference after all will be little more than that of burthening the luggage cart with more books or with fewer,[4] yet I wish it could be saturday, but make no effort about it, only let me know as soon as ever you can.

I have seen Captain Burney and his cargo.[5] You may remember, I thought Banks had not gained much by circumnavigating the world. I am, Madam, your most etc.

SAM. JOHNSON

2. No details of this affair have been recovered.

3. The Thrales and SJ traveled to Brighton, but stayed less than a month (*Post* to JB, 17 Oct. 1780; Clifford, 1952, p. 192).

4. SJ took with him to Brighton the materials he needed to write his "Pope" (*Ante* To John Nichols, Early Aug. 1780; F. W. Hilles, "The Making of *The Life of Pope*," in *New Light on Dr. Johnson*, ed. Hilles, 1959, p. 259).

5. James Burney (1750–1821), R.N., eldest son of Dr. Charles Burney, had sailed with Capt. Cook on his second and third voyages and returned home earlier that month, commanding the *Discovery* after Cook's death (Joyce Hemlow, *The History of Fanny Burney*, 1958, p. 144; *The Early Journals and Letters of Fanny Burney*, ed. L. E. Troide, 1988, I.xliii).

James Boswell

TUESDAY 17 OCTOBER 1780

PRINTED SOURCE: JB's *Life*, 1791, II.328.

Dear Sir,   October 17, 1780

I am sorry to write you a letter that will not please you, and yet it is at last what I resolve to do. This year must pass without an interview;[1] the summer has been foolishly lost, like many other of my summers and winters. I hardly saw a green field, but staid in town to work, without working much.

1. JB had written several times that autumn to suggest that he and SJ meet at Carlisle or York (*Life* III.438–39).

Mr. Thrale's loss of health has lost him the election;[2] he is now going to Brighthelmston, and expects me to go with him, and how long I shall stay I cannot tell.[3] I do not much like the place, but yet I shall go, and stay while my stay is desired. We must, therefore, content ourselves with knowing what we know as well as man can know the mind of man, that we love one another, and that we wish each other's happiness, and that the lapse of a year cannot lessen our mutual kindness.

I was pleased to be told that I accused Mrs. Boswell unjustly, in supposing that she bears me ill-will. I love you so much, that I would be glad to love all that love you, and that you love; and I have love very ready for Mrs. Boswell, if she thinks it worthy of acceptance. I hope all the young ladies and gentlemen are well.

I take a great liking to your brother.[4] He tells me that his father received him kindly, but not fondly; however, you seem to have lived well enough at Auchinleck, while you staid.[5] Make your father as happy as you can.

You lately told me of your health: I can tell you in return, that my health has been for more than a year past, better than it has been for many years before. Perhaps it may please God to give us some time together before we are parted.[6] I am, dear Sir, Yours, most affectionately,

SAM. JOHNSON

2. *Ante* To William Strahan, 13 Sept. 1780.

3. *Ante* To Hester Thrale, 16 Oct. 1780 and n. 3.

4. *Ante* To Hester Thrale, 21 June 1780 and n. 9.

5. JB and his brother had enjoyed a "comfortable" reunion at Auchinleck, 16 Aug.–13 Sept. (*Life* III.438; *Boswell, Laird of Auchinleck*, ed. J. W. Reed and F. A. Pottle, 1977, p. 223).

6. SJ and JB saw each other again during JB's London jaunts of 1781, 1783, and 1784.

John Nichols

THURSDAY 26 OCTOBER 1780

MS: British Library.

ADDRESS: To Mr. Nicol.

Sir: Brighthelmston,[1] Oct. 26, 1780

I think you never need send back the revises unless something important occurs.[2] Little things, if I omit them, you will do me the favour of setting right yourself.[3] Our post is awkward as you will find, and I fancy you will find it best to send two sheets at once. I am, Sir, Your most humble servant,

SAM. JOHNSON

1. MS: "Brighthelmston" added in an unidentified hand

2. "Revises" were final proofs (J. D. Fleeman, "Some Proofs of Johnson's *Prefaces to the Poets*," *The Library* 17, 1962, p. 214). No proofs from this stage (the last before the final printed version) have been recovered (Fleeman, "Proofs," p. 215 n. 2).

3. "The proofs show that Nichols accepted this charge. Though one cannot always easily distinguish between Johnson's and Nichols's corrections of minute details, Nichols's hand is unmistakably involved in matters of spelling, punctuation, and typography" (J. H. Middendorf, "Johnson as Editor: Some Proofs of the 'Prefaces,'" in *Eighteenth-Century Studies in Honor of D. F. Hyde*, ed. W. H. Bond, 1970, p. 91).

John Nichols

c. DECEMBER 1780[1]

PRINTED SOURCE: Chapman III. 265.[2]

Mr. Nicol is desire[d] to procure the dates of Pope's Works upon the Dunciads. Mr. Reed can probably supply them.[3]

1. "By mid-November [1780] the Thrales had settled once more in Streatham, where they were joined by Johnson, and it was there in all probability that the *Life of Pope* was actually written. Mrs. Thrale, who transcribed various documents for Johnson mentions in *Thraliana* the foul copy of Pope's Homer under date of 10 December" (F. W. Hilles, "The Making of *The Life of Pope*," in *New Light on Dr. Johnson*, ed. Hilles, 1959, p. 259).

2. Chapman's reference (Dobell's Catalogue, 1937) is inaccurate, but the correct source has not been traced.

3. Isaac Reed (1742–1807), editor and literary scholar, upon whose "extensive and accurate knowledge of English literary History" SJ drew extensively during the composition of his *Lives of the Poets* (*Life* IV.37). Reed supplied additional biographies for the edition of 1790, and assisted JB in the composition and revision of his *Life* (Waingrow, p. 314 and n. 1). "In the Bodleian (MS. Malone 30) is a

chronology of Pope's writings in the hand of Isaac Reed with MS. notes by John Nichols" (F. W. Hilles, "Johnson's Correspondence with Nichols," *Philological Quarterly* 48, 1969, p. 229).

Mary Prowse

SATURDAY 9 DECEMBER 1780

MS: Hyde Collection.
ENDORSEMENT: Dr. Johnson, Decr. 1780.

Madam: Decr. 9, 1780

I return You very sincere and respectful thanks for all your favours. You have, I see, sent Guineas when I expected only pounds.[1]

It was beside my intention that You should make so much enquiry after Johnson. What can be known of him must start up by accident. He was not a Native of your town or country, but an adventurer who came from a distant part in quest of a livelihood, and did not stay a year. He came in 36 and went away in 37. He was likely enough to attract notice while he staid, as a lively noisy man, that loved company. His memory might probably continue for some time in some favourite alehouse. But after so many years perhaps there is no man left that remembers him. He was my near relation.[2]

The unfortunate woman for whom your excellent Mother has so kindly made provision is, in her way, well. I am now sending her some cloaths. Of her cure there is no hope.[3] Be pleased, Madam, to accept the good wishes and grateful regard of, Madam, Your most obedient and most humble Servant,

SAM. JOHNSON

1. *Ante* To Mary Prowse, 14 Aug. 1780 and n. 4.
2. *Ante* To Mary Prowse, 14 Aug. 1780, n. 7.
3. *Ante* To Mary Prowse, 14 Aug. 1780, n. 3.

William Vyse

SATURDAY 30 DECEMBER 1780

PRINTED SOURCE: JB's *Life*, ed. Malone, 1804, III.480.

Sir:
December 30, 1780

I hope you will forgive the liberty I take, in soliciting your interposition with his Grace the Archbishop:[1] my first petition was successful,[2] and I therefore venture on a second.

The Matron of the Chartreux[3] is about to resign her place, and Mrs. Desmoulins, a daughter of the late Dr. Swinfen, who was well known to your father,[4] is desirous of succeeding her. She has been accustomed by keeping a boarding school to the care of children, and I think is very likely to discharge her duty. She is in great distress, and therefore may properly receive the benefit of a charitable foundation.[5] If you wish to see her, she will be willing to give an account of herself.

If you shall be pleased, Sir, to mention her favourably to his Grace, you will do a great act of kindness to, Sir, Your most obliged, and most humble Servant,

SAM. JOHNSON

1. *Ante* To William Vyse, 19 July 1777, n. 2.
2. *Ante* To William Vyse, 19 July 1777 and n. 6.
3. Charterhouse School (*Ante* To Richard Congreve, 25 June 1735, n. 14).
4. William Vyse the elder (*Ante* To Lucy Porter, 18 June 1768, n. 5).
5. The surviving records suggest that Elizabeth Desmoulins did not receive the Charterhouse appointment: with the exception of an interval in 1783, she appears to have continued as SJ's pensioner and household member until his death.

Charles Allen[1]

1780[2]

PRINTED SOURCE: William Shaw, *Memoirs of the Life and Writings of the Late Dr. Samuel Johnson*, 1785, pp. 156–57.

1. The Rev. Charles Allen (?1730–95), Vicar of St. Nicholas, Rochester, 1765–95 (*GM* 1795, p. 351; Edward Halsted, *The History and Topographical Survey of the County of Kent*, 1782, II.51; *Alum. Oxon.* II.i.16).
2. "Upon his [Shaw's] going to settle in Kent, in 1780, as a curate, the Doctor wrote to Mr. Allen . . . the following letter" (Shaw, *Memoirs*, p. 156).

Sir,

Mr. William Shaw, the gentleman from whom you will receive this, is a studious and literary man; he is a stranger, and will be glad to be introduced into proper company; and he is my friend, and any civility you shall shew him, will be an obligation on, Sir, your most obedient servant,

SAM. JOHNSON

John Nichols
LATE 1780[1]

MS: British Library.
ADDRESS: To Mr. Nicol.

Sir:

This life of Dr. Young was written by a friend of his son.[2] What is crossed[3] with black is expunged by the author, what is crossed with red is expunged by me,[4] if you find any thing more that can be well omitted I shall not be sorry to see it yet shorter.[5]

1. SJ had completed work on "Young" sometime between 8 Aug. and 18 Sept. 1780 (*Ante* To Hester Thrale, 8 Aug. 1780; *Works*, Yale ed. 1.301).

2. The biographical section of SJ's "Young" was contributed by Herbert Croft (1751–1816), barrister and man of letters, a close friend of Edward Young's only son, Frederick (b. *c.* 1732) (*Life* v.548–49).

3. *cross*: "to cancel; as, *to* cross *an article*" (SJ's *Dictionary*).

4. According to John Hussey, SJ "expunged nearly half" of Croft's original memoir (*Lives of the Poets* III.361).

5. According to Edmund Burke, Croft's memoir was "a bad imitation of Johnson: . . . all the panting and convulsions of the Sibyl without the inspiration" (*Boswell, Laird of Auchinleck*, ed. J. W. Reed and F. A. Pottle, 1977, p. 347).

John Nichols

MS: British Library.

Mr. Nichol is entreated to save the proof sheets of Pope because they are promised to a Lady who desires to have them.[2]

1. F. W. Hilles argues convincingly that SJ "completed his manuscript [of 'Pope'] early in 1781" ("The Making of *The Life of Pope*," in *New Light on Dr. Johnson*, ed. Hilles, 1959, p. 260). *Post* To John Nichols, *c.* March 1781 and n. 2.

2. On her father's behalf Frances Burney had asked for the proofs of "Pope" (Madame d'Arblay, *Memoirs of Doctor Burney*, 1832, II.178).

Warren Hastings

MONDAY 29 JANUARY 1781[1]

MS: British Library.

Sir:

Jan. 29, 1781

Amidst the importance and multiplicity of affairs in which your great Office engages you I take the liberty of recalling your attention for a moment to literature, and will not prolong the interruption by an apology which your character makes needless.

Mr. Hoole, a Gentleman long known and long esteemed in the India house,[2] after having translated Tasso, has undertaken Ariosto. How well he is qualified for his undertaking[3] he has already shown.[4] He is desirous Sir, of your favour in

1. Following common diplomatic practice when long sea voyages were involved, SJ sent two other versions of this letter, at roughly six-month intervals. These are dated 12 June 1781 (B.L. Add. MS: 39871, f. 12) and 21 Jan. 1782 (Add. MS: 39871, ff. 27–28). Substantive variants have been recorded in the notes.

2. John Hoole had worked as a clerk in the East India Office since *c.* 1745 (*Life* II.289 n. 2; Hazen, p. 60).

3. "how well he is qualified for such a work" (12 June 1781); "How he is qualified for the work" (21 Jan. 1782)

4. Hoole's translation of *Orlando Furioso* (five vols.) was published by subscription in 1783.

promoting[5] his proposals, and flatters me by supposing that my testimony may advance his interest.[6]

It is a new thing[7] for a Clerk of the India house to translate Poets. It is new for a Governour[8] of Bengal to patronise Learning. That he may find his ingenuity rewarded, and that Learning may flourish under your protection[9] is the wish of, Sir, Your most humble Servant,

SAM. JOHNSON

5. "forwarding" (21 Jan. 1782)

6. In the postscript to Volume 5, Hoole thanks the subscribers to his translation, and singles out the "august names" at the head of the list: "I must not forget my obligations to the Governor-General of Bengal, and to the rest of the Gentlemen of the East India Company's service at that settlement, for their very generous patronage" (*Orlando Furioso*, 1783, v.iv).   7. "It is new" (12 June 1781)

8. "Poets, nor less for a Governour" (21 Jan. 1782)

9. "Patronage" (21 Jan. 1782)

John Nichols
c. MARCH 1781[1]

MS: British Library.

Mr. Johnson being now at home desires the last leaves of the Criticism on Popes Epitaphs, and he will correct them.[2]

1. See below, n. 2.

2. SJ's "criticism upon Pope's *Epitaphs*" was appended to his "Pope," the last biography to be finished (*Lives of the Poets* III.254–72). Proofs had been corrected by 14 Mar. (*Post* To JB, 14 Mar. 1781), and the second installment of prefaces was published in May (J. D. Fleeman, "Some Proofs of Johnson's *Prefaces to the Poets*," *The Library* 17, 1962, p. 213 n. 8).

Thomas Cadell
MONDAY 5 MARCH 1781

MS: Hyde Collection.

Sir: March 5, 1781

In making up my account for the lives, I desire that you will satisfy Mr. Dilly for a set of Poets and lives which he sent on my account to Mrs. Boswel,[1] and a set of lives sent by him to Lord Hailes.[2]

I am glad that the work is at last done.[3] I am, Sir, Your humble servant,

SAM. JOHNSON

1. *Ante* To JB, 21 Aug. 1780 and n. 8.   2. *Ante* To JB, 13 Mar. 1779.

3. The second and final installment of SJ's *Prefaces to the Poets* was published 18 May (*Bibliography Supplement*, p. 156).

William Strahan

MONDAY 5 MARCH 1781

MS: Hyde Collection.

ADDRESS: To William Strahan, Esq.

Sir:
                                    March 5, 1781

Having now done my lives I shall have money to receive,[1] and shall be glad to add to it, what remains due for the Hebrides, which You cannot charge [me] with grasping very rapaciously. The price was two hundred Guineas or pounds; I think first pounds then Guineas. I have had one hundred.[2]

There is likewise something due for the political pamphlets, which I left without bargain to your liberality and Mr. Cadel's.[3] Of this You will likewise think that I may have all together.[4] I am, Sir, Your humble servant,

SAM. JOHNSON

1. The original agreement was for 200 guineas (*Lit. Anec.* VIII.416), but in 1783 SJ received a further *ex gratia* payment of £100 (J. D. Fleeman, "The Revenue of a Writer: Samuel Johnson's Literary Earnings," in *Studies in the Book Trade in Honour of Graham Pollard*, 1975, pp. 218, 227–28).

2. The surviving records suggest that "Johnson contracted with Strahan to write the book [*A Journey to the Western Islands of Scotland*] for 200 guineas (£210), and that in addition he parted with a third share in the copyright (valuing the whole at £210) for £70" (Fleeman, p. xxiii). In Jan. 1775 he had been paid £170; he was therefore owed £110 (Fleeman, p. xxiii).

3. According to J. D. Fleeman, "we do not know what Johnson received for the political pamphlets of the early 1770s, or for the collected *Political Tracts* of 1776. Johnson did not perhaps know himself" ("The Revenue of a Writer," p. 222).

4. The next recorded payment from Strahan to SJ, 29 Mar., amounted to £52 11s. (Fleeman, "The Revenue of a Writer," p. 217).

MS: National Library of Wales.
ADDRESS: To Miss Owen at Penrhos near Shrewsbury.
POSTMARK: 8 MR.

Madam: Boltcourt, Fleetstreet, March 8, 1781

Though I have omitted to answer your letter I have not forgotten it, nor betrayed it. I have kept your Secret, and pitied your Situation.[1] If I could send you any[thing] more useful than pity, I should be in more haste to write. I can only repeat the advice which I formerly gave You, to act as well as You can, and to suffer those evils which you cannot help to take as little hold as is possible of your thoughts. You will tell me that You cannot look on the disgrace of your family, and the waste of an ancient estate without great distress of mind. And what you say must be allowed to have great weight; but every passion is stronger or weaker as it is more or less indulged and what I recommend to You is not insensi[bi]lity, but a constant endeavour to divert your thoughts by reading, work, and conversation, and when You are alone to compose them by trust in God.

Write to me with full confidence whenever You are inclined, You shall have a more speedy answer. I sincerely wish you well, and should think it great happiness to contribute in any manner to your ease, and tranquillity.

If You find that your presence does any good endeavour to continue it, but if not, take care of yourself, and retire from the sight of evil which you cannot hinder, and which wears out your life in misery.

All is not happiness in other places. Mr. Thrale's apoplexy has much weakened him, and though in my opinion, he may live many years,[2] he will, I fear, always be weak and put into

---

1. Margaret Owen was suffering from the excesses of her alcoholic, spendthrift, mentally unstable older brother John (1741–1823) (*Thraliana* I.441, II.818, 1152).   2. *Post* To Joshua Reynolds, 4 Apr. 1781.

danger by slight irregularities. I am, for my part, better than when you knew me,[3] and I am with great sincerity, Madam, Your affectionate and most humble Servant,

SAM. JOHNSON

3. It is likely that SJ is thinking not of their most recent meeting, July 1780 (*Ante* To Hester Thrale, 10 July 1780), but of the time they spent together during the winter of 1776 and the spring of 1777 (Clifford, 1952, pp. 148–51).

Lucy Porter

THURSDAY 8 MARCH 1781

MS: Hyde Collection.
ADDRESS: To Mrs. Lucy Porter in Lichfield.
POSTMARK: 8 MR.
ENDORSEMENT: 1781.

Dear Madam: London, March[1] 8, 1781

It is indeed a long time since I wrote to You, I have been taken up more than I needed with some little employment, and have neglected You and my other friends. But I did not quite forget You. I hope as the Spring advances your health will improve, and that before oisters go out of season you will be able to eat other meat. I hope You receive the weekly barrel which I have ordered since I knew that your Stomack was so much disordered.[2] If I can send any thing else that will do you good, I shall be very willing. Take care of your self.

I missed last year my annual visit to my own country, and I hardly went any whither else. I hope this year to make myself amends.[3] My health has lately fluctuated a little, but I am still better than when You saw me last. Poor Mr. Thrale has had many strokes of an apoplexy, and is very feeble, but I think in

1. MS: "March" superimposed upon "May"
2. One of SJ's customary gifts to Lucy Porter was a barrel of oysters.
3. SJ left for Lichfield on 15 Oct. and returned to London *c.* 11 Dec. (*Post* To Hester Thrale, 17 Oct. 1781; 8 Dec. 1781).

no immediate danger.⁴ Mrs. Thrale and Miss are well. Pray for me, and may God bless You.

Make my compliments to all my friends. Tell Miss Adey that I will write to her;⁵ and give my sincere respects to Mr. Pearson. I am, dear Love, Your most humble servant,

SAM. JOHNSON

4. *Post* To Joshua Reynolds, 4 Apr. 1781.

5. MS: "her" superimposed upon "You"

James Boswell

WEDNESDAY 14 MARCH 1781

PRINTED SOURCE: JB's *Life*, 1791, II.370.

Dear Sir, March 14, 1781

I hoped you had got rid of all this hypocrisy of misery. What have you to do with Liberty and Necessity?¹ Or what more than to hold your tongue about it? Do not doubt but I shall be most heartily glad to see you here again, for I love every part about you but your affectation of distress.²

I have at last finished my Lives, and have laid up for you a load of copy, all out of order, so that it will amuse you a long time to set it right.³ Come to me, my dear Bozzy, and let us be

1. JB had written to SJ "in February, complaining of having been troubled by a recurrence of the perplexing question of Liberty and Necessity" (*Life* IV.71). JB's journal records his "dreadful melancholy" at thoughts of predestination: "I saw a dreary nature of things, an unconscious, uncontrollable power by which all things are driven on, and I could not get rid of the irresistible influence of motives" (*Boswell, Laird of Auchinleck*, ed. J. W. Reed and F. A. Pottle, 1977, p. 283).

2. When they were reunited on 20 March, SJ told JB, "'I love you better than ever I did'" (Reed and Pottle, *Laird of Auchinleck*, p. 292).

3. *Ante* To JB, 13 Mar. 1779 and n. 2. According to JB, SJ "was so good as to make me a present of the greatest part of the original" (*Life* IV.36). This gift came in two installments: on 21 Mar. SJ turned over "a deal of the original *copy*"; on 21 Aug. "Dr. Dunbar of Aberdeen called . . . with a small parcel of MS. of *Prefaces to the Poets*" (Reed and Pottle, *Laird of Auchinleck*, pp. 293–94, 392). Two holograph MSS have been recovered: those of "Rowe" (Hyde Collection) and "Pope" (Pierpont Morgan Library) (J. D. Fleeman, *A Preliminary Handlist of Documents and*

as happy as we can. We will go again to the Mitre, and talk old times over. I am, dear Sir, Yours, affectionately,

SAM. JOHNSON

Manuscripts of SJ, 1967, pp. 27–28). For a checklist of the surviving proofs, see J. D. Fleeman, "Some Proofs of Johnson's *Prefaces to the Poets*," *The Library* 17, 1962, pp. 228–30.

Joshua Reynolds

WEDNESDAY 4 APRIL 1781

MS: Beinecke Library.

Wednesday

Mr. Johnson knows that Sir Joshua Reynolds and the other Gentlemen will excuse his incompliance with the call,[1] when they are told that Mr. Thrale died this morning.[2]

1. SJ had been expected to attend the scheduled meeting of The Club (*Life* IV.84).
2. Henry Thrale, attended by SJ, died of apoplexy in the family's rented house on Grosvenor Square (*Thraliana* I.490; Clifford, 1952, pp. 198–99).

Hester Thrale

THURSDAY 5 APRIL 1781

MS: Beinecke Library.
ADDRESS: To Mrs. Thrale at Brighthelmston, Sussex.[1]
POSTMARK: 5 AP.

Dearest Madam:

London, Apr. 5, 1781

Of your injunctions to pray for You and write to You I hope to leave neither unobserved, and I hope to find You willing in a short time to alleviate your trouble by some other exercise of

1. "Mrs. Thrale's usual reaction to death was to run away. This time, not waiting for the funeral, she hurried with Queeney immediately to Streatham and from there to Brighton, where she remained for two weeks" (Clifford, 1952, p. 199).

the mind. I am not without my part of the calamity. No death since that of my Wife has ever oppressed me like this.[2] But let us remember that we are in the hands of him who knows when to give, and when to take away, who[3] will look upon us with mercy through all our variations of existence, and who invites [us] to call on him in the day of trouble.[4] Call upon him in this great revolution of life, and call with confidence. You will then find comfort for the past, and support for the future. He that has given You happiness in marriage to a degree of which without personal knowledge, I should have thought the description fabulous, can give You another mode of happiness as a Mother, and at last the happiness of losing all temporal cares in the thoughts of an eternity in heaven.

I do not exhort You to reason yourself into tranquillity, we must first pray, and then labour, first implore the Blessing of God and then [those] means which he puts into our hands.[5] Cultivated ground has few weeds, a mind occupied by lawful business, has little room for useless regret.

We read the will to day, but I will not fill my fi[r]st letter with any other account than that with all my zeal for your advantage I am satisfied, and that the other executors, more used to consider property than I, commended it for wisdom and equity.[6] Yet why should I not tell You that You have[7] five hundred pounds for your immediate expences, and two thousand pounds a year with both the houses and all[8] the goods?

Let us pray for one another, that the time whether long or short that shall yet be granted us, may be well spent, and that

2. On 13 Apr. SJ recorded in his diary, "On Wednesday, 11, was buried my dear Friend Thrale who died, on Wednesday, 4, and with him were buried many of my hopes and pleasures" (*Works*, Yale ed. 1.304).

3. MS: "and" del. before "who"

4. "And call upon me in the time of trouble: so will I hear thee, and thou shalt praise me" (Psalm 50:15).

5. "The safe and general antidote against sorrow, is employment" (*Rambler* No. 47, *Works*, Yale ed. III.257).

6. The four executors of Henry Thrale's will were SJ, John Cator, Henry Smith, and Jeremiah Crutchley (Clifford, 1952, p. 200).

7. MS: "h" superimposed upon "f"   8. MS: "a" superimposed upon "h"

when this life which at the longest is very short, shall come to an end, a better may begin which shall never end. I am, Dearest Madam, Your most humble servant,

SAM. JOHNSON

Hester Thrale

SATURDAY 7 APRIL 1781

MS: Houghton Library.

Dear Madam:

April 7,[1] 1781

I hope You begin to find your mind grow clearer. My part of the loss hangs upon me. I have lost a friend of boundless kindness at an age when it is very unlikely that I should find another. ⟨*five or six words*⟩.[2]

If You think change of place likely to relieve you, there is no reason why You should not go to Bath,[3] the distances are unequal, but with regard to practice and business they are the same. It is a day's journey from either place, and the Post is more expeditious and certain to Bath.[4] Consult only your own inclination, for there is really no other principle of choice. God direct and bless You.

Mr. Cator has offered Mr. Perkins money, but it was not wanted.[5] I hope we shall all do all we can to make you less unhappy, and you must do all you can for yourself. What we or what You can do will for a time be but little, yet certainly

1. MS: "7" superimposed upon "11"

2. MS: erasure and heavy deletion

3. *Ante* To Hester Thrale, 5 Apr. 1781, n. 1. Hester Thrale remained at Brighton, and returned to Streatham *c.* 21 Apr. (Clifford, 1952, p. 200; *Post* To Hester Maria Thrale, 19 Apr. 1781 and n. 1).

4. The western road that connected London with Bath was one of the best in England. As a consequence, the stagecoach journey took only sixteen or seventeen hours, and mail service between the two cities was extremely efficient (Howard Robinson, *The British Post Office*, 1948, p. 130).

5. John Cator, in his capacity as executor, was concerned with keeping the brewery running smoothly.

that calamity which may [be] considered as doomed to fall inevitably on half mankind, is not finally without alleviation.

It is something for me that as[6] I have not the decripitude I have not the callousness of old age. I hope in time to be less afflicted. I am, Madam, Your most humble servant,

SAM. JOHNSON

6. MS: "a" superimposed upon "I"

Hester Thrale

MONDAY 9 APRIL 1781

MS: Houghton Library.

Dearest Madam: London, Apr. 9, 1781

That You are gradually recovering your tranquillity is the effect to be humbly expected from trust in God. Do not represent life as darker than it is. Your loss has been very great, but You retain more than almost any other can hope to possess. You are high in the opinion of mankind; You have children from whom much pleasure may be expected, and that you will find many friends You have no reason to doubt. Of my friendship, be it worth more or less, I hope You think yourself certain, without much art or care. It will not be easy for me to repay the benefits that I have received, but I hope to be always ready at your call. Our sorrow has different effects, you are withdrawn into solitude, and I am driven into company. I am afraid of thinking what I have lost. I never had such a friend before. Let me have your prayers and those of my dear Queeny.

The prudence and resolution of your design to return so soon to your business and your duty deserves great praise, I shall communicate it on Wednesday to the other Executors.[1] Be pleased to let me know whether you would have me come

1. *Ante* To Hester Thrale, 5 Apr. 1781, n. 6; 7 Apr. 1781, n. 3.

to Streatham to receive [you], or stay here till the next day. I am, Madam, Your most humble servant,

SAM. JOHNSON

William Vyse
TUESDAY 10 APRIL 1781

MS: Hyde Collection.
ENDORSEMENT: Dr. Johnson.

Reverend Sir: Bolt court, Fleetstreet, Apr. 10, 1781

The Bearer is one of my old Friends, a man of great Learning, whom the Chancellor has been pleased to nominate to the Chartreux.[1] He attends his Grace the Archbishop to take the oath required,[2] and, being a modest Scholar, will escape embarrasment if You are so kind as to introduce him; by which You will do a kindness to a Man of great merit, and add another to those favours which have been already conferred by You, on, Sir, Your most humble Servant,

SAM. JOHNSON

1. In Oct. 1780 Lord Thurlow promised SJ, who had provided Alexander Macbean with a "distinct" and "authoritative" recommendation, to exert his influence at the next opportunity (pensioners in the hospital were limited to eighty). Accordingly, when a vacancy occurred Macbean was nominated "a poor brother of the Charterhouse," where he spent the last three years of his life (*Life* 1.187, III.441; Wheatley and Cunningham 1.364; *Post* To Hester Thrale, 26 June 1784).

2. *Ante* To William Vyse, 19 July 1777 and n. 2.

Hester Thrale
WEDNESDAY 11 APRIL 1781

MS: Hyde Collection.

Dear Madam: London, Apr. 11, 1781

I am glad to hear from my dear Miss, that You have recovered tranquillity enough to think on bathing but there is no disposition in the world to leave you long to yourself. Mr. Perkins pretends that your absence produces a thousand difficulties which I believe it does not produce. He frights Mr. Crichley. Mr. Cator is of my mind that there is no need of hurry. Perkins has disclosed to Mr. Crichley his appetite for partnership,[1] which he has resolved not to gratify. I would not have this importunity give you any alarm or disturbance, but to pacify it come as soon as You can prevail upon your mind to mingle with business.[2] I think business the best remedy for grief as soon as it can be admitted.

We met to day and were told of mountainous difficulties, till I was provoked to tell them, that if there were really so much to do and suffer, there would be no Executors in the world. Do not suffer yourself to be terrified.

I comfort you, and hope God will bless and support You, but I feel myself like a man begining a new course of life. I had interwoven myself with my dear Friend. But our great care ought to be that we may be fit and ready when in a short time we shall be called to follow him.

There is however no use in communicating to You my heaviness of heart. I thank[3] dear Miss for her letter. I am, Madam, Your most humble servant,

SAM. JOHNSON

1. The death of Henry Thrale provided John Perkins with "his chance to bid for partnership. His first trump in the play, which started when Thrale was removed from the scene, was his technical ability. He had been at the centre of operations, the real architect of success, for a lifetime. . . . His second, and decisive, trump was that he had married, as his second wife, Amelia Bevan, widow of Timothy Paul Bevan, son of one of the richest Quaker bankers of Lombard Street and himself a wealthy druggist and merchant, whose extensive cousinhood stood ready to bring capital in plenty for the purchase, and able cadets for partners" (Peter Mathias, *The Brewing Industry in England, 1700–1830*, 1959, pp. 272–73). *Post* To John Perkins, 2 June 1781 and n. 1.

2. *Ante* To Hester Thrale, 7 Apr. 1781, n. 3.

3. MS: "think"

Hannah More[1]

THURSDAY 12 APRIL 1781

MS: Hyde Collection.

ADDRESS: To Miss Moore.

Madam: Thursday, Apr. 12

When I came home yesterday, Mr. Boswel reminded me that I was pre-engaged on Monday to General Paoli.[2] Shall I come on Monday to Breakfast? or will Mrs. Garrick be so kind as to receive me on Tuesday?[3] Be pleased to set all as right as You can, for, Madam, Your most humble Servant,

SAM. JOHNSON

1. Hannah More (1745–1833), dramatist, poet, social reformer, and political and religious writer, author of *Percy* (1777), *Le Bas Bleu* (1786), and *Strictures on the Modern System of Female Education* (1799). More met SJ in June 1774, on the first of her annual visits to London (William Roberts, *Memoirs of the Life and Correspondence of Mrs. Hannah More*, 1834, 1.48; *Life* IV.341 n. 6). After David Garrick's death More became Mrs. Garrick's constant companion, and at her request functioned as household "chaplain" (*Life* IV.96), with responsibility for "the moral and spiritual care of the servants" (M. G. Jones, *Hannah More*, 1952, pp. 39–40).

2. In 1781 JB's spring jaunt to London lasted for two and a half months, 19 Mar. – 2 June (*Boswell, Laird of Auchinleck*, ed. J. W. Reed and F. W. Pottle, 1977, pp. 292, 370). There is no record in his journal of the dinner at Pasquale Paoli's.

3. On Friday, 20 Apr., Mrs. Garrick entertained for the first time since her husband's death (20 Jan. 1779). The guests included SJ and JB (*Life* IV.96).

Lucy Porter

THURSDAY 12 APRIL 1781

MS: Hyde Collection.

ADDRESS: To Mrs. Lucy Porter in Lichfield.

POSTMARK: 12 AP.

Dear Madam: London, Apr. 12, 1781

Life is full of troubles, I have just lost my dear friend Thrale.[1] I hope he is happy; but I have had a great loss.

1. *Ante* To Joshua Reynolds, 4 Apr. 1781.

I am otherwise pretty well, I require some care of myself, but that care is not ineffectual, and when I am out of order I think it often my own fault.

The Spring is now making quick advances; as it is the season in which the whole world is enlivened and invigorated, I hope that both You and I shall partake of its benefits. My desire is to see Lichfield,[2] but being left Executor to my Friend,[3] I know not whether I can be spared but I will try, for it is now long since we saw one another, and how little we can promise ourselves many more interviews, we are taught by hourly examples of mortality. Let us try to live so as that mortality may not be an evil. Write to me soon, my Dearest; your letters will give me great pleasure.

I am sorry that Mr. Porter has not had his Box but by sending it to Mr. Mathias, who very readily undertook its conveyance, I did the best, I could, and perhaps before now he has it.[4]

Be so kind as to make my compliments to my Friends, I have a great value for their kindness, and hope to enjoy it before the summer is past. Do write to me. I am, dearest Love, Your most humble Servant,

SAM. JOHNSON

2. *Ante* To Lucy Porter, 8 Mar. 1781 and n. 3.
3. *Ante* To Hester Thrale, 5 Apr. 1781 and n. 6.
4. *Ante* To Lucy Porter, 8 Apr. 1780.

Hester Thrale

THURSDAY 12 APRIL 1781

MS: Hyde Collection.

Dearest Madam: London, Apr. 12, 1781

You will not suppose that much has happened since last night, nor indeed is this a time for talking much of loss and gain. The business of Christians is now for a few days in their own bosoms.[1] God grant us to do it properly. I hope You gain ground on your affliction. I hope to overcome mine. You and Miss must comfort one another. May You long live happily together. I have nobody whom I expect to share my uneasiness, nor if I could communicate it, would it be less. I give it little vent, and amuse it as I can. Let us pray for one another. And when we meet, we may [try] what fidelity and tenderness will do for us.

There is no wisdom in useless and hopeless sorrow, but there is something in it so like virtue, that he who is wholly without it cannot be loved, nor will by me at least be thought worthy of esteem. My next letter will be to Queeney. I am, Madam, Your most humble servant,

SAM. JOHNSON

1. In 1781 Good Friday fell on 13 Apr. In his diary entry for Easter SJ noted: "The decease of him from whose friendship I had obtained many opportunities of amusement, and to whom I turned my thoughts as to a refuge from misfortunes, has left me heavy. But my business is with myself" (*Works*, Yale ed. 1.304).

Hester Thrale

SATURDAY 14 APRIL 1781

MS: Hyde Collection.
ADDRESS: To Mrs. Thrale at Brighthelmston, Sussex.
POSTMARK: 14 AP.

Dear Madam:

My intention was to have written this day to my dear Queeney, but I have just heard from you, and therefore this letter shall be yours. I am glad that You find the behaviour of your acquaintance such as you can commend. The world is not so unjust or unkind as it is peevishly represented, those who deserve well seldom fail to receive from others such services as they can perform, but few have much in their power, or are so stationed as to have great leisure from their own affairs, and kindness must be commonly the exuberance of content. The

337

wretched have no compassion, they can do good only from strong principles of duty.

I purpose to receive You at Streatham, but wonder that you come so soon.

I sent immediately to Mr. Perkins to send you twenty pounds and intended to secure you from disappointment by inclosing a note in this, but yours written on Wednesday 11th came not till Saturday the fourteenth, and mine written to night will not come before You leave Brighthelmston, unless You have put Monday next for monday sevennight, which I suspect as You mention no alteration of your mind.[1] I am, Madam, Your most humble servant,   SAM. JOHNSON

1. *Ante* To Hester Thrale, 7 Apr. 1781, n. 3; *Post* To Hester Thrale, 16 Apr. 1781.

John Nichols
MONDAY 16 APRIL 1781

MS: British Library.
ADDRESS: To Mr. Nicol.
                                                    Monday, Apr. 16

Mr. Johnson desires Mr. Nicol to send him a set of the last lives, and would be glad to know how the octavo edition goes forward.[1]

1. The second installment of SJ's *Prefaces* was officially published in six volumes on 18 May. The format (small octavo) was often described as duodecimo. All the prefaces then appeared (divorced from the *Works*, and officially rechristened *Lives*) in four large octavo volumes on 16 June (*Bibliography Supplement*, pp. 155–56, 159).

Hester Thrale
MONDAY 16 APRIL 1781

MS: Beinecke Library.
ADDRESS: ⟨To⟩ Mrs. Thrale at Brighthelmston, Sussex.
POSTMARK: 16 AP.

Dear Madam: London, Apr. 16, 1781

As I was preparing this day to go to Streatham according to the direction in your letter of the 11th which I could not know, though I suspected it, to be erroneous, I received two letters of which the first effect was that it saved me a fruitless Journey. Of these letters that which I perceive to have been written first has no date of time or place, the second was written on the 14th, but they came together.

I forbore, because I would not disturb you, to tell you that last week Mr. Perkins came to talk about partnership, and was very copious.[1] I dismissed him with nothing harsher than, *that I was not convinced.*

You will have much talk to hear. Mr. Cator speaks with great exuberance, but what he says, when at last he says it, is commonly right. Mr. Robson made an oration flaming with the terrifick, which I discovered[2] to have no meaning at all; for the result was that if [we] stopped payment we should lose credit.

I have already so far anticipated Mr. Scrase's advice,[3] as to propose to the Executors advantages for Perkins which Mr. Cator thinks too liberal. "Mr. Perkins says that the trade will produce in profit 12000£ a year; for the first four thousand which will come of itself, P. shall have 200£; for the second four thousand, P. shall [have] 400£, and for the third four thousand which will give yet a higher proof of good management, P. shall have 600£. If the trade gains much, P. shall gain much even to 1200£ a year." This connects his interest with ours. It has however not yet been mentioned to him, and such profit, I suppose, will make him afraid to leave us.

I have written to Mr. Robson to send the will. There were two copies, but I know not who has them.

You are to receive five hundred pounds immediately. Mr. Scrase shall certainly see the will, if You and I go to Bright-

1. *Ante* To Hester Thrale, 11 Apr. 1781 and n. 1.
2. MS: "di" altered from "?de"
3. "Mr. Scrase says 'tis Madness to try at carrying on such a Trade with only five Girls" (*Thraliana* I.491).

helmston on purpose, which if we have any difficulty, may be our best expedient.

I am encouraged, dearest Lady, by your Spirit. The season for *Agnes* is now over.[4] You are in your civil character a man. You may sue and be sued.[5] If you apply to business perhaps half[6] the mind which You have exercised upon knowledge and elegance, you will need little help, what help however I can give you, will I hope, be always at call.

(make my compliments to Mr. Scrase.)

⟨   ⟩[7]

I am, Madam, Your most humble Servant,

SAM. JOHNSON

4. *Ante* To Hester Thrale, 25 Oct. 1777 and n. 3.

5. "By marriage the very being or legal existence of a woman is suspended . . . it is incorporated and consolidated into that of the husband; . . . she can bring no action for redress without her husband's concurrence, . . . neither can she be sued without making the husband a defendant" (*The Lawes Respecting Women*, 1777, p. 64). As a wife Hester Thrale had been technically *in potestate viri*, "and therefore disabled to make any bargain or contract, without her husbands consent or privity"; as a widow she was a *feme sole*, an independent legal agent (Thomas Blount, *Glossographia*, 1670, pp. 171–72; *The Lawes Respecting Women*, p. 117).

6. MS: "half" altered from "have"

7. MS: mutilated; several lines missing

Hester Thrale

TUESDAY 17 APRIL 1781

MS: Hyde Collection.

ADDRESS: To Mrs. Thrale at Brighthelmston, Sussex.

POSTMARK: 17 AP.

Dear Madam: London, Apr. 17, 1781

Mr. Norris (Mr. Robson's Partner) promised to send the will to morrow,[1] You will therefore have it before You have this

1. Randall Norris (*fl.* 1775–1827), of the Inner Temple, had conducted legal business for Henry Thrale. He later represented Queeney Thrale in a dispute with her mother over the Oxfordshire estate (information supplied by Professors E. A. Bloom and L. D. Bloom).

letter. When You have talked with Mr. Scrase write diligently down all that You can remember, and where You have any difficulties ask him again, and rather stay where you are a few days longer, than come away with imperfect information.

The executors will hardly meet till You come, for we have nothing to do, till we go all together to prove the will.

I have not had a second visit from Mr. Perkins, for he found his discourse to me very unavailing. I was dry, but if he goes to Cator he will be overpowered with words as good as his own. Smith appears a very modest inoffensive Man, not likely to give any trouble. The difficulty of finding Executors Mr. Scrase has formerly told You, and among all your acquaintance except Pepys whom You pressed into the service and who would perhaps have deserted it,[2] I do not ⟨know⟩ with whom you could have been more commodiously connected. They all mean well, and will, I think, all concur. ⟨*six or seven words*⟩[3]

Miss told me that You intended to bathe; it is right, all external things are diversions; Let her bathe too. I regain that tranquillity which irremediable misfortunes necessarily admit, and do not, I hope, think on what I have left, without grateful recollection of what I have enjoyed. I am, Dear Madam, Your most humble servant,

SAM. JOHNSON

2. "When Mr. Thrale made his Will . . . he kindly asked me who I would appoint Joint Executors with myself—I named Johnson, Cator, and [William Weller] Pepys. . . . he however is scrupulous, as all honest and refined Characters are, and will not bear the Burthen with me" (*Thraliana* I.418).

3. MS: heavy deletion

Hester Maria Thrale

THURSDAY 19 APRIL 1781

MS: The Earl of Shelburne.
ADDRESS: To Miss Thrale at Brighthelmston, Sussex.
POSTMARK: 19 AP.

My dearest Miss: London, Apr. 19, 1781

This is the last night on which I can write to Brighthelmston,[1] and therefore I resolve to pay the letter which I owe to You, for I would not have you think that I want either tenderness or respect for You.

We are now soon to meet, our meeting will be melancholy, but we will not give way too long to unprofitable grief. The world is all before us—and Providence our Guide. Life has other duties, and for You, my dearest, it has yet, I hope, much happiness. The Friendship which has begun between us, may[2] perhaps by its continuance give us opportunities of supplying the deficiencies[3] of each other. I hope we shall never lose the kindness which has grown up between us. The loss of such a Friend as has been taken from us encreases our need of one another, and ought to unite us more closely. I am, my dear Love, your most humble servant,

SAM. JOHNSON

1. Queeney and her mother were about to return to Streatham after their fortnight's respite in Brighton (*Ante* To Hester Thrale, 5 Apr. 1781, n. 1).
2. MS: "may" altered from "my"   3. MS: "cies" repeated as catchword

Margaret Strahan
MONDAY 23 APRIL 1781

MS: Hyde Collection.

Dear Madam: Apr. 23, 1781

The Grief which I feel for the loss of a very kind friend is sufficient to make me know how much You must suffer by the death of an amiable son, a man of whom, I think, it may be truly said, that no one knew him who does not lament him.[1] I look upon myself as having a friend, another friend taken from me.

1. William Strahan the younger (1740–81), first his father's partner and then an independent printer, had died 19 Apr. (J. A. Cochrane, *Dr. Johnson's Printer*, 1964, pp. xiv, 130–31).

Comfort, dear Madam, I would give You if I could, but I know how little the forms of consolation can avail. Let me however counsel You, not to waste[2] your health, in unprofitable sorrow, but to go to Bath, and endeavour to prolong your own life, but when we have all done all that we can, one friend must in time lose the other. I am, Dear Madam, Your most humble Servant,

SAM. JOHNSON

2. MS: "waste" superimposed upon "let" partially erased

John Nichols

c. APRIL 1781

MS: British Library.
ADDRESS: To Mr. Nicol.

Please to deliver to Mr. Steevens a complete set of the lives in 12mo.[1]

SAM. JOHNSON

1. *Ante* To John Nichols, 16 Apr. 1781, n. 1.

Mary Prowse

MONDAY 7 MAY 1781

MS: Hyde Collection.
ENDORSEMENT: Dr. Johnson, May 1781.

Madam: N.B. *Boltcourt*, Fleetstreet, London, May 7, 1781

Having lately had a melancholy occasion to search my Chest for mourning,[1] I found in one of the pockets this tattered letter, which seems to prove that You have remitted to me more money than was due.[2]

1. Henry Thrale died 4 Apr. and was buried a week later (*Works*, Yale ed. 1.304).   2. *Ante* To Mary Prowse, 14 Aug. 1780.

You see, Madam, that I was paid, or might have been paid by your good Mother to—76. It is not likely that I neglected to call on the Banker, yet it is possible, but the Bankers books will clear the question. I am willing to suppose that I received it, for it would be hard that Charity should be cheated.

In a few weeks will be published with my name some Lives of the Poets,[3] of which if You will be pleased to favour me by accepting a copy, I beg that You will let me know to whom in London I may send them, that they may be conveyed to You.[4] I am, Madam, your most humble Servant,

SAM. JOHNSON

3. SJ refers to the four-volume (large octavo) edition of his *Lives*, published 16 June (*Bibliography Supplement*, pp. 156, 159).

4. "On searching Child's Accounts I found the year 76 had been paid. I therefore omitted the present years payment and acknowledged the Books which I soon after received" (MS: note).

John Taylor
SATURDAY 12 MAY 1781

MS: Berg Collection, New York Public Library.
ADDRESS: To the Reverend Dr. Taylor in Ashbourne, Derbyshire.
POSTMARK: 12 MA.
ENDORSEMENTS: 1781, 12 May 81.

Dear Sir: London, May 12, 1781

You went out of town without giving me any notice, and considering the state of your health, I did not think You to blame, but why you have since given me no account of yourself I cannot discover, for I hope your disorders are not grown worse.

Dr. Butter talked to me of writing you some directions for your diet, and other parts of regimen; I called at his door lately but did not find him, if he has sent you any advice, be sure to try it. I have just lost one friend by his disobedience to his physicians;[1] let me not lose another. If Butter has forgotten

1. Henry Thrale had died 4 Apr.

or delayed his purpose, let me know, that I may remind or quicken him. But write to me immediately. Neither you nor I can now afford to lose time.

I have by negligence and indulgence lost something of the health which I had regained, but I purpose to fall again to work. But I am not near so bad as You have known me. Whether I can come down into the country soon I know not, but having missed the journey last year I seriously desire to see[2] my old friends this summer.[3] Of old Friends You know how few are left to a Man past seventy, and how much danger there is that every Year should make them fewer. I have lately heard that Charles Congreve is dead. I am sorry that in his last years I could not love him better. But he had put himself to nurse, a state to which an old Man is naturally tempted, and which he should resolutely disdain, till his powers really desert him. I am, Sir, yours affectionately,

SAM. JOHNSON

2. MS: "s" superimposed upon "c"

3. *Ante* To Lucy Porter, 8 Mar. 1781, n. 3.

Hester Thrale

TUESDAY 22 MAY 1781

MS: Rylands Library.

Dear Madam: May 22, 1781

I will be ready for You when You call, do not let that trouble You. It does not appear that Mr. B. want[s] to see us separately from Mr. C. He wants to see us all together, as he must sometime do, and nothing is necessary but to commission Mr. Perkins to let him know that we shall all be *ready* to meet him, upon any time which he shall appoint.[1] Mr. P. has probably

1. In his campaign to purchase the Thrale brewery (*Ante* To Hester Thrale, 11 Apr. 1781, n. 1), John Perkins had enlisted the assistance of the banker David Barclay (1728–1809). On 17 May Hester Thrale noted: "David Barclay the rich Quaker will treat for our Brewhouse, and the Negotiation is already begun. My

something to say, respecting his own particular hopes and fears, which he naturally wishes to tell You, and which it can do You no harm to hear, but we shall perhaps to morrow hear it together, for, next to You, he, I believe, thinks me his friend.

In a negotiation of such importance we must expect something of artifice, but less has yet appeared than is practiced upon much slighter occasions. Keep P. in as good humour as You can. Much must depend upon his representation.—Remember that You are to call to morrow for, Madam, Your most humble servant,

SAM. JOHNSON

---

heart palpitates with hope and fear, my Head is bursting with Anxiety and Calculation" (*Thraliana* I.494). Negotiations necessarily involved the four executors (*Ante* To Hester Thrale, 5 Apr. 1781, n. 6); "Mr. C." could refer to either Crutchley or Cator, with Crutchley the likelier possibility (*Thraliana* I.496).

Unidentified Correspondent

TUESDAY 22 May 1781

MS: Hyde Collection.

Sir: May 22, 1781

I have sent You the Manuscripts which I have retained too long; they have been of great use to me, and therefore all by whose interest or favour I obtained them, are considered by me as encouragers and benefactors, and You, Sir, have, in particular a claim to the gratitude and[1] acknowledgments of, Sir, Your most humble servant,

SAM. JOHNSON

1. MS: "and" superimposed upon "of"

Hester Thrale

MONDAY 28 MAY 1781

MS: National Library of Scotland.
ADDRESS: To Mrs. Thrale.

Madam: May 28, 1781

I shall have on Tuesday an opportunity of making it up with
Beattie,[1] and therefore beg your permission to stay here till I
wait on You at the Borough on Wednesday. I am, Madam,
Your most obedient,

SAM. JOHNSON

1. James Beattie and his elder son had taken rooms in Middle Scotland Yard,
where they stayed from late April to late July. On 1 June Beattie reported to Sir
William Forbes: "I have been visiting all my friends again and again, and found
them as affectionate and attentive as ever. . . . Johnson grows in grace as he grows
in years. He not only has better health . . . but he has contracted a gentleness of
manner which pleases everybody" (Margaret Forbes, *Beattie and His Friends*, 1904,
pp. 170–71, 174).

John Nichols
MAY 1781

MS: British Library.

May 1781[1]

An
Account of the Lives and Works
of some of the most eminent
English Poets   by etc.

The
English Poets
biographically and critically considered
by Sam. Johnson

Let Mr. Nicol take his choice or make another to his mind.[2]

1. MS: date in Nichols's hand
2. The title of the four-volume edition of 1781 reads: *The Lives of the Most Eminent English Poets; with Critical Observations on their Works. Ante* To John Nichols, 16
Apr. 1781, n. 1.

John Perkins

SATURDAY 2 JUNE 1781

MS: Hyde Collection.
ADDRESS: To Mr. Perkins in Southwark.
ENDORSEMENT: 2 June 1781.

Sir: June 2, 1781

However often I have seen You, I have hitherto forgotten the
note, but I have now sent it, with my good wishes for the Prosperity of You and your Partner, of whom from our short conversation I could not judge otherwise than favourably.[1] I am,
Sir, Your most humble servant,

SAM. JOHNSON

1. On 31 May the Thrale brewery had been sold for £135,000 to Perkins and
Robert Barclay (c.1740–1828), David Barclay's nephew (*Life* IV.493; Clifford,
1952, p. 201). Responsibility for the purchase money was shared by the two
Barclays, Perkins, and Silvanus Bevan (1743–1830), a Quaker banker and the
brother-in-law of Perkins's wife (*Thraliana* I.498 and n. 2; *Life* IV.86 n. 2; Peter
Mathias, *The Brewing Industry in England, 1700–1830*, 1959, p. 288; *Ante* To Hester
Thrale, 11 Apr. 1781, n. 1).

Frederick Augusta Barnard

WEDNESDAY 6 JUNE 1781

PRINTED SOURCE: Chapman II.428.

Sir:

I have sent you the remaining Lives,[1] and as I must complete
those which His Majesty was pleased to accept,[2] I beg that you
will favour me with one of the volumes, that the additional
part may be bound uniformly. My booksellers have not be-
haved very well, and therefore, I have not been able to ac-
comodate my friends as I wish.[3] You must excuse me yourself,

1. *Ante* To John Nichols, 16 Apr. 1781, n. 1.
2. *Ante* To Hester Thrale, 10 Mar. 1779 and n. 5.
3. *Ante* To Thomas Cadell, 13 Apr. 1779 and n. 3.

and save my credit with any that may blame me. I am, dear Sir, Your most humble servant,

SAM. JOHNSON

Lucy Porter

SATURDAY 9 JUNE 1781

MS: Hyde Collection.
ADDRESS: To Mrs. Lucy Porter in Lichfield.
POSTMARK: 9 IV.
ENDORSEMENT: 1781.

Dear Madam: London, June 9, 1781

I hope the Summer makes You better. My disorders which had come upon me again, have again given way to medicine, and I am a better sleeper than I have lately been.

The death of dear Mr. Thrale has made my attendance upon his house necessary, but we have sold the trade which we did not know how to manage, and have sold it for an hundred and thirty thousand pounds.[1]

My lives are at last published,[2] and You will receive them this week by the carrier. I have some hopes of coming this summer amongst you for a short[3] time.[4] I shall be loath to miss You two years together. But in the mean time let me know how You do. I am, dear Madam, Your affectionate Servant,

SAM. JOHNSON

1. *Ante* To John Perkins, 2 June 1781, n. 1.
2. *Ante* To John Nichols, 16 Apr. 1781, n. 1.
3. MS: "short" repeated as catchword
4. *Ante* To Lucy Porter, 8 March 1781, n. 3.

John Nichols

SUNDAY 10 JUNE 1781

MS: British Library.

ADDRESS: To Mr. Nicol.

Sir: June 10, 1781

My desire being to complete the sets of lives which I have formerly presented to my Friends, I have occasion for few of the first volumes, of which by some misapprehension I have received a great number, which I desire to exchange for the latter volumes. I wish success to the new edition.[1] I am, Sir, Your most humble Servant,

SAM. JOHNSON

1. *Ante* To John Nichols, 16 Apr. 1781, n. 1.

Bennet Langton

SATURDAY 16 JUNE 1781

MS: Hyde Collection.

ADDRESS: To Captain Langton in St. Margarets, Rochester.

POSTMARK: 16 IV.

Dear Sir: Boltcourt, June 16, 1781

How welcome your account of yourself and your invitation to your new house was to me, I need not tell you, who consider our friendship not only as formed by choice but as matured by time.[1] We have been now long enough acquainted to have many images in common, and therefore to have a source of conversation which neither the learning nor[2] the wit of a new companion can supply.

My Lives are now published, and if you will tell me whither

1. That spring Langton had moved his family to a small house in Rochester, overlooking the Medway. On his visit in 1783, SJ found the house "very airy, and pleasant . . . a habitation . . . likely to promote health" (*Post* To William Strahan, 15 July 1783; Fifer, p. 111 n. 10).   2. MS: "nor" altered from "not"

I shall send them that they may come to you, I will take care that You shall not be without them.

You will perhaps be glad to hear that Mrs. Thrale is disencumbred from her Brewhouse, and that it seemed to the purchaser so far from an evil, that he was content to give for it an hundred and thirty five thousand pounds.[3] Is the Nation ruined?

Please to make my respectful compliments to Lady Rothes, and keep me in the memory of all the little dear family, particularly pretty Mrs. Jane. I am, Sir, Your affectionate, humble Servant,

SAM. JOHNSON

3. *Ante* To John Perkins, 2 June 1781, n. 1.

Joshua Reynolds
SATURDAY 23 JUNE 1781

MS: New York Public Library.
ADDRESS: To Sir Joshua Reynolds.

Dear Sir:
June 23, 1781

It was not before yesterday that I received your splendid benefaction.[1] To a hand so liberal in distributing, I hope, nobody will envy the power of acquiring. I am, Dear Sir, Your obliged and most humble servant,

SAM. JOHNSON

1. "I am indebted to Mr. Malone, one of Sir Joshua Reynolds's executors, for the following note, which was found among his papers after his death, and which, we may presume, his unaffected modesty prevented him from communicating to me with the other letters from Dr. Johnson with which he was pleased to furnish me. However slight in itself, as it does honour to that illustrious painter, and most amiable man, I am happy to introduce it" (*Life* IV.133).

Frances Reynolds

MONDAY 25 JUNE 1781

MS: Hyde Collection.
ADDRESS: To Mrs. Reynolds.
ENDORSEMENT: Dr. Johnson, June 81.

Dear Madam: June 25, 1781

You may give the books to Mrs. Horneck, and I will give you another set for yourself.[1]

I am afraid there is no hope of Mrs. Thrale's custom for your pictures but, if you please, I will mention it. She cannot make a pension out of her jointure.[2]

I will bring the papers myself. I am, Madam, Your most humble servant,

SAM. JOHNSON

1. *Ante* To John Nichols, 10 June 1781.

2. "As early as 1768, during a trip to Paris, she [Frances Reynolds] had purchased a large number of fine paintings that she hoped she could sell to Mrs. Thrale in return for a comfortable annuity. Her scheme apparently failed, and she kept the paintings as her private treasure" (Richard Wendorf and Charles Ryskamp, "A Blue-Stocking Friendship," *Princeton University Library Chronicle* 41, 1980, p. 181).

John Perkins[1]

MONDAY 2 JULY 1781

PRINTED SOURCE: Hill II.222.

Sir,   July 2, 1781

Mrs. Thrale has informed me of the iron resolution of Mr. Cator and Mr. Crutchley. They have law on their side, and

1. Though the addressee is not recorded, internal evidence, supported by *Thraliana*, makes Perkins the only possible candidate. On 7 July Hester Thrale noted: "We have had another hot storming Day last Tuesday 3 July about this everlasting Brew house, but 'tis over. Perkins wanted more Indulgence than we as Executors could give him; so I lent him the Money I had saved and put in the Stocks" (*Thraliana* I.501 and nn. 2, 3). For his part in the acquisition and management of the brewery, *ante* To John Perkins, 2 June 1781, n. 1.

cannot be opposed. What then can be done? If time will do any thing for you, that you may apply to your friends, I will struggle for that. I think Mr. Barclay's interest so much requires your concurrence and assistance, that if you cannot procure security, he must help you. His difficulties are only niceties. Do not be bashful, use all the efforts that you can. I am, Sir, Your humble Servant,

SAM. JOHNSON

I shall come to you this morning, but I will meet Mrs. Thrale to-morrow about twelve.

Frances Burney
MONDAY 9 JULY 1781

PRINTED SOURCE: Chapman II.431.

Dear Madam,   July 9, 1781

Pray let these books be sent after the former to the gentleman whose name I do not know.[1] I am, Madam, Your most humble servant,

SAM. JOHNSON

1. William Bewley (1726–83), a Norfolk surgeon, close friend of Charles Burney, and "one of the earliest and most ardent of all Johnsonians" (Roger Lonsdale, *Dr. Charles Burney*, 1965, p. 277). SJ was completing his gift of an inscribed set of the *Lives of the Poets* (Lonsdale, *Burney*, pp. 277–78; *Life* IV.134).

Unidentified Correspondent
TUESDAY 10 JULY 1781

MS: Beinecke Library.

Dear Sir: July 10, 1781

I am desired by Mrs. Lennox to solicit your assistance. She is in great distress; very harshly treated by her husband, and oppressed with severe ilness. Do for her what you can, You were perhaps never called to the relief of a more powerful mind. She has many fopperies, but she is a great Genius, and nullum magnum ingenium sine mixtura.[1]—I hope, You will call on her to morrow. She lives at the house of Pauson, Pewterer, in Queenstreet, Westminster. I am, Sir, Your most humble Servant,

SAM. JOHNSON

1. *nullum magnum ingenium sine mixtura dementiae fuit*: "no great genius has ever existed without some touch of madness" (Seneca, *De Tranquillitate Animi* XVII.10, trans. J. W. Basore, Loeb ed.).

Thomas Astle[1]
TUESDAY 17 JULY 1781

MS: Hyde Collection.
ADDRESS: To T. Astle, Esq.
ENDORSEMENT: July 12th 1781, Doctor Johnson.

Sir: July 17, 1781

I am ashamed that You have been forced to call so often for your books, but it has been by no fault on either side. They have never been out of my hands, nor have I ever been at home without seeing You, for to see[2] a Man so skilful in the Antiquities of my country, is an opportunity of improvement not willingly to be missed.

Your Notes on Alfred appear to me very judicious and accurate, but they are too few.[3] Many things familiar to You are unknown to me and to most others, and You must not think too favourably of your readers, by supposing them knowing

1. Thomas Astle (1735–1803), F.S.A., F.R.S., collector, antiquarian, and palaeographer, first Chief Clerk (1775–83) and then Keeper of the Tower Records (1783–1803). Astle's numerous publications included *The Will of King Henry VII* (1775), *A Catalogue of the MSS. in the Cottonian Library* (1777), and *The Origin and Progress of Writing* (1784) (*Lit. Anec.* III.202–6).   2. MS: "a see"

3. Astle's edition of the will of King Alfred was published in 1788 (*Life* IV.133 n. 2).

You will leave them ignorant. Measure of Land, and value of money, it is of great importance to state with care. Had the Saxons any gold coin?

I have much curiosity after the manners and transactions of the middle ages, but have wanted either diligence or opportunity or both; You, Sir, have great opportunities, and I wish you both diligence and Success. I am, Sir, Your most humble servant,

SAM. JOHNSON

Charles Dilly

TUESDAY 17 JULY 1781

MS: Hyde Collection.

Sir:
July 17, 1781

Pray deliver to the Bearer a set of lives half bound 8vo, and send me two sets of Ramblers, neatly bound. I am, Sir, Your humble servant,

SAM. JOHNSON

Frances Reynolds

SATURDAY 21 JULY 1781

MS: Yale Center for British Art.
ADDRESS: To Mrs. Reynolds.

Dearest Madam:
July 21, 1781

There is in these such force of comprehension, and such nicety of observation as Locke or Pascal might be proud of.[1]

1. SJ responds to a preliminary version of Reynolds's "Enquiry Concerning the Principles of Taste, and of the Origin of Our Ideas of Beauty, etc." In the judgment of J. L. Clifford, "the *Enquiry* is what one might expect from an intelligent amateur, from one not a professional writer, yet one who has given much thought to the problems of aesthetics. ... It is packed with fresh arguments and novel suggestions" (*The Augustan Reprint Society*, No. 27, 1951, p. viii).

This I say with intention to have you think that I speak my opinion.

They cannot however be printed in their present state.[2] Many of your notions seem not very clear in your own mind, many are not sufficiently developed and expanded for the common reader; the expression almost every where wants to be made clearer and smoother. You may by revisal and improvement make it a very elegant and curious work. I am, Dearest Dear, Your most humble servant,

SAM. JOHNSON

2. After further revisions (*Post* To Frances Reynolds, 8 Apr. 1782), the "Enquiry" was privately printed in 1785.

John Perkins
MONDAY 6 AUGUST 1781

MS: Hyde Collection.
ADDRESS: To Mr. Perkins.

Dear Sir: Bolt court, Aug. 6, 1781

I have a mind to go for a few weeks into the Country,[1] and shall be glad to borrow thirty pounds of your house,[2] for which if You are willing, I will wait upon You on Monday. I am, Sir, Your most humble Servant,   SAM. JOHNSON

1. In the event, SJ did not leave for Lichfield until 15 Oct. (*Works*, Yale ed. 1.310).   2. *Ante* To John Perkins, 2 June 1781, n. 1.

Thomas Patten[1]
MONDAY 24 SEPTEMBER 1781

MS: Hyde Collection.

Dear Sir: N.B. Bolt court, Fleetstreet, Sept. 24, 1781

It is so long since we passed any time together, that you may

1. Thomas Patten (1714–90), D.D., Rector of Childrey, Berkshire (1755–90),

be allowed to have forgotten some part of my character, and I know not upon what other supposition, I can pass without censure or complaint the ceremony of your address. Let us not waste time in words, to which while we speak or write them[2] we assign little meaning. Whenever you favour me with a letter, treat me as one that is glad of your kindness, and proud of your esteem.[3]

The Papers which have been sent for my perusal I am ready to inspect if you judge my inspection necessary or useful; but indeed I do not see what advantage can arise from it. A Dictionary consists of independent parts, and therefore one page is not much a Specimen of the rest. It does not occur to me that I can give any assistance to the authour, and, for my own interest, I resign it into your hands, and do not suppose that I shall ever see my name with regret where[4] you shall think it proper to be put.

I think it, however, my duty to inform a Writer who intends me so great an honour, that in my opinion he would better consult his interest by dedicating his work, to some powerful and popular neighbour, who can give him more than a name. What will the world do, but look on and laugh, when one Scholar dedicates to another?[5]

If I had been consulted about this Lexicon of Antiquities while it was yet only a design, I should have recommended rather a *division* of Hebrew, Greek, and Roman particulars,

---

and an "excellent friend" of SJ (*Life* IV.508; *Post* To Thomas Wilson, 31 Dec. 1782). At the request of the Rev. Thomas Wilson (1747–1813), who was working on an archaeological dictionary, Patten had written to SJ on 4 Sept., asking that he "cast ... [his] eye over a few articles" relating to Wilson's project. Patten told SJ that Wilson was "ambitious to send it [his book] into the world under your patronage, and, with your permission, to dedicate it to you, if you shall judge it worthy of so splendid an introduction to the public notice" (*GM* 1819, p. 291).

2. MS: "write them" superimposed upon undeciphered erasure

3. A ceremonious letter from Richard Congreve had provoked a similar response. *Ante* To Richard Congreve, 25 June 1735.

4. MS: "where" superimposed upon "which" partially erased

5. Thomas Wilson did not heed this warning: his *Archaeological Dictionary; or Classical Antiquities of the Jews, Greeks, and Romans, Alphabetically Arranged* (one vol., 1782) is dedicated in lavish terms to SJ.

into three volumes, than a combination in one. The Hebrew part at least I would have wished to separate, as it might be made a very popular book, of which the use might be extended from men of learning down to the English reader and which might become a concomitant to the family Bible.

When works of a multifarious and extensive kind are undertaken in the country, the necessary books are not always known. I remember a very learned and ingenious Clergyman of whom, when he had published notes upon the Psalms, I enquired what was his opinion of Hammond's Commentary, and was answered, that he had never heard of it.[6] As this Gentleman has the opportunity of consulting you, it needs not be supposed that he has not heard of all the proper books, but unless he is near some library, I know not how he could procure them, and if he is conscious that his *supellex* is *nimis angusta*,[7] it would be prudent to delay his publication till his deficiencies may be supplied.

It seems not very candid to hint[8] any suspi[ci]ons of imperfection in a work which I have not seen, yet what I have said ought to be excused, since I cannot but wish well to a learned Man, who has selected me for the honour of a dedication, and to whom I am indebted for a correspondence so valuable as yours, and I beg that I may not lose any part of his kindness, which I consider with respectful gratitude.[9] Of you, dear Sir, I entreat that you will never again forget for so long a time, your most humble servant,

SAM. JOHNSON

6. *Ante* To Hester Thrale, 26 July 1775, n. 2.

7. SJ combines Persius (*Ante* To Thomas Birch, 22 June 1756, n. 5) with Juvenal's *res angusta domi* (*Satires* III.165). Literally, he means that Wilson's "furniture" may be "too narrow," i.e. his means too straitened.

8. MS: "hints" with "s" partially del.

9. *Post* To Thomas Wilson, 31 Dec. 1782.

John Taylor
MONDAY 24 SEPTEMBER 1781

MS: British Library.
ADDRESS: ⟨To the Rev.⟩ Dr. Taylor ⟨in⟩ Ashbourne, Derbyshire.
POSTMARK: 25 SE.
ENDORSEMENT: 1781.

Dear Sir: London, Sept. 24, 1781

All the expedients which You propose are so peremptorily rejected, that I see not what advice can be given you.[1] Nothing seems to remain but that You write immediately to the Duke, by which you will offend his Unkle,[2] and what hope you can have of his acting not only without advice, but contrarily to it, You must consider. If You write, I can suggest no more than you have already, nor can much more be urged.

Mr. Barker, who must know the family, seems to despair which is a great discouragement; and indeed it is hard to persist long in importuning men to do what they say they cannot do, and what indeed they cannot do but by indirect and artificial means, which they have not zeal enough to seek, and which can hardly be expected from friendship merely political. However, if you can recollect any other train of interest by which they might proceed, I would have you mention it, with pressing urgency, for I think You have nothing to fear more than disappointment of this preferment.

But let your health be your great care; suffer not vexation to lay hold upon your mind. I am glad to hear that you grow stronger. Be alone, or unemployed as little as You can. Remember that your disappointment is one of the common incidents of life, and if it is not seen to depress You, will supply no

---

1. Taylor was hoping for preferment to the deanery of Lincoln, which fell vacant on the death of Robert Richardson (1731–81). His campaign was unsuccessful: in Apr. 1782 Richard Cust (c. 1728–83), D.D., was installed as dean (John Le Neve and T. D. Hardy, *Fasti Ecclesiae Anglicanae*, 1854, II.36; *Alum. Oxon.* II.ii.208; *Post* To Hester Thrale, 10 Nov. 1781; 14 Nov. 1781). *Ante* To John Taylor, 9 Sept. 1779.   2. *Ante* To Hester Thrale, 19 May 1777 and nn. 3, 4.

triumph to your enemies. I still intend to visit You.[3] I am, dear Sir, affectionately yours,

SAM. JOHNSON

3. *Post* To Hester Thrale, 10 Nov. 1781.

John Perkins
MONDAY 8 OCTOBER 1781

MS: Hyde Collection.
ADDRESS: To Mr. Perkins.

Dear Sir: Oct. 8, 1781

I have received the notes, and have signed and sent the acknowledgement.

I hope You found all your family well, and particularly my little Boy,[1] make my compliments to them all. I am, Sir, Your obliged and most humble servant,

SAM. JOHNSON

1. Of Perkins's three young sons, SJ may be referring to the eldest, John (1775–?1818), who was Hester Thrale's godchild (Hyde, 1977, pp. 127, 362).

Lucy Porter
MONDAY 15 OCTOBER 1781

MS: Houghton Library.
ADDRESS: To Mrs. Lucy Porter in Lichfield.
POSTMARK: 15 OC.

Dear Madam: London, Oct. 15, 1781

You bade me send you word when I was to be at Lichfield. I am this day going to Oxford, where I shall probably make very little stay, and shall come forward by Birmingham. I hope to be with You in less than a Week, and to find You and all my other friends well. I am, Dear Madam, Your most humble servant,

SAM. JOHNSON

Unidentified Correspondent

MONDAY 15 OCTOBER 1781

MS: Hyde Collection.

Sir: Oct. 15, 1781

I have put Mr. Kearsley's[1] note[2] into the hands of Mr. Allen to whom I owe rent; if any assistance of yours is necessary, You will certainly give it. If something is not done before my return, I think his last proposal such as leaves him very little claim to tenderness. I am, Sir, Your most humble servant,

SAM. JOHNSON

1. George Kearsley (d. 1790), London bookseller, who published on 24 Nov. *The Beauties of Johnson*, a collection of "maxims and observations" (*Life* IV.500; Ian Maxted, *The London Book Trade 1775–1800*, 1977, p. 127).

2. *note*: "a paper given in confession of a debt" (SJ's *Dictionary*).

Hester Thrale

WEDNESDAY 17 OCTOBER 1781

MS: Hyde Collection.

Dear Madam: Oxford, Oct. 17, 1781

On monday evening arrived at the Angel Inn at Oxford Mr. Johnson and Mr. Barber without any sinister accident.

I am here but[1] why am I here? on my way to Lichfield, where I believe Mrs. Aston will be glad to see me. We have known each other long, and by consequence are both old, and She is paralytick, and if I do not see her soon, I may see her no more in this world. To make a visit on such considerations is to go on a melancholy errand. But such is the course of Life.

This place is very empty, but there are more here whom I know, than could have [been] expected. Young Burke has just been with me,[2] and I have dined to day with Dr. Adams, who

1. MS: "by"

2. Richard Burke, who had been called to the bar in Nov. 1780, was returning from the Northern Circuit (Fifer, pp. xliii–xliv; *Burke's Correspondence* IV.371).

seems fond of me. But I have not been very well. I hope I[3] am not ill by sympathy, and that You[4] are making hast to recover your plumpness and your complexion. I left you *skinny and lean.*[5]

To morrow, if I can, I shall go forward, and when I see Lichfield, I shall write again.

Mr. Parker the Bookseller sends his respects to you.[6] I send mine to your young Ladies. I am, Madam, Your most humble Servant,

SAM. JOHNSON

3. MS: "tha" partially erased before "I"

4. MS: "Y" superimposed upon "I"

5. "Early in September Mrs. Thrale was troubled with a rash which proved to be St. Anthony's Fire, and the inflammation continued for a whole month" (Clifford, 1952, p. 205). On 21 Oct. she reported to SJ: "I was many Years before I felt Sickness, but it is now in no haste to leave me, I must be still Leaner before I venture to grow fat; I have now pass'd seven Weeks completely without one comfortable Meal and I think seven more must be so spent before I recover" (MS: Rylands Library).

6. Sackville Parker (1707–96), bookseller on Logic Lane, Oxford, and an old friend of SJ (*Life* IV.308, 536).

Hester Thrale

SATURDAY 20 OCTOBER 1781

MS: Hyde Collection.

Dear Madam: Lichfield, Oct. 20, 1781

I wrote from Oxford, where I staid two days; on thursday I went to Birmingham, and was told by Hector that I should not be well so soon as I expected, but that well I should be. Mrs. Careless took me under her care, and told me when I had tea enough. On fryday I came hither and have escaped the post-chaises all the way.[1] Every Body here is as kind as I expected, I think Lucy is kinder than ever. I am very well. Now We are bothe valetudinary, we shall have something to write about.

1. *Ante* To Hester Thrale, 6 June 1775.

We can tell each other our complaints, and give reciprocal comfort and advice as—Not to eat too much—and—Not to drink too little, and we may now and then add a few strictures of reproof. And so we may write and write, till we can find another subject. Pray make my compliments to all the Ladies great and little. I am, Madam, Your most humble servant,

SAM. JOHNSON

Hester Thrale

TUESDAY 23 OCTOBER 1781

MS: Hyde Collection.
ADDRESS: To Mrs. Thrale at Streatham, Surry.
POSTMARKS: LITCHFIELD, 26 OC.

Dear Madam: Lichfield, Oct 23, 1781

I had both your letters, and very little good news in either of them. The diminution of the Estate though unpleasing and unexpected must be borne, because it cannot be helped, but I do not apprehend why the other part of your income should fall short.[1] I understood that You were to have 1500£ yearly from the money arising from the sale,[2] and that your claim was first.

I sincerely applaud your resolution not to run out, and wish You always to save something, for that which is saved may be spent at will, and the advantages are very many of having some money loose and unappropriated. If your ammunition is always ready, you may shoot advantage as it starts, or pleasure as it flies.[3] Resolve therefore never to want money.

1. In her letter of 17 Oct. Hester Thrale had reported: "The Oxfordshire [Crowmarsh] Estate . . . turns out but 300£ a Year at last, and scarcely that . . . My Income will therefore be a good deal less than I thought for, in Consequence of which I shall lay down a Pair of my Horses in the first Place, for I will not run out" (MS: Rylands Library).   2. *Ante* To John Perkins, 2 June 1781, n. 1.
3. Perhaps a reminiscence of Pope's *Essay on Man*: "Eye Nature's walks, shoot Folly as it flies, / And catch the Manners living as they rise" (I.13–14).

The Gravedo is not removed, nor does it encrease.[4] My nights have commonly been bad. Mrs. Aston is much as I left her, without any new symptoms, but between time and Palsy wearing away. Mrs. Gastrel is brisk and[5] lively.

Burney told me that she was to go,[6] but You will have my dear Queeney, tell her that I do not forget her, and that I hope she remembers me. Against our meeting we will both make good resolutions, which on my side, I hope to keep, but such hopes are very deceitful. I would not willingly think the same of all hopes, and particularly should be loath to suspect of deceit my hope of[7] being always, Dearest Madam, Your most humble Servant,

SAM. JOHNSON

4. *gravedo*: "a cold in the head" (*OED*).   5. MS: "and and"
6. Frances Burney had spent most of the summer at Streatham Park, but in October she left for Chessington and work on her second novel, *Cecilia* (Hester Thrale to SJ, 18 Oct. 1781, MS: Rylands Library; Clifford, 1952, p. 205).
7. MS: "my hope of my hope of"

Hester Thrale

SATURDAY 27 OCTOBER 1781

MS: Hyde Collection.
ADDRESS: To Mrs. Thrale at Streatham, Surry.
POSTMARKS: LITCHFIELD, 29 OC, [Undeciphered].

Dearest dear Lady: [Lichfield] Oct. 27, 1781

Your Oxford letter followed me hither with Lichfield put upon the direction in the place of Oxford, and was received at the same time as the letter written next after it.[1] All is therefore well.

Queeny is a naughty captious girl, that will not write because

1. SJ refers to Hester Thrale's letters of 17 and 18 Oct. (MSS: Rylands Library). On 24 Oct. she had written, "Nothing vexes me but my Folly in writing to Oxford. I wonder where that Letter is gone to" (MS: Rylands Library).

I did not remember to ask her.[2] Pray tell her that I ask her now, and that I depend upon her for the history of her own time.

Poor Lucy's ilness has left her very deaf, and I think, very inarticulate. I can scarcely make her understand me, and she can hardly make me understand her. So here are merry doings.[3] But she seems to love me better than she did. She eats very little, but does not fall away.

Mrs. Cobb and Peter Garrick are as You left them.[4] Garrick's legatees at this place are very angry that they receive nothing.[5] Things are not quite right, though we [are] so far from London.[6]

Mrs. Aston is just as I left her. She walks no worse, but I am afraid speaks less distinctly as to her utterance; her mind is untouched. She eats too little, and wears[7] away. Her extenuation is her only bad Symptom. She was glad to see me.

That naughty Girl Queeny, now she is in my head again. How could she think that I did not wish to hear from her, a dear Sweet—But he must suffer who can love.[8]

All here is gloomy, a faint struggle with the tediousness of time, a doleful confession of present misery, and the approach

---

2. "Queeney ... says you did not bid her write to you; and you *used* to *bid* her write to you" (Hester Thrale to SJ, 24 Oct. 1781, MS: Rylands Library).

3. Cf. *Ante* To Hester Thrale, 28 Oct. 1779.

4. The Thrales had visited Lichfield on their way to Wales in July 1774 (*Life* v.428–29).

5. By the terms of David Garrick's second will, 2 Feb. 1779, his brother Peter had been left £3,000, his sister Merial £3,000, and his brother George £10,000. "And if there shall not be sufficient to answer and pay all the said last mentioned Legacies The Legatees shall abate in proportion to their Legacies and wait until the Death of my Wife" (*The Letters of David Garrick*, ed. D. M. Little and G. M. Kahrl, 1963, III.1366: "Appendix G, Garrick's will"). According to Joseph Farington, "Garrick made a will very much exceeding his real fortune. ... His property might be abt £50,000 and he reckoned it at more than £100,000" (*The Diary of Joseph Farington*, ed. Kenneth Garlick and Angus Macintyre, 1978, I.109).

6. SJ may be alluding ironically to his own poem: "Resolved at length, from Vice and London far, / To breathe in distant Fields a purer Air" (*London*, ll. 5–6).

7. MS: undeciphered deletion before "wears"

8. *Ante* To Hester Thrale, 17 July 1775, n. 1.

seen and felt of what is most dreaded and most shunned. But such is the lot of Man. I am, Dearest Madam, Your most humble Servant,

SAM. JOHNSON

Hester Thrale

WEDNESDAY 31 OCTOBER 1781

MS: Hyde Collection.
ADDRESS: To Mrs. Thrale at Streatham, Surry.
POSTMARKS: 2 NO, [Undeciphered].

Dear Madam: Lichfield, Oct. 31, 1781

It almost enrages me to be suspected of forgetting the discovery of the papers relating to Cummins's claim.[1] Those papers we must grant the liberty of using, because the Law will not suffer us to deny them. We may be summoned to declare what we know, and what we know is in those papers. When the evidence appears, Lady Lade will be directed by her Lawyers to submit in quiet. I suppose it will be proper to give at first only a transcript.

Your income diminished as it is, you may without any painful frugality make sufficient.[2] I wish your health were as much in your power, and the effects of abstinence were as certain as those of parcimony.[3] Of your regimen I do not think with much approbation; it is only palliative, and crops the disease but does not eradicate it. I wish you had at the begining digested full meals in a warm room, and excited the humour to exhaust its power upon the Surface. This, I believe, must be done at last.

Miss Seward has been enquiring after Susan Thrale of

1. H. L. Piozzi identified "Cummins" as a man "to whom Mr. T.'s Estate owed Money, as it appear'd on the first Blush of the Transaction" (Piozzi II.212). No further details of his claim have been recovered. This "Cummins" should not be confused with "Mrs. Cummins" the schoolmistress (paragraph 3).
2. *Ante* To Hester Thrale, 23 Oct. 1781 and n. 1.
3. *Ante* To Hester Thrale, 17 Oct. 1781 and n. 5.

whom she has heard so much from Mrs. Cummins as excites her curiosity. If my little dear Perversity continues to be cross, Susy may be my Girl too,[4] but I had rather have them both. If Queeney dos not write soon she shall have a very reprehensory letter.[5]

I have here but a dull scene. Poor Lucy's health is very much broken. She takes very little of either food or exercise, and her hearing is very dull, and her utterance confused. But she will have *Watts's Improvement of the Mind.*[6] Her mental powers are not impaired, and her social virtues seem to encrease. She never was so civil to me before.

Mrs. Aston is not that I perceive worse than when I left her, but she eats too little, and is somewhat emaciated. She likewise is glad to see me, and I am glad that I have come.

Here is little of the sunshine of life, and my own health does not gladden me. But to scatter the gloom I went last night to the ball, where, You know, I can be happy even without You. On the Ball which was very gay I looked a while, and went away. I am, Dear Madam, Your most humble servant,

SAM. JOHNSON

4. *Ante* To Hester Thrale, 6 Oct. 1777 and n. 3.

5. *Post* To Hester Maria Thrale, 7 Nov. 1781.

6. *The Improvement of the Mind* (1741) by Isaac Watts. "Few books have been perused by me with greater pleasure than his *Improvement of the Mind* . . . a work in the highest degree useful and pleasing. Whoever has the care of instructing others may be charged with deficience in his duty if this book is not recommended" (*Lives of the Poets* III.309).

Hester Thrale

SATURDAY 3 NOVEMBER 1781

MS: Hyde Collection.

Dearest Madam: Lichfield, November 3, 1781

You very kindly remind me of the dear home which I have left, but I need none of your aids to recollection, for I am here gasping for breath, and yet better than those whom I came to visit. Mrs. Aston has been for three years a paralytic crawler, but, I think, with her mind unimpaired. She seems to me such as I left her, but she now eats little, and is therefore much emaciated. Her Sister thinks her, and she thinks herself passing fast away.

Lucy has had since my last visit a dreadful illness, from which her Physitians declared themselves hopeless of recovering her, and which has shaken the general fabrick, and weakened the powers of life. She is unable or unwilling to move, and is never likely to have more of either strength or spirit.

I am so visibly disordered that a medical man who only saw me at Church sent me some pills. To those whom I love here I can give no help, and from those that love me, none can I receive. Do You think that I need to be reminded of Home and You?

The time of the year is not very favourable to excursions. I thought myself above assistance or obstruction from the seasons,[1] but find the autumnal blasts sharp and nipping and the fading world an uncomfortable prospect. Yet I may say with Milton that I do not *abate* much *of heart or hope*.[2] To what I have done I do not despair of adding something, but *what it shall be I know not*.[3] I am, Madam, most affectionately yours,

SAM. JOHNSON

1. "He that shall resolutely excite his faculties, or exert his virtues, will soon make himself superiour to the seasons, and may set at defiance the morning mist, and the evening damp, the blasts of the east, and the clouds of the south" (*Idler* No. 11, *Works*, Yale ed. II.39).

2. "Yet I argue not / Against heaven's hand or will, nor bate a jot / Of heart or hope" (Milton, "To Mr. Cyriack Skinner Upon his Blindness," ll. 6–8).

3. SJ may have in mind lines from Lear's "O! reason not the need" speech: "I will do such things, / What they are, yet I know not, but they shall be / The terrors of the earth" (*King Lear* II.iv.278–80).

Hester Maria Thrale

WEDNESDAY 7 NOVEMBER 1781

MS: The Earl of Shelburne.

ADDRESS: To Miss Thrale at Streatham, Surry.

POSTMARKS: LITCHFIELD, 9 NO.

My dear Sweeting: Lichfield, Nov. 7, 1781

How could you suppose that by not asking you to write, I meant to show dislike or indifference.[1] It had been more reasonable to suppose that having asked you often, and having had no reason to change my mind, I considered it as a general compact that we should write to one another. The truth is that I did not reflect or remember that I had not asked you.

I am not sorry that this little suspicion has been discovered, because it gives me an opportunity of telling you that before you mingle in the crowd of life I wish you to exterminate Captiousness from your mind, as a very powerful and active cause of discontent, of such discontent as is very often without reason, and almost always without remedy. Captiousness is commonly the resentment of negative injuries, or offences of omission, of which the ill intention cannot be proved, and should therefore very rarely be supposed. As the provocations of captiousness can seldom be declared, they operate in sullen silence, and undermine those friendships which could perhaps have withstood the battery of an open quarrel. Captiousness is a slow poison which destroys confidence and kindness by imperceptible corrosion. The captious man often determines wrong though he always determines against himself, and after years passed in gloom and malevolence, often discovers at last that he was never injured. The rule to be observed is, never to impute to design those negligences or omissions which can be imputed to forgetfulness, nor ever to resent as deliberate and malignant enmity, such offences as may be the effect of accidental levity or hasty petulance.

---

1. *Ante* To Hester Thrale, 27 Oct. 1781 and n. 2.

This, my lovely dear, is a very grave and long lesson, but do not think it tedious, I have told you not many things more worthy of your attention and memory.

I have been this day returning my visits, and am going as I suppose, to Ashbourne to morrow;[2] I do not suppose my stay will be long,[3] and hope that you will not be sorry to see again, Dear Miss, Your most humble servant,   SAM. JOHNSON

2. *Post* To Hester Thrale, 10 Nov. 1781.
3. *Post* To Hester Thrale, 8 Dec. 1781.

Hester Thrale

SATURDAY 10 NOVEMBER 1781

MS: National Portrait Gallery, London.

Dear Madam: Ashbourne, Nov. 10, 1781

Yesterday I came to Ashbourne, and last night I had very little rest. Dr. Taylor lives on Milk, and grows every day better, and is not wholly without hope of Lincoln.[1] Every[one] enquires after You and Queeny, but whatever Burney may think of the celerity of fame,[2] the name of Evelina had never been heard at Lichfield, till I brought it. I am afraid my dear Townsmen will be mentioned in future days as the last part of this nation that was civilised. But the days of darkness are to be soon at an end. The reading Society ordered it to be procured this week.[3]

Since I came into this quarter of the earth I have had a very sorry time, and I hope to be better when I come back. The little padock and plantations here are very bleak. The Bishop

1. *Ante* To John Taylor, 24 Sept. 1781 and n. 1.
2. SJ combines the two senses of *fame* as defined in his *Dictionary*: "celebrity; renown" and "report; rumour."
3. A later reference by Anna Seward to "our book-club" and "its directors" suggests that a Lichfield "reading Society" may well have existed at this period (*Letters of Anna Seward*, 1811, VI.335; information supplied by Dr. G. W. Nicholls).

of Chester is here now with his Father in law;[4] he sent us a message last night, and I intend to visit him.

Most of your Ashbourne friends are well. Mr. Kennedy's daughter has married a Shoemaker,[5] and he lives with them and has left his parsonage. I am, Madam, Your most humble servant,

SAM. JOHNSON

4. SJ refers to Beilby Porteus (1731–1808), Bishop of Chester (1776–87), who was married to the second daughter of Brian Hodgson (*c.* 1709–84), an Ashbourne innkeeper and friend of John Taylor (*Life* III.505–6).

5. Catherine Kennedy (1739–1810) married John Burton of Ashbourne (*Johns. Glean.* VI.193).

Hester Thrale

MONDAY 12 NOVEMBER 1781

MS: Hyde Collection.

Dear Madam: Ashbourne, Nov. 12, 1781

I have a mind to look on Queeny as my own dear Girl, and if I set her a bad example, I ought to counteract it by good precepts,[1] and he that knows the consequences of any fault is best qualified to tell them. I have through my whole progress of authorship honestly endeavoured to teach the right, though I have not been sufficiently diligent to practice it, and have offered Mankind my opinion as a rule, but never proposed my behaviour as an example.

I shall be very sorry to lose Mr. Perkins, but why should he so certainly die?[2] Nesbit needed not have died if he had tried to live. If Mr. Perkins will drink a great deal of water the acrimony that corrodes his bowels will be diluted, if the cause be only acrimony, but I suspect dysenteries to be produced by animalcula, which I know not how to kill.

1. *Ante* To Hester Maria Thrale, 7 Nov. 1781.

2. On 24 Oct. Hester Thrale had reported, "Perkins is ill, not ill but broken somehow; and looking like a Man that would not live two years" (MS: Rylands Library).

If the medical man did me good, it was by his benevolence, for his pills I never touched.[3] I am, however, rather better than I was.

Dear Mrs. Biron, she has the courage becoming an Admirals Lady, but courage is no virtue in a bad cause.[4]

I have been at Lichfield persecuted with solicitation to read a poem, but I sent the authour word, that I would never review[5] the work of an anonymous authour, for why should I put my name in power of one who will not trust me with his own.[6] With this answer Lucy was satisfied, and I think it may satisfy all whom it may concern.

If Crutchly did nothing for life but add weight to its burden, and darkness to its gloom, he is kindest to those from whom he is furthest.[7] I hope when I come not to advance perhaps your pleasures, though even of that I should be unwilling to despair, but at least not to encrease your inconveniences which would be a very unsuitable return for all the kindness that you[8] have shown to, Madam, Your most humble servant,

SAM. JOHNSON

3. *Ante* To Hester Thrale, 3 Nov. 1781.

4. The "bad cause" in question may have been one of Admiral Byron's sexual escapades, for which he was notorious (L. A. Marchand, *Byron*, 1957, p. 12).

5. *review*: "to survey; to overlook; to examine" (SJ's *Dictionary*).

6. G. B. Hill (implicitly endorsed by R. W. Chapman) suggests that the "anonymous author" was Erasmus Darwin and the poem Darwin's *Loves of the Plants*. However, Darwin had left Lichfield for Radburn Hall, Derbyshire, in Mar. 1781; moreover, in Oct. 1781 he was engrossed in translating Linnaeus (information supplied by Dr. G. W. Nicholls). No plausible alternative candidate has been identified.

7. Jeremiah Crutchley, the putative illegitimate son of Henry Thrale, had been paying unwanted attentions to Queeney (*Thraliana* 1.497; Clifford, 1952, p. 205).

8. MS: "your"

Hester Thrale

WEDNESDAY 14 NOVEMBER 1781

MS: A. Brooks.

ADDRESS: To Mrs. Thrale at Streatham, Surry.

POSTMARKS: ASHBORNE, 17 NO.

Dearest Madam: Ashbourne, Nov. 14, 1781

Here is Doctor Taylor by a resolute adherence to Bread and Milk, with a better appearance of health than he has had for a long time past, and here am I, living very temperately but with very little amendment. But the balance is not perhaps very unequal, he has no pleasure like that which I receive from the kind importunity with which You invite me to return. There is no danger of very long delay. There is nothing in this part of the world that can counteract your attraction.

The hurt in my leg has grown well slowly according to Hector's prognostick,[1] and seems now to be almost healed, but my nights are very restless, and the days are therefore heavy, and I have not your conversation to cheer them.

I am willing, however to hear that there is happiness in the world, and delight to think on the pleasure diffused among the Burneys. I question if any ship upon the ocean goes out attended with more good wishes than that which carries the fate of Burney.[2] I love all of that breed, whom I can be said to know, and one or two whom I hardly know, I love upon credit, and love them because they love each other. Of this consanguineous unanimity I have had never much experience, but it appears to me one of the great lenitives of life, but it has this deficience that it is never found when distress is mutual—, he that has less than enough for himself has nothing to spare, and as every man feels only his own necessities he is apt to

---

1. *Ante* To Hester Thrale, 20 Oct. 1781.

2. Earlier that month James Burney had been appointed to the command of the *Latona*, "one of the best frigates in the navy," newly built and equipped with 38 guns (*Diary and Letters of Madame D'Arblay*, ed. Austin Dobson, 1904, I.453, II.54; *Royal Kalendar*, 1780, p. 147).

think those of others less pressing, and to accuse them of witholding what in truth they cannot give. He that has his foot firm upon dry ground may pluck another out of the water, but of those that are all afloat, none has any care but for himself.

We do not hear that the deanery of Lincoln is yet given away, and, though nothing is said, I believe much is still thought about it.[3] *Hope travels through.*[4]— I am, Dearest of all dear Ladies, Your most humble servant,

SAM. JOHNSON

3. *Ante* To John Taylor, 24 Sept. 1781 and n. 1.
4. "Hope travels thro', nor quits us when we die" (Pope, *Essay on Man* II.274).

Hester Thrale

SATURDAY 24 NOVEMBER 1781

PRINTED SOURCE: Piozzi, *Letters* II.226–28.

Dear Madam,   Ashbourne, Nov. 24, 1781

I shall leave this place about the beginning of next week, and shall leave every place as fast as I decently can, till I get back to you, whose kindness is one of my great comforts. I am not well, but have a mind every now and then to think myself better, and I now hope to be better under your care.

It was time to send Kam to another master;[1] but I am glad that before he went he beat Hector,[2] for he has really the appearance of a superior species to an animal whose whole power is in his legs, and that against the most defenceless of all the inhabitants of the earth.

Dr. Taylor really grows well, and directs his compliments to be sent. I hope Mr. Perkins will be well too.

But why do you tell me nothing of your own health?

1. "Kam was Kamschath Dog very savage" (Piozzi II.227).
2. In the annotated set of *Letters* (1788) now at Trinity College, Cambridge, H. L. Piozzi identifies "Hector" as "The Greyhound."

Perhaps since the fatal pinch of snuff I may have no care about it.[3] I am glad that you have returned to your meat, for I never expected that abstinence would do you good.

Piozzi,[4] I find, is coming in spite of Miss Harriet's prediction, or second sight,[5] and when *he* comes and *I* come, you will have two about you that love you; and I question if either of us heartily care how few more you have. But how many soever they may be, I hope you keep your kindness for me, and I have a great mind to have Queeney's kindness too.

Frank's wife has brought him a wench;[6] but I cannot yet get intelligence of her colour, and therefore have never told him how much depends upon it.

The weather here is chill, and the air damp. I have been only once at the waterfall, which I found doing as it used to do, and came away. I had not you nor Queeney with me. Your, etc.

SAM. JOHNSON

3. "I remember feeling that once when I was half distracted with a dreadful Headache brought on by Anguish of Mind he cooly recommended me to take a Pinch of Snuff" (Piozzi II.227).

4. Gabriel Mario Piozzi (1740–1809), Italian singer, composer, and music teacher, had become a favorite of Hester Thrale during the summer of 1780. By the following winter Piozzi was "a constant visitor at Streatham, where he taught Queeney singing, played the harpsichord for the entertainment of the Master, and set the Mistress to work translating Italian poetry" (Clifford, 1952, p. 193). From early July 1781 until late November, Piozzi was absent in Italy; when he returned, the tender friendship that had begun following the death of Henry Thrale developed into an intense but secret courtship (Clifford, 1952, pp. 204–6).

5. "Instead of trying the Sortes Virgilianae for our absent friends, we agreed after dinner today to ask little Harriet what they were doing now who used to be our common guests at Streatham. Dr. Johnson (says she) is very rich and wise, Sir Philip is drown'd in the water—and Mr. Piozzi is very sick and lame, poor man!" (Piozzi, *Letters* II.217).

6. The Barbers' second child, Elizabeth Ann (1781–1802), was baptized at St. Andrew's, Holborn, on 28 Nov. (A. M. Berrett, "Francis Barber's Marriage and Children: A Correction," *Notes and Queries*, June 1988, p. 193).

Edmund Allen

PRINTED SOURCE: JB's *Life*, ed. Croker, 1848, pp. 699–700.
HEADING: Johnson to Allen.

Dear Sir: Ashbourne, November 26, 1781

I am weary enough of the country to think of Bolt Court, and purpose to leave Ashbourne, where I now am, in a day or two, and to make my way through Lichfield, Birmingham, and Oxford, with what expedition I decently can, and then we will have a row[1] and a dinner, and now and then a dish of tea together.

I doubt not but you have been so kind as to send the oysters to Lichfield, and I now beg that you will let Mrs. Desmoulins have a guinea on my account.

My health has been but indifferent, much of the time I have been out, and my journey has not supplied much entertainment.

I shall be at Lichfield, I suppose, long enough to receive a letter, and I desire Mrs. Desmoulins to write immediately what she knows. I wish to be told about Frank's wife and child. I am, dear Sir, Your most humble servant,

SAM. JOHNSON

1. The text appears to be corrupt at this point.

Hester Maria Thrale

MS: The Earl of Shelburne.
ADDRESS: To Miss Thrale at Streatham, Surry.
POSTMARKS: ASHBORNE, 1 DE.

My dearest Love: Ashbourne, Nov. 28, 1781

The day after to morrow will carry me back to Lichfield, whence I purpose to find the way to London with all convenient speed. I have had a poor, sickly, comfortless journey, much gloom and little sunshine. But I hope to find you gay, and easy, and kind, and I will endeavour to copy you, for what can come of discontent and dolour? Let us keep ourselves busy and do what good we can to one another.

Dr. Taylor says that he has a bigger Bull than he ever had, and the cow which he sold for an hundred and twenty guineas, has brought the purchaser a calf for which he ask[s] a hundred pounds. The Dr. has been unsuccessful in breeding horses, for he has had sixteen fillies without one colt, an accident beyond all computation of chances. Such is the uncertainty of Life. He is, I believe, yet in hopes of the deanery.[1]

> Thus we sigh on from day to day
> And wish and wish the soul away.

He is however happier than if he had no desire. To be without hope or fear, if it were possible would not be happiness; it is better that life should struggle with obstructions than stagnate and putrefy. Never be without something to wish, and something to do.

I believe I shall be at Lichfield long enough to receive a letter from you, and therefore hope that you will send one, for I have great pleasure in being, Madam, your most humble servant,

SAM. JOHNSON

1. *Ante* To John Taylor, 24 Sept. 1781 and n. 1.

Hester Thrale

MONDAY 3 DECEMBER 1781

MS: Hyde Collection.

Dear Madam: Lichfield, Dec. 3, 1781

I am now come back to Lichfield, where I do not intend to stay long enough to receive another letter. I have little to do here but to take leave of Mrs. Aston, I hope not the last leave. But Christians may [say] with more confidence than Sophonisba

> Hauremo tosto lungo lungo spatio
> Per stare insieme, et sarà forse eterno.[1]

My time past heavily at Ashbourne, yet I could not easily get away though Taylor, I sincerely think, was glad to see me go. I have now learned the inconveniences of a winter campai[g]n. But I hope home will make me amends for all my foolish sufferings.

I do not like poor Burney's vicarious captainship.[2] Surely the tale of Tantalus was made for him. Surely he [will] be in time a Captain like another captain, of a Ship like another Ship.[3]

You have got Piozzi again notwithstanding pretty Harriets dire denunciations.[4] The Italian translation which he has brought you will find no great accession to your library, for the writer seems to have understood very little English.[5] When we meet we can compare some passages. Pray contrive a multitude of good things for us to do when we meet, something that may *hold all together*. Though if any thing makes *me* love You more, it is going from You. I am, Dear Madam, Your most humble servant,

SAM. JOHNSON

1. *Ma tu pur cerca mantenerti in vita; / Che tosto aremo un lungo lungo spazio / Di stare insieme, e sarà forse eterno*: "May you however seek to live, for soon we will have a long, long time together, perhaps even eternity" (Giangiorgio Trissino, *Sofonisba*, ll. 1794–96, in *Two Renaissance Plays*, ed. Beatrice Corrigan, 1975, pp. 141–42).

2. *Ante* To Hester Thrale, 14 Nov. 1781, n. 2. James Burney had been appointed "during the absence of the Honourable Captain Conway" (*Diary and Letters of Madame D'Arblay*, ed. Austin Dobson, 1904, I.453).

3. James Burney was promoted to the rank of captain in 1782 (*The Early Journals and Letters of Fanny Burney*, ed. L. E. Troide, 1988, I.xliii).

4. *Ante* To Hester Thrale, 24 Nov. 1781 and n. 5.

5. It is likely that Gabriel Piozzi had presented Hester Thrale with C. M. Mei's translation of *Rasselas: Istoria di Rasellas Principe d'Abissinia*, Padua, 1764 (information supplied by Professors E. A. Bloom and L. D. Bloom).

Hester Thrale
SATURDAY 8 DECEMBER 1781

MS: Hyde Collection.

Dear Madam: Birmingham, Decr. 8, 1781

I am come to this place on my way to London and to
Streatham. I hope to be in London on Tuesday or Wednesday,
and at Streatham on Thursday by your kind conveyance. I
shall have nothing to relate either wonderful or delightful. But
remember that You sent me away, and turned me out into the
World, and you must take the chance of finding me better or
worse. This you may know at present, that my affection for
You is not diminished, and my expectation from you is encreased. Do not neglect me, nor relinquish me. Nobody will
ever love You better, or honour You more than, Madam, Your
most obliged and most humble Servant,

SAM. JOHNSON

John Nichols
WEDNESDAY 26 DECEMBER 1781

MS: British Library.
ADDRESS: To Mr. Nicols.

Dec. 26, 1781[1]

Mr. Johnson being much out of order sent in search of the
book but it is not found. He will, if he is better look himself
diligently to morrow. He thanks Mr. Nichols for all his favours.

1. MS: "1781" added in Nichols's hand

INDEX

This is an index of proper names alone; the comprehensive index to the entire edition appears in Volume v. The following abbreviations are used: Bt. (Baronet), Kt. (Knight), ment. (mentioned). Peers are listed under their titles, with cross-references from the family name.

Entries for each of SJ's correspondents begin with a comprehensive listing of all letters to the individual in question. Page numbers for footnotes refer to pages on which the footnotes begin, although the item which is indexed may be on a following page.

The index was compiled mainly by Phyllis L. Marchand with the assistance of Marcia Wagner Levinson and Judith A. Hancock.

M

P

S

T

X

Y